Concert Music, Rock, and Jazz since 1945:
Essays and Analytical Studies

EASTMAN STUDIES IN MUSIC

The Poetic Debussy: A Collection of His Song Texts and Selected Letters
(Revised Second Edition)
Edited by Margaret G. Cobb

Concert Music, Rock, and Jazz since 1945: Essays and Analytical Studies
Edited by Elizabeth West Marvin and Richard Hermann

Music and the Occult: French Musical Philosophies, 1750–1950
Joscelyn Godwin

"Wanderjahre of a Revolutionist" and Other Essays on American Music
Arthur Farwell, edited by Thomas Stoner

French Organ Music from the Revolution to Franck and Widor
Edited by Lawrence Archbold and William J. Peterson

Concert Music, Rock, and Jazz since 1945: Essays and Analytical Studies

Elizabeth West Marvin and Richard Hermann

editors

UNIVERSITY OF ROCHESTER PRESS

First published 1995
Soft cover edition published 2002

The University of Rochester Press
668 Mount Hope Avenue, Rochester, NY 14620, USA

and at Boydell & Brewer, Ltd.
P.O. Box 9, Woodbridge, Suffolk 1P12 3DF
United Kingdom

ISBN 1-878822-42-X (Hard cover)
ISBN 1-58046-096-8 (Soft cover)
ISSN 1071-9989

Library of Congress Cataloging-in-Publication Data
Concert music, rock, and jazz since 1945: essays and analytical
studies edited by Elizabeth West Marvin and
Richard Hermann,
p.cm.— (Eastman studies in music, ISSN 1071-9989; 2)
    Includes bibliographical references and index.
        ISBN 1-58046-096-8
1.   Music – 20th century –History and criticism. 2. Popular
    music— History and criticism. I. Marvin, Elizabeth West,
    1955-. II. Hermann, Richard, 1950-. III. series.
            ML 160.C737 1995
        780'.9'04— dc20   94— 30277

British Library Cataloguing-in-Publication Data
        Concert Music, Rock, and Jazz since 1945:
Essays and Analytical Studies. (Eastman Studies in Music,
        ISSN 1071-9989; Vol 2
1.   Marvin, Elizabeth West II. Hermann, Richard III. Series
            780.9045
        ISBN 1-58046-096-8

A catalogue record for this item is available from the British
Library.

Printed in the United States of America.
This publication is printed on acid-free paper.

Contents

Contributors

JONATHAN W. BERNARD
University of Washington (Seattle, Washington)

JANE PIPER CLENDINNING
Florida State University (Tallahassee, Florida)

ROBERT COGAN
New England Conservatory of Music (Boston, Massachusetts)

NICHOLAS COOK
University of Southampton (Southampton, UK)

JOHN COVACH
University of North Carolina (Chapel Hill, North Carolina)

WALTER EVERETT
University of Michigan (Ann Arbor, Michigan)

CYNTHIA FOLIO
Temple University (Philadelphia, Pennsylvania)

DAVE HEADLAM
Eastman School of Music of the University of Rochester (Rochester, New York)

RICHARD HERMANN
University of New Mexico (Albuquerque, New Mexico)

ELLIE M. HISAMA
The Ohio State University (Columbus, Ohio)

JONATHAN D. KRAMER
Columbia University (New York, New York)

ELIZABETH WEST MARVIN
Eastman School of Music of the University of Rochester (Rochester, New York)

ANDREW MEAD
University of Michigan (Ann Arbor, Michigan)

ROBERT D. MORRIS
Eastman School of Music of the University of Rochester (Rochester, New York)

Acknowledgements

We gratefully acknowledge Robert Freeman and the Eastman School of Music for granting a publication subvention to offset the cost of producing musical examples for this book; our thanks also to Ralph P. Locke and the members of the *Eastman Studies in Music* Editorial Board. For preparation of musical examples, we wish to acknowledge Eastman graduate students, Ed Jurkowski, Pat Long, Jeff Markarian, and David Palmer. For their continuing support, we thank our families: Elizabeth L. Hermann, and Glenn, Russell, and Caroline West.

E.W.M. and R.H.

Note

Throughout this volume, pitch designations conform to the guidelines established by the Acoustical Society of America (middle C = C4).

Introduction

Elizabeth West Marvin and Richard Hermann

As the twentieth century moves toward its final years, researchers on Western music—especially those working on music of this century—are increasingly turning their attention to more diverse repertoires than were previously represented in publications and at professional meetings.[1] Those working on the theory and analysis of recent music have necessarily developed diverse ways of understanding these works as well—in some cases by extending established analytical methods to new repertoires, and in others by drawing upon research in other disciplines, such as linguistics, philosophy, mathematics, or literary theory. This collection brings together fourteen essays, all previously unpublished, that represent some of the most notable current research on music from the latter part of this century; the authors explore a wide range of musics, and do so by means of an equally wide range of music-analytical techniques.

---

1 Consider, for example, the "Song" session, chaired by Arthur Komar, at the 1992 annual meeting of the Society for Music Theory. The four papers presented were "Chromatic Third-Relations and Tonal Structure in the *Trois poèmes de Mallarmé* of Debussy," by Avo Somer; "Love Forever Lost: Musical Expression and the Plagal Domain in Two Songs from Tchaikovsky's *Six Romances*, Op. 28," by Joseph C. Kraus; "The Pop Album as Song Cycle: Paul Simon's 'Still Crazy After All These Years,'" by Peter Kaminsky; and "Voice Leading and Harmony in the Early Music of The Beatles," by Walter Everett.

In addition, analytical articles on jazz and popular musics have recently appeared in scholarly music journals (see, for example, Steven Block, "Pitch-Class Transformation in Free Jazz," *Music Theory Spectrum* 12 (1990): 181–202; and Allen Forte, "Secrets of Melody: Line and Design in the Songs of Cole Porter," *The Musical Quarterly* 77 (1993): 607–47). One journal that has been at the forefront in presenting analyses of both concert and popular musics is the *College Music Symposium*, which published at least one article on popular music each year from 1989–1992. See Paul S. Machlin's "Pygmalions of Pop: Reinterpreting Jazz and Rock Standards" (1989), Robert Gauldin's "Beethoven, Tristan, and The Beatles" (1990), E. Michael Harrington's "Rock Music as a Resource in Harmonic, Melodic, and Metric Dictation" (1991), Walter Everett's "Voice Leading and Harmony as Expressive Devices in the Early Music of the Beatles: *She Loves You*" (1992), and Peter Kaminsky's "The Popular Album as Song Cycle: Paul Simon's *Still Crazy After All These Years* (1992)—this, in addition to a number of articles on broadening the repertoires taught in undergraduate classrooms to include non-Western musics, Western popular music, more music composed by women, and influences from feminist scholarship.

It is our intent in this volume to blur the distinction between "classical" and "popular" musics, so as to avoid the implication that one class of music is more worthy of serious analytical study than the other. Of course, the division of musics into distinct classes has a long history. Among the now-famous divisions is Christoph Bernhard's mid-seventeenth century account, in the *Tractatus compositionis augmentatus*, which divides compositional styles into the *stylus gravis* (also called *stylus ecclesiasticus*), the *stylus luxurians communis* and the *stylus comicus*.[2] The three styles—more commonly known as church, chamber (or concert), and theatre music—arguably still exist, though our definitions have broadened considerably. Thus, our equivalent of the seventeenth-century "chamber" or late eighteenth-century concert room ranges from a large symphony hall, to a bar or restaurant, to an outdoor amphitheatre; and our "chamber" and "concert" repertoires range from concerti to jazz sets to rock songs. Likewise, "theatre" music now includes not only opera scores but also music for films, TV shows, and commercials, while "church" music now ranges from Gospel choir music to choral-orchestral Mass settings. Indeed, a further division into "low-, middle-, and high-art" music might be perceived by some for each of these styles. High-art concert music, for example, might feature computer music or "serious" orchestral or chamber compositions. Middle-art concert music might include orchestral "pops" repertoire or improvised jazz, while low-art concert music might encompass rock, rap, or country music, among other types.

It is hardly a surprise that problems arise in extending Bernhard's taxonomy to today's music. First, cross-over among categories is not uncommon: rock concerts are surely part concert music and part theatre, and film music uses many of the same idioms as today's concert music, though in a "theatrical" venue. Even more problematic is the division into "low-, middle-, and high-art" music. As the articles in this collection show, the musical relationships in some rock and jazz compositions are every bit as complex and interesting as those in some "high-art" compositions. Second, recorded music from around the world has influenced composers as diverse as Lou Harrison and another Harrison: ex-Beatle, George. Older music, too, reaches new audiences through recordings: as this essay is written, a recording of Gregorian chant has reached the top of the pop music "charts," thus merging the *stylus ecclesiasticus* with populist entertainment. Indeed, art music is no longer restricted in locale to the church, chamber, or theatre; music of many types has become ubiquitous in our society—in elevators, supermarkets, automobiles, and shopping malls.

Clearly, the repertoires studied by musical scholars deserve to be expanded, given our pluralistic society and the mass market for diverse musics. This

---

2 Bernhard's *Tractatus* is fully translated by Walter Hilse in *The Music Forum III*, edited by William J. Mitchell and Felix Salzer (New York: Columbia University Press, 1973). This discussion is found on pages 34–35 of that translation.

expansion will necessitate new approaches to music scholarship—some of which will be sociological, cultural, or historical examinations of the origins, the critical reception, and the influences of these musics. Other approaches will deal more directly with the musical artworks themselves, using analytical tools adapted from music theory, as well as from other disciplines. It is this latter road that is traversed in this volume.

All of these factors converged upon us as editors, when faced with the task of naming this collection. An early title juxtaposed the words *Modern/Postmodern*; yet this did not capture the diversity of music to be included. In another version, *Musical Pluralism* captured the diversity, but implied a more sociological/ cultural study than our book delivers. We tried *Classical and Popular Music Since 1945*, but feared that the title's initial words might imply to some that we were dealing in large part with Mozart and Haydn. Further, this title set up a dichotomy between the two repertoires that we had hoped to avoid. Even so, our book's final title represents a compromise: *Concert Music, Rock, and Jazz* should not be taken to mean that the latter two musics cannot be heard in concerts, nor should *Rock . . . since 1945* be taken to imply that there was such a thing as rock music before 1945. This date, however—with its post-World War II imagery— evokes an era of musical experimentation and diversity upon which we wish to build. So much so, that we have chosen to include the date in our title in spite of the fact that at least one of the compositions analyzed here—Ruth Crawford's *String Quartet*—predates 1945. Crawford's quartet is included because it belongs to the modernist aesthetic that we wished to capture in at least some of the repertoire represented here, because Crawford's music has attained full recognition only in recent years, and because the analyst's integration of feminist thought with formal analysis is an important contribution to our collection.

Concert Music, Rock, and Jazz since 1945 is divided into three parts: "Compositional Poietics," "Some Structuralist Approaches," and "Influences from Other Disciplines." It should be clear from the discussion above that we could not hope to represent the diversity of post-1945 music exhaustively in a single volume. Thus we were forced to omit many categories of music and analytical methodologies that might appropriately have been included here. We have chosen essays that break new ground with respect to the compositions that they address, the perspectives from which they are written, or the analytical methodologies that they introduce or extend.

Essays on "compositional poietics" open the volume. In music, the term "poietics" (or "poetics") has frequently been interpreted to refer to the pre- compositional activities of composer-theorists. These discussions have a long history in music-theoretical discourse; among the most famous is Thomas Morley's *A Plaine and Easie Introduction to Practicall Musicke* (London, 1597). A recent contribution to this literature is *Composition with Pitch-Classes*, written by one of our contributors, Robert Morris.[3] Both volumes are concerned with the technical know-how of composing music, such as dissonance treatment (Morley) or array interpretation (Morris). Conventional definitions certainly support this pre-compositional view of poietics. For instance, according to *Webster's International Dictionary of the English Language*, the English words "poem," "poetics," and "poet" all derive from a Greek verb meaning "to make, to compose, to write, especially in verse."[4]

A different perspective is provided by Aristotle, who in the *Poetics* separates artistic knowledge into three classes: poietic knowledge (from *poiesis*—to make), practical knowledge (from *praxis*—to do), and theoretical knowledge (from *theoria*—to contemplate). According to traditional interpretations of Aristotle, the first of the three classes, *poiesis*, has a two-part meaning: the first being the inspiration that guides the composer in creation, and the second being the rational planning that realizes the inspiration.[5] The contributors to this first section do not here contemplate *poiesis* in the latter, rational (or precompositional) sense; instead, each author shows selected aspects of the current cultural condition that influences some composers to create; thus they align themselves with the first sense of *poiesis* just noted.

While these three authors are acclaimed scholars in music theory, they are also accomplished composers. Discussions by composers about the aesthetic or technical bases of their own compositions are hardly rare, yet these essayists do not dwell here upon their own creative work, nor are they attempting a systematic survey of today's musical aesthetics or more general cultural conditions. Rather, they interpret certain aspects of those cultural conditions that provide context and motivation for the repertoire this volume examines. Jonathan Kramer begins his essay with an anecdote about a composition student's derivation of new musical material from old, then uses this story as a point of departure to explore the concept of musical "unity." This exploration provides a context for Kramer's discussion of "modernism" and "postmodernism" in music composition, in which he cites exemplars from music literature and descriptions of postmodernism in other disciplines by literary and art critics. Robert Cogan also addresses unity (or invariance) in music composition, placing this feature in a binary opposition: invariant/variant. He proposes other oppositions as well, and uses the concept of opposition as an analytical approach to works by Olivier Messiaen and Elliott Carter. Cogan argues for musical aesthetics and theories that have a place for

---

3   Robert D. Morris, *Composition with Pitch-Classes* (New Haven: Yale University Press, 1987).

4   *Webster's International Dictionary of the English Language*, rev. Noah Porter (Springfield, Mass.: G. C. Merriam, 1896), p. 1105.

5   *Aristotle's Poetics*, trans. S. H. Butcher, intro. Francis Fergusson (New York: Hill and Wang, 1961), pp. 8–11. In those pages, Fergusson brings in valuable interpretations from Aristotle's writings on ethics that clarify the terms *praxis*, *poiesis*, and *theoria*.

oppositions and for diversity. Finally, Robert Morris describes an "ethnomusicological perspective" shared among composers of many different types of music; these are composers who hold that there is more than one legitimate art music, who understand that musics differ with respect to social stratum and musical function, and who are sensitive to the interrelations between music and culture. This perspective allows many types of music composition to thrive. Morris provides a brief history of twentieth-century composition and ethnomusicology to illustrate some parallels between the two fields, and closes by considering issues of musical universals.

By exploring compositional poietics, our essayists have entered into the infrequently explored territory (for music theorists) of current cultural contexts for compositional thought. Because these three commentators are recognized in two of the three Aristotelian classes of artistic knowledge (*poiesis* and *theoria*), these essays could become catalysts for discussion by future scholars studying musical composition in the last decades of this century.

Each of the authors in the collection's second section, "Some Structuralist Approaches," draws upon previous music-theoretical research, extending these theories to new repertoires and/or to new musical dimensions. Andrew Mead, for example, notes that Elliott Carter does not consider himself to be a twelve-tone composer; yet Mead provides compelling evidence that procedures drawn from twelve-tone composition are at work in this music. Mead uses musical examples from three works—the Third String Quartet, *Night Fantasies*, and the Piano Concerto—to demonstrate Carter's use of twelve-tone operations upon rows that are ordered in register rather than in time, the resulting invariances that permit trichordal and hexachordal combinatoriality, and the compositional realizations of rows and pitch-class collections among instruments or groups of instruments in these works. Walter Everett similarly demonstrates the applicability of an established analytical technique to a new repertoire—in this case, Schenkerian analysis and the music of the Beatles. Everett uses graphic analysis to show large-scale tonal and motivic coherence in *Abbey Road*, Side Two. By detailing aspects of the album's compositional history and its studio production, Everett also provides a context for the work's large-scale structure, its text painting, and the timbral effects achieved in the studio.

Jane Clendinning's essay approaches Ligeti's music on three levels: the microstructure, the audible surface, and the macrostructure. Her concern with the "audible surface" is shared by the remaining essays in Part II. Clendinning represents strikingly concrete features of the music—such as expansion of range, pacing of activity, and density of pitch material—through graphic analyses of *Lontano*, *Lux aeterna*, and the ninth of the *Ten Pieces for Wind Quintet*. Cynthia Folio approaches perceptual issues through the findings of researchers in music perception, through her interview with an African master drummer on performers' perception of polyrhythm, and through her own process of transcribing improvised jazz solos by Thelonious Monk, Ornette Coleman, and Eric Dolphy. Folio categorizes polyrhythm into three distinct types and draws upon previous work in rhythmic analysis, particularly that of Maury Yeston, to formalize a measure of polyrhythmic dissonance. Her essay combines polyrhythmic analyses with a discussion of underlying linear step progressions and large-scale form. Finally, Elizabeth West Marvin's contribution also addresses perceivable patterning in music, by extending the contour theories of Robert Morris and others to various musical dimensions; thus, she focuses her attention not only on melodic contours of relatively high and low notes, but also on audible dynamic contours of relatively loud and soft notes, rhythmic contours of relatively long and short notes, and chordal densities of relatively wide and narrow spacing patterns. In excerpts drawn from Dallapiccola's *Quaderno musicale di Annalibera*, Stockhausen's *Kontakte*, and the first movement of Stockhausen's *Klavierstücke*, No. 2, she demonstrates instances in which equivalent contours are expressed in differing dimensions—for example, as both dynamic and rhythmic contours.

Part III of the collection explores avenues of music analysis that are influenced by research in other disciplines. Jonathan Bernard notes that the minimalist compositional stance in art and in music stands as an obstacle to theory and analysis, but he proposes possible solutions to this dilemma, drawing upon models in the visual arts. After defining minimalism in music—primarily by dispelling myths about what it is not—Bernard offers diverse analytical views of excerpts from Alvin Lucier's *I am sitting in a room*, Philip Glass's *Music in Twelve Parts*, Steve Reich's *Music for 18 Musicians*, and Glass's *Satyagraha*; for each he finds an analogue in the visual arts. Ellie Hisama's interdisciplinary approach combines feminist theory with a formalist analysis of Ruth Crawford's *String Quartet*, third movement. Following a biographical sketch that outlines some of the barriers Crawford encountered as a woman composer in the 1930s, Hisama presents the hypothesis that the movement's climax parodies nineteenth-century musical norms— that the work is distinctly feminist because it undercuts the "masculinist musical narrative" by its incorporation of an independent second narrative. She describes this second narrative in terms of the interweaving sound-strands occupied by each instrument in its characteristic register. By measuring the "degree of twist" among strands from moment to moment, a progression emerges whose course differs from the surface motion toward and away from climax.

Dave Headlam characterizes the analysis of popular music as an area in which the worlds of modernism and postmodernism collide. He turns to postmodernist writers, such as Roland Barthes and Michel Foucault, to help define "authorship," as he traces the origins of some of Led Zeppelin's signature works to songs from the Delta blues tradition. In three analyses, of "Whole Lotta Love," "Babe, I'm Gonna Leave You," and "When the Levee Breaks," Headlam compares Led Zeppelin's reworkings of these songs with their original versions to illustrate facets of these recordings that support the attribution of Led Zeppelin as "author."

Richard Hermann views Berio's *Sequenza IV for Piano* from a number of perspectives—that of the performer, that of the formalist music analyst, and that of the analyst influenced by linguistic theories. In the latter role, he creates analogies between musical elements and lexical elements, and likens his chordal shape functions to transformation rules. Hermann's functions operate upon referential chords of the work to generate related variant chords, all within the context of two chaconne-like chordal successions. Finally, John Covach explores philosophies of humor in relation to musical parody, specifically in the rock music composed for the film *This is Spinal Tap*. His analyses draw upon recognition of stylistic features of the music that is parodied, as well as upon incongruous departures from that style.

To tie together some of the common threads that these essays share—despite their admitted diversity—the University of Rochester Press commissioned Nicholas Cook to write an Afterword to close the collection.[6] In his insightful offering, "Music Theory and the Postmodern Muse," Cook has used issues raised by Kramer in the opening essay to structure his response. His discussion is divided into three sections, representing three of the issues around which postmodernism revolves: the death of the author, the principle of unity, and the relationship of work and text. Drawing upon Roland Barthes's idea (cited by Kramer) that the birth of the reader is at the expense of the death of the author, Cook's opening section contrasts the ways in which Mead, Bernard, and Hisama discuss the reader (listener) and the author (composer). In the second section of his essay—on musical unity and disunity—Cook highlights common themes in the Kramer, Cogan, and Morris essays, then notes that Kramer's and Cogan's calls for analytical attention to musical disunity remain unheeded in some of the analyses that follow. Both Headlam and Covach, for example, seek in their articles to identify the norms that unify a musical "style," in order to attribute authorship to the musicians reworking earlier music (Headlam) and to examine the humorous incongruities of stylistic departure and parody (Covach). Likewise, Mead and Everett demonstrate connected structures in the music of Carter and the Beatles, using set-theoretical and Schenkerian analytical methods, respectively. In the closing section, Cook ponders the role of music notation in structuring and influencing the analytical process. Since several articles in the collection present scores transcribed from recordings, Cook begins this section with a discussion of the relation between sounding music and transcriptions, referring to examples drawn from essays by Headlam, Folio, and Cogan. Finally, Cook turns to three "text-based" analyses—by Marvin, Hermann, and Clendinning—that inspire him

---

6 Recent precedents for such an Afterword include Paul Robinson's "A Deconstructive Postscript: Reading Libretti and Misreading Opera," in *Reading Opera*, ed. Arthur Groos and Roger Parker (Princeton: Princeton University Press, 1988), pp. 328–46; and Hayden White's "Commentary: Form, Reference, and Ideology in Musical Discourse," in *Music and Text: Critical Inquiries*, ed. Steven Paul Scher (Cambridge: Cambridge University Press, 1992), pp. 288–319.

to hypothesize a "dream machine" for analysis and composition that could implement the analytical approaches described in these three essays, and others as well.

With this collection, we hope to foster an atmosphere in which analysts of twentieth-century music will think of both Ligeti and Monk, Varèse and Zappa, and Crawford and McCartney as composers of interest, and will perhaps be inspired to look to new repertoires in their own research, adapting and extending analytical methodologies presented here or developing new ones as the music demands. We likewise hope that one article or another in this volume will pique the interest of a popular musician, an ethnomusicologist, a student of contemporary culture, a composer or performer of "concert" music, or any type of music enthusiast—and that, once here, the reader will choose to read further.

I
Compositional Poietics

Beyond Unity: Toward an Understanding of Musical Postmodernism

Jonathan D. Kramer

As a teacher of music composition, I have often experienced the following: a student appears for his or her weekly lesson with some newly composed material. I notice some problems with it, which I try to explain. The student then defends the questionable passage by pointing to its rigorous derivation from materials composed in previous weeks. The student apparently believes that his or her efforts at making the piece tight and economical somehow guarantee coherence, render any suspect passage immune from structural problems, and magically make the composition succeed aesthetically.

I find such an attitude extremely hard to combat in most students. Their almost religious belief in the power, utility, and necessity of musical unity starts young and dies hard. The value many of today's student composers place on unity should not be surprising. This quality has been important to composers and their teachers at least from the beginning of the nineteenth century and perhaps from the start of the tonal era. It has been accepted as self-evident that good pieces are coherent, consistent, and parsimonious in their choice of material. All parts are ideally understood to be essential, yet the whole is believed to transcend the sum of its parts. Commentary has routinely praised unity in what was understood to be the greatest music.

Until quite recently, no one seems to have asked why unity is universally valued in Western music. Yet today we are finding in so-called postmodern music serious challenges to the necessity of unity, and we are beginning to hear calls for analytical methods that are no longer biased toward the elucidation of unity.

But just what *is* musical unity? Anton Webern wrote a seemingly straight-forward definition:

> Unity is surely the indispensable thing if meaning is to exist. *Unity,* to be general, *is the establishment of the utmost relatedness between all component parts.* So in music, as in all other human utterance, the aim is to make as clear as possible the relationships between the parts of the unity; in short, to show how one thing leads to another [emphasis added].[1]

---

1 Anton Webern, *The Path to the New Music,* trans. Leo Black (Bryn Mawr, Penn.: Theodore Presser, 1963), p. 42.

Webern's definition is typical of twentieth-century modernist thought. The nineteenth century accepted a weaker concept of unity: a work was thought to be unified if all its parts were understandable in relation to the whole.[2] The twentieth-century idea that the parts had to be related not only to the whole but also to each other is a stronger condition. Since we will be concerned largely with recent ideas on unity, we will accept Webern's stronger formulation.

Traditional twentieth-century analytical methodologies encourage us to listen for and to value Webern's brand of unity in music. When a passage of striking discontinuity or apparent disunity is considered (if it is considered at all), the normal way of approaching it is to remark on, or even marvel at, the power of the surprise, but then to demonstrate that the unexpected does, in fact, belong to the piece. Traditional analysis strives to show similarities, whether obvious or hidden, between disparate events. Disunity may be noticed, but it is the underlying unity that is explained. This discrepancy indicates both our analytical prejudices and the fact that we have well-developed theories of musical unity but nothing comparable for disunity. Traditional analysis studies similarity, not difference (difference is central to postmodern thinking in other disciplines, but not yet in music analysis). This is hardly surprising, since unity has long been universally valued and disunity has always been a bit suspect. We have been conditioned to think of disunity as a negative value; it is the absence of something we are told is an indispensable feature of all good music. Thus we tend to believe in our demonstrations of how a piece is unified, but the notion of showing that or how a piece might be disunified probably strikes us as more than a little bizarre.

As Joseph Kerman has pointed out,[3] the concept of unity works better for German instrumental music than for other bodies of music. We need not go too far afield to appreciate the truth of his contention; we do not need to invoke the music of happenings to find compositions that are less than comfortably served by the idea of unity, music for which at least some of our analytical strategies do not work so well. Consider certain Eastern European concert music. Nineteenth-century Russian music, for example, is still sometimes denigrated for its "episodic forms" and "lack of development." The fact that the introductory themes of Tchaikovsky's Violin and First Piano Concertos are never referred to later in those pieces continues to trouble some commentators,[4] who seem to believe in some universal law that requires themes to return. Similarly, the lack of linear, teleological development in Mussorgsky is still sometimes disparaged.

Eastern European music lacking in pervasive unity is not exclusively Russian.

---

2 I am indebted on this point to Karen Painter.

3 Joseph Kerman, "How We Got into Analysis, and How to Get Out," *Critical Inquiry* 7 (1980): 320.

4 I confess to being among the guilty. See my book of program notes, *Listen to the Music* (New York: Schirmer, 1988), pp. 762–63, 765.

What can an analyst who believes in the inevitability of structural unity make of, for example, a nondevelopmental and varied work like Janáček's Sinfonietta? In fact, the one blatant gesture toward formal unity in that piece—the recapitulation of the entire first movement as coda of the fifth movement—strikes at least this listener as a gratuitous gesture toward traditional (i.e., Western European) closure. This superficial bowing to the dictates of Germanic organicism surely does some harm to the work; any resulting unification certainly does not adequately compensate.

I am complaining not that the Sinfonietta's one unifying passage is incongruous (or even disunified) with respect to the rest of the piece, but that the composer felt the need to wrap things up by grafting onto his wonderfully disparate piece a traditional, internally unmotivated, and rather automatic recapitulation. If the coda is indeed structurally unmotivated, then one might argue that it is actually a gesture of disunity. Thus there is a contradiction between its literal relationship to the opening and its unexpectedness in context. This contradiction might be intriguing were it not gratuitous, and were the coda not so long: it is a *complete* rehash of the first movement. Indeed, there are other returns in the Sinfonietta that do not seek to destroy the prevailing disunity. While some passages are unrelated to other one another, other passages do interrelate: the work is not thoroughly disunified. It is hard to imagine a piece that would be totally lacking in unity. When the first movement returns at the end in an apparent attempt to round out the Sinfonietta, however, the artificiality and superficiality of this attempt at closure compromises the work's quirkiness.

If we study discontinuous or nondevelopmental compositions in the normal ways, our analyses will most likely find unity in (or force unity onto) the music. Yet the analytical project is problematized if methodologies are designed to search for unity even in pieces that strike us as less than pervasively unified. When an analysis fails to unify all aspects of a piece, we tend to blame the analytical method as imperfect or the analyst as lacking sufficient skill or insight. We rarely think to blame the piece: perhaps it is difficult to demonstrate pervasive unity in a given composition simply because it is not totally unified![5]

What should our response be to an allegedly disunified piece of music? We might reject it outright, or we might try to constitute it as unified in our minds. Studies in psychology support the notion that perception is an ordering process: to enter a stimulus into our minds, we must encode it in some way. If it has clear cues to its structure, we use them; if not, we invent them. Thus all music that is perceived (i.e., that is not ignored or rejected) is unified to some degree, in some

---

5   For an analysis that attempts to study the disunity as well as unity of a work, see Jonathan D. Kramer, "Unity and Disunity in Carl Nielsen's Sixth Symphony," in Mina Miller (ed.), *A Nielsen Companion* (London: Faber and Faber, 1995), pp. 293–344.

way. So it is hardly surprising that analysis seeks to elucidate unity. There is always a handy analytical method available to demonstrate how (if not that) the music coheres. All we need do is try hard enough, bend the piece or the method sufficiently, or ignore disunifying factors, in order for the piece to come out unified. Thus the analytic mind mimics the listening mind, as analysts have been telling us for a long time. Both listening and analyzing create as well as discover unity. But is that unity really in the music? Or is it in the listener's mind and the analyst's charts and prose?

These challenging questions suggest that we should differentiate between the alleged unity of a composition (whether studied in score or in performance) and that of music as heard, understood, and remembered. I call the former *textual unity,* and the latter *perceptual unity.* We cannot point directly to the textual unity in a score or a performance, but we can isolate the elements that create it: textual unity exists in relationships between events or qualities of music. Textual unity has a degree of objectivity. It is assumed to be demonstrable, whether or not it is experienced. Perceptual unity also resides in relationships—but not among aspects of the music-out-there but among aspects of music-in-here: music as perceived, as encoded in short- and then long-term memory, and as recalled.

It is all too easy to project the perceptual unity of listening back onto the stimulus. The postmodern aesthetic, however, encourages us to separate the two, by conceiving of the text—the music—as autonomous. There is some degree of textual unity in most pieces; there is also a measure of textual disunity in a lot of music. There is a considerable amount of perceptual unity in the mind of the listener; and, indeed, there is a degree of perceptual disunity, or irrationality, in the listener's mind. But the listener's perceptual unity/disunity is not identical to the music's textual unity/disunity.[6]

Since perceiving is an ordering process, perceptual unity is certainly not remarkable. Any music that makes even a modicum of sense to a listener is understood to possess perceptual unity. Thus the title of this essay is an exaggeration: it is impossible to get completely beyond unity in perceived music.

This important point needs to be emphasized: the textual unity of music, the textual unity of performance (which results from the performer's perceptual unity), and the perceptual unity of listening are not the same. The demonstrable unity of a score may have something to do with the perceived unity of a performance

---

6 Thomas Clifton wrote that the word "ordered" is "a description of an experience which may be independent of, and other than, the kinds of orderings injected into the work by the composer. Once again, then, the experience of order says nothing about whether order is there in fact. Order is constituted by the experiencing person, who is just as likely to experience it in a collection of natural sounds as in improvised music or a finely wrought fugue by J. S. Bach" *Music as Heard* (New Haven: Yale University Press, 1983), p. 4.

(although it may not!), but the two are not identical. If we have a perceptually unified experience and if we can demonstrate quasi-objective patterns of textual consistency in a score, it is difficult to resist the temptation to relate the two. Yet perceptual unity and the factors that purportedly create it *are* distinguishable.[7] As Alan Street has stated, "There is simply no reason, still less a necessity, to infer unity of form from that of structure."[8] Or, as Leonard Meyer puts it, perceptual

> unity is neither an objective trait like frequency or intensity, nor a specifiable relationship like an authentic cadence or a *crescendo*. Rather, it is a psychological effect—an impression of propriety, integrity, and completeness— that depends not only on the stimuli perceived, but on cultural beliefs and attitudes ingrained in listeners as standards of cognitive/conceptual satisfaction.[9]

Once we realize that a unified experience is psychological and cultural, that it is not guaranteed by—nor even necessarily related to—motivic or any other kind of consistency, then we should be in a position to appreciate a work's surprises, *non sequiturs,* detours, etc., *for themselves,* without having to find their fundamental principles of textual unification. We have these experiences of surprise all the time, and analysis *can* help us understand them, if only because it tells us what our thwarted expectations might have been.[10] What I am objecting to is the obsession of analysts to find how the surprising events also fit the unified plan of the work. I do not say that such information is not interesting, but only that it can be less important than the impact of the discontinuity.

Schenkerian theory and set theory, arguably the two most common analytic methodologies currently (or at least recently) practiced, are both intense statements on the necessity of, more or less respectively, textual organicism and unity. They are popular because they try to answer a question that has bothered music theorists for generations. But this question—how are works of music unified?—is not the only one to ask, nor is it the most basic. Today we are witnessing not only a widespread acceptance of these two theories but also a growing dissatisfaction with them, somewhat parallel to the uneasy coexistence of latter-day modernism and postmodernism in composition (about which I have something to say below). The more thoughtful of the disaffected do not reject Schenkerian or set theory outright;

---

7 Stephen Davies, "Attributing Significance to Unobvious Musical Relationships," *Journal of Music Theory* 27 (1983): 207.

8 Alan Street, "Superior Myths, Dogmatic Allegories: The Resistance to Musical Unity," *Music Analysis* 8 (1989): 100.

9 Leonard B. Meyer, *Style and Music* (Philadelphia: University of Pennsylvania Press, 1989), p. 326.

10 An intriguing analysis of this sort can be found in Joseph Dubiel, "Senses of Sensemaking," *Perspectives of New Music* 30 (1992): 210–21. Dubiel analyzes what he calls a "gratuitous" move to F minor in the first movement of Haydn's Quartet in D Minor, Opus 76, no. 2.

these methodologies do what they do exceedingly well. But we are coming to realize, now that we have amassed a substantial body of very good analyses, that they do not really explain all that much about the *impact* of music. Only now that the mania for unity is being answered in sophisticated and/or rigorous analyses have we begun to realize how hollow it is. We have begun to understand, as Joseph Kerman has told us in an often quoted passage: "From the standpoint of the ruling ideology, analysis exists for the purpose of demonstrating organicism, and organicism exists for the purpose of validating a certain body of works of art." [11]

One theorist who is willing to confront discontinuities without smoothing them over into textual unities is Brian Hyer.[12] He has studied a passage in Mozart's G Minor Symphony, although he is careful to point out that the discontinuity in this excerpt is typical rather than unique. "The point is that if discontinuities can be found in this most unified of all compositions, then discontinuities can be found anywhere." He demonstrates that mm. 247–51 from the first movement's recapitulation are locally necessary, because of the need to return from a far-flung but structurally inessential motion away from the tonic, although they are not organically necessary to the unfolding of the piece. They have neither motivic precedent nor consequent, they do not appear in the corresponding place in the exposition, and—most significantly—they are motivated not by any global harmonic plan but only by the tonal logic of the preceding few measures, which move the music into a strange and distant area from which return is locally imperative. This passage is exciting because of its textual disunity rather than any sense of belonging organically. The textual unity it contains is, by comparison, rather ordinary: the realization of implied tonal return. A traditional analysis would point to the voice-leading connections between this passage and the previous and subsequent music, thereby positing both unity and continuity; this passage is not, after all, divorced from the movement's continuity in every possible way. But such an analysis privileges continuity over discontinuity, textual unity over disunity. This excerpt in some ways fits in and in other ways does not; it is the prejudices of analysis that make us more able, and more willing, to understand and accept the former over the latter.

In his 1965 book, *Man's Rage for Chaos,* literary critic Morse Peckham quotes a writer who praises artistic unity in a typical manner: "What the poem discovers— and this is its chief function—is order amid chaos, meaning in the middle of confusion, and affirmation in the heart of despair." [13] Peckham then comments,

---

11 Kerman, p. 315.

12 In a preliminary version (read at Columbia University, April 1989) of the unpublished paper "Them Bones, Them Bones, Them Dry Bones: Discontinuities in the First Movement of the Mozart G Minor Symphony."

13 The citation Peckham uses is from Elizabeth Jennings, *Poetry Today,* quoted by a reviewer of her volume *Recoveries* in the *London Times Literary Supplement* (June 11, 1964): 512.

What heartening words those are! What a cozy glow they offer! It is a pity that they are quite false. At least they are false if what is meant is what all such statements mean: order is a defining character of art.[14]

Peckham does not deny that people like, crave, and need order. He devotes a number of pages to what he calls the "rage for order," which relates to the psychological concept of perception as a unifying process.[15] But he does deny that the purpose of art is to provide order in a chaotic world; the world, he feels, is overly ordered. If order is everywhere, it can hardly be the purpose of art to bring order out of chaos. "Everyman experiences order every second of his life. If he did not, he could not cross the room, let alone the street . . . That order is a defining character of art is so utterly untrue that it is downright absurd."[16] Peckham believes that the purpose of art is to present disorienting and disunified experiences, that we in turn are forced to order in our minds if we are to make sense of them. By this process of ordering, we grow as individuals and as a culture.

When it was new, *Man's Rage for Chaos* was particularly popular with the artistic avant garde. More recently, however, the book seems to be routinely ignored, perhaps because it poses a deep threat to the beliefs of modernists and traditionalists alike. But it is, in fact, one of the first statements of the postmodern aesthetic of disunity. Furthermore, Peckham's ideas anticipate recent applications of mathematical chaos theory[17] to the arts.

Despite similarities, however, Peckham's chaos is not the same thing as the chaos of contemporary science. For Peckham chaos is profoundly disorienting, while chaos theory characterizes it as "an orderly disorder."[18] According to the theory, a small, unpredictable, seemingly insignificant event can have enormous consequences (or no consequences at all). This causal event is characterized as disordered because of its randomness, but the large-scale result remains within predictable and hence ordered limits. A frequently used example of chaos theory concerns weather prediction.[19] It is not simply difficult but virtually impossible to

---

14 Morse Peckham, *Man's Rage for Chaos* (New York: Schocken, 1965), p. 31.

15 Peckham has written (p. 30): "Unity of any kind is something the human being always tries to perceive if he possibly can. Indeed there is no set of perceptual data so disparate that human perception cannot create order and unity out of it." Also (p. 41): "Since we value and often madly overvalue whatever is ordered, we tend to impute order to whatever we value, even to the point of distorting perceptual data so that we see something as ordered which in fact is not; . . . perception is not mere passive response to a stimulus but a creative, dynamic act, an act of interpretation."

16 Ibid., p. 33.

17 For highly readable accounts of this new theory, see James Gleick, *Chaos: Making a New Science* (New York: Viking, 1987); Ian Stewart, *Does God Play Dice?* (Oxford: Basil Blackwell, 1989); and N. Katherine Hayles, *Chaos Bound: Orderly Disorder in Contemporary Literature and Science* (Ithaca: Cornell University Press, 1990).

18 Gleick, p. 15.

19 Ibid., pp. 11–23; Hayles, p. 12.

make accurate long-range predictions, because tiny changes in air currents, undetectable in themselves, can lead to ever larger changes, ultimately having considerable impact on the weather. Yet weather is not totally random; some degree of prediction is indeed possible. Weather behavior lies someplace between the orderly and the disorderly. This combination of chaos and order lies at the heart of the science of chaos. "Chaotic systems," writes Katherine Hayles, a scholar with advanced degrees in both chemistry and English, "are both deterministic and unpredictable." [20]

A similar case arises in music: an unexpected, unjustified, unexplained event can have a huge impact on the subsequent music (or even on our retrospective understanding of what we have already heard), even if—*particularly* if—it is not eventually integrated, either motivically or harmonically. We hear the subsequent music differently, even when it involves literal recapitulation, because the context has changed radically. Especially when the music refuses in any substantive way to integrate the unexpected into the fabric or logic of the piece, we listeners take on the burden of making sense of it. I mean that quite literally. We create sense, in order to render the passage coherent. This is our rage for order at work.

Consider, for example, the A-major tune in the finale of Bartók's Fifth String Quartet. I remember first coming to know this piece while I was an undergraduate. I was struck, intrigued, overpowered by the seeming irrationality of this simple tune intruding on the last movement. More than one of my professors was quick to point out that what was truly admirable about this seeming *non sequitur* was how it fundamentally *did* fit in, *did* partake of and even strengthen the tight logical consistency of the piece. I am not sure whether or not these learned professors went on to demonstrate the alleged underlying unity, and I am not particularly interested in justifying the A major passage in terms of tonal, motivic, melodic, harmonic, rhythmic, or abstract set relationships. [21] Nor was I impressed when, after I explained this point in a lecture, a theorist gleefully responded that a contour analysis reveals that the tune is "actually" a transformation of a prominent earlier melody. The power of that passage lies in its unexpectedness and also in just when in the piece we experience the simple/familiar/tonal interrupting the complex/abstract/nontonal. An analysis—such as my friend's contour study—that shows how the tune is, in fact, integrated into the movement may not be false; probably it is demonstrably and objectively true. But it misses the point, if we take the point of analysis to be the explanation of how a piece is heard, how it works, and what it means. Of course if our analytical purpose is more traditional—to find

---

20 Hayles, p. 14.

21 After calling the tune "a grotesque contrast," Elliott Antokoletz offers several such justifications for its harmonic and melodic derivation. See *The Music of Béla Bartók: A Study of Tonality and Progression in Twentieth-Century Music* (Berkeley: University of California Press, 1984), p. 179.

consistencies whether audible or not, whether structural or not, whether significant or not—then explaining the textual unity behind the perceptual disunity of the tune can be a tempting challenge. But I hope for more from musical analysis.

There are two aspects of chaos theory of potential relevance to music. In a chaotic system (1) unexpected events happen, which (2) may or may not have far-reaching consequences. A small air current may be unpredictable in itself, yet it may (or may not) be so situated in space and time that it contributes to a chain of events that culminates in a hurricane. In traditional music, unexpected events do happen. They need not be as massively unpredictable as Bartók's A-major passage, as the analyses (cited above) by Dubiel and Hyer show.[22] An unexpected event may or may not have large-scale consequences for how the music is subsequently understood and/or for how it subsequently unfolds. Chaos theory suggests that the unexpected need not be explained in reference to what has preceded it. In this sense, postmodern music well exemplifies the orderly disorder of a chaotic system. In a piece like John Zorn's *Forbidden Fruit,* the impact of unexpected musical events on the listener's mental representation of the music can be considerable and can alter his or her understanding of the entire work. While one particular quotation of the many in *Forbidden Fruit* may not be capable of generating the musical equivalent of a hurricane, having heard it may nonetheless irrevocably alter a listener's experience. A piece may succeed in ignoring the possible implications of an unanticipated event (just as not every unexpected air current leads to a storm), but this event may still suggest to the listener a profoundly altered context in which to understand the remainder of the piece.

Music that totally avoids the unpredictable—such as randomly generated, pure minimalist, or totally serialized music, for example—is no longer very widely composed. These types (even the random, which usually produces a thorough if grey consistency) represent extremes of textual unity about which increasing numbers of composers are skeptical. Thus, while only a few theorists have yet fully confronted the challenges of chaos theory or the devaluation of textual unity, substantial numbers of postmodern composers *are* responding to these challenges. Disillusioned with the extremes to which the mania for unity can be pushed, they have given up trying to make all or even most aspects of their pieces relate to a germinating cell or to an overriding generative idea—to what philosophers of postmodernism call a "meta-narrative." These composers are working at a time when chaos theory has shown how natural the unpredictable is, even within an orderly system. I do not necessarily suggest direct influence (although I do know some composers who are fascinated by chaos theory), but

---

22 Another such analysis, of a passage from the first movement of Beethoven's Quartet in A Minor, Opus 132, can be found in Jonathan D. Kramer, *The Time of Music,* (New York: Schirmer, 1988), pp. 29–32.

rather that chaos in both the arts and sciences emanates from common cultural concerns.

Why has late twentieth-century culture begun to turn away from order toward chaos? Those who see chaos as a negative[23] will necessarily take a cynical view, but there are those for whom the concept of order has become oppressive and who embrace chaos as a source of freedom. Katherine Hayles states: "As chaos came to be seen as a liberating force, order became correspondingly inimical."[24]

The loss of faith in textual unity and the acceptance of chaos are two important aspects of postmodernism, a term that has recently become common in discussions and criticism of new music, just as it has been applied to architecture, literary theory, and social criticism in countless books and articles.[25] Among musicians as among critics and practitioners of these other arts, there is little agreement on just what the word means. The problem of definition becomes particularly acute when we understand postmodernism as neither a straightforward rejection nor simply an extension of modernism, but rather as having aspects of both.

Furthermore, there is even considerable disagreement over just what constitutes musical modernism. For our purposes, I take twentieth-century modernism to include the progressive and often atonal music composed after approximately 1909. Just as the advent of atonality did not prevent many composers from continuing to create tonal music after 1909, so the rise of postmodernism in music in the mid-1970s did not preclude the continued activity of modernist composers, who thrive today, particularly in academic music departments. Early modernist composers sought new languages in uncompromising and challenging works of great purity, complexity, and originality. These composers and their descendants today are often unconcerned with popular acceptance; sometimes they are contemptuous of the average listener, for whom they rarely compromise. They remain true to their own private expression, continuing to create art for art's sake. This isolation, or alienation, is a common characteristic of modernism.

But postmodernism has other values. Jean-François Lyotard, one of the leading theorists of postmodernism, defines the postmodern simply as "incredulity towards meta-narratives."[26] Similarly, urban theorist David Harvey considers post-

---

23 George Rochberg is one. In his strongly worded response to an earlier article of mine (which is, in turn, a response to his "Can the Arts Survive Modernism?"), he sees only the negative side of disunity, equating it with "divorce, wife abuse, drug abuse, street crime, and intensifying neurosis." See "Kramer vs. Kramer," *Critical Inquiry* 11 (1984): 509–17.

24 Hayles, p. 22.

25 As Rose Rosengard Subotnik remarks with regard to the spread of new critical methods, "for better or worse, music is almost invariably the last art to be affected." Although Subotnik is referring not to postmodernism but to semiology and structuralism, her idea applies widely. See *Developing Variations: Style and Ideology in Western Music* (Minneapolis: University of Minnesota Press, 1991), p. 169.

26 Quoted in David Harvey, *The Condition of Postmodernity* (Oxford: Basil Blackwell, 1989), p. 45.

modernism's rejection of meta-narratives as one important factor that sets it apart from modernism.[27] In music the great meta-narrative, the one constant that romanticism and modernism share, is organic unity. A truly postmodern music, like a truly postmodern music theory, demotes textual unity from the status of a totalizing meta-narrative to one of many possible smaller narratives. Textual unity becomes nothing more than a strategy available to be used (or ignored) in generating or analyzing a piece, or even just a part of a piece.

Particularly relevant to today's music is the division of postmodernism into two camps or styles: neoconservative and radical postmodernism.[28] Neoconservative postmodernism, which art critic Hal Foster feels is better known, is

> conceived in therapeutic, not to say cosmetic, terms: as a return to the verities of tradition ... Modernism is reduced to a style ... and condemned, or excised entirely as a cultural mistake; pre- and postmodern elements are then elided, and the humanist tradition is preserved. But what is this return if not a resurrection of lost traditions set against modernism, a master plan imposed on a heterogeneous present?[29]

When a composer or a piece is labelled postmodern, the postmodernism referred to is usually neoconservative. In these terms, George Rochberg is a quintessential postmodernist, although he rejects the term. He has written an article that condemns modernism as a mistake,[30] and his compositions elide pre- and post-

---

27 Harvey, pp. 8–9. Harvey believes that postmodernism is distinguished not only by a rejection of totalizing meta-narratives but also by an acceptance of discontinuity over continuity, difference over similarity, and indeterminacy over rational logic. I particularly recommend Harvey's introductory critical overview. Harvey is a professor of geography, specializing in urban problems.

28 Other writers have made this distinction. Hal Foster, for example, distinguishes a "postmodernism of reaction" from a "postmodernism of resistance" in "Postmodernism: A Preface," in Foster (ed.), *The Anti-Aesthetic: Essays on Postmodern Culture* (Port Townsend, Wash.: Bay Press, 1983), p. xii. In a subsequent essay Foster expands on his distinction. He substitutes the terms "neoconservative postmodernism" and "poststructuralist postmodernism" in "(Post)modern Polemics," in *Recodings: Art, Spectacle, Cultural Politics* (Seattle: Bay Press, 1985), pp. 120–35. See also E. Ann Kaplan's discussion of Foster's ideas in *Postmodernism and its Discontents* (London: Verso, 1988), pp. 2–3. Jann Pasler applies Foster's categories to music, and she sketches a third species of postmodernism. See "Postmodernism, Narrativity, and the Art of Memory," in Jonathan D. Kramer (ed.), *Time in Contemporary Musical Thought*, which is *Contemporary Music Review* 7 (1993): 19–20. George Edwards sketches a similar distinction between "postmodernism as utopia" and "postmodernism as protest." See "Music and Postmodernism," *Partisan Review* 58 (1991): 701–04.

29 Foster, "Postmodernism: A Preface," p. xii.

30 Rochberg, "Can the Arts Survive Modernism?" *Critical Inquiry* 11 (1984): 317–40. Although I still have trouble with several of Rochberg's ideas, particularly those in his response to me in "Kramer vs. Kramer," I would revise some of the formulations in my response to his original article. See Jonathan D. Kramer, "Can Modernism Survive George Rochberg?" *Critical Inquiry* 11 (1984): 341–54.

modernist elements. Other composers whose recent (but often not earlier) music exemplifies neoconservative postmodernism include John Harbison, Steve Reich, Bernard Rands, Eric Stokes, and Fred Lerdahl. In Lerdahl's pieces, such as *Waves* and *Cross-Currents,* the sonorities and materials sometimes suggest modernism, sometimes premodernism. The organization, based on principles elucidated in the composer's theoretical work,[31] is decidedly organic. In these works Lerdahl subjects a background structure to successive elaborations of ever greater complexity of detail. The results are powerful: organicism may have been reduced to a "mere" possibility in the postmodern age, but it remains a rich possibility. Lerdahl's music represents the best of a neoconservative, but not radical, postmodernism. It is the latter, however, that eschews meta-narratives such as organic unity.

At least some of John Zorn's work exemplifies radical postmodernism. *Forbidden Fruit,* for example, is not textually unified. It offers a considerable dose of postmodern chaos, despite its nostalgia for other musics. Zorn writes about his stylistic eclecticism:

> I grew up in New York City as a media freak, watching movies and TV and buying hundreds of records. There's a lot of jazz in me, but there's also a lot of rock, a lot of classical, a lot of ethnic music, a lot of blues, a lot of movie soundtracks. I'm a mixture of all those things . . . We should take advantage of all the great music and musicians in this world without fear of musical barriers, which sometimes are even stronger than racial or religious ones. That's the strength of pop music today. It's universal.[32]

Listening to *Forbidden Fruit* can be as dizzying as it is electrifying. You never know what is coming next, nor when. The stylistic juxtapositions are amazingly bold. If there were any discernible thread of continuity, the music would surely be more tame, more predictable, more ordinary. But there is not.

Like most taxonomies of the arts, particularly of the contemporary arts, the dichotomy between the two postmodernisms is difficult to apply rigidly. In music, it can sometimes be hard to distinguish neoconservative postmodernism from what might better be called antimodernism—an extreme conservativism in which artists try to return to what is perceived as a golden age before the advent of modernism. "New Romantic" works like Rochberg's *Ricordanza* and Michael Torke's piano concerto *Bronze*—both of which are almost indistinguishable from nineteenth-century music—are good examples, as are many compositions by Stefania M. de Kenessey. Both postmodern and antimodern composers reject some of the sounds

---

31 As formulated in the influential book by Fred Lerdahl and Ray Jackendoff, *A Generative Theory of Tonal Music* (Cambridge, Mass.: MIT Press, 1983), and as refined and extended in several subsequent articles.
32 John Zorn, notes to recording of *Forbidden Fruit* (Elektra/Asylum/Nonesuch 9 79172-2, 1987).

and procedures of modernism and embrace some of the sounds of music from the past, but there are decided differences in the ways those sounds are put together and in aesthetic attitudes. To complicate the matter further, there is still a healthy number of modernists composing today, such as Pierre Boulez, Elliott Carter, Charles Wuorinen, Karlheinz Stockhausen, Milton Babbitt, Harrison Birtwistle, Mario Davidovsky, and Brian Ferneyhough. Aspects of postmodernism, modernism, and antimodernism sometimes mingle in the works of one composer (Luciano Berio, for example). Thus the taxonomy offered here is useful only as an overview, not as a means to place individual works or composers into convenient "isms." It is not very informative to label particular works *exclusively* as postmodernist, antimodernist, or latter-day modernist, or as neoconservative vs. radical postmodernist. These classifications and oppositions, fuzzy as their boundaries may be, do relate to real cultural divisions, however. These categories have exerted a discernible influence on composers, and to some extent recent music has participated in shaping the categories. Thus the relevance to music of these dichotomies is undeniable, even if it is not a particularly useful exercise in tedium to try to ally compositions exclusively with one camp.

The coexistence of latter-day modernists, antimodernists, and postmodernists is not particularly cordial.[33] Several of today's modernists—whether they are composers who continue to create in a modernist style, performers who play mostly modernist music, or reviewers who praise only modernist music—scornfully dismiss postmodernism, in which they see a rejection not only of modernism's purity and austerity but also of the cultural relevance (which should not be confused with popular acceptance) that modernism once had. Hal Foster writes of

---

33 Latter-day modernists may well find themselves in an increasingly difficult position. High modernists (such as Schoenberg and Webern, for example) may have thrived on the lack of public acceptance of their work (at the same time that they deplored it): they knew, whether consciously or not, that the music they were producing was unprecedented, radically new, and profoundly challenging. Thus they could console themselves by saying that the public was not yet ready for the new music. But today's audiences have made little progress toward accepting and enjoying the works of high modernism, so it is hardly surprising that latter-day modernism has few adherents. (There remains a nucleus of enthusiasts in the general public, but their number is small.) Today's modernists cannot comfort themselves with the knowledge that they are breaking new ground, because they are not. Thus modernists in the 1990s can hardly look to the future the way modernists in the 1920s may have. Since listeners still have trouble with the music of Schoenberg and Webern, how likely is it that a large public will rally around the music of, say, Wuorinen or Xenakis? This dilemma, it seems to me, is producing a widespread despondency among our modernists, particularly as they see segments of the public excited by the neoconservative postmodernism they despise.

Lest I be misunderstood, let me state that I tremendously respect the tenaciousness of latter-day modernists, who continue to compose the music in which they deeply believe, despite dwindling financial support, shrinking audiences, disdainful reviews, and the death of some brilliant ensembles that specialized in performing modernist music. I also, for what it is worth, readily admit to admiring and enjoying several recent pieces in the late-modernist mold.

"a modernism long ago purged of its subversive elements and set up as official culture in the museums, the music halls, the magazines";[34] and, we might add, in musical academia and in the awarding of composition grants and prizes. Since in my experience latter-day modernists generally do not recognize a difference between neoconservative and radical postmodernism, they reject all postmodern music as conservative, superficial, simplistic, pandering to popular taste, or—ironically, from my point of view—disunified.

It can indeed be difficult to distinguish postmodern music from antimodern music. For example, Rochberg's Third Quartet[35] strikes me as postmodern, but its neoconservative composer thinks of it as a return to earlier, premodern values.[36] Similarly, I find much of the recent music of John Harbison to be neoconservative, although his tastes as a listener and conductor run from the modernist to the postmodernist. These categories are particularly difficult to sort out because both radical and neoconservative postmodern music may use triads, stylistic eclecticism, diatonic tunes, metric regularity, etc. One difference, though, is the concern with unity: neoconservatives, like latter-day modernists, still value textual unity and organicism as totalizing musical structures, while many radical postmodernists have forsaken this allegiance. Cultural critic Andreas Huyssen discusses the way modernist critics confuse radical postmodernism with neoconservatism:

> [Critics] took them to be compatible with each other or even identical, arguing that [radical] postmodernism was the kind of affirmative art that could happily coexist with political and cultural neoconservatism. Until very recently, the question of the postmodern was simply not taken seriously on the left, not to speak of those traditionalists in the academy or the museum for whom there is still nothing new and worthwhile under the sun since the advent of modernism.[37]

The continued viability of modernism is evident in both recent music and polemics by certain recent composers. In the latter category is a 1984 article by German composer York Höller. Höller's music adheres to a modernist aesthetic (at least it did at the time of his article); it is not at all conservative. Yet his vehement defense of organicism certainly *is* conservative:

> The work of art seems to me to be above all an *organism*, like an organico-energizing system, comparable to a living organism in nature. In

---

34 Foster, *Recodings: Art, Spectacle, Cultural Politics,* p. 125.

35 See my comments about this work in *The Time of Music,* pp. 210–11. See also Pasler's comments in "Postmodernism, Narrativity, and the Art of Memory."

36 Notes to recording of Rochberg's Third String Quartet (Nonesuch Records H-71283, 1973).

37 Andreas Huyssen, *After the Great Divide: Modernism, Mass Culture, Postmodernism* (Bloomington: Indiana University Press, 1986), p. 199.

such a system, all elements are linked by functional relations; they do not result from arbitrary formulation, but from the evolution of a process.[38]

Höller takes as desirable the "congruence" between top-down and bottom-up generative processes of composition, and he assumes that this congruence is "a guarantee of the quality of a musical work."[39] As he goes on, he reveals an attitude toward musical organicism that is markedly close to the views of Schoenberg. Höller typifies a group of middle-aged modernists who are working to preserve the organicist aesthetic of the preceding generation. In the topsy-turvy world of postmodernism, we find a composer like Höller—whose music uses many of the techniques and devices of high modernism—espousing a conservative aesthetic, while on the other hand the ideas of radical postmodernists are often actualized in music of almost comfortable consonance and pseudo-tonality.

Consonance does not guarantee a postmodern aesthetic, however. Some pathbreaking early minimalist works strike me as more modernist than postmodernist. The purity, the strong statement, and the radical newness of such pieces as Steve Reich's *Violin Phase* or Philip Glass's *Music in Fifths* are thoroughly modernist. These composers' attempts to define a new kind of music reflects early twentieth-century experiments, although the actual sounds of their music are dissimilar from those of early atonality. Significantly, early minimalist music is thoroughly unified, and sometimes is even pervasively organic: consider the way Reich's *Four Organs* grows inexorably from its initial material.

Perhaps the grandest achievement of early minimalism is Glass's first opera, *Einstein on the Beach,* written in collaboration with Robert Wilson. In its attempt to redefine opera and to create a new kind of musical theater, *Einstein* is a modernist work; the austerity and purity of both the music and the staging are equally modernist. I do not deny underlying postmodern sensibilities: it is not surprising (at least in retrospect) to find Glass moving into the world of postmodernism in his subsequent operas. But the means are modernist. Concomitantly, the work is thoroughly unified. There are large-scale musical recapitulations, each scene is motivically consistent, there are recurrent visual as well as musical motives, such as the ubiquitous oblong and the finger dancing. I do not mean to detract from *Einstein's* originality. However, for all its discoveries and expansiveness, it remains a unified conception, as do most modernist artworks.

If minimalist diatonicism and repetition can produce both modernist works (such as *Einstein*) and postmodernist works (such as Reich's *Tehillim*), then it is hardly surprising that it is sometimes difficult to untangle modern and postmodern aesthetic attitudes. Another source of confusion between these categories is the use

---

38 York Höller, "Composition of the Gestalt, or the Making of the Organism" *Contemporary Music Review* 1 (1984): 35. Street (p. 78) discusses this article briefly.
39 Ibid., pp. 35–36.

of collage and pastiche by composers of both aesthetic persuasions. There is a difference, however: the postmodernist does not feel the need to retreat behind a mask of ironic commentary, of art as critique. Thus postmodern music often eschews irony.[40] It takes from history, but it does not interpret, analyze, or revise. Furthermore, the quotations in postmodern music are not defended as acts of homage nearly as readily as modernist quotations were and are.

The conflict between modernist (i.e., ironic) and postmodernist (i.e., not ironic) approaches to pastiche was reinforced for me in 1990, when I lectured at the Summer Courses for Young Composers in Kazimierz Dolny, Poland, under the auspices of the International Society for Contemporary Music. I was expected to share several of my own compositions. I presented works chronologically, demonstrating my gradual transformation from a 1960s modernist to a 1980s postmodernist. Most of the students had been educated in and were working within the central European tradition of modernism. They found themselves intrigued with my pseudo-serial piano piece from 1968, somewhat interested in my quasi-minimalist works from 1974 (clarinet and electronics) and 1980 (piano), but utterly mystified by a stylistically eclectic orchestral piece from 1987.[41] One student, an Austrian, expressed what he intended as a criticism: all the diverse styles in this piece were presented without irony, without commentary. I had just let them be what they are. His attitude was decidedly modernist: the only viable way to incorporate the past into the present is with distortion. This attitude shows one reason why postmodernism, at least in music, has thrived more in America than in Europe. Contemporary European composers often seem less willing simply to savor unmediated historicist juxtapositions. They feel they must impose order and purpose, even if that happens through ironic commentary and distortion of sources.

Modernist pastiche acknowledges history: the past is reinterpreted in the present. But postmodern pastiche is anti-historical: the past coexists with, and indeed is indistinguishable from, the present. Critic Madan Sarup discusses pastiche:

The great modernisms were predicated on the invention of a personal, private style. The modernist aesthetic was originally linked to the conception of an

---

40 For a contrary opinion, see Demetri Porphyrios, "Architecture and the Postmodern Condition," in Lisa Appignanesi (ed.), *Postmodernism: ICA Documents* (London: Free Association Books, 1989), p. 89. Porphyrios believes that, at least in architecture, postmodernists are preoccupied with ironic commentary and parody.

41 These four works (plus a fifth) are available on the compact disc *Jonathan Kramer: Five Compositions* (New York: Leonarda Productions, 1990). The five compositions are: *Musica Pro Musica* for orchestra (1987), *Atlanta Licks* for chamber ensemble (1984), *Music for Piano Number 5* (1980), *Renascence* for clarinet and electronics (1974, rev. 1985), and *Music for Piano Number 3* (1968).

authentic self and a private identity which can be expected to generate its own unique vision of the world and to forge its own unmistakable style. The [postmodernists] argue against this; in their view the concept of the unique individual and the theoretical basis of individualism are ideological . . . In a world in which stylistic innovation is no longer possible all that is left . . . is pastiche.[42]

If stylistic innovation is truly no longer possible, if pastiche is all that remains, then all new music must in some sense be quotation. While I am not comfortable with this blanket generalization—I think there is still innovative vitality in computer, spectral, and microtonal music, for example—it is true that many composers have forsaken the quest for novel sounds, new organizing principles, and original compositional strategies for their own sake. Since its materials (although not their combination) are rarely new, postmodern music is often a pastiche of quotations, even when the composer does not consciously intend to refer to other music. Thus, in contrast to modernism's (and romanticism's) commitment to expression, postmodernism is simply presentational.

In his important essay "The Death of the Author," Roland Barthes writes of the inescapability of postmodern quotation and of the attendant shift of unity from the creator to the perceiver (a theme which parallels my earlier ideas on textual vs. perceptual unity):

> We know now that a text is not a line of words releasing a single "theological" meaning (the "message" of the Author–God) but a multi-dimensional space in which a variety of writings, none of them original, blend and clash. The text is a tissue of quotations drawn from . . . many cultures and entering into mutual relations of dialogue, parody, contestation, but there is one place where this multiplicity is focused and that place is the reader, not, as was hitherto said, the author. The reader is the space on which all the quotations that make up a writing are inscribed without any of them being lost; a text's unity lies not in its origin but in its destination.[43]

---

42 Madan Sarup, *An Introductory Guide to Poststructuralism and Postmodernism* (Athens, Ga.: University of Georgia Press, 1989), p. 133.

43 Roland Barthes, "The Death of the Author," in *ImageMusicText,* trans. Stephen Heath (New York: Noonday, 1977), pp. 146, 148. This article is discussed in Michael Newman, "Revising Modernism, Representing Postmodernism: Critical Discourses of the Visual Arts" in Appignanesi, pp. 114–24. At the end of his essay (p. 148), written in 1968, Barthes throws down a challenge to which literary critics have responded but which music analysts are only now, a quarter century later, beginning to consider: "Classic criticism has never paid any attention to the reader; for it, the writer is the only person in literature . . . To give writing its future, it is necessary to overthrow the myth: the birth of the reader must be at the cost of the death of the Author."

Pastiche and collage, primary forms of postmodern discourse,[44] encourage the perceiver to make his or her own perceptual sense of a work of art. In particular, the less a work is textually unified, the more the perceiver must assume the burden of rendering his or her perception of it coherent. To make sense of a chaotic piece like *Forbidden Fruit,* for example, the listener must invest some effort. And, since the ordering is largely the listener's, the piece might well mean or even be very different things to different perceivers. It of course matters what references or quotations present themselves to the listener, just as it matters in what order and for what durations they are heard; these aspects of the structure will presumably be common to all listeners' understanding of the music. But, since the piece apparently lacks unequivocal unifying structures, each perceiver constitutes the work's unity mentally in his/her own way. The resulting multiplicity of responses suggests that there are as many pieces as there are listeners, an idea thoroughly appropriate to postmodern thinking.

Discontinuity and pastiche have been important aspects of some modernist art from early in the twentieth century. Why, then, am I positing textual disunity as a postmodern more than a modernist phenomenon? One reason is that postmodernism in some ways continues and intensifies the modernist project. The discontinuities of modernism can be extreme, but those of the late twentieth-century culture can be more so. They are readily accepted to the extent that we have become all but immune to their power. Cultural critic O. B. Hardison, Jr., invokes MTV to exemplify the recent increase of discontinuity:

> When Jean Cocteau used abrupt discontinuities in his surrealist film *Orpheus* the art world was enchanted. How advanced, how outrageous! The discontinuities of *Orpheus* are trivial compared to the discontinuities accepted as the normal mode of television by TV aficionados of the developed world. The psychoanalytic surrealism of *The Cabinet of Dr. Caligari* or of Ingmar Bergman's *Wild Strawberries* is timid compared to the surrealism that teenagers ingest as a daily diet from musical videos, to say nothing of the spectacular happenings that have become standard fare at concerts by popular entertainers like Michael Jackson or Kiss or Madonna.[45]

Hayles, like Hardison, sees the discontinuities of music videos as quintessentially postmodern. Her ideas can with few changes be adapted to postmodern concert music.

Turn it on. What do you see? Perhaps demon-like creatures dancing; then a

---

45 O. B. Hardison, Jr., *Disappearing through the Skylight: Culture and Technology in the Twentieth Century* (New York: Viking, 1989), pp. 178–79.

cut to cows grazing in a meadow, in the midst of which a singer with blue hair suddenly appears; then another cut to cars engulfed in flames. In such videos, the images and medium collaborate to create a technological demonstration that any text can be embedded in any context. What are these videos telling us, if not that the disappearance of a stable, universal context *is the context* for postmodern culture?[46]

It is interesting that these two theorists, neither of whom as far as I know is a musician or music scholar, turn to popular music videos as a prime exemplar of postmodernism. Of the modest amount of writing to appear concerning musical postmodernism, the majority focuses on popular music. Yet several postmodern composers are seeking to weaken the barrier between pop and art music. While the split between these two may have existed for some time,[47] it intensified in the late nineteenth century (with, for example, the waltzes of Johann Strauss). By the middle of the twentieth century the alienation of modernism brought the music of the concert hall to its farthest remove from pop music. Their purposes were different, their intended audiences were different, their economics were different, and their musical materials and procedures were different. Postmodernism respects no such boundaries, however. Unconcerned with textual unity, and wishing to create a music for people rather than for humankind, postmodern composers are happy to cross the line that separates vernacular from art music. In so doing they may create discontinuities as chaotic as those of MTV and more extreme than those in, for example, modernist works like Stravinsky's *Rite of Spring* or *Symphonies of Wind Instruments*. Crossover music, like Zorn's *Forbidden Fruit* or William Bolcom's Third Symphony, creates powerful discontinuities that are possible only with the suspension of underlying textual unity—not only of materials and style but also of musical genre (e.g., pop vs. classical).

Bolcom's symphony is sometimes dismissed by latter-day modernists as a sprawling, seemingly random series of unrelated styles. True, the piece does include modernist passages, vernacular passages, and many styles between those extremes, all within the second movement. That movement is not a hodgepodge but rather a dynamic opposition of seemingly incompatible idioms. In particular, the

---

46 Hayles, p. 272.

47 For a brief yet interesting discussion of the split between popular and art music through the ages and the attempts of postmodernists to close the gap, see Kyle Gann, "Boundary Busters: How To Tell New Music from Music that Happens To Be New," *Village Voice* (September 3, 1991): 85–87. Gann's ideas are controversial: other scholars place the popular/art split far more recently. Lawrence W. Levine, for example, demonstrates convincingly that in America the split is a product of late nineteenth- and early twentieth-century social conditions. See *Highbrow/Lowbrow: The Emergence of Cultural Hierarchy in America* (Cambridge, Mass.: Harvard University Press, 1988), pp. 84–168.

opposition of high modernism and American pop music gives the symphony its vitality. While he has not produced a whirlwind like *Forbidden Fruit,* Bolcom's subtle mastery of timing and surprise make the symphony a thorough delight. Its seemingly illogical progressions have in fact deep meaning, whether they are humorous or poignant. Bolcom juxtaposes different kinds of music without distortion, without commentary, without irony, without the feeling that any of them is the natural language of the symphony upon which the others are intruding.[48]

How, when, where, and why did postmodernism arise? Huyssen considers it primarily an American phenomenon, with roots in the 1960s' attempt to recreate a vital avant garde and thereby renew modernism. He labels this '60s avant garde the "Duchamp–Cage–Warhol axis." Huyssen explains[49] that the artistic revolts of the '60s were not directed against modernism *per se.* After all, the works of the Duchamp–Cage–Warhol axis certainly have a lot in common with modernism. What such artists were rejecting, rather, was the image high modernism had attained, its welcome into society as chic, its use in advertising and media, its cultural acceptability. Thus the revolt against what modernism had come to mean was carried out in the spirit of what modernism had originally meant. The avant garde music of Cage and similar composers and artists tried to be as revolutionary as the music of Schoenberg, Webern, Stravinsky, and Ives had been a half century earlier. The avant garde music of the '60s was not yet, therefore, postmodern, although it differed in some fundamental ways from earlier high modernist music. Part of the reason '60s music was still modernist was that it still accepted—indeed, strove for—textual unity, although of a new kind: consistency more than organicism.

Huyssen believes that the '60s experimentation in Europe, particularly Germany, was also an attempt to recapture the modernist impulse, but for a different reason: modernism had been cut off by the Second World War. This explains why music of the Darmstadt school, for example, and also of the avant garde in Poland, represented a resurgence of modernism rather than a birth of postmodernism. America had not been torn apart by the war; it had, furthermore, accepted many modernist artists as refugees from Europe, against whom native artists eventually rebelled. Thus by the '60s the time was ripe for an artistic revolution in this country.

The music of Cage came closer to breaking with its modernist antecedents than did its European counterparts. Particularly in the '60s Cage created and promoted a music that was chaotic in one sense, since in it no event responds to any other

---

48 By his Fifth Symphony, composed ten years later, Bolcom permits these different styles to flow one into the next, allowing the listener to accept the work's diversity rather than confront its oppositions.

49 Huyssen, pp. 189–90.

event, but not at all chaotic in another sense; it was a music if not of organicism, then at least of overwhelming consistency, at least as usually performed. In all performances I have heard of *Atlas Eclipticalis,* for example, every event is so much like every other event that, even though they are not interrelated in any functional or implicative manner, they belong together and to the piece. In performance, this music *is* textually unified: while one thing may not lead to another, there is certainly an utmost relatedness between all the parts (I am again invoking Webern's definition of unity, quoted above). Many of Cage's '60s pieces may, in Peckham's terms, present the listener with profound disorder, since they lack anything resembling typical musical structure and often do not even contain anything like traditional musical sound. But they are not chaotic in the sense of chaos theory, because the lack of relationship between constituent events precludes any individual event having large structural impact. Since no event responds to any other event, a seemingly random fluctuation cannot affect an entire piece. For that to happen would require more compositional control over interrelationships than Cage was willing to exercise. Because of its consistent textual unity, the music of the Duchamp–Cage–Warhol axis was finally more modernist than postmodernist but—because of its lack of integrated form—nearer to postmodernism than were its European counterparts.

It must be acknowledged that several theorists of postmodernism prefer to characterize Cage as a postmodernist rather than a modernist.[50] Indeed, Cage's music displays several of the traits of postmodernism, including open form, chance, anarchy, listener participation, and indeterminacy. Nonetheless, because of its avant-garde experimentation and its continued engagement with textual unity (at least as usually performed), I prefer to understand it as late modern, or at least as transitional—although that is strange term to apply to such an original and influential body of work.

Cage remained an avant gardist as long as the concept had any currency. His intense desire to show us how to experience life as we experience art was the rallying cry for the American avant garde of the 1960s. This very American attitude is at odds with the aesthetic of high modernism, which sought to create works of such purity and austerity that they were destined to remain far removed from daily life. Yet the art-as-life works are as unified as life itself and hence retained one crucial component of the modernist (and, indeed, the romantic) aesthetic. The artist-as-genius of romanticism and high modernism may have given way to the artist-as-prophet in a figure like Cage, but it remained for the true postmodernists to give us the artist-as-everyman.[51]

---

50 Gregory L. Ulmer, for example, discusses the manner in which Cage "postmodernizes" verbal texts. See "The Object of Post-Criticism" in Foster, *The Anti-Aesthetic,* pp. 102–07.

51 Modernist Udo Kasemets anticipated this idea in his 1968 exhortation that "for a better life

31

The defeat of the totalizing meta-narrative of textual unity may not be a defining characteristic of all musical postmodernism, but it is one of the stronger aspects of radical postmodernism. The demise of the notion that the unity of musical texts is intimately related to the unity of the listening experience suggests that we should also be skeptical of the relationship between the composer and the music. The act of composing may (to some degree) be unified behavior, the musical text may (to some degree) be unified, a performance may (to some degree) be unified, an analysis may (to some degree) be unified, and the listening experience may (to some degree) be unified, but these five possible unities are only weakly interrelated. The focus of the creative act is moving away from the composer toward the text and, ultimately, the listener.[52] Significantly, several music theorists are shifting their attention away from the score and the composer's methods toward the music as constituted in listeners' minds. This scholarly abandonment of the composer is anti-romantic and, by extension, anti-modernist. It goes along with Roland Barthes' idea of the death of the author, which may be translated into the death of the composer. Locating unity, expression, and creativity in the listener implies that, as mentioned above, there are as many musical texts—as many pieces—for a given compositional act or performance as there are listeners. Is this idea incompatible with the analytical project? No, it suggests rather that studies of compositional procedures, scores, performances, and above all perceptual mechanisms are different, perhaps even independent, enterprises.

As is appropriate in this postmodern age, many composers and music theorists are asking some critical and difficult questions, several of which I have considered in this essay. Is music truly unified, or is it just perceived as and understood to be unified? Must we accept that music is unified simply because it can be analyzed as unified? Where does musical unity reside: in the compositional act, on the printed page which analysis assiduously studies, in the sounds performers present to our ears, or in our minds? What does the demonstrated textual unity of a score have to do with the experienced perceptual unity of a performance? Can we achieve an analytical understanding of discontinuity, surprise, disunity, disorder, and even chaos?

More and more composers are creating music that demands such an understanding if it is to be studied in any meaningful way. Their music has

---

everybody should become an artist." See "Eight Edicts on Education, with Eighteen Elaborations," *Source: Music of the Avant Garde* 4 (1968): 42.

52 This tripartite division of the analytical subject parallels Jean-Jacques Nattiez's three parts of musical semiology: the poietic level (i.e., processes of creation), the esthesic level (i.e., meanings constructed by active listeners during the process of perceiving), and the neutral level—physical traces that result from the poietic process (i.e., the material reality of the music, whether a live performance, recorded performance, or printed score). See *Music and Discourse: Toward a Semiology of Music,* trans. Carolyn Abbate (Princeton: Princeton University Press, 1990), pp. 10–16.

decisively rejected textual unity as a ruling metaphor, as a totalizing meta-narrative. I am intrigued by this postmodern music, which strikes me as profoundly relevant to its cultural milieu. And I am encouraged that some theorists and analysts are responding to the postmodern challenge by studying musical values and processes that actually are *beyond unity*.[53]

---

53 I am indebted to John Halle, Severine Neff, Karen Painter, Jann Pasler, and John Rahn for penetrating readings of earlier drafts of a longer version of this essay and for several useful suggestions. Warren Burt, George Fisher, Stefan Litwin, and Allen Otte also were helpful. I appreciate Elizabeth West Marvin's urging me to write the article. Papers derived from this article were presented in several public forums: as the keynote address to the Florida State University Music Theory Society, January 19, 1991; in a lecture at the University of Kentucky, March 20, 1991; as an informal talk at the third annual Montanea International Composers Conference, Talloires, France, July 11, 1991; as a paper read at the Fourth International Music Analysis Conference, City University of London, September 19, 1991; as the keynote address to the Indiana Theory Symposium, Indiana University, April 4, 1992; as a keynote address to a regional conference of the Society for Composers, Bates College, April 25, 1992; and in lectures at Northwestern University on November 19, 1992, the City University of New York Graduate Center on February 22, 1993, and Carleton College on January 29, 1994. I appreciate useful comments and criticisms from several audience members on these occasions. At the Montanea Conference, Robert Cogan told me about his recently completed article "Composition: Diversity/Unity," *Interface* 20 (1991): 137–41. He has revised and expanded this intriguing essay as "The Art-Science Music after Two Millennia," which follows this essay.

The Art-Science of Music after Two Millennia

Robert Cogan

This essay addresses several themes: first, music as the art-science of sound; second, the fundamental aesthetic notions of unity and diversity reconsidered; third, the beginnings of music, connecting early traces of surviving music to the present. Several voices of the author will be heard: the composer, the music theorist, and finally the person who simply (simply?) listens and tries to understand. Multiplicity of voices itself is an important theme.

The approach to a new century and a new millennium induces a certain historical vertigo: where are we, where have we been, where are we going? The music world's current rear-view orientation is somewhat illusory. Despite "early music," despite an obsessive individual and institutional nostalgia, our culture's musical past still tends to be quite shallow, largely oblivious to music's historical beginnings and global diversity. Our views of the musical future, when we bother to have them, incline to be equally thin: often directed towards the technology of musical production rather than towards a vision of what might be produced.

Look and listen about us! Primeval forests fall, mountains explode, cities and empires crumble—daily we are amazed—but it is equally amazing that a few dozen sounds (verbal or musical), a few pen or brush strokes on paper, a scroll, or a wall, can survive the chaos and destruction of millennia. In the global human panorama, where is music? Our direct experience of it is rather recent, short-termed. We have virtually no music of the Greek epoch, no equivalent of Homer, Sophocles, or Plato; no *Bible*; no musical Lascaux caves, pyramids, or Parthenon. If the amazing creative outburst of the "axial period" of the sixth century B.C. was musical, if parallel to the contemporary giants Confucius and Buddha, Jeremiah and Heraclitus, Pythagoras and Aeschylus, there were comparable musical giants, we hardly know them.[1] Music seems young, or our knowledge of it.

During the past two millennia the music we know flowered. Of earlier music only verbal rumors remain: biblical mention; chanted choruses of Greek drama,

---

1 The idea of the fifth and sixth centuries B.C. as the "axial period" in human history derives from the philosopher Jaspers: Karl Jaspers, *The Origin and Goal of History* (London: Routledge, 1953), pp. 1–21.

now spoken or silent. Often in those early rumors, however, there are intimate ties to mathematics and science: Pythagorean ratios, Sanskrit tuning calculations, Chinese bell metallurgy—the art-science of sound, continued in the medieval quadrivium of arithmetic, astronomy, geometry, and music.[2]

I

Where is the deepest surviving musical past, the edge of our audition into the historical void, the second-biggest bang? Example 1 shows the first phrase of a ten-minute instrumental piece, *Yu-lan* ("Elegant Orchid"). Its surviving notation, given in Figure 1, dates from 550 A.D.; the specified instrument is the *ch'in*, the plucked table-lute that is the principal instrument of Chinese classical music.[3] The given composer—can it be true?—is Confucius, which may mean that its actual composition occurred a millennium earlier. Whether we date it 550 B.C. or A.D. it remains one of our earliest large-scale instrumental musical relics.

Example 1: *Yu-lan*, First Phrase

---

2   On Chinese bell-tuning see Huang Xiang-Peng, "Archeology in Morphomusicology, on Zeng Houyi's Bells," *Sonus* 4/2 (1984): 1–13.

3   *Yu-lan* lies as far back as we can see with any clarity; of course it too had antecedents, now almost entirely lost. On the history and manuscripts of *Yu-lan* (*Youlan*), and on its historical attribution to Confucius see [David] Ming-Yueh Liang, *Music of the Billion* (New York: Heinrichshofen, 1985), pp. 200–01. On the *ch'in* (*qin*) see: R. H. Van Gulik, *The Lore of the Chinese Lute* (Tokyo: Sophia, 1968). The transcription of excerpts from *Yu-lan* derives from [David] Ming-Yueh Liang, *The Chinese Ch'in* (San Francisco: Chinese National Music Association, 1972), p. 249–61. *Yu-lan* appears in two recordings: "Exotic Music of Ancient China" (Lyrichord LL 122 [LP]) and "Chine: L'art du Qin" (Ocora 560001 [CD], 1990). This essay's spectrographs derive from the latter; Li Xiangting is the performer.

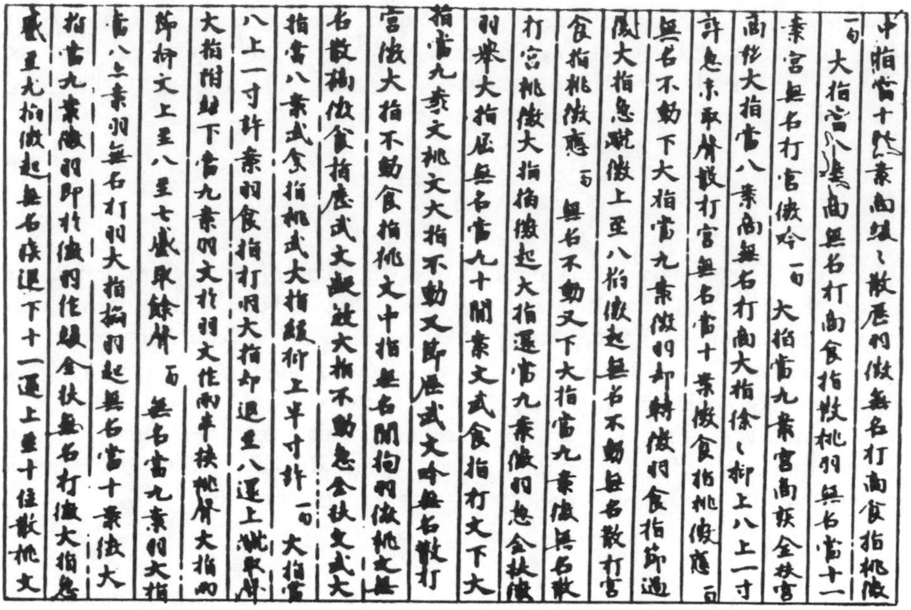

Figure 1: *Yu-lan*, **Tang Dynasty Manuscript**

What does *Yu-lan* tell about music then and now—now, because I happily embrace it as my earliest precursor? To begin, it reveals that music is an art of sounds and design: sonic design. Let me suggest what I mean by design. Example 2 is a sketch of the piece's first section (*P'ai* I). Immediately you will notice its long linear double arch: a scalar ascent reaching across two octave registers, which then curves back to its origins. Of the four parts of this design, the middle two form twin crests, close variants of each other. The outer two provide a low-register frame for the motion, a fixed takeoff and landing point.

The smaller parts of *Yu-lan* reflect the larger, so that the design is what we now, following the mathematician Mandelbrot, call *fractal*—self-similar on different scales.[4] For example, the manuscript's first phrase is subdivided into four gestures, or *chü*; four *chü* comprise the phrase, four phrases comprise the section (*p'ai*), four sections comprise the piece. The piece is, thus, at every level an example of the archetypal four-part Chinese *ch'i-ch'êng-chuan-ho* structure.[5]

4 Benoit Mandelbrot, *The Fractal Geometry of Nature* (New York: Freeman, 1977).
5 Liang, *The Chinese Ch'in*, pp. 224–29.

Example 2: *Yu-lan*, **Linear Design of First Section (*P'ai* I)**

This design consists of sounds—and what sounds! Here, however, is the rub: musicians have historically been unable to describe, analyze, or understand sounds. We analyze pitches frequently, rhythms occasionally, sounds almost never. Elsewhere I have quoted Wittgenstein, whose first example of our inability to describe our knowledge was "how a clarinet sounds."[6]

We have just lived through two centuries of discovery and exploration of wave phenomena: of light and color beginning in the nineteenth century (from electromagnetism to Impressionist color painting, to the camera, film, and more recently, television and lasers); and of sound in the twentieth century (recording, sound synthesizers, computer music, digital sound, sampling, voice prints). We understand, analyze, and synthesize the wave phenomena of light, colors, and sounds in utterly new ways. The ability to open the previously closed black box of

6   Ludwig Wittgenstein, *Philosophical Investigations*, trans. G. E. M. Anscombe (New York: Macmillan, 1953), p. 36e, cited in Robert Cogan, *New Images of Musical Sound* (Cambridge, Mass.: Harvard University Press, 1984), p. 1.

Yu-lan's distinctive, subtle sounds is at hand. After more than two millennia of sonic ignorance, we are beginning to address the mysteries of the magic encoded in the sounds that bewitch us: a genuinely new ability that we hope will lead to new enchantments.

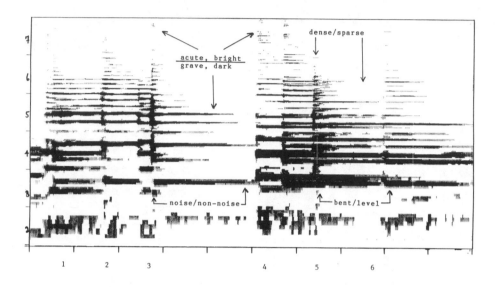

Figure 2: *Yu-lan*, Spectrographic Detail: Six Repeated G's from *P'ai* I

When we do this, what do we find? One tool developed to unlock sonic secrets is spectrographic analysis, which samples and reveals the varying partial or overtone structures of complex sounds and sound sequences—the previously hidden features that create our changing sonic impressions.[7] In the midst of *Yu-lan*'s first phrase the note G repeats six times. Analysis of the spectrograph reproduced as Figure 2, reveals not repetitive similarity, but rather a wealth of opposing sonic differences and nuances in the performance of the six G's: dense, cluttered spectra (many spectral lines) opposing sparse, empty spectra (few lines); sharp, noisy attack spectra (the shaded bands) opposing non-noisy, decaying resonances (absence of bands); level spectra opposing bent spectra; acute, bright spectra opposing grave, dark spectra. To obtain all these diverse spectral contrasts from a single note, each sound requires different instrumental techniques: open

7 On spectrographic analysis and the oppositional interpretation of spectra see Cogan, *New Images of Musical Sound*. This essay's spectrographs have been produced with Hypersignal Plus software, and with the technical assistance of Mr. Harry Norris.

string or stopped, presence or absence of an elaborating note, note-bending, plucking with the fingerflesh or fingernail—all specified in Yu-lan's ancient verbal notation.

(harmonics, entire example)

Figure 3: *Yu-lan*, **Spectrographic Detail: Harmonics from** *P'ai* II

These changing, opposing G's form a striking set of events within the double arch design of the first section (*P'ai* I). In the second section (*P'ai* II) the initial ascent resumes, climbing to a yet higher region. At the apex of this new ascent we observe an entirely new spectral quality, shown in Figure 3. A superb sonic contrast is revealed by the spectrograph: the frail, sparse, ghostly spectrum of *ch'in* harmonics that is vividly opposed to the richer, more dense earlier spectra of the instrument's open and stopped strings.

This sonic contrast, this new opposition of spectral registers, densities, and qualities is the goal of the entire unfolding design. As the ethnomusicologist [David] Ming-Yueh Liang observed, "All *ch'in* schools believed that *ch'in* music should reflect the way of the universe, its basic organization of positive and negative forces, hard and soft, or light and dark. These concepts oppose each other, and opposition creates change or movement, the vital force of living." [8]

The remainder of *Yu-lan* consists of ever more intense juxtapositions of these opposing qualities, the play of sonic *yang* and *yin*. At the farthest edge of our musical universe, we find this extraordinary object with its rich subtle design of opposing colors and forces.

---

8 Liang, *The Chinese Ch'in*, p. 125.

II

So in our earliest known musical beginnings, we find a fascinating music of design and sounds: opposing, contrasting sonic qualities and features. This fact poses a serious challenge to many traditional notions about music. In the first place, there is the rich sophistication of the ancient object itself, far removed from conventional notions of simple, crude beginnings.

In addition, *Yu-lan* requires that we recognize *opposition* as a primary constructive principle. Consequently, I propose here an *oppositional poetics*, similar to that of contemporary linguistics: "One thing can be distinguished from another thing only insofar as it is contrasted with or opposed to something else, that is, insofar as a relationship of contrast or opposition exists between the two."[9] Indeed, let us borrow from linguistics its fundamental contrast: the *invariant/variant* opposition. Much thought and energy in the aesthetics and theory of music have been devoted to processes of unity (invariance), while comparatively little have been devoted to the necessary complementary processes of diversity and opposition (variance). Our fundamental assumptions about music, about musical works and values, are wholly imbued with the notion of unity. Most often we regard the musical work as a single object— fixed, knowable, immutable, unified—rather than as a set of opposing, mutable, surprising, open-ended possibilities. Why one, and not the other? Why is the one assumed to be superior, preferable—indeed the only proper possibility?

From this fundamental unitary assumption many others have followed. For example, the nineteenth-century saw improvisation displaced to the outer margins of European music. The improvised elaboration and cadenzas of earlier seventeenth- and eighteenth-century European music gave way to the composed elaboration and cadenzas of Beethoven, Chopin, and Brahms.[10] Did the improviser, free and uncontrolled, threaten an ideal, predetermined unity with unbridled, unchanneled diversity?

Improvisation came to be viewed not as spontaneous fantasy and individual expressive nuance, but rather as irrelevance. We have pursued the dream, or nightmare, of the totally controlled musical object far into the twentieth century, into electronic and computer music. But its effect is far deeper. It dominates our notion of the ideal edition (the single editorial truth), the authentic instrument, the

---

9 N. S. Trubetzkoy, *Principles of Phonology*, trans. C. A. M. Baltaxe (Berkeley: University of California Press, 1969), pp. 13–31. Also see Roman Jakobson and Linda Waugh, *The Sound Shape of Language* (Bloomington: Indiana University Press, 1979).

10 Even earlier, J. S. Bach was criticized for notating the previously improvised elaborations; see *The Bach Reader*, ed. Hans David and Arthur Mendel (New York: W. W. Norton, 1945), p. 238. Current editorial practice tends to obscure Bach's penchant for variants, for changing (slightly or greatly) a piece each time he recopied it—an improvisation of the pen.

definitive performance, the perfect recording, and even the authoritative unchallengable analysis!

Musics as distant and different as Afro-American (now global) jazz and North Indian *ragas* testify to the eternal power of improvisation, but their presence has created a new polarization, with dogmatic absolutists on both sides: improvisation never vs. improvisation only.[11] The conflict about improvisation is, however, only a symptom of a more general confusion that surrounds variance and invariance — or unity, opposition, and diversity.

III

In writing about the sonic oppositions of *Yu-lan* and about an oppositional poetics, I am of course writing about my own compositional preoccupations. For almost thirty years, my works have invited the active improvised participation of the performer in the creation of sonic experiences and a sonic universe.[12] I find this invitation, this improvisation, necessary, for the sonic is inescapably intimate and subtle, affected by and tied to the slightest unpredictable move, the most intimate breath of the performer. To wholly predetermine and notate every detail of sonic nuance (in addition to everything we now notate) would be to create a monstrosity of control and complication, a notation at once unreadable and unperformable.

Having invited performers into the creation of sonic (as well as rhythmic) nuance, and having deeply appreciated and enjoyed their contributions to it, I have concluded that to exclude them from the design of the musical structures at the highest level is inconsistent and arbitrary; so they are now invited there too. The opposition *composed/improvised* has become an essential feature of my work, although the listener may never specifically know which is which!

For these reasons among others, many of my works take the form of open-ended folios in which not only the finest details but also the large flow is created by the performer, selecting from options I provide. *Utterances*, for one or two solo voices, is such a folio.[13] Page nineteen of this work is the only page (of the sixty now

---

11 The word "improvisation" is a problem; its current aura hardly includes the elaborate, highly rationalized theoretical basis (including tuning, scalar structure, consonance and dissonance, meter, ornamentation, and forms) that underlie North Indian improvisation, or its traditions of apprenticeship and learning.

12 The word "performer" is also a problem; I use it to mean a creatively active participant in a performance, as opposed to a vocal or instrumental technician. This definition corresponds, I believe, to performance practice throughout most of European music history and in many other music cultures.

13 Robert Cogan, *Utterances* (Cambridge: Publication Contact International, 1977). Two different recordings exist, both by Joan Heller, soprano (Spectrum SR–128 [LP], 1980; and Neuma 450–72 [CD], 1988). The recordings reveal some of the variant possibilities of the open-ended

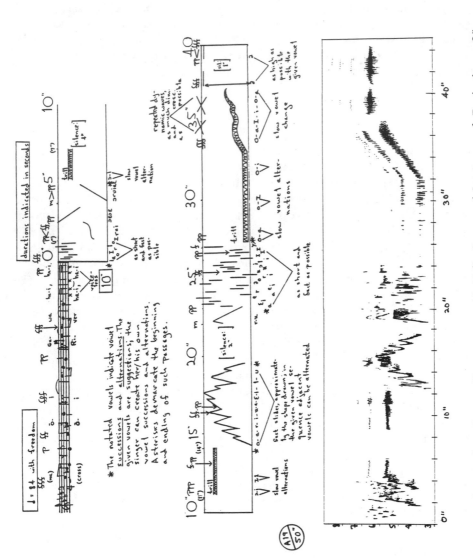

Example 3: Robert Cogan, *Utterances*: p. 19, Folio Score and Spectrograph Beginning at 0"

existing; more may appear) that must occur in every performance. The bulk of page nineteen is based entirely on linguistic vowels; other opposing pages are based on consonants, or on linguistic combinations derived from a wide variety of quotations—from poetic, philosophical, or other texts in a variety of languages. (Some segments of *Utterances* are based on synthetic language: freely created syllables and words.) Example 3 reproduces page nineteen of the score and a spectrograph of its performance; there appear vowel points, vowel trills, vowel slides—opposing acute and grave vowels in various oscillations, combinations, and successions, each vowel having a different spectrum.

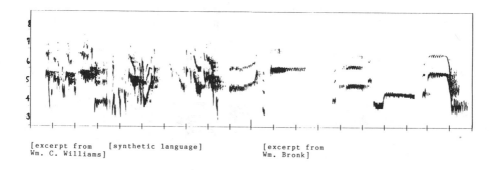

[excerpt from   [synthetic language]   [excerpt from
Wm. C. Williams]   Wm. Bronk]

Figure 4: Robert Cogan, *Utterances*: p. 32, Spectrograph

Figure 4 (a spectrograph of page 32 of the score) illustrates a segment in synthetic language: syllables that do not occur in English. This segment is opposed by settings of textual bits drawn from two American poets: William Carlos Williams and William Bronk. In *Utterances* every fragment, every utterance, has not only an opposing text and spectrum, but also an opposing musical space deployment, an opposing rhythm, and an opposing musical language (for example, number of notes and note-collection).

Figure 5 (from pages 2, 10, and 27) opposes additional bits from Williams and Bronk, set with twelve notes, to four- and five-note Kwakiutl and Japanese quotations. The textual linguistic oppositions are magnified by musical settings in the most extreme vocal registers, and (in one case) by the singer's use of a rattle.

The idea of expanding the array of vocal oppositions by means of vocal resonators (hands, tubes, physical objects, bullhorns) pervades my *whirl . . . ds II*:

---

folio format; the spectrographs (Figures 4–6) derive from the Neuma CD. The two-voice versions are called *Polyutterances*; see the Neuma CD 450–89 on which Ms. Heller sings both tracks.

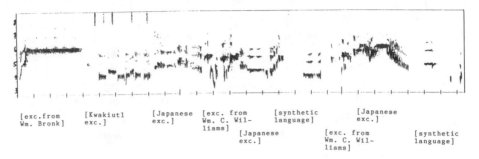

[exc.from Wm. Bronk]	[Kwakiutl exc.]	[Japanese exc.]	[exc. from Wm. C. Wil- liams]	[synthetic language]		[Japanese exc.]	
				[Japanese exc.]		[exc. from Wm. C. Wil- liams]	[synthetic language]

Figure 5: Robert Cogan, *Utterances*: p. 10, preceded by p. 2, followed by p. 27;
Spectrograph

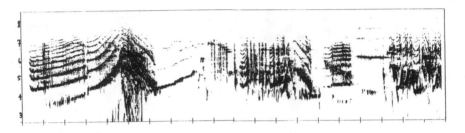

Figure 6: Robert Cogan, *whirl . . . ds II: red allen hock it*: pp. 18–20, "kIdz;"
Spectrograph

red allen hock it, for two amplified voices and projections,[14] excerpted as the spectrograph of Figure 6. But there the plot thickens further. It is evident that there is no clear boundary between language and music—both are sonic phenomena. *whirl . . . ds II* revolves on the axis of language, exploring both its auditory and visual features. It is a work of parallels and oppositions between light, color, and sound—waves seen and waves heard—all set in motion by language. The twin train of visual projections consists of language as calligraphy, graffiti, textures, colors, physical associations, and finally spectrographs of the vocal sounds themselves—all thrown into opposition with each other and with the twin train of voices. The texts' words become projected pictures and amplified sounds; and the sounds themselves become projected spectrographs, part of the train of visual projections.

---

14 Robert Cogan, *whirl . . . ds II: red allen hock it* (Cambridge: Publication Contact International, 1969). Recorded by Joan Heller and Patrice Pastore, sopranos (Spectrum SR–163 [LP], 1982). The spectrograph (Fig. 6) derives from this recording.

IV

"It is only opposites which powerfully move our souls." [15]
Claudio Monteverdi

What can oppositional theory tell us about other musics? In the book *New Images of Musical Sounds*, I explored its uses for illumination of tone color and for development of an analytical sonic theory, examining European music from Gregorian chant to Risset, as well as examples of Balinese, Tibetan, and American music. Others, for example Wayne Slawson in his book *Sound Color* have made similar, complementary contributions.[16] We all owe much to the structural, oppositional linguistic theories of De Saussure, Trubetzkoy, and especially Roman Jakobson—and equally to a dialectical tradition reaching back to the very beginnings of philosophy as a human discipline.[17]

I have written elsewhere about oppositional thinking in the music of Edgard Varèse.[18] Roberta Lukes has documented the independent, oppositional approach of Varèse and the architect–designer Le Corbusier in the creation of their multi-media *Poème Electronique*; each artist agreed to work autonomously, without specific knowledge of or reference to the input of the other.[19] There the visual and the sonic unfolded as distinct, opposing worlds, an opposition further reflected in the colliding structure Varèse created in the sonic domain itself.

It would be interesting to continue such investigations in music of the "radical" American tradition, for example those composers from Ives to Cage who offer such obvious grounds for an oppositional approach, with its conceptual space for improvisation, contradiction, and diversity. However, I prefer to focus here, however briefly, on the oppositional approaches of two of the most distinguished traditional composers of our time, Olivier Messiaen and Elliott Carter.

The opening "Liturgie de cristal" of Messiaen's *Quatuor pour la fin du temps* juxtaposes four independent, opposing instruments; each instrument (clarinet, piano, violin and cello) revolves in its own time and space, speaking its own musical language in its own opposing cycle of repetitions and variations. The cello speaks only in the whole-tone scale, Mode 1 in Messiaen's system of symmetrical modes.[20] The piano speaks not in Mode 1, but rather in Mode 2 (the octotonic

---

15 Claudio Monteverdi, Foreword to *Madrigali guerrieri ed amorosi*, 1638.

16 Wayne Slawson, *Sound Color* (Berkeley and Los Angeles: University of California Press, 1985).

17 Roman Jakobson, *Six Lectures on Sound and Meaning* (Cambridge, Mass.: MIT Press 1978); and Roman Jakobson, *Language in Literature* (Cambridge, Mass.: Harvard University Press, 1987).

18 Robert Cogan, "Varèse: An Oppositional Sonic Poetics," *Sonus* 11/2 (1991): 26–35.

19 Roberta Lukes, "The Poème Electronique of Edgard Varèse," doctoral dissertation in progress, Harvard University.

20 Olivier Messiaen, *Technique de mon langage musical* (Paris: Leduc, 1942), pp. 51–56.

scale) and in Mode 3, as well as in a recurring dialect of juxtaposed pentatonics unique to it (see Example 4). It incorporates these different opposing dialects into a single large repetitive arch design. The piano's cycles of pitch repetition ("color," to use the medieval term) do not coincide with its cycles of rhythmic repetition (the medieval "talea," or iso-rhythm); consequently, on each repetition of the piano's harmonic cycle the rhythmic durations of the harmonies are different. Thus the piano part by itself unfolds several distinct opposing threads—different musical dialects and different cyclical rhythmic patterns, none coinciding. And all of these unfold in opposition to the aforementioned cello, an independent chirping violin, and an extended, enveloping clarinet song, somewhere between bird and human— all unfolding at the same time.

In his *String Quartet No. 2* Elliott Carter created a four-part debate, a tetra-logue, each instrument with its distinctive, personal, opposing intervàllic musical language and rhythmic character. The metronomic, march-like second violin is dominated by major thirds, sixths, and sevenths; in contrast, the accelerating, on-rushing cello is distinguished by perfect fourths, minor sixths, and registrally expanded tritones. Each of the other instruments is also uniquely characterized, rhythmically and intervalically.[21]

Carter had already preceded this work by the Cello Sonata, whose regular, metronomic world of the piano is opposed to the rhapsodic, rhythmically free world of the cello; and by the *String Quartet No. 1*, whose core is a prolonged superimposed conflict between a soaring sustained chorale duet in the violins and a violent ejaculative declamatory duet in the viola and cello.[22] Carter's *String Quartet No. 3* takes the notion of superimposed contrasting voices to a higher level of complexity: the entire work consists of juxtaposed contrasting duets simultaneously in different tempi: opposing duos of increasing rhythmic contrast and intensity.[23]

Every mature work, even the smallest, reveals the oppositional side of Carter's imagination. The one minute "Canon In Memoriam Igor Stravinsky" would seem to be thoroughly unified by its canonic and serial processes. Example 5, however, reveals its apparent series to be a kind of "illusion." It is formed by the interfolding of three opposing cells, each cell proceeding at its own speed: a five-note cell with a new attack every six eighth-notes (or MM = 28); a four-note cell with a new attack every nine eighth-notes (or MM = 18.67); and a three-note cell with a new attack every ten eighth-notes (or MM = 16.8). As the piece unfolds, the illusion is

21 Robert Cogan and Pozzi Escot, *Sonic Design: The Nature of Sound and Music* (Englewood Cliffs: Prentice-Hall, 1976), pp. 59–71, 205–07, and 284–89.
22 Martin Schreiner, "Expansion as Design in the 'Fantasia' of Elliott Carter's First String Quartet," *Sonus* 12/2 (1992): 11–26.
23 Daniel Godfrey, "A Unique Vision of Musical Time: Carter's String Quartet No. 3," *Sonus* 8/2 (1987): 40–59. Andrew Mead discusses pitch structure in this work in his essay in this volume.

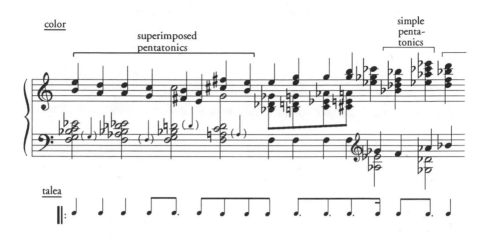

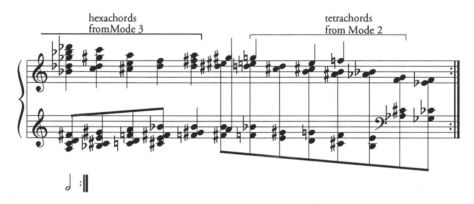

**Example 4: Olivier Messiaen, *Quatuor pour la fin du temps*,
"Liturgie de cristal,"
Opposing Piano Cycles: *Color* (29 Harmonies) and *Talea* (17 Durations).**
(Accidentals apply only to the note they immediately precede.)

Example 5: Elliott Carter: "Canon In Memoriam Igor Stravinsky,"
Superimposed Pitch-Duration Cells and Resulting Series

unmasked as the individual cells take on more and more body. The fluid serial texture of the beginning imperceptibly solidifies into the frozen texture of the close with the three distinct cellular strands each proceeding at its own given, opposing pace. Here, on the smallest scale, is the germinal essence of the later, large-scale *Night Fantasies*, with its incessant underlying superposition of strata governed by the opposing speeds MM = 10.8 and MM = 8.75; but also with its intrinsic fundamental opposition of the fluid to the frozen.[24]

In his approach to musical language, Carter is equally oppositional. Harmony was previously conceived as selective and unified: for example tonal harmony, based on a single chosen sonority model (the triad), moving along a single scalar path according to a single governing root progression (the fifth), to a single ultimate goal (the tonal center). In contrast, Carter's "harmony book" aims to discover *all* available harmonies, from two notes to twelve.[25] By analyzing the interval structure (the "vector," or available interval content) of each, he aims to discover the whole range of their similarities and oppositions. In this way a system is created with a space for every possible harmonic sonority, every possible linguistic structure and nuance, each sounding (in his music) in opposition to any and all the others. The open, welcoming spirit of this system, which includes and embraces all harmonic sounds, stands in direct contrast to other exclusive, hierarchical systems that have preceded it.

---

24 David Schiff, *The Music of Elliott Carter* (London: Eulenburg Books, 1983), pp. 318–21.
25 Ibid., pp. 60–70 and 324–25.

V

In conclusion let us go back more than two millennia, to an old debate. Heraclitus described reality as flux: "Everything flows; nothing remains. One cannot step twice into the same river."[26] According to him, all is opposition: "Without opposition all things would cease to exist." His preferred images are *fire* and *stream*. "Everything becomes fire, and from fire everything is born. All is everlasting fire, rhythmically flaring." In the *Fire Sermon*, his contemporary Buddha echoed, "All things are on fire; the mind is on fire, ideas are on fire."[27]

Plato and Aristotle succeeded Heraclitus. Plato taught that underlying all apparent flux are unified permanent forms; for example, the regular solids: the cube, pyramid, and sphere.[28] His pupil Aristotle formulated a poetics of *unity* and *likeness*: in place of ongoing flux, the dramatic unities of time and place; in place of oppositions, imitative similarity (mimesis).[29]

For two millennia, aesthetics—including music theory—has generally followed the Platonic–Aristotelian reduction of flux and diversity to permanence and unity. Music theory today is dominated by two traditions, the Schenkerian and Schoenbergian, both obsessed by a radical ideal of unity embodied equally in Schenker's fundamental line (*Urlinie*) and Schoenberg's generative series.[30] Schoenberg's cry "Let there be unity!" was their only agreement.

What I propose is not Platonic, but Heraclitean: music as a stream, a flaring flux of opposing sounds. I advocate musical aesthetics and theories with a place for oppositions and diversity. This is not meant as fashionable Schoenberg- or Schenker-bashing. Their greatness offers us a serious challenge: to create a music

---

26 The quoted fragments of Heraclitus are drawn from *Herakleitos and Diogenes*, trans. Guy Davenport (San Francisco: Grey Fox, 1976).

27 Lin Yutang, ed., *The Wisdom of China and India* (New York: Random House, 1942), pp. 363–64.

28 Plato, *The Collected Dialogues*, ed. Edith Hamilton and Huntington Cairns (Princeton: Princeton University Press, 1961).

29 Aristotle, *On Poetry and Music*, trans. S. H. Butcher (New York: Liberal Arts, 1948).

30 The metaphysical assumptions of Schenker and Schoenberg shaped, and perhaps distorted their theories. Schenker's theory is essentially *oppositional*: only at a work's conclusion does the linear path, or *Urlinie*, resolve to the tonic goal; until then, the essential tension of the work results from the open conflict, the irresolution, between that line and its ultimate goal. This is a profoundly more dynamic, oppositional view of tonality than other, simpler tonal theories. Schoenberg discovered, almost from the beginning of serial composition, the desirability of subdividing the series into hexachords characterized by opposition of both pitch-class and interval emphasis. Serialism could fruitfully be viewed as regularizing these oppositions, rather than as a simple unifying mechanism. Such a view would directly connect Schoenberg's serial works with his earlier "interval-group" works (for example, *Das Buch der hängenden Gärtens*, I, and *String Quartet No. 2*, IV) as well as with later composers who aimed to expand the serial twelve-tone language. In this light, unity and opposition become equal forces in both Schenkerian tonality and Schoenbergian serialism.

of diversity, of sounds, of oppositions as rich as the music of unity that they celebrate (if their largely unexamined assumptions of unity are correct).

This is not merely a musical issue; a similar problem has emerged in other fields as well. Mandelbrot, the creator of fractal geometry, has contrasted his intention with Euclid's and Plato's. Rather than the Euclidean–Platonic reduction of natural phenomena to regular figures, Mandelbrot proposes a mathematics that generates the full complexity and diversity of natural forms—cloud-formations, trees, streams, coastlines. "Clouds are not spheres, mountains are not cones, coastlines are not circles . . . Many patterns of Nature are so irregular and fragmented, that compared with Euclid—a term used to denote all of standard geometry—Nature exhibits an altogether different level of complexity. The number of distinct scales of length of natural patterns is for all practical purposes infinite. The existence of these patterns challenges us to study those forms that Euclid leaves aside as being 'formless,' to investigate the morphology of the 'amorphous.' " [31]

The biologist Richard Lewontin has observed that with Mendel and Darwin the fundamental issues of biology shifted from understanding the unity and regularity of species to understanding their diversity, variation, and change—their impermanence, dynamism, and flux. [32] The historian of ideas Sir Isaiah Berlin, surveying European thought from Socrates through the nineteenth-century Russians, finds a common Platonic core based on three assumptions: 1) all questions must have only one true answer; 2) there must be a dependable path toward this single truth; 3) the true answers must form a single unified whole. [33] For Berlin these assumptions were undermined by two Italians: Machiavelli and Vico. Machiavelli recognized two opposing ideals: resourceful rulers who knew how to seize opportunities, and unworldly Christians. In that dual light he could not establish a single consistent criterion of the right life for humans. Vico's concern was with the diversity of human cultures, each with its own vision of reality, its own values and modes of creation. Berlin concludes that values can be incompatible and can clash: "The notion of the perfect whole, the ultimate solution seems conceptually incoherent."

Finally, the psychoanalytic theorist James Hillman reflects, "Which fantasy governs our view of soul-making, the many or the one? The very question shows to what extent we are ruled by a bias toward the one. Unity, integration, and individuation seem an advance over multiplicity and diversity. So seems monotheism superior to polytheism. Jung [however] used a polycentric description for the psyche. The light of nature was multiple, like stars or sparks." [34] Hillman

---

31 Mandelbrot, pp. 1–3.
32 Richard Levins and Richard Lewontin, *The Dialectical Biologist* (Cambridge, Mass.: Harvard University Press, 1985), pp. 9–11.
33 Sir Isaiah Berlin, *The Crooked Timber of Humanity* (New York: Alfred A. Knopf, 1991), pp. 5–19.
34 James Hillman, *A Blue Fire* (New York: Harper and Row, 1989), pp. 38–45.

concludes, "A polytheistic psychology would find place for each spark. It would aim less at gathering them into a unity, and more at integrating each fragment according to its own principle. It would accept the multiplicity of voices."

Accept the multiplicity of voices: novelists as different as Mary McCarthy and Milan Kundera find the essence of novels to be their multiplicity of viewpoints and voices.[35] The seminal Russian philosopher–critic Mikhail Bakhtin has clearly identified the new aesthetic attitude in his influential book *Problems of Dostoevsky's Poetics*. "The book deals essentially with a problem of structure, the formal procedures by which Dostoevsky permits each of his characters to speak in their own voices with a minimum of interference from him as author, the effect of which is to create a new genre. Bakhtin calls this genre the 'polyphonic novel' because it has many points of view, many voices, each of which is given its full due by Dostoevsky."[36] Dialogue, polyphony, polyglossia, and heteroglossia consequently became characteristic features of Bakhtin's critical approach.

We must recognize that diversity and opposition are equal and complementary to unity as aesthetic ideals. To make a music maximally diverse is not a trivial ambition. As creators, whether composers or theorists, our task is to explore the possibilities, the inherent liveliness of each principle. Unity is one of the possibilities of diversity. Aesthetically as well as socially, in the current global world we require an ideal of multiplicity: multiplicity of peoples, voices, opposing sounds. An *a priori* assumption of unity as the sole or primary value is an aesthetic and social danger.

Is it not clear that we are still working through the artistic, aesthetic visions and debates of our great contemporaries of two-and-a-half millennia ago: Confucius, Heraclitus, Plato, and their colleagues? Our feeling of alliance is not at all nostalgic; it is not even Guy Davenport's formula that the newest derives from the oldest.[37] Rather, these thinkers are focused on and struggling with many of the same issues we are. Today, if lucky, we might take a step or two towards deeper musical understanding, towards lively sonic creation. Such recent developments as linear and registral analysis, set and probability theory, fractal geometry, sound synthesis and spectroscopy, and oppositional or dialogic awareness have added (and some still newer developments might add further) to our always insufficient

---

35 "Variousness and amplitude are characteristic of the novel . . . each human unit was allotted an eye of its own." Mary McCarthy, "Novel, Tale, Romance," *New York Review of Books* 30/8 (1983): 50–55. "The novel is the imaginary paradise of individuals . . . where everyone has the right to be understood." Milan Kundera, "Man Thinks, God Laughs," *New York Review of Books* 32/10 (1985): 11.

36 Katerina Clark and Michael Holquist, *Mikhail Bakhtin* (Cambridge, Mass.: Belknap Press of Harvard University Press, 1984), p. 240. Bakhtin's entire aesthetic anticipates positions taken in this essay; I regret that I came to know his work only after the essay was largely completed.

37 Guy Davenport, *The Geography of the Imagination* (San Francisco: North Point, 1981), p. 21.

insights, our always limited resources—unlocking another door, another black box, removing one more barrier. So, approaching a new century and a new millennium, the art-science of music might remain open, diverse, and young.[38]

---

38 This essay, now revised for publication, was originally presented at a lecture–concert devoted to the author's work: the Ellen Sitgeaves Vail Motter Lecture, Hilles Cinema, Harvard University, October 16, 1991. It expands a brief earlier paper, "Composition: Diversity/ Unity," *Interface* 20/3–4 (1991): 137–141.

Aspects of Confluence between Western Art Music and Ethnomusicology

Robert D. Morris

As we survey Western Art music of this century from our own *fin de siècle* stand-point, we are struck by its ever proliferating diversity. Whether one attributes the present pluralism to compositional "contextualism" as does Milton Babbitt, describes it like Leonard B. Meyer as a "fluctuating stasis," or simply deems it "postmodern,"[1] the fact is that there are dozens of aesthetic paradigms simultaneously flourishing today in Western Art music alone, each with its own dedicated creators, performers, critics and ideologies. And despite the almost violent sequences of aesthetic change and fashion that distinguish the twentieth century, each new compositional orientation has tended to survive rather than being superseded by the next. Having been informed, for example, that serialism, aleatoric music, stochastic process, east/west fusion, minimalism, and/or the "new romanticism" are dead, one quickly discovers that such pronouncements are inept, for all of these directions still evolve, each producing new music and continuing to work on its own set of postulated technical problems.

Once contemporary art music's pluralism is acknowledged, one notices that the ecological balance among contemporary music cultures is hardly static, but quite fluid. Each culture is aware to various degrees of accuracy and acceptance of the doings of the others. There are borrowings, acculturations, rejections, evaluations, and even alliances going on all the time. Many individual artists, usually performers, have simultaneous citizenship in many of these cultures. Although the stances of neoclassicism, nationalism, and exoticism provide well-documented, if older, examples of some interactions among contemporaneous music cultures, such contacts are now often more casual and less generalizable. Recent interactions are exemplified by the mutual, two-way influences between avant garde jazz and improvised new music, Western and non-Western art music, popular and so-called "serious" music, and deterministic and stochastic composition, to mention only a few of the most obvious cases.

---

1 See Milton Babbitt, *Words about Music*, eds. Stephen Dembski and Joseph N. Straus (Madison: University of Wisconsin Press, 1987), pp. 166–72; Leonard B. Meyer, *Music, the Arts, and Ideas: Patterns and Prediction in Twentieth-Century Culture* (Chicago: University of Chicago Press, 1967).

Only one other musical field has had to deal with such a radical mix of musical orientations. For decades, ethnomusicology has provided a framework for the study of the character, role, and place of music within and among vastly diverse cultures in all parts of the world. Detailed studies of music in, and/or as, culture—gleaned from fieldwork, transcription, and verbal description—have resulted in an immense, highly diverse, and specialized literature. As a result, ethnomusicologists have found it difficult to provide a concise definition of the scope of their discipline.[2] This difficulty parallels, of course, the similar problem of describing current art music directions in a nut shell. But beyond diversity in subject and method, there are other parallels between modern art music composition and ethnomusicology. Both enterprises have had to develop new methods and models to carry on their work. The simultaneous invention and/or rejection of musical notations, the reliance on recording and music processing technology, the emphasis on the relation of music to culture, the rejection of traditional Western ideologies, philosophies, and world-views as ethnocentric, and the borrowing of concepts and ideas from both contemporary academic and not-so-scholarly disciplines marks both fields. In addition, the necessity of open-mindedness and practical creativity are characteristically shared by the new music composer and the ethno-musicologist.

Of course, the music and influences of many Western art music composers shows a considerable connection with very musics that ethnomusicologists have studied. Perhaps the best known of these composers are Henry Cowell, Lou Harrison, John Cage, and Alan Hovaness, who were directly influenced by various forms of Near Eastern and Asian art music. Their music is certainly not a form of "nationalism," but rather represents an early stage of world music awareness in the minds of Western composers. A more general Eastern influence is prevalent in works of John Cage and Pauline Oliveros,[3] which spring from the philosophies and practices of Taoism and Buddhism.[4] But to limit our view to Eastern influence is to miss a bigger picture; reference in twentieth-century Western art music has become generalized to encompass any and all world musics. Thus, the musics of Charles Ives, George Gershwin, Leonard Bernstein and William Bolcom, the "Third Stream" experiments of the late 1950s and early 1960s that combined "classical" and jazz musics,[5] the "magic theater" music of George Rochberg, the Lorca settings of George Crumb, the recent operas of Karlheinz Stockhausen, the

---

2   See Alan P. Merriam, "Definitions of 'Comparative Musicology' and 'Ethnomusicology': An Historical–Theoretical Perspective," *Ethnomusicology* 21 (1977): 189–204.

3   See John Cage, *Silence* (Middletown, Conn.: Wesleyan University Press, 1961) and Heidi Von Gunden, *The Music of Pauline Oliveros* (Metuchen, NJ: Scarecrow Press, 1973).

4   For an interesting survey of Buddhist-influenced Western music see "Buddhism in the Performing Arts in North America," *Spring Wind: Buddhist Cultural Forum* 5/3 (1985): 14–95.

5   I am thinking of such pieces as Babbitt's *All Set* (1957) and Gunther Schuller's *Conversations for Jazz Quartet and String Quartet* (1959).

electronic music travelogues of Jon Appleton, the revival of the music of Scott Joplin and Louis Gottshalk, and so forth, all tangibly represent an important aspect of the self-conscious pluralism discussed above.[6]

In view of all this activity, it is not surprising that a certain view of new music and its place in society has arisen in the past 30 years, one shared by musical creators of very different stripes. I shall call this view the "ethnomusicological perspective," since it mirrors the view of many ethnomusicologists when they say that their field is not simply "what ethnomusicologists do," but a set of shared attitudes about how one construes music-making in and as culture.[7] This perspective involves three basic but interrelated components. The first of these holds that there is more than one kind of legitimate art music. A composer will allow that someone else's contrasting musical practice is valid and worthwhile. The view may be exercised historically, so the various musics of the past that are not part of one's actual or adopted tradition are respected and enjoyed. This ecumenical attitude is found in composition departments of music schools and universities where composers get along and support each other, even if they are of utterly different habits and inclinations.

Second, composers sharing the ethnomusicological perspective understand that musics differ with respect to social strata and musical function. Moreover, popular, folk, and ritual music are understood to involve entirely different value criteria from Western art music and are not regarded as inferior in principle to art music; As a result, those who live and compose within the ethnomusicological perspective tend to remain at least value-neutral with respect to musical practices and orientations that do not concern them. Other composers within this perspective will actively embrace other musics, and often engage in some sort of "professional" performance. Such poly-musicality may not lead to eclecticism however; some creators will attempt to keep their musical interests separated, but not necessarily with a hierarchical partitioning into "primary" and "secondary." For example, William Bolcom, William Albright, and James Tenney have composed and played piano rag-time music. In the case of Bolcom and Albright, rag-time has filtered into a good number of their other compositions, whereas Tenney's compositions have not been generally influenced by this kind of American music.

The third tenet of the ethnomusicological perspective follows naturally from the others. Persons creating music from within the perspective tend to be more

---

6 See Gary Clarke, *Essays on American Music* (Westport, Conn.: Greenwood Press, 1977), pp. 194–97 and 207–08; "Stockhausen on Opera (in Conversation with Jerome Kohl)," *Perspectives of New Music* 23 (1985): 24–39; and Jon Appleton, "The World Music Theater of Jon Appleton" (Folkways Records FTS 33437, 1974). The disc includes such pieces as Appleton's *Nevsehir*, which "is a capsulated memory of village life (in a small town in central Turkey) . . . of the market with the sudden intrusion of a string trio playing Strauss for the benefit of Western tourists."

7 See Marcia Herndon and Norma McLeod, *Music as Culture* (Darby, Penn.: Norwood Editions, 1981).

sensitive to the interrelations between music and culture than their Western art music colleagues in performance, musicology, and theory. This leads a composer to consider candidly the nature of the audience for traditional art music and how to improve and revitalize this audience, as well as build new audiences for today's often non-traditional musical productions. The problems and projects that result cannot be solved or completed overnight, or even over years, and at times the attempt to reach people with new art music leads many into long productive pedagogical careers. Some become dedicated faculty members at musical and academic institutions; others write books and articles with varying levels of scholarly weight.

In view of all this, one might expect that there has been a tremendous amount of direct contact between composers and ethnomusicologists; yet this is not so. To be sure, there are celebrated cases: for example, the Hungarian composer/ethnomusicologists Bartók and Kodaly, who actually did fieldwork and published the results; or Henry Cowell, who spent his 1931 Guggenheim grant working in Berlin with comparative musicologist Erich von Hornbostel, Professor Sambamoorthy, the noted south Indian musicologist, and Radan Mas Jodjhana of Java.[8] Of course, upon reflection we might not expect such direct links between composition and ethnomusicology after all, due to the nature of activity in each field. Composers create music (but often at a desk), whereas ethnomusicologists study existing musics (but often in the field). From any point of view, we see how exceptional a musical citizen Cowell was. He devoted much of his time to furthering the acceptance and appreciation of non-Western music. This led him to travel to the East and collect music that eventually appeared in the classic set of Folkway record albums entitled "Music of the World's Peoples."[9] Cowell's attempt to synthesize world music with the American "ultramodern style" of the 1920's was furthered by two of his most noted students, Lou Harrison and John Cage. So, despite the fact that Cowell was the lifelong friend of the ethnomusicologist Charles Seeger, it was within the sphere of composition—not scholarship—that interest in World music first developed among American composers.

If, in general, direct links between ethnomusicologists and composers are hard to find, how can we account for the many parallels between the two fields? Part of the answer lies in the history of each field, and to this end (and only to this end) I will undertake a very brief chronological summary of the relevant issues in both areas, commencing with composition.

To start, it is important to remember that American art music, as such, was beginning to declare its independence from European models as early as the 1930s. In 1933, Cowell published his *American Composers on American Music: A*

---

8 See Frederick Koch, *Reflections on Composing: Four American Composers* (Pittsburgh: Carnegie–Mellon University Press, 1983), pp. 62–75, for a brief biography of Cowell.
9 "Music of the World's Peoples" (Folkways Records FE 4604, Vol I–IV, 1951).

Symposium,[10] a book written by and about important American composers of the time, including Carl Ruggles, George Gershwin, Howard Hanson, Charles Seeger, Ruth Crawford, Aaron Copland, Carlos Chavez, Wallingford Reigger, Dane Rudhyar, and John Becker. Chapter titles, including the following, testify to the growing interest in non-Western music and music acculturation of that time: "The Music of Mexico," "The Development of Cuban Music," "An Afro-American Composer's Point of View," "The Relation of Jazz to American Music," "Oriental Influences in American Music," and, most notably, "Imitation versus Creative Music in America." Such ideas gathered momentum until the 1950s, when the new influence of European Serialism severely retarded the independent growth of American art music—an ironic fact, since Milton Babbitt, George Perle, and many others were developing extensions of Schoenberg's twelve-tone system quite independently of Boulez and Stockhausen.[11] I might add that the McCarthy era had other more global negative repercussions on American musical culture, and, indeed, on all aspects of culture.

The period from 1960–80 heightened the desire for complete American musical autonomy. The advances of musical recording and transmission allowed one to refer to and reflect upon the music of all peoples and times. In addition, the activities of the so-called "New-York School" of Cage, the musical revolutions in Jazz, from Bebop to modern jazz and beyond, and the rise of rock 'n' roll thickened the plot. Such new directions provided alternatives to following in the steps of the European composers who had themselves renounced serialism for a number of different musical ideologies that tended to ignore the main body of American art music.

The products of ethnomusicology played an important role in this period. In addition to the new availability of recordings of non-Western music collected and produced by ethnomusicologists, and bolstered by the populist interest in Indian Music initiated by the Beatles, many musicians from Asia were beginning to be imported to teach in ethnomusicology programs in the West. Mantle Hood's pedagogical concept of bi-musicality put an emphasis on learning musical cultures by participating in performance, as opposed to studying music only intellectually.[12] Many young composers in American graduate programs were therefore exposed to the actual repertoire of non-Western music. In the climate of the civil-rights movement, the Vietnam conflict, and the Cultural Revolution in China, musicians with inclinations to the political left found more than a haven within ethnomusicological provinces to study the anthropology and sociology of folk and urban music.

---

10 Henry Cowell, *American Composers on American Music: A Symposium* (Stanford: Stanford University Press, 1933).

11 See Milton Babbitt, "Some Aspects of Twelve-Tone Composition," *The Score and I.M.A. Magazine* 12 (1955): 53–61.

12 Mantle Hood, *The Ethnomusicologist* (New York: McGraw-Hill, 1971).

In accord with the new alternatives for musical creativity and the radical sentiments of the 1960s, many composers on the left began to raise questions about the relevance of almost any aspect of traditional Western music to the issues of their day. Cornelius Cardew's collection of essays, *Stockhausen Serves the Hands of Imperialism*, was one such critique which attacked all of the avant garde from a Marxist perspective.[13] Less total, but far more influential were the activities of composer collectives such as the New York *Fluxus* Group or the Ann Arbor, Michigan *Once* Group.[14] Critical issues were raised not only in print but via "happenings," concept music, and occasional spoofs. One can get a good feeling for this period by perusing the twelve volumes of the now defunct *Source: Music of the Avant Garde*, a periodical edited by Larry Austin at the University of California at Davis. Concomitant with the search for alternatives to European music traditions was a move away from the structures of music to an intense concern for context. Composers, beginning with Cage, began to experiment with musical devices that broke down the stereotypical hierarchy of composer, performer, and audience. The use of electronics to create new types of musical acoustical and performance spaces (for example, Stockhausen's *Kontakte* and John Chowning's *Phoné*), the creation of musical environments (David Rosenboom's "sound sculptures," David Mott's *Maze*, and David Tudor's *Rain Forest*), and the consideration of the audience as actively involved in performance (Alvin Lucier's Queen of the South, and Pauline Oliveros's set of "sonic meditations"), all resonate with the concerns of ethnomusicologists of the same period.

As for avant-garde European composers after 1950, connections with world music were initially considered a form of "nationalism"—an ideology that clashed with the attempt, following World War II, to develop a pan-European style, based on the "rational" foundation of post-Webern serialism and using the new technology of electronic music. It was only after 1960, when the main European composers had become relatively independent from one another, did a concern for music of other cultures become a promontory on the European musical terrain. On the other hand, there had been an important, if unacknowledged, musico-cultural influence on European composers from America, even in the heyday of Darmstadt. Composers, such as John Cage and later Steve Reich, travelled to Europe[15] spreading forms of musical experience derived in part from Asian and African

---

13 Cornelius Cardew, *Stockhausen Serves Imperialism and Other Articles: With Commentary and Notes* (London: Latimer New Dimensions, 1974).

14 See Michael Nyman, *Experimental Music: Cage and Beyond* (London: Studio Vista, 1974); "Groups: New Music Ensemble, ONCE group, Sonic Arts Group, Musica Elettronica Viva" *Source: Music of the Avant Garde* 3 (1968): 14–27.

15 Indeed, it was Reich's European success in 1974, and later the critical acclaim of Phillip Glass's opera *Satyagraha* (*c̀.* 1980) in Amsterdam (1980) that secured minimalism's high prestige, or at least notoriety, at home.

music.[16] All other forms of American music were more or less ignored, and jazz continued to be touted as the only "true" American music.[17] In the 1960s and 70s, many of the major European composers taught in American universities and had their music played extensively throughout North and South America.[18] This was not taken lightly by many of the more chauvinistic American composers. Perhaps it was partially due to their charge that the European composers were musically out to colonize America,[19] that most of these composers eventually returned to Europe. It is interesting to note that almost all of these composers ended up practicing some form of poly-musicality.[20] (Incidentally, an account of the importation of American computer music technology into Europe would tell the same story in another way.)[21]

The history of ethnomusicology provides a fuzzy isomorphism with the development of American musical independence. The emergence of American "ethnomusicology" out of European "comparative musicology" was due in large part to the efforts of Charles Seeger. Seeger began his musical contributions as a composer, a key figure in the aforementioned ultramodern movement in New York, encouraging composers such as Carl Ruggles and Ruth Crawford.[22] While Joseph Kerman's association of Seeger and Charles Ives as reacting "against the

---

16 See Steve Reich, "Music as a Gradual Process," *Source: Music of the Avant Garde 5/2* (1971): 30–39.

17 This is exemplified by the contents of André Hodeir, *Since Debussy: A View of Contemporary Music* (New York: Grove Press, 1961), a book which enjoyed some degree of popularity in North America in the early 1960s. American composers not associated with the avant garde are ignored and European composers who migrated to America (such as Stravinsky, Schoenberg, and Bartók) are found wanting. Other books by Europeans on new music such as Erhard Karkoschka, *Notation in New Music: A Critical Guide to Interpretation and Realization*, trans. Ruth Koenig (New York: Praeger, 1972) or Hans Heinz Stuckenschmidt, *Twentieth-Century Music*, trans. Richard Deveson (New York: McGraw-Hill, 1969) are of the same flavor.

18 For instance, György Ligeti taught at Berkeley, Karlheinz Stockhausen at the University of California at Davis, Luciano Berio at Juilliard, Krzysztof Penderecki at Yale—not to mention Pierre Boulez's position as Musical Director of the New York Philharmonic.

19 Certainly, such anti-European feelings among American composers were exacerbated by the Chicago Lyric Opera's announcement that it had commissioned Penderecki for a new opera to be premiered in 1976, the American Bicentennial season.

20 Among such pieces are Stockhausen's operas (Japanese Noh plays), Ligeti's *Piano Concerto* (African rhythms), and Boulez's *Rituel* (Javanese Gamelan music).

21 Among many examples: Berio's idea to found an electronic studio in Milan was inspired in part by the experimental concrete music of Vladimir Ussachevsky and Otto Leuning in the later 1950s; Boulez recruited John Chowning, Barry Vercoe, and many other leading computer music engineers and programmers for work at IRCAM in the 1970s, but American computer music composers not known for their technical expertise were not invited.

22 At present, there is no book-length biography of Seeger in print. Many of his essays are reprinted in Charles Seeger, *Studies in Musicology 1935–75* (Berkeley: University of California Press, 1977).

elite art music of their time" is insightful,[23] the similarity between them breaks down after the onset of the American depression when Seeger's interests became socially radical and his musical concerns followed suit. Like Ives, Seeger began to compose music involving folk or popular elements—features that presumably all people could understand and enjoy—but he went on to the study of American folk and non-Western art music. During and after a series of administrative posts, including music technical adviser in Roosevelt's Resettlement Administration, Seeger turned his attention to more scholarly matters, holding positions of influence in all of the American learned musical societies of his time. While one cannot seriously doubt that the birth of ethnomusicological studies in the United States was largely due to Seeger's influence and eminence, George Herzog, Mieczyslaw Kolinski, and Claus Wachsmann—major scholars of European comparative musicology who had emigrated to America—were also important to the development of the field.

The 1950s saw ethnomusicologists struggling with two divergent points of view. The first involved the continuation of comparative musicology under the new banner of "ethnomusicology," coined by Jaap Kunst in the early fifties.[24] Comparative musicology, supposedly carrying out a category of music scholarship originally defined by Guido Adler,[25] actually had been concerned with the structure and function of "traditional music": music that is orally transmitted without notation, but analyzed according to taxonomies reflecting a Western scholarly perspective.[26] Throughout the first third of the century, archives had been founded and maintained to hold the recordings, transcriptions, and catalogues of folk, tribal, and non-Western music. The work accomplished during the fifties by such Americans as Harry S. Powers (on South Indian music) and William Malm (on Japanese music) might be seen as more modern and sophisticated examples of comparative musicology.[27]

The second direction in ethnomusicology consisted of study of the "Anthropology of Music," the title of Allan Merriam's groundbreaking book of 1964.[28] This kind of inquiry was particularly well suited for understanding music

---

23 See Joseph Kerman, *Contemplating Music* (Cambridge, Mass.: Harvard University Press, 1985), pp. 160–62.

24 Jaap Kunst, *Ethno-Musicology: a Study of its Nature, its Problems, Methods, and Representative Personalities* (The Hague: M. Nijhoff, 1955).

25 Guido Adler, "Umfang, Methode und Ziel der Musikwissenschaft," *Vierteljahrsschrift für Musikwissenschaft* 1 (1885): 5–20.

26 Charles Seeger, "Systematic Musicology: Viewpoints, Orientations and Methods," *Journal of the American Musicological Society* 4 (1951): 240–48.

27 See Harold S. Powers, *The Background of the South Indian Raga-System* (Ph.D diss., Princeton University, 1958) and William Malm, *Japanese Music and Musical Instruments* (Rutland, Vt.: Charles E. Tuttle Company, 1959).

28 Alan P. Merriam, *The Anthropology of Music* (Evanston: Northwestern University Press, 1964).

in culture, especially outside the traditional Western art music context. These two directions were codified by the kinds of academic positions which their proponents held: either in music departments or in departments or archives of anthropology. While these directions are not really as far apart as some aver, they did map onto a Europe versus America dichotomy: the continuation of the older European enterprise versus the American application of empirical anthropological theory and methodology to music. An intermediate position of "bi-musicality" was advanced by Mantle Hood, who asserted that active participation in performance should be the primary crucible for understanding music, as mentioned previously. In any case, by 1980, ethnomusicology was dominated by the anthropological paradigm.[29]

Although these historical sketches are hardly complete or even up-to-date, they serve my purpose to show that while new music composition and ethnomusicology have strong roots in the work of Cowell and Seeger, they have also been driven by more global internal and external cultural forces. As a result, their developments and contributions are intertwined in complex and unexpected ways, many of which are considered in two recent books by Bruno Nettl: *The Study of Ethnomusicology: Twenty Nine Issues and Concepts* and *The Western Impact on World Music*.[30]

Two issues that prove controversial both to composers and ethnomusicologists are the assertion of musical universals and the preservation of traditional musics. Of course, the bold assertion that there are musical universals is perhaps a Eurocentric preoccupation, exemplified by Paul Hindemith's theories of tonality or Leonard Bernstein's, *The Unanswered Question*.[31] Hindemith sought to construct an overarching theory of tonality that would apply to the entire corpus of Western art music, with his own music as the most sophisticated expression of his harmonic and contrapuntal principles. Less self-serving, but equally ethnocentric, is Bernstein's more modern and polemical attempt to ground musical gesture in a linguistically-influenced grammatical theory. While such researches might be of limited descriptive usefulness, basic ethnomusicological research indicates they are certainly not expressions of universals in music.

Older conceptions of musical universals in ethnomusicology derive from the concerns of European comparative musicology which had its intellectual roots in the Laplacean science of the late nineteenth century. For instance, the contributions of Kolinsky and others have their origins in the Gestalt psychology

---

29 See Timothy Rice, "Toward the Remodeling of Ethnomusicology" *Ethnomusicology* 31 (1987): 469–88.

30 Bruno Nettl, *The Study of Ethnomusicology: Twenty Nine Issues and Concepts* (Urbana: University of Illinois Press, 1983) and *The Western Impact on World Music* (New York: Schirmer Books, 1985).

31 See Paul Hindemith, *The Craft of Musical Composition*, trans. Arthur Mendel (New York: Associated Music Publishers, 1941–2); Leonard Bernstein, *The Unanswered Question: Six Talks at Harvard* (Cambridge, Mass.: Harvard University Press, 1976).

of Max Wertheimer and Wolfgang Köhler.[32] The *a priori* principles supporting the global application of such ethnomusicological methods were finally examined and criticized by Marcia Herndon and others in the early 1970s.[33] Charles Seeger also had problems with absolute views and methodologies, but couched his response in such general and abstract philosophical terms that his own position might be considered a form of universalism itself.[34] Explicit denials of any universals in music have been advanced by George List and Claus Wachsmann.[35]

Kolinski's ideas about musical universals are mirrored in many composers' writings since Hindemith. The musical theories of Stockhausen and Xenakis either specify or rely on the tenets of Gestalt psychology, information science (which had its brief day in ethnomusicological research), and phenomenology.[36] Perhaps the clearest exposition of this family of compositional theories is found in the 1961 treatise, *Meta + Hodos* (and its sequels) by James Tenney[37] which postulates a remarkably consistent and sophisticated theory of musical perception and structure. But regardless of the intellectual stature of Tenney's work, it implies that music perception can and does operate outside of grammatical constraints such as those imposed by tonality. Tenney therefore does not address issues suggested by the diversity of musical languages found throughout the world; like Kolinski's work, the theory is not very responsive to the social and anthropological contexts of music. Such meta-cultural features makes it share the proprieties of Cage's ideas about music, that all structure in art can be ignored, presumably allowing one to perceive musical things "just as they are" without expectation, outside of any intellectual or psychological framework. This connection of Tenney to Cage suggests how the quest for musical universality might be intimately related to the negation of musical categories.

The reason that the question of musical universals has remained alive probably stems from Noam Chomsky's vital contributions to linguistics in the late 1950s and 60s.[38]

---

32 See Kurt Koffka, *The Principles of Gestalt Psychology* (London: Routledge and Kegan Paul Ltd., 1962).

33 Marcia Herndon, "Analysis, The Herding of Sacred Cows?" *Ethnomusicology* 18 (1974): 219–62.

34 For instance, see Charles Seeger, "The Music Process as a Function in a Context of Functions," *Inter-American Institute for Musical Research* 2 (1966): 1–36 or "Reflections upon a Given Topic: Music in Universal Perspective," *Ethnomusicology* 15 (1971): 385–98.

35 See George List "On the Non-Universality of Musical Perspectives," *Ethnomusicology* 15 (1971): 389–401, and Claus P. Wachsmann "Universal Perspectives in Music," *Ethnomusicology* 15 (1971): 381–84

36 See, for example, Karlheinz Stockhausen, ". . . How Time Passes . . ." in *Die Reihe 3: Musical Craftsmanship* (Bryn Mawr: Theodore Presser, 1959), pp. 10–40; Yannis Xenakis, *Formalized Music* (Bloomington: Indiana University Press, 1971).

37 *Meta + Hodos*, originally written in 1961, was revised and reprinted in James Tenney, *META + HODOS and META Meta + Hodos*, 2nd ed. (Oakland, Cal.: Frog Peak Music, 1988).

38 See, for instance, Noam Chomsky, *Syntactic Structures* (The Hague: Mouton, 1957).

Chomsky's new concepts of transformational grammars and his inquiry into the universal features of natural language structure not only directly influenced both ethnomusicological and compositional thought but provided a sophisticated underpinning for Chomsky's own anti-establishment political views. While Bernstein's work only flirted with advances in linguistics, Fred Lerdahl (with the linguist Ray Jackendoff) began applying linguistic theory to the study of Western tonality,[39] suggesting that hierarchic structures are crucial to the perception and retention of musical structure. Chomsky's idea of surface diversity as a paraphrase of deep structural "meaning" suggests that while the faces of World music might be demonstrably different, deeper similarities will be unearthed by appropriate research.

Nevertheless, some ethnomusicologists, such as Steven Feld,[40] have taken exception to applying linguistic theory to ethnomusicological study. In a similar vein, Carol Robertson has shown that sonic or behavioral notions of music held by a certain culture can not be invariably used to indicate that musical activity is going on at all levels of the culture.[41] Rather, her research shows that music is defined by its place in culture, not by any of its endemic structural features.[42] Ellen Koskoff, in an examination of values held by Western classical music performers, has pointed out that the assertion of musical universals within the context of a music culture might be a musico-cultural universal itself, and that universals can only be discussed if one carefully defines one's universe.[43]

A similar ambivalence to that surrounding musical universals is raised when one considers the preservation of traditional music. Certainly the issue has many political overtones, as exemplified by the perennial conflict between the modern Western composer and the conservative, often reactionary, worldview of the classical music establishment. But as indicated above, there are deeper misgivings about our traditional European art music heritage. Today, a good many people feel either intimidated or stifled by the cultural aura associated with the music of Bach, Beethoven, and Brahms. While this might be considered evidence that American culture remains under the influence of European cultural values, it certainly is a residue of our desire to transcend Euro-centric music domination. Sometimes this manifests itself in a generalization of the "ugly American syndrome," where one bemoans the introduction of European musical practices and concepts into non-Western art musics, threatening to ruin such music's special subtleties and

---

39 Fred Lerdahl and Ray Jackendoff, *A Generative Theory of Tonal Music* (Cambridge, Mass.: MIT Press, 1983).

40 Steven Feld, "Linguistics and Ethnomusicology," *Ethnomusicology* 18 (1974): 197–219.

41 Carol Robertson, "'Pulling the Ancestors': Performance, Practice, and Praxis in Mapuche Ordering" *Ethnomusicology* 23 (1979): 395–416.

42 The remark, usually attributed to John Cage, "Don't call it music, if the term bothers you," comes to mind here.

43 Ellen Koskoff, "Thoughts on Universals in Music" *The World of Music* 26/2 (1984): 66–87.

traditional uniqueness. Stockhausen has offered this solution, that we

> maintain as many crystallizations of other cultures in their present form as is at all possible. The stage of the cultural museum of the earth, in which the musical museum plays a really essential role, cannot be avoided.[44]

But anthropologists have pointed out that such views are not really so benign, since it is the outsider's view of the culture, not the native's, that asserts the value judgement against change.

Both composers and ethnomusicologists have come to understand that music cultures of true vitality are not static and aloof, but are normally in a state of flux, influencing and being influenced by other music cultures. Moreover, if culture may be defined as the information needed to function in a set of given situations and occasions, then musical cultures can overlap and be nested within a group or individual. Such is the background for much recent ethnomusicological research on acculturation, the transmission of "power," and role of "gender" within and among musical cultures. Certainly this orientation resonates with musical directions in the performance art of, for instance, Laurie Anderson[45] and the recent brand of international popular music deemed "World Music." Whether these issues will surface in the discussion or practice of art music is of interest, for, if they do, light will thrown on the question of whether art music, as such, must be necessarily conservative.

---

44 Stockhausen, "Weltmusik," in *Texte zur Musik* (Köln: Du Monte, 1975), pp. 468–76.
45 For instance, see Anderson's mixed media piece, *United States*.

II
Some Structuralist Approaches

Twelve-Tone Composition and the Music of Elliott Carter

Andrew Mead

Elliott Carter has emerged as one of the most significant composers of the second half of the twentieth century. While his developments in the rhythmic domain have received much attention, his pitch language is no less remarkable.[1] His solutions to writing music using the total chromatic collection are strikingly original, yet deeply related to developments of other major twentieth century composers. Carter has distanced himself from any school of composition, and his writings and recorded conversations suggest that he does not consider himself a twelve-tone composer.[2] Nevertheless, the analytical and theoretical tools developed in conjunction with twelve-tone compositions reveal a great deal about Carter's music, and his particular approach to working with "twelve tones which are related only with one another"[3] suggests a wealth of extensions to existing twelve-tone theory. This essay examines certain pitch structures in Carter's music using tools of twelve-tone theory in order to suggest commonalities with other composers' practice, while highlighting the individual and creative ways Carter has enriched and extended certain familiar theoretical ideas.

The fundamental problem for composers writing in the total chromatic is finding ways to determine roles for the various musical elements in some sort of sensible syntax. Traditional tonal syntax depends to a great degree on the structure of the diatonic collection.[4] Not only does the collection's intervallic structure allow us to register each contained pitch class in a unique position, it also identifies the

---

1 Prominent writings on the music of Elliott Carter include Jonathan Bernard, "The Evolution of Elliott Carter's Rhythmic Practice," *Perspectives of New Music* 26 (1986): 164–203; Jonathan Bernard, "Spatial Sets in Recent Music of Elliott Carter," *Music Analysis* 2 (1983): 5–34; Jonathan Bernard, "An Interview with Elliott Carter," *Perspectives of New Music* 28 (1990): 180–214; David Schiff, *The Music of Elliott Carter* (London: Eulenberg Books, 1983); and *The Writings of Elliott Carter: An American Composer Looks at Modern Music*, ed. Else Stone and Kurt Stone (Bloomington: Indiana University Press, 1977).

2 See, for example, the extensive interview with Elliott Carter in Allen Edwards, *Flawed Words and Stubborn Sounds* (New York: W. W. Norton, 1972), pp. 79–89 in particular.

3 This is Schoenberg's phrase, found in Arnold Schoenberg, *Style and Idea*, ed. Leonard Stein, trans. Leo Black (Berkeley: University of California Press, 1975), p. 218.

4 See, for example, Richmond Browne, "Tonal Implications of the Diatonic Set," *In Theory Only* 5 (1981): 3–21.

positions of the remaining pitch classes as chromatic inflections of its contained pitch classes. Additionally, the diatonic collection arranged as a scale places each class of the intervals it contains at a fixed scale degree difference. For example, minor (and major) seconds are only found as scale degree adjacencies, or a difference of one scale degree, while fourths, both perfect and augmented, are only found at a difference of three scale degrees. One consequence of this property is that within the diatonic collection no interval class can function both as a step and as a skip.

Chromatic enrichment of the diatonic collection will tend to break down both of these modes of distinction (e.g., interval-class roles and pitch-class scale degree positions), and highly chromatic music depends more and more on the specificity of its own composition to clarify ambiguity. Pushed to an extreme, the modes of distinction provided by the diatonic collection become totally submerged, and the composer is faced with the problem of creating a musical syntax based on a collection, the total chromatic, whose elements are all equally related to each other.[5]

For some composers, the solution has involved the use of a row class, the equivalence class of twelve-tone rows related to each other under a defined set of operations. It is important to consider how a row class can provide a musician with a syntax for composing within the total chromatic. A twelve-tone row may be described in two complementary ways, reflecting two points of view whose interactions underlie all sorts of different musical syntaxes. It is useful to describe a row both as an ordered succession of pitch classes and as a sequence of directed interval classes.[6] This reflects a fundamental duality of content and order

---

5 Milton Babbitt, in "Since Schoenberg," *Perspectives of New Music* 12 (1973): 3–28, uses this notion to articulate the fundamental difference between the collectional nature of tonality and the permutational nature of twelve-tone composition.

6 Directed interval classes are interval classes ordered in a single (unspecified) musical dimension. Our familiar notions of "rising fourths" or "falling thirds" invoke order in two dimensions, time and register. Simultaneities clearly articulate interval classes ordered solely in register, while the effect of an interval class solely ordered in time might be approximated by voices on one or more instances of a given pitch class moving in opposite registral directions to instances of another pitch class. Such is the effect of the opening of Milton Babbitt's Second String Quartet (1954). For the purposes of this essay, directed interval classes will be notated with a value, 0–6, combined with a sign, +/-, when we speak in the abstract. When we speak of such successions realized in register, we shall use values from 0–11, to correspond to our intuitions about intervals in chords. A discussion of related issues may be found in John Rahn, *Basic Atonal Theory* (New York: Longman, 1980), pp. 27–30. More on intervals in twelve-tone rows may be found in Robert Morris, *Composition with Pitch-Classes* (New Haven: Yale University Press, 1987), and "On the Generation of Multiple-Order-Function Twelve-Tone Rows," *Journal of Music Theory* 21 (1971): 238–63. An extremely elaborate investigation of the notion of interval in a host of musical interpretations, along with an analysis of portions of Carter's String Quartet No. 1 may be found in David Lewin, *Generalized Musical Intervals and Transformations* (New Haven: Yale University Press, 1987).

Considered as sequences of directed interval classes, a row and its transformations create a distribution of all possible directed interval-class sequences in the total chromatic. Some directed interval-class sequences, for example, are available from adjacencies in a member of the row-class, while others can only be derived by skipping one or more pitch-class elements, or by spanning more than one member of the row class. Considered as ordered pitch-class successions, a row within a row class may be viewed as a set of distinctions among all of the possible pitch-class collections in the total chromatic, based on their order number positions.[7] Once again, some types of collections will be available as adjacencies, while others will be available from non-adjacent positions. Taken together, both descriptions allow us to trace the interactions of content and order through the transformations of a twelve-tone row. We can readily recognize a familiar pitch-class collection in a new order, or a familiar intervallic pattern associated with a new set of pitch classes; indeed we are required to do so constantly to understand tonal syntax. These abilities help us to comprehend music composed in the total chromatic as well.

These two interdependent descriptions of twelve-tone rows suggest how a row class creates hierarchy among the elements of the total chromatic. Basic decisions made in building a row can create dramatic differentiations among the potential roles that the most fundamental elements of the total chromatic might play. The choice, for example, of [0, 1, 2, 6, 7, 8]-type hexachords for the discrete hexachords of a row creates a profound differentiation between the ways interval-class 3's and interval-class 6's can be made to behave.[8] Because the former interval class is excluded from the hexachord type, in a given row it can only arise between discrete segmental hexachords. On the other hand, interval-class 6's are only available *within* members of the hexachord class. Since transposition by 6 of any pitch class in one of these hexachords will yield another element of the same hexachord, this interval will *never* be found between the row's discrete segmental hexachords.[9] This is but one consequence of such a decision, and subsequent

---

7   This description of twelve-tone rows originates in Milton Babbitt, "Twelve-Tone Invariants as Compositional Determinants," *Musical Quarterly* 46 (1960): 246–59, reprinted in *Problems of Modern Music*, ed. Paul Henry Lang (New York: W. W. Norton, 1962). Some of the consequences of describing twelve-tone rows in this way may be found in Andrew Mead, "Some Implications of the Pitch-Class/Order Number Isomorphism Inherent in the Twelve-Tone System: Part One," *Perspectives of New Music* 26 (1988): 96–163.

8   *Editors' note*: As in the other articles in this collection, pitch class sets and rows use integer notation to represent pitch classes: C = 0, C♯/D♭ = 1, D = 2, and so on. Mead's notation differs slightly in that he uses lower case "t" and "e" to represent pitch classes 10 and 11 (A♯/B♭ and B). Interval numbers are calculated by summing half steps: minor second = 1, major second = 2, and so on. For intervals 10 and 11, Mead uses integer representation (rather than t and e). Finally, boldface integers **0–9** and boldface **t** and **e** are used to denote order numbers.

9   Milton Babbitt discusses these particular consequences with regard to his composition *All Set* in *Words about Music*, ed. Stephen Dembski and Joseph N. Straus (Madison: The University of Wisconsin Press, 1987), pp. 114–17.

decisions only increase the specificity of the various roles that diverse chromatic elements might play.

While a row class' structure imposes a hierarchy upon the total chromatic collection, it does not establish a hierarchy among the row class' members, the rows themselves. This can only arise though the activity of composition, the decisions of what materials shall be projected on the surface of a piece. The selection of a particular pitch-class collection or sequence of directed interval classes can be used to establish families of rows based on various types of invariance relations, and the interaction of a number of such choices can allow a particular moment in a piece to articulate simultaneously a great number of different strands of relationships. Hierarchies among different moments and passages in a composition arise from the varying degrees to which they invoke different relational strands.[10]

Two crucial points should emerge from the preceding description of row classes' function. First, the fairly cumbersome terminology of pitch classes and directed interval classes is used here to emphasize that twelve-tone rows are themselves *abstractions*, ordered in but one musical dimension that is not specified pre-compositionally in any way. The musical articulation of a row is a *compositional act*, both in terms of what musical dimension manifests the row's elements and its order, and in terms of what collectional and ordinal groupings within the row are highlighted. Second, and even more important, a row class does not determine how a composition goes; in itself it provides a distribution of all the materials of the total chromatic, and in conjunction with the compositional selection of materials, it provides *opportunities* for creating hierarchies of relationships in a composition. But it is the *act* of composition that marshalls these potentialities into the living process that is a piece of music.

In the light of the preceding discussion we can see that many of Elliott Carter's ways of dealing with issues of pitch in the total chromatic are directed towards similar ends. Carter too is concerned with creating distinct roles for the elements of the total chromatic, both in terms of collection and order. He does this in a variety of different ways in his compositions, and we shall investigate some examples below. However, one of the most crucial compositional differences between Carter's general practice and that usually associated with "twelve-tone composition" entails the dimension in which specified order is articulated. Most descriptions of the twelve-tone system tend to make the assumption that "order"

---

10 The analytical consequences of the preceding are discussed with regard to the music of Arnold Schoenberg in Andrew Mead, "Large-Scale Strategy in Arnold Schoenberg's Twelve-Tone Music," *Perspectives of New Music* 24 (1985): 120–57, and Stephen Peles, "Interpretations of Sets in Multiple Dimensions: Notes on the Second Movement of Arnold Schoenberg's *String Quartet #3*," *Perspectives of New Music* 22 (1983–84): 303–52. Ideas about hierarchies in underlying pitch-class designs may be found in Morris, *Composition with Pitch-Classes*, pp. 233–80, and inform the volume as a whole.

is equivalent to "order in time." This, though, is a compositional decision, as more than one musical dimension manifests pitch-class order.[11] In Carter's initial decisions about the distribution of roles in the total chromatic, order is manifested in register. This is immediately apparent in his steadfast distinction between intervals of the same interval class, but has consequences throughout his compositional decisions.

Virtually all of Carter's music from the String Quartet No. 2 (1959) and the *Double Concerto* (1961) has been based on some exhaustive distribution of the eleven intervals plus their compounds (in general, the octave is avoided) among distinct ensembles, individual instruments, particular movements or playing styles, or some combination thereof. Additionally, in many works specific intervals are associated with particular tempi.[12] In some instances, a given interval is reserved to combine modes of projection; that is, it is used as a boundary interval between them. Such distributions immediately affect the ways larger collections may arise, as well as the ways their elements are ordered (in register, as we shall assume for the remainder, unless otherwise specified). Particular combinations of intervals will tend to specify particular combinations of instruments, ensembles, tempi, and so forth, while different orderings of a fixed pitch-class collection might unite disparate combinations of musical projection. Furthermore, disparate types of collections might be associated in the ways each could manifest intervals, and thus be projected by similar means.

In addition to specific interval distributions, Carter's compositions frequently employ exhaustive distributions of collection classes of a given cardinality.[13] The String Quartet No. 3 (1971), for example, uses all of the four-element collection classes, while the Piano Concerto (1965) uses all the three-element collection classes and the Concerto for Orchestra (1969) uses all of the five- and seven-element classes.[14] As suggested above, the compositional assignment of intervals will to a large extent control the distribution of collection classes of a given size, based on their interval content, but Carter frequently further limits their roles in various ways. For example, certain collection classes may be used within a given ensemble or instrument or movement, while others are reserved for connecting two or more modes of projection. Individual collection classes can also themselves be associated with a tempo or repertoire

---

11 See John Rahn, "On Pitch and Rhythm: Interpretations of Orderings of and in Pitch and Time," *Perspectives of New Music* 13 (1975): 182–203 for an extended discussion of the musical dimensions in which order may be manifested.

12 This is discussed in Bernard, "The Evolution of Elliott Carter's Rhythmic Practice."

13 The term "collection class" carries the same meaning as the more familiar "set class," referring to the class of all pitch-class collections equivalent under T and I. Occasionally the locution "trichord type" or "hexachord type" will be used, as a less cumbersome way of specifying a collection class of which a particular collection is a member.

14 All of these points are noted in Schiff, *The Music of Elliott Carter*.

of tempi.[15] In effect, these decisions limit possible orderings for a given collection class, by restricting it to the repertoire of intervals associated with its assigned roles.

Still another feature of Carter's pitch structure helps determine the distribution of musical roles for the elements in the total chromatic. Starting as early as the *Double Concerto*, Carter's music has contained twelve-note chords which frequently serve as points of reference in the unfolding argument. These chords are, of course, twelve-tone rows whose order is manifested in register rather than time. As we shall see, they interact in a variety of ways with the smaller collections and intervals to provide a world within which to compose. Example 1, drawn from *A Symphony of Three Orchestras* (1976), illustrates the four classical twelve-tone transformations of a given ordering.[16] As the example shows, the transformations that appear as the four referential chords of the work contain collectional invariances permitting trichordal and hexachordal combinatoriality.

P:	5	1	0	3	9	t	7	2	4	8	6	e
I₃P:	t	2	3	0	6	5	8	1	e	7	9	4
RP:	e	6	8	4	2	7	t	9	3	0	1	5
RI₃P:	4	9	7	e	1	8	5	6	0	3	2	t

Brackets mark aggregate collections for trichordal combinatoriality; hexachordal combinatoriality occurs in row pairs P and RP, I₃P and RI₃P.

**Example 1: Carter, *A Symphony of Three Orchestras*
Twelve-Tone Rows Ordered in Register**

---

15 See, for example the chart of the trichords and associated tempi from the Piano Concerto in Schiff, *The Music of Elliott Carter*, p. 68.

16 Example 1 is adapted from Schiff, p. 68.

A few examples from Carter's String Quartet No. 3 illustrate some of the techniques discussed here.[17] The four players are divided for the duration of the work into two duos consisting of the first violin and cello, and the second violin and viola. Each duo has a repertoire of "movements," four in the first duo, and six in the second.[18] The two duos are distinguished in a variety of ways including approaches to rhythm and general expressive tenor. Each movement has its own characteristic playing mode and affect, flagging its return through the work. A number of different articulative and expressive factors are used to identify movements, as well as to link movements within duos. The entire composition unfolds all the possible pairings of movements between duos, as well as solo statements for each of the ten movements. Figure 1 diagrams the work's combination of movements.

Duo I:
A *Furioso* (major 7th)
B *Leggerissimo* (perfect 4th)
C *Andante espressivo* (minor 6th)
D *Pizzicato giocoso* (minor 3rd)

Duo II:
1 *Maestoso* (perfect 5th)
2 *Grazioso* (minor 7th)
3 *Pizzicato giusto, meccanico* (tritone)
4 *Scorrevole* (minor 2nd)
5 *Largo tranquillo* (major 3rd)
6 *Appassionato* (major 6th)

```
Duo II:  1  1  1  -  2  2  3  3  3  -  4  4  4  3  3  2  2  2
Duo I:   A  -  B  B  B  C  C  -  D  D  D  -  B  B  A  A  -  D

Duo II:  1  1  -  5  5  5  6  6  5  5  -  4  4  6  6  6  6 (Coda)
Duo I:   D  C  C  C  -  B  B  D  D  A  A  A  C  C  -  A  ABCD
```

Figure 1: General Scheme of Movement Appearance
in Elliott Carter's String Quartet No. 3

---

17 For a more extensive discussion of the Quartet, see the author's "Pitch Structure in Elliott Carter's *String Quartet #3*," *Perspectives of New Music* 22 (1983–84): 31–60.

18 The term "movement" can be a bit misleading with regard to Carter's music. As is the case with several pieces, including the String Quartet No. 3, the *Concerto for Orchestra* and *A Symphony of Three Orchestras*, the musical fabric consists of a constant [footnote continued on p. 75]

Figure 1 also specifies a "characteristic interval" for each movement, with complementary intervals distributed between duos. As mentioned previously, the piece employs all 29 four-element collection classes. The work also contains a recurring referential ordering of the twelve pitch classes, always in the same transposition. The row, of course, is ordered in register rather than time, and in the numerous spots where it is present, each movement is filtered through the resulting set of fixed pitches. A sample passage, along with an illustration of the row articulated in register, is illustrated in Example 2.

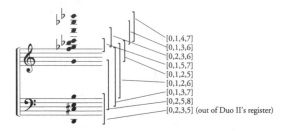

[0,1,4,7]
[0,1,3,6]
[0,2,3,6]
[0,1,5,7]
[0,1,2,5]
[0,1,2,6]
[0,1,3,7]
[0,2,5,8]
[0,2,3,5] (out of Duo II's register)

Tetrachordal collection classes represented as overlapping row segments

Example 2: Carter, String Quartet No. 3, m. 15
Compositional Realization of Row Ordered in Register
Duo II, *Maestoso* (P. 5th); Duo I: *Furioso* (M. 7th) and *Leggerissimo* (P. 4th)

Because the work's referential ordering is based on an all-interval row, each movement will have a specific order number adjacency containing its characteristic interval.[19] In those passages in which the referential ordering is present, four-element collection classes are differentiated by the various ways they may appear spread out across the registrally-fixed pitches; the example lists the collection classes of those tetrachords found at adjacent order positions.

Although the row or some part of it is frequently present in the surface of the music, it also exerts its presence in less literal ways, affecting those passages where it does not appear. Example 3 illustrates one way the row controls the distribution

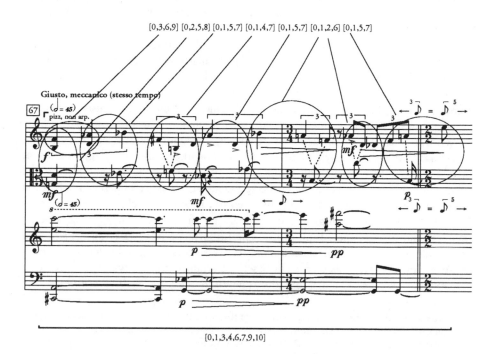

Example 3: Carter, String Quartet No. 3, mm. 67–68
Collection Classes Drawn from the Twelve-Tone Row

interweaving of discrete yet evolving musical continuities. Carter himself refers to these as "movements," as in the preface to the String Quartet No. 3, (New York: AMP, 1973), which also contains a chart comparable to the information found in Figure 1. This use of the term "movement" has also been employed by David Schiff in *The Music of Elliott Carter*.

19 See Robert Morris and Daniel Starr, "The Structure of All-Interval Series," *Journal of Music Theory* 18 (1974): 364–89 for a description and a discussion of the properties underlying all-interval rows.

of four-element collection classes in the composition. In the illustrated passage, all of the four-element collections found in Duo II, with one important exception (a member of [0, 3, 6, 9]), are members of those collection classes represented at adjacent order numbers in the row, as listed in Example 2. Further analysis of the work has suggested that one of the strategies for distributing four-element collection classes between the duos is based on whether or not they may be represented as row adjacencies.[20]

Example 3 also illustrates indirectly another principle at work that may be traced back to the referential ordering. The member of the [0, 3, 6, 9] collection class in the second violin (the exception mentioned above) is the aggregate complement of the collection found in Duo I. Complementation within the aggregate abounds in the composition, involving a wealth of different combinations of members of the various collection classes, but combinations of the sort represented by [{0, 3, 6, 9}, {1, 2, 4, 5, 7, 8, t, e}] play a particularly significant role.[21] Example 4 illustrates three passages employing an eight-element collection of the same class found in Duo I in Example 3. The first two passages are by no means unique in the composition in their use of the collection in question, but I have chosen them as particularly striking moments in the musical discourse. The first (measure 28) is drawn from the opening of the first solo passage for Duo I and the second (measure 136) marks the first return of any movement in the work. The significance of their shared eight-element collection is revealed in the coda (measure 469 and following), where Duo II completes the aggregate at the registers determined by the referential ordering. This is the only member of the collection class [0, 3, 6, 9], that Duo II can play in the registers determined by the referential ordering, due to registral and instrumental limitations. The importance of the passage is revealed by the fact that Duo I summarizes its four movements using a particular member of an eight-element collection class, itself determined by the way the other duo can extract its complement from the referential ordering.[22] (In Example 4, the

---

20 Carter's own chart of the uses of collections in this piece (Schiff, pp. 262–63) bears this out to a degree with only three exceptions: two collection types that are indicated as connecting the two duos ([0, 1, 3, 6] and [0, 2, 3, 6]) and one type assigned to Duo I ([0, 1, 2, 5]). Nevertheless, these collection types are frequently represented independently in Duo II, arising from the same sorts of segmentation as do the other collections (see Mead, "Pitch Structure in Elliott Carter's *String Quartet #3*").

21 Such a formulation is called a mosaic, a term used to describe collections of discrete collections partitioning the aggregate (the total chromatic collection). The term originates in Donald Martino, "The Source Set and its Aggregate Formations," *Journal of Music Theory* 5 (1961): 224–73. The concept is further examined in Mead, "Some Implications of the Pitch-Class/Order Number Isomorphism Inherent in the Twelve-Tone System," and in Robert Morris and Brian Alegant, "The Even Partitions in Twelve-Tone Music," *Music Theory Spectrum* 10 (1988): 74–101. The term is used in slightly different ways in Mead and in Morris and Alegant; the differences are discussed in Morris and Alegant's footnote 8, p. 76.

22 In *Flawed Words and Stubborn Sounds*, Carter states, rather surprisingly, "The actual notion

references to Duo I's four movements are labeled with the letters found in Figure 1.) As may be inferred, the presence of a registrally-articulated twelve-tone row in this work has ramifications far beyond its literal appearance, and its most immediate manifestations.

Ex. 4a-1

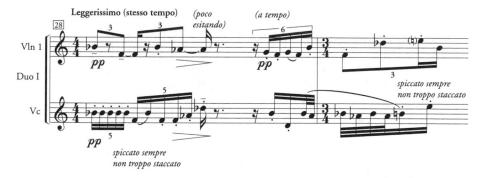

Ex. 4a-2

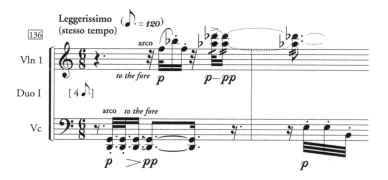

Examples 4a-1 and 2: Expressions of [0, 1, 3, 4, 6, 7, 9, t] in Carter's String Quartet No. 3

of 'absolute pitch' is not significant in my pieces. The pitches are chosen registrally as a matter of instrumental practicality" (p. 110). Carter's subtle handling of both pitch and pitch class leads one not to take this statement too literally. At the least, the presence of a particular transposition of a referential twelve-note chord guarantees the registral assignment of its elements a priviledged positions, even when the entire chord is not present, and the preceding example seems musically persuasive. While the composition of his String Quartet No. 3 followed the interview, the evidence of his earlier music seems to suggest a greater attention to "absolute pitch" than the composer's statement might lead one to believe.

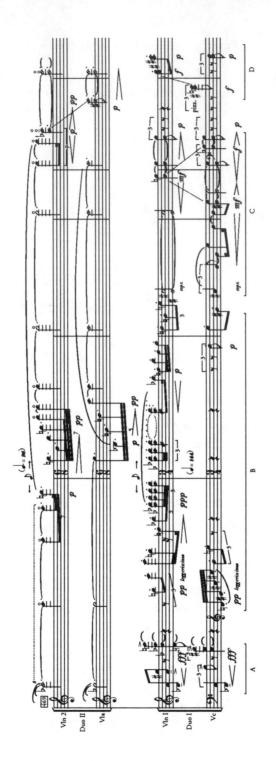

Example 4b: Expressions of [0, 1, 3, 4, 6, 7, 9, t] in Carter's String Quartet No. 3

We shall examine two more of Elliott Carter's compositions to illustrate some of the ways he has combined his various methods of distributing elements of the total chromatic to form his compositional worlds. The Piano Concerto (1965) is one of the first works in which he used the interaction of rows and collections to define his pitch language. This is a massive work in two movements, pitting a solo piano accompanied by an entourage of seven solo sustaining instruments against an essentially monolithic force, the orchestra. What follows here is not an analysis of the piece itself, but an examination of aspects of its pitch, pitch-class and collection-class structure, the compositional limitations within which the piece was made to move.[23]

The Concerto (particularly the first movement) is based on two referential orderings of the twelve pitch classes, and employs all twelve three-element collection classes. Each ensemble (the soloist with its companions, and the orchestra) has its own row, and the twelve three-element collection classes are divided between the two playing groups.[24] Eight of the twelve collection classes are represented by the four discrete segmental trichords of the two rows, as Example 5a shows. The ordering of the two rows further suggests that complementary pairs of intervals are split up between the two ensembles, as diagrammed in Example 5b. (The single exception, a duplication of the solo group's perfect fourth near the center of the orchestra's row probably arose as an unavoidable by-product of other constraints.)

Examination of the rows and the trichordal distribution between ensembles reveals some of the specific ways they are related, and suggests some more general principles used in the piece. First, the two rows, while clearly not simple order transformations of each other, project the same pair of hexachordal collections. As Example 5b shows, the top six pitch classes of one are the bottom six pitch classes of the other. Hexachordal combinatoriality, created by the combination of hexachords at like order numbers, may be found in the piece, as illustrated in Example 6.

The hexachordal relationship between the two rows invites an examination of the distribution of trichordal collections within the hexachords, beyond merely their segmental partitions. The two hexachords do not belong to the same collection class, and therefore have different trichordal distributions. Figure 2 lists the two hexachords' trichordal partitions. Note that one hexachord is a member of the all-trichord collection class, [0, 1, 2, 4, 7, 8], a property not shared by the class of its complement.[25]

---

23 An extensive overview of the work's dramatic shape and compositional origins may be found in Schiff, pp. 227–38, along with additional analytical insights.

24 See also the chart of this information in Schiff, p. 68.

25 David Schiff has noted the use of this collection class in later works of Carter in *The Music of Elliott Carter*, p. 65. Hexachords of this type, along with their complements, also appear in

(a) Discrete Trichordal Segments

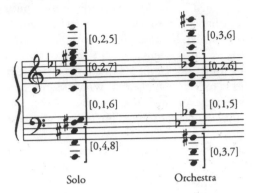

Solo　　　　　　Orchestra

(b) Hexachordal Structure and Complementary Pairing of Intervals

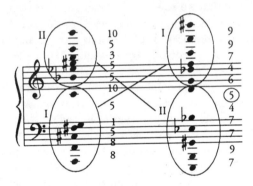

Hexachord I: [0, 1, 2, 4, 7, 8] (all-trichordal)
Hexachord II: [0, 1, 2, 5, 6, 8]

Examples 5a-b: Twelve-Tone Rows in Carter's Piano Concerto

Milton Babbitt's *Sounds and Words* (1960), certain aspects of which are analyzed in Joseph Dubiel, "Review Essay: Robert Morris, Composition with Pitch-Classes: A Theory of Compositional Design," *The Journal of Musicological Research* 10 (1990): 47–80.

Example 6: Hexachordal Combinatoriality in Carter's Piano Concerto, mm. 59–60

The trichordal partitions of the two hexachords found in Figure 2 reveal a fascinating aspect of Carter's distribution of the twelve trichordal collection classes between his two ensembles. As may be seen, almost all of the trichordal partitions of the all-trichordal hexachord contain one trichord type belonging to the solo group, and one belonging to the orchestra. The two exceptions are those found segmentally in the two rows. In contrast, with only one exception, the trichordal partitions of the other hexachord contain two trichord types belonging to the same ensemble, either solo or orchestra. Carter's distribution of trichord types forces his two segmental hexachords into contrasting roles. When they are produced by discrete trichords, hexachords of the former type must almost always arise through the combination of the two ensembles, while the hexachords of the latter type must appear most frequently within one ensemble or the other.

We can generalize two principles from the preceding. First, larger collections of a single class may variously arise as the combination of collections of a variety of classes. For example, sections characterized by different trichordal collection classes might be linked through the production of members of a given hexachordal collection class. (Such a procedure is already implicit in our abbreviated discussion above of Duo I's summational statements of its four movements in the String

81

Ensemble:
[0,2,5]
[0,2,7]
[0,1,6]
[0,4,8]
[0,1,2]
[0,1,3]

Orchestra:
[0,3,6]
[0,2,6]
[0,1,5]
[0,3,7]
[0,1,4]
[0,2,4]

Trichordal Partitions	Collection Class Membership	Trichordal Partitions	Collection Class Membership

```
[0, 1, 2, 4, 7, 8]                        [0, 1, 2, 5, 6, 8]

0  1  2        [0,1,2]  –        0  1  2        [0,1,2]  S
      4  7  8  [0,1,4]                  5  6  8  [0,1,3]

0  1     4     [0,1,4]  –        0  1     5     [0,1,5]  O
   2       7 8 [0,1,6]              2       6 8 [0,2,6]

0  1       7   [0,1,6]  –        0  1       6   [0,1,6]  –
   2  4      8 [0,2,6]              2  5      8 [0,3,6]

0  1         8 [0,1,5]  –        0  1         8 [0,1,5]  O
   2  4  7     [0,2,5]              2  5  6     [0,1,4]

0     2  4     [0,2,4]  –        0     2  5     [0,2,5]  S*
   1       7 8 [0,1,6]              1       6 8 [0,2,7]

0     2     7  [0,2,7]  –        0     2     6  [0,2,6]  O
   1     4   8 [0,3,7]              1     5   8 [0,3,7]

0     2        [0,2,6]  O*       0     2        [0,2,6]  O
   1     4  7  [0,3,6]              1     5  6  [0,1,5]
        8                                8

0        4  7  [0,3,7]  –        0        5  6  [0,1,6]  S
   1  2      8 [0,1,6]              1  2      8 [0,1,6]

0        4  8  [0,4,8]  S*       0        5  8  [0,3,7]  O*
   1  2    7   [0,1,6]              1  2    6   [0,1,5]

0           7 8 [0,1,5] –        0           6 8 [0,2,6]  O
   1  2  4     [0,1,3]              1  2  5     [0,1,4]
```

* Segmental Partition	S Both are solo trichords
– One trichord each from solo and orchestra	O Both are orchestral trichords

Figure 2: Trichordal Partitions for Elliott Carter's Piano Concerto

Quartet No. 3.) Second, because each hexachordal collection class has its own set trichordal subsets, Carter's distribution of the twelve trichord types between the two ensembles creates a distribution of relative availablity within and between ensembles for all the hexachord types, based on the ways they might be partitioned into trichords. While it is easy to extend both principles to collections of all different sizes and classes, we shall limit ourselves for the purpose of illustration to the interaction of trichords and hexachords.

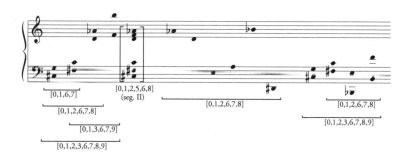

Example 7: Carter's Piano Concerto, mm. 1–5

The very opening of the Piano Concerto contains a particularly elegant demonstration of the principles underlying its trichordal and hexahordal inter-actions at work. the piece opens with an extended passage for the solo ensemble preceding the entrance of the full orchestra. Example 7 contains the first five measures of the work, along with its reduction. The primary trichordal type found in the passage is [0, 1, 6], and the example shows some of the six- and eight-element collections articulated in the musical surface. Of note are the

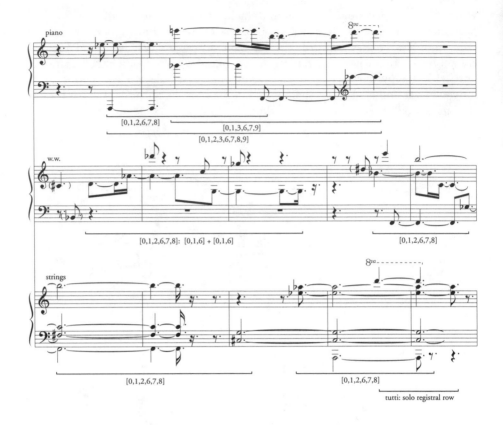

Example 8: Carter's Piano Concerto, mm. 12–16

presence of members of two hexachordal collection classes, [0, 1, 2, 6, 7, 8] and
[0, 1, 3, 6, 7,9], each containing three tritones, and each containing members of
[0, 1, 6]. The members of the former collection class, in fact, can be generated by
members of [0, 1, 6]. Carter's careful durational notation yields a member of the
intra-ensemble segmental hexachordal collection class, [0, 1, 2, 5, 6, 8].[26]

Example 8 illustrates a portion of the continuation of this passage, which
continues to employ the materials of the first five measures. Members of the
previously mentioned hexachordal collection classes are present, and members of
[0, 1, 2, 6, 7, 8] are unfolded simultaneously in three different strands, differ-

---

26 A contrasting analysis of this passage emphasizing registral ordering of trichords is found in
Bernard, "Spatial Sets," pp. 6–14.

-entiated by timbre. A wide variety of modes of articulation present members of the trichordal class [0, 1, 6] by register, instrumental grouping, and temporal proximity. The aggregate found in the last two bars is in the referential ordering of the solo ensemble's row, and is partitioned by winds and strings into a complementary pair of members of [0, 1, 2, 6, 7, 8]. This last is a vivid instance of an aggregate manifesting two different interpretations in two different musical dimensions, permitting its participations in a number of different streams of reference.

The special significance of the hexachordal collection class [0, 1, 2, 6, 7, 8] is made clear with the entrance of the orchestra, illustrated in Example 9. The orchestra enters with a trichord of its own, a member of [0, 2, 6]. This class of trichord shares the interval-class 6 with the trichord type used by the solo ensemble, and the linkage may be readily heard.[27] More interesting, however, is the production of a member of [0, 1, 2, 6, 7, 8] by means of a member of each trichordal collection class present, the soloist's [0, 1, 6] and the orchestra's [0, 2, 6]. The orchestral passage continues with a burst of overlapping material, within which the unmuted brass prominently project another member of [0, 1, 2, 6, 7, 8], partitioned as a pair of members of [0, 1, 5], an orchestral trichordal collection class. The persistent hexachordal type thus provides a mode of continuity over the change of ensembles by functioning first as the source of the solo ensemble's trichords, then as a link between the ensembles, and finally as a source of the orchestra's trichords. This is made possible by the distribution of trichords within this type of hexachord interacting with Carter's assignment of trichord types to the two ensembles. It is worth noting that the other prominent hexachord type in the opening passage, [0, 1, 3, 6, 7, 9], may also be partitioned into an [0, 2, 6] and an [0, 1, 6]. Hexachords of both types are found prominently in the passages surrounding the entrance of the orchestra.

Similar strategies are found throughout the Concerto. Example 10 illustrates a particularly vivid series of exchanges between the solo ensemble and the full orchestra. members of [0, 2, 3, 4, 5, 7] are exchanged between ensembles, first generated by members of [0, 2, 4] in the orchestra, then [0, 2, 5] in the piano, and then [0, 1, 5] in the orchestra again. The orchestra's strategy of holding one member of [0, 2, 4] while moving another member is taken up with members of [0, 1, 5], in this case generating a new class of hexachord, a member of [0, 1, 2, 6, 7, 8], the type found in the work's opening bars. The piano responds by producing another [0, 1, 2, 6, 7, 8] with a pair of trichords from its [0, 2, 7] class. Thus the passage proceeds by unfolding different kinds of trichords within a

---

27 David Schiff notes in discussing this passage that "the tritone functions throughout as a common element, linking the two instrumental groups" (*The Music of Elliott Carter*, p. 231). Since the tritone is its own complement, this would seem happily to coincide with our previous observation concerning the distribution of intervals between ensembles.

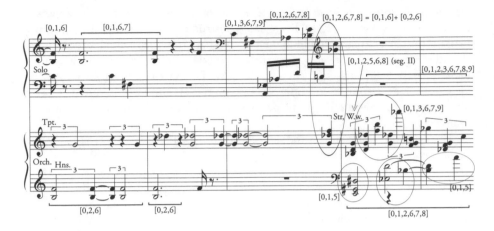

Example 9: Carter's Piano Concerto, mm. 19–24

certain hexachord type, and changing hexachord class by preserving the class of trichordal generators.[28] All of this is influenced by the availability of trichords in each ensemble, and the availability of hexachords between and within each ensemble.

The preceding discussion hardly exhausts the wealth of strategies underlying the Piano Concerto, but illustrates one particular pathway into the work. The principles underlying this discussion may be generalized in a number of ways, involving both larger and smaller collection classes, and are found in a number of Carter's other compositions.[29]

Night Fantasies (1980), an extended work for solo piano, is more explicitly dependent on twelve-tone ordering than the two pieces discussed so far. As David Schiff has pointed out, the work is based on the 88 all-interval classical row classes in which the second hexachord is the retrograde of the first, transposed by T_6.[30] As in the compositions discussed previously, the rows of the work are ordered in register, rather than time. The rows are used as a background grid against which

---

28 The use of single trichordal generators to create and modulate among hexachords is discussed in Milton Babbitt, "Since Schoenberg." Extended discussion of trichords and hexachords are found in Martino, "The Source Set," and Morris and Alegant, "Even Partitions."

29 See Morris, *Composition*, pp. 90–98, for some interesting possibilities; in particular, see his discussion of chains of collections based on shared subsets.

30 Schiff, pp. 316–317. A classical row class is the familiar 48-member row class generated by the use of the classical twelve-tone operations. Larger and smaller row classes may be generated using other operational specifications.

Example 10: Carter's Piano Concerto, mm. 68–72

collections of smaller cardinality are projected. For the purposes of the following discussion, we shall concentrate on the relations among the rows, rather than on the ways the smaller collections arise, but as shall be suggested, the nature of the rows will strongly affect the ways smaller collections may appear on the musical surface.

The composition contains sections employing complete twelve-tone rows, and sections using merely the ordered hexachords of rows, to create variety in its registral spacing. Virtually all of the material of the piece may be located explicitly in some specific row. While not every row is completely present, the inherent properties of these rows permits unambiguous identification with relatively few elements. Example 11 illustrates a passage near the beginning of the piece in which a row is followed by a transformation by pitch-class inversion, showing certain interesting invariance properties. The four languidly sustained notes of the opening are found in the same registral positions in both rows. We shall discuss the conditions for those properties and others below.

At first blush, the use of 88 classical row classes might seem to permit so much variety as to overwhelm any possible organization they might provide. However, a number of factors combine the classical row classes into larger equivalence classes, and provide a number of sensible routes among them.

Because of their shared retrograde-symmetrical all-interval property, all of the classical row classes must employ one of four hexachordal collection classes. The four are [0, 1, 2, 3, 4, 5], [0, 2, 3, 4, 5, 7], [0, 2, 4, 5, 7, 9], and [0, 1, 3, 4, 5, 8]. The first three are the first order all-combinatorial hexachordal collection classes,

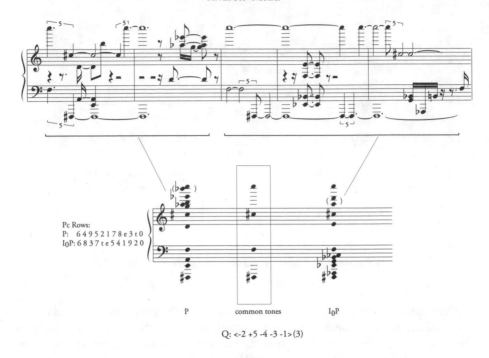

Example 11: Carter's *Night Fantasies*, mm. 10–14

labeled in Figure 3 as A, B, and C, respectively, after Martino.[31] The fourth is the unique transpositionally-combinatorial hexachordal collection class, labeled Q for the purposes of this paper. These four classes of collections are very closely related. The four are closed under the cycle-of-fifths transformations (M and MI, or M_5 and M_7), and with the addition of the [0, 1, 4, 5, 8, 9] collection class (E after Martino), they form a closed family based on the transposition of any number of elements by the excluded interval, the tritone. This last collection class is the third order all-combinatorial hexachord type; it cannot be used to generate all-interval rows since it lacks all of the interval classes. All five of these hexachordal collection

---

31 These labels are found in Martino, "The Source Set." It is interesting to note that these four hexachords, A, B, C and Q are found together in Carter's own list of the three- to six-note chords (Schiff, pp. 324–25). Jonathan Bernard makes some additional observations about Carter's list in "An Interview." As Bernard's remarks suggest, the list itself offers many interesting insights into Carter's thinking about chromatic pitch space.

0 1 3		[0, 1, 3]	A: {0, 1, 3, t, e, 2}
	4 5 8	[0, 1, 4]	
0 1 4		[0, 1, 4]	B: {0, 1, 4, 9, e, 2}
	3 5 8	[0, 2, 5]	
0 1 5		[0, 1, 5]	Q: {0, 1, 5, 9, t, 2}
	3 4 8	[0, 1, 5]	
0 1 8		[0, 1, 5]	A: {0, 1, 8, 9, t, e}
	3 4 5	[0, 1, 2]	
0 3 4		[0, 1, 4]	Q: {0, 3, 4, 7, e, 2}
	1 5 8	[0, 3, 7]	
0 3 5		[0, 2, 5]	C: {0, 3, 5, 7, t, 2}
	1 4 8	[0, 3, 7]	
0 3 8		[0, 3, 7]	Q: {0, 3, 8, 7, t, e}
	1 4 5	[0, 1, 4]	
0 4 5		[0, 1, 5]	C: {0, 4, 5, 7, 9, 2}
	1 3 8	[0, 2, 7]	
0 4 8		[0, 4, 8]	Q: {0, 4, 8, 7, 9, e}
	1 3 5	[0, 2, 4]	
0 5 8		[0, 3, 7]	B: {0, 5, 8, 7, 9, t}
	1 3 4	[0, 1, 3]	

Analogous Partition of A and C:

0 2 5		[0, 2, 5]	C: {0, 2, 5, 7, 9, t}
	1 3 4	[0, 2, 3]	

Figure 3: Generation of A, B, C, and Q Hexachords
from Trichordal Partitions of Q

classes can also be characterized exclusively as those generated by taking a minor third from each of the three distinct members of the collection class [0, 3, 6, 9] and combining them.[32]

---

32 For example, {0, 3}, {4, 7} and {5, 8}, drawn from {0, 3, 6, 9}, {1, 4, 7, t} and {2, 5, 8, e}, respectively, yield an instance of Q; any other comparable combination would remain within the set of five collection classes discussed above. Significant related discussions of collections in

A special feature of the Q hexachord type's trichordal partitions is illustrated in Figure 3. As may be seen, when Q is partitioned into trichords and one of the trichords is transposed by T_6, the resulting hexachord belongs to the class of A, B, C, or Q. Furthermore, the resulting trichordal partitions of the A, B and C hexachords are those found in the work's extended row classes. One more trichordal partition of A and C can be found, containing a member of [0, 1, 3] and a member of [0, 2, 5] in both cases. These close the system by yielding each other under the analogous moves (holding one trichord while transposing the other by T_6). This is also illustrated in Figure 3.

Because of the close relationship among these four hexachordal collection classes, it is possible to reduce the 88 row classes to 11 families based on directed interval classes. These directed interval-class sequences are listed in Figure 4. The directed interval-class sequences are read as follows. The numbers represent interval classes, ordered with regard to their successive appearance in a row. The relative directions of the interval classes are indicated by + and -, which might be musically represented in a number of ways, either in time, or in register. (When we examine their realization in register, we shall change our notational approach somewhat to correspond with musical intuition; for the present abstract discussion, however, it is useful to avail ourselves of the flexibility afforded by interval classes combined with plus or minus signs.)

A row may be constructed from a directed interval-class sequence by following it with the interval-class 6, and continuing with the sequence again, written out backwards, with the signs reversed. Thus, for example <+1 +2 -5 +4 -3> would yield <+1 +2 -5 +4 -3 6 +3 -4 +5 -2 -1> as the sequence of directed interval classes for an all-interval row class; a member of the row class may be constructed by inserting a pitch class anywhere and following the intervals.[33]

Each distinct interval-class sequence in Figure 4 can create eight classical row classes, based on the combination of three binary operations. They are the cycle-of-fifths operation (which preserves directed interval-classes +/-2 and +/-4, reverses the sign of +/-3, and exchanges +1 for -5 and -1 for +5), the interval-class 3 sign-switching operation (which does what its name suggests), and T_6, the order number transposition that swaps the position of the hexachords without changing their interior order. Switching the sign of interval-class 3 is equivalent to mapping the material between +3 and -3 in the row onto itself by T_6, the excluded interval.

---

terms of subsets of cyclical generators may be found in Robert Morris, "Set Groups, Complementation and Mappings Among Pitch-Class Sets," *Journal of Music Theory* 26 (1982): 101–43. The present example would be considered an equivalence class under his ß.

33 The classical twelve-tone transformations affect such a sequence as follows: transposition leaves both signs and numbers unchanged; inversion reverses the signs while leaving the numbers unchanged; retrograde inversion reverses the sequence of numbers while leaving their signs unchanged; and retrogression both reverses the sequence of numbers and their signs. Interval-class 6 takes no sign, as it is its own complement.

Directed Interval-Class Sequences:

NB: Interval-class 3 may have either sign; +3 would generate one row class and -3 another row class (resulting, for example, in Hexachords B and Q, for sequence 2). A-C denotes either Hexachord A or C; these are equivalent under the M operation, as described in the text. B and Q map onto themselves under M.

1:	<+1 +2 -5 +4 3>	(A-C, B)
2:	<+1 3 -2 -5 -4>	(B, Q)
3:	<+1 3 +4 -5 +2>	(A-C, Q)
4:	<+1 +4 3 +2 +5>	(A-C, Q)
5:	<+1 -4 -5 -2 3>	(B, Q)
6:	<+2 -1 3 +5 -4>	(A-C, Q)
7:	<+2 -1 3 -5 +4>	(A-C, Q)
8:	<+2 +1 -5 3 +4>	(B, Q)
9:	<+2 +1 -4 +5 3>	(A-C, Q)
10:	<+2 3 -1 +5 +4>	(Q)
11:	<3 -1 +2 -5 -4>	(Q)

Figure 4: Generators of the 88 Retrograde-Symmetrical All-Interval Row Classes in Carter's *Night Fantasies*

Thus the operation stays within the family of hexachords, while preserving the all-interval property of the row.[34] Figure 5 illustrates the various combinations of these operations applied to the sequence <+1 +2 -5 +4 -3>.

Viewing the extended families of row-classes in the ways outlined above provides several strategies for relating material in the background grid of the

---

34 See a similar discussion in Morris and Starr, "All-Interval Series."

<+1 +2 -5 +4 3>

P:	<+1 +2 -5 +4 -3 6 +3 -4 +5 -2 -1>	
	0 1 3 t 2 e 5 8 4 9 7 6	(A)
Ic3SsP:	<+1 +2 -5 +4 +3 6 -3 -4 +5 -2 -1>	
	0 1 3 t 2 5 e 8 4 9 7 6	(B)
MP:	<-5 +2 +1 +4 +3 6 -3 -4 -1 -2 +5>	
	0 7 9 t 2 5 e 8 4 3 1 6	(C)
Ic3SsMP:	<-5 +2 +1 +4 -3 6 +3 -4 -1 -2 +5>	
	0 7 9 t 2 e 5 8 4 3 1 6	(B)
T_6P:	<+3 -4 +5 -2 -1 6 +1 +2 -5 +4 -3>	
	0 3 e 4 2 1 7 8 t 5 9 6	(A)
$T_6Ic3SsP$:	<-3 -4 +5 -2 -1 6 +1 +2 -5 +4 +3>	
	0 9 5 t 8 7 1 2 4 e 3 6	(B)
T_6MP:	<-3 -4 -1 -2 +5 6 -5 +2 +1 +4 +3>	
	0 9 5 4 2 7 1 8 t e 3 6	(C)
$T_6Ic3SsMP$:	<+3 -4 -1 -2 +5 6 -5 +2 +1 +4 -3>	
	0 3 e t 8 1 7 2 4 5 9 6	(B)

Figure 5: Rows Generated from Interval-Class Sequence

composition. In Example 12, the musical surface has been composed to project instances of interval-class 3, the intervallic generator of all four hexachord types. It is worth noting that in this passage the appearance of members of our basic hexachord types arise not only as row segments, but also as combinations of elements from more than one row.

Example 13, to which we shall return, contains an example of two adjacent rows, labeled III and IV, related by the interval-class 3 sign switching operation. As may be seen, the outer trichords are held as registrally-fixed common tones between the two rows, while the interior trichords exchange registral position and change order. Both rows are, of course, derived from the same directed interval-class sequence.

Example 14 is a reduction of a striking passage in the work. The passage is based solely on hexachords, and it is a catalogue of those hexachordal orderings containing an end dyad that may be realized as a major second. The hexachords have been displayed to have their commonly situated interval articulated by a fixed pair of pitches as the uppermost dyad in each. The strategy employed here not only associates orderings within families, but also reveals a shared property among families.

The strategy employed in Example 14 may be generalized using Figure 4.

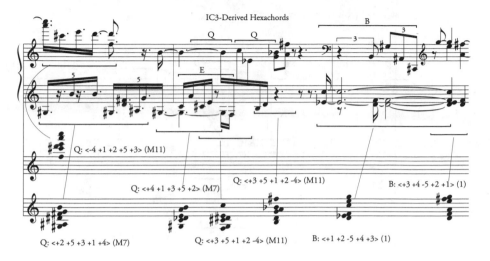

Example 12: Carter's *Night Fantasies,* mm. 15–17

Because different directed interval-class sequences have identically-ordered subsets, we can generate rows from different row-class families containing identically-ordered segmental pitch-class subsets. Due to the symmetrical nature of the rows in question, an invariant segment in one hexachord guarantees one in the other hexachord. This is illustrated in Figure 6.

Because Carter has ordered pitch classes in register in his music, we can investigate the conditions underlying "common tone" relations between two orderings, those situations in which *pitches* are held in common between two registrally ordered aggregates. The order numbers of pitches held in common between two registrally-ordered rows will not always be the same, so it is useful to develop a tool for examining those conditions under which common tone relations may occur. Figure 7 provides a format for doing so.

Up to this point we have used interval-class numbers and signs to indicate directed interval classes, as that is the most useful notation for abstract discussion. In Figure 7, however, we change our notation slightly to conform to our intuitions concerning directed interval classes as they are musically realized in register. Here they are represented by the total number of half-steps between adjacent order numbers, and thus may be summed to indicate the total number of half-steps between any pair of order numbers when a row is ordered in register. Thus, for example, the directed interval-class sequence <-2 +5 -4 -3 -1 6 +1 +3 +4 -5 +2> would become the registrally-projected intervals <10 5 8 9 11 6 1 3 4 7 2>. (The numerals 10 and 11, representing in this case the number of half-steps between

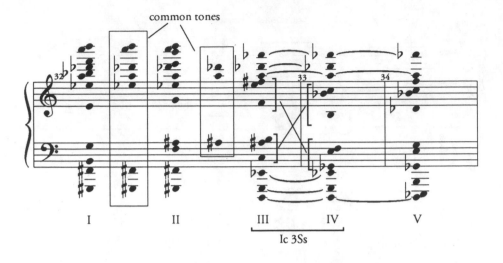

I: Q: <-2 +5 -4 -3 -1> (3)
II: B: <-2 -1 +5 -3 -4> (8)
III: Q: <+5 -4 -3 -2 +1> (M4)
IV: A: <+5 -4 +3 -2 +1> (M4)
V: Q: <+1 -4 -5 -2 +3> (5)

Pc Rows:
8 6 e 7 4 3 9 t 1 5 0 2
8 6 5 t 7 3 9 1 4 e 0 2
2 7 3 0 t e 5 4 6 9 1 8
2 7 3 6 4 5 e t 0 9 1 8
2 3 e 6 4 7 1 t 0 5 9 8

Example 13: Carter's *Night Fantasies*, mm. 32–34 (reduction)

1: <+1 +2 -5 +4 -3>:   0 1 3 t 2 e 5 8 4 9 7 6

3: <+2 -5 +4 -3 +1>:   1 3 t 2 e 0 6 5 8 4 9 7

6: <+2 -1 +3 +5 -4>:   0 2 1 4 9 5 e 3 t 7 8 6

7: <+2 -1 +3 -5 +4>:   0 2 1 4 e 3 9 5 t 7 8 6

Figure 6: Invariant Segments in Rows from Different Families

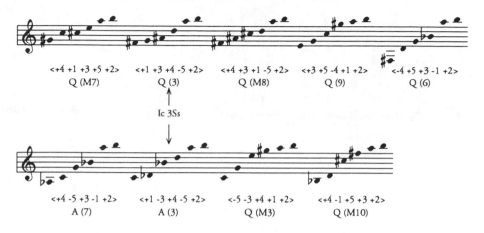

Example 14: Carter's *Night Fantasies,* m. 157 and following (reduction)

order numbers, do not get abbreviated as t and e, as is the case for pitch-class names.)

In Figure 7, each column represents the number of half-steps between the order number at the bottom of the column and the order numbers at the left-hand side, of a row ordered in register, from the bottom to the top. Order numbers are notated using **boldface**. To find the number of half-steps between pitches associated with two order numbers, one finds their intersection in the chart. Thus, in the first chart of Figure 7, the number of half-steps between pitches at order numbers **2** and **8** is 38; as this represents a chart of the row found at the beginning of Example 13, we can see the information realized between the B in the lower staff and the D♭ three octaves and a major second above.

These charts may be interpreted to represent inversion by flipping the list of half-steps around a diagonal axis, marked with an arrow in Figure 7. (As the rows under consideration are retrograde-symmetrical, we need not consider transformations under this operation for our present purposes.)

Charts such as those found in Figure 7 can be used to make comparisons among rows from different families, or among rows of a given row class. For example, comparing the column **0** with the horizontal **e** in the first chart, we find the numbers 23, 43 and 66 in common. This means that there will be four pitches held as common tones between a row of this chart and the inversion of it that maps the pitch classes at order numbers **0** and **e** onto themselves. This is the source of the common tone relationship found in the passage illustrated in Example 11.[35]

---

35 The resulting invariance relations are special cases of order relations, [footnote continued on p. 97]

3: <-2 +5 -4 -3 -1>:   8 6 e 7 4 3 9 t 1 5 0 2

	0	1	2	3	4	5	6	7	8	9	t
e	66	56	51	43	34	23	17	16	13	9	2
t	64	54	49	41	32	21	15	14	11	7	
9	57	47	42	34	25	14	8	7	4		
8	53	43	38	30	21	10	4	3			
7	50	40	35	27	18	7	1				
6	49	39	34	26	17	6					
5	43	33	28	20	11						
4	32	22	17	9							
3	23	13	8								
2	15	5									
1	10										

8:   <-2 -1 +5 -3 -4>:   8 6 5 t 7 3 9 1 4 e 0 2

	0	1	2	3	4	5	6	7	8	9	t
e	66	56	45	40	31	23	17	13	10	3	2
t	64	54	43	38	29	21	15	11	8	1	
9	63	53	42	37	28	20	14	10	7		
8	56	46	35	30	21	13	7	3			
7	53	43	32	27	18	10	4				
6	49	39	28	23	14	6					
5	43	33	22	17	8						
4	35	25	14	9							
3	26	16	5								
2	22	11									
1	10										

M4: <+5 -4 -3 -2 +1>:   2 7 3 0 t e 5 4 6 9 1 8

	0	1	2	3	4	5	6	7	8	9	t
e	66	61	53	44	34	33	27	16	14	11	7
t	59	54	46	37	27	26	20	9	7	4	
9	55	50	42	33	23	22	16	5	3		
8	52	47	39	30	20	19	13	2			
7	50	45	37	28	18	17	11				
6	39	34	26	17	7	6					
5	33	28	20	11	1						
4	32	27	19	10							
3	22	17	9								
2	13	8									
1	5										

Figure 7: Invariance Charts for Registrally-Projected Rows

Comparisons with other rows are performed through comparison of columns and horizontals between charts. The six circled numbers between the first two charts of Figure 7 represent seven common tones available between rows of each chart whose pitches at order number **0** are the same, and the boxed intervals between the second two charts indicate three common tones between a row of the middle chart whose pitch at order number **3** is the same as the pitch at order number **4** of a row of the bottom chart. Both of these common-tone relations are illustrated in Example 13, the first between the rows labeled I and II, and the second between those labeled II and III. The registrally-fixed common tones are listed separately, between the pairs of rows. Common tone relations need not depend on order number invariance, and the differences are indicated by the differences in the columns in which the common half-step distances are found.

An aspect of the relationship between common tone relations and order number invariance in rows of this extended row class is also illustrated in Example 13. As may be seen, the common tones A♭ and A in the highest register of the rows marked III and IV, associated in both cases with the order numbers **e** and **9**, produce common tones D and E♭ in the lowest register, associated with the order numbers **0** and **2**. This is a result of the symmetrical nature of the rows under discussion. However, when the A♭ and A are preserved as common tones between the rows labeled as IV and V, the pitch at order number **2** changes, as the A is associated with two different order numbers in the two rows, **9** and **t** respectively. This dramatizes a special feature of common tone relations in these rows based on order number position. Figure 8 illustrates a shared characteristic of all the rows of the 88 row classes projected in register. All rows of the system are based on a symmetrical tritone nest, so, when ordered in register, the number of half-steps between symmetrically placed order numbers will always be fixed, no matter which directed interval class succession or which hexachord type is present.[36] In terms of Figure 7, the values of the diagonal marked with an arrow of every possible chart from the system will always be 66, 54, 42, 30, 18, and 6. These values are all equivalent to 6, mod 12. This condition grants the tritone a special role within *Night Fantasies'* musical world.

The close of the work features a persistently recurrent chord that rings out through a welter of different textures. The chord, based on a pair of tritones (pitch

---

drawing out instances of collections ordered in the same way in two members of a row class. There is a large literature on order relations, including Philip Batstone, "Multiple Order Functions in Twelve-Tone Music," *Perspectives of New Music* 10 (1972): 60–71 and 11 (1972): 92–111; David Kowalski, "The Construction and Use of Self-Deriving Arrays," *Perspectives of New Music* 25 (1987): 286–362; Morris, "Multiple-Order-Function Rows"; Daniel Starr, "Derivation and Polyphony," *Perspectives of New Music* 23 (1984): 180–257; and Peter Westergaard, "Toward a Twelve-Tone Polyphony," *Perspectives of New Music* 4 (1966): 90–112.

36 Morris and Starr develop the concept of tritone nests in "All-Interval Series," making the preceding point, as well as a number of others.

Boldface numbers are order numbers of all rows in *Night Fantasies*.

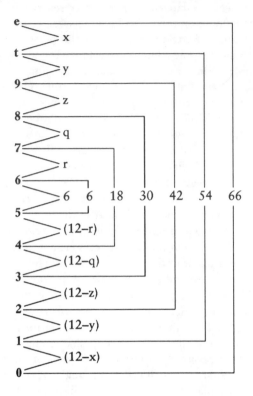

Figure 8: Shared Tritone Nests in the Extended Row Class of Carter's
Night Fantasies

classes 2 and 8 nested between 7 and 1), may be found at the left of Example 15, which contains a reduction of a brief portion of this passage. These registrally-fixed tritones are held invariant through a variety of rows, always at the same order numbers. The passage links rows from throughout the work's extended row class by projecting their fixed order number pitch invariance.[37]

The particular nature of the rows used in *Night Fantasies* will condition the ways smaller collections may appear in the musical surface. Any collection containing a tritone, for instance, must cross the boundary marked by the division between the rows' discrete segmental hexachords, as Figure 8 shows. Closed-

---

37 This is pointed out in Schiff, pp. 317–18.

Example 15: Carter's *Night Fantasies,* Sustained Chord

position tritones that do not arise as connections between successive rows are restricted to the middle register. This is dramatically manifested in the passage marked *recitativo collerico* at measure 234 and following. The ways collections may be held invariant between rows as common tones will be intimately affected by the various ways of connecting rows and their conditions discussed above.

The preceding discussion has attempted to provide some bases for more extended analyses of Elliott Carter's compositions. It is at this point, with some grounding in the worlds he constructs for each piece, that we may begin to follow the drama of his explorations in a more than anecdotal way. As many people have pointed out, Carter's music is powerfully expressive, and that expression arises from the interaction of the many facets of his musical language, including much more than simply the pitch domain. Nevertheless, much of the poignancy and power of his music arises from the ways in which established collections of notes are recontextualized by their ordered reinterpretations, donning new temporal and timbral garb with each new intervallic disposition. A full appreciation of the richness and subtlety of Carter's music can be greatly aided by an understanding of the principles that underlie his approach to composing within the total chromatic.

One pleasant consequence of examining Carter's pitch world is that we may observe both his striking originality as a composer, and the common bases his music shares with the work of a variety of other twentieth century musicians. The use of ordering to control hierarchies of collections within the aggregate demonstrates a commonality with Schoenberg's practice, as do the hints of hexachordal combinatoriality and fixed order number invariance. As noted above, the four related rows used in Carter's *A Symphony of Three Orchestras* form a trichordallycombinatorial array, so that each registral slice including the respective discrete segmental trichords of each row will form and aggregate. The top aggregate, that formed from the top three elements of the four rows, may be heard at the opening of the work. Such arrays, articulated in time rather than register, may be found in the works of several composers, including Donald Martino and Milton Babbitt. The exploration of the interaction of trichords and hexachords, and by implication the extension of such interactions to collections of all sizes, has been a central aspect of the music of many composers, starting with both Schoenberg and Webern. Milton Babbitt's compositional practice during the 1950s involved a careful exploration of just the sorts of trichordal and hexachordal inter-dependencies we observed at the opening of Carter's Piano Concerto, in the context of trichordal arrays. The drama of Babbitt's *Composition for Four Instruments*, for example, hinges on the fact that hexachords of the class [0, 1, 2, 3, 4, 5] may be partitioned into a pair of [0, 1, 3]s, and a pair of [0, 1, 4]s, or one of each. Other works of Babbitt from this period capitalize on the ways a given trichord type may generate more than one kind of hexachord.[38]

Most striking, however, is the ways that Carter's original approach to dealing with such issues and structures suggests interesting extensions and elaborations of twelve-tone theory and practice. Some new ways of thinking arise from his use of register to manifest pitch-class order. These would include the various types of invariance based on common tones discussed above, dependent both on order number positions and the sums of half-steps between order numbers in registrally ordered rows. Others are not immediately the result of Carter's choice of compositional manifestation. While some of the modes of linkage among rows of the vastly extended row class of *Night Fantasies* are dependent on their manifestation of pitch-class order in register, the operations uniting families of classical row classes by directed interval-class sequences are abstract and would have consequences in any sort of manifestation.

Perhaps most interesting of all is the interaction of referential orderings and the exhaustion of collection classes of a given cardinality in Carter's music. In all of the works examined above, the use of one or more members of one or more row classes contributes to the hierarchy of the smaller collections used. In the String Quartet No. 3, one of several ways of distributing tetrachordal collection classes is determined by their available representation at consecutive order numbers in the work's row. In the Piano Concerto, the hexachordal partitions of the two rows along with the distribution of trichordal collection classes between the solo and orchestral ensembles leads to a hierarchy of hexachordal collection classes, based on trichordal partitioning. Hexachordal collection classes may be characterized by the number of ways they may arise within or between

---

38 Babbitt's own account of a number of these properties may be found in Babbitt, *Words about Music*, pp. 85–107.

ensembles, and the degree to which they are restricted to one or the other ensemble. There is a wide variety of functional distributions among the hexachord types based on the Concerto's arrangement of the trichords – from a distribution of five partitions within and five between ensembles, to instances of all within and nine between. The distribution of the trichord types creates a differentiation among the hexachord types roughly analogous to the functional distribution of intervals of various classes by difference of scale degree in the diatonic system.[39] Similarly, the rows of *Night Fantasies*, through their special distributions of intervals, pose limits and restraints on the ways collections of all sizes may appear in the musical surface.

All of these aspects of Carter's music have ramifications far beyond their specific musical manifestations, and hearken directly back to our initial discussion of twelve-tone composition. Different orderings of the twelve pitch classes, as may be inferred from our remarks at the outset, will create different distributions among collection classes of a given cardinality, based on segmental representation. In both the String Quartet No. 3 and *Night Fantasies*, Carter employs all-interval rows as past of his strategy to create hierarchies among larger collection classes. Thus in the Quartet, for example, all the intervals are equally available segmentally, while the difference in segmental availability is used to distinguish roles among the tetrachord types. One could reverse the strategy: there exist so-called ten-trichord rows, rows that contain segmentally members of all trichordal collection classes except [0, 3, 6] and [0, 4, 8]. These rows *cannot* be all-interval, so that one could in a situation equalizing the availability of a large selection of trichord types, create hierarchies among the intervals themselves by their availability a row adjacencies.[40] Taking still another approach, we can see that different sorts of distributions of the trichord types among two or more ensembles would create different ways of building hierarchies among the hexachord types. Such notions can be extended to collections of all different sizes.

Finally, we should emphasize that observations concerning the various intersections between Carter's music and the work of others should in no way diminish our sense of the composer's originality. On the contrary, such intersections are unavoidable given the inevitable restrictions imposed by the

---

39 I am indebted to Stephen Peles for this observation, as well as a number of conversations on related issues.

40 Ten-trichord rows are discussed in Babbitt, *Words about Music*, pp. 106–7, and a complete list of the row classes exhibiting this property may be found in the appendix of Daniel Starr, *Derivation and Polyphony in Twelve-Tone Music* (Ph.D. diss., Princeton University, 1981). There are additionally two all-trichord rings containing members of all twelve trichord classes and related by the circle-of-fifths transformation. They may be found in Walter O'Connell, "Tone Spaces," *Die Reihe* 8 (English ed., 1968): 35–67. Still more techniques for controlling the collectional nature of row segments may be found in Robert Morris, "Set-Type Saturation Among Twelve-Tone Rows," *Perspectives of New Music* 22 (1983–84): 187–217.

inherent abstract structure of the twelve-pitch-class total chromatic, and our appreciation of those commonalities can only increase our enjoyment of the individualities of each composer's music. Carter's music reflects a high degree of sensitivity on the composer's part to the properties of the total chromatic, and his compositional approach suggests new ways of comprehending familiar terrain in the chromatic world. What is truly original about this singular musician is the fresh viewpoint he has taken towards composing with the twelve pitch classes, and we may celebrate not only the body of works that he has given us, but also those new insights he has consequently provided into twelve-tone composition.

An Analysis of Polyrhythm in Selected Improvised Jazz Solos

Cynthia Folio

Thelonious Monk, Ornette Coleman, and Eric Dolphy, three of the great jazz innovators of the late-1950s and 1960s, were masters of timing and rhythmic spacing. Each of these artists used polyrhythm, by setting up one or more implied meters against the underlying meter of the tune to create tension. Within their respective styles, all three musicians employed different types of polyrhythmic passages for different musical and dramatic functions, as the following analyses show.

This essay is organized into four parts. The first part defines rhythm and polyrhythm, then discusses some general principles of polyrhythm. This leads naturally to the second part: some questions about the perception of polyrhythm. The third part and main body of the paper presents several transcriptions of polyrhythmic passages,[1] with analysis and discussion of metric layers, composite rhythm, implied hypermeasures, relative consonance and dissonance of rhythmic streams, recurrence of particular patterns and groupings over various timespans, creation of structural downbeats, relation to pitch and harmonic progression, and stylistic aspects. The essay concludes with some general remarks about the analysis of jazz.

I. Definitions and General Principles

Polyrhythm is an area of study that is only touched upon in the recent blossoming of rhythmic studies. One notable exception is Maury Yeston's work,[2] which catalogues and discusses various proportions and their composite rhythms. David Locke's book notates and discusses performance aspects of polyrhythms in West African music.[3] Simha Arom's study describes the principles underlying the musical

---

1 The sources of these excerpts are listed in the Discography.

2 Maury Yeston, *The Stratification of Musical Rhythm* (New Haven: Yale University Press, 1976).

3 David Locke, *Drum Gahu: The Rhythms of West African Drumming* (Crown Point, Indiana: White Cliffs Media Co., 1987).

system of traditional Central African polyphony and polyrhythm, and includes many transcriptions.[4] Stephen Handel considers the perception of polyrhythm, concluding that rhythmic interpretation is contextual with respect to the tempo, the polyrhythmic configuration, the element frequency of each pulse train, and the duration and intensity of the elements of each pulse train.[5] Finally, Jonathan Kramer discusses polyrhythm briefly, defining it broadly as the simultaneous existence of different rhythmic groups in different voices; he further suggests:

> . . . no one has yet devised a viable method for studying simultaneously sounding groups that conflict . . . The problem is not so much in delineating concurrent groups . . . but in explaining how they interact. Is a composite rhythm created? If so, how?[6]

This essay explores some of Kramer's questions with the help of specific examples.

Improvised polyrhythm has become a standard tension-creating device in jazz improvisation, and also appears in music of other cultures, for example in the music of India and Ghana. A number of jazz and ethnomusicology researchers, including Lloyd Miller[7] and David Locke, believe that the use of polyrhythm in jazz can be traced directly to the practices of West Africa. Also, many jazz musicians from the 1960's to the present, such as drummer Ed Blackwell, have travelled to West Africa to study African drumming. In short, polyrhythm can't help but "resonate" with the jazz tradition.

Since authors frequently differ in defining terms relating to rhythm, it is necessary to begin by clarifying their meanings as used in this essay. Some of these are defined succinctly in Fred Lerdahl's and Ray Jackendoff's *A Generative Theory of Tonal Music*: *beats* are elements that make up a metrical pattern and do not have duration; *timespans* are durations of time between beats; *accents* are of three main types—phenomenal, structural, and metrical; *metrical hierarchy* is defined as two or more levels of beats; a *structural downbeat* is a point (coinciding with a beat) at which grouping structure, metrical structure, and harmonic structure converge; and *structural anacrusis* is a passage or section that leads to a structural downbeat.[8] *Hypermeasures* are defined by Kramer as metric units on all levels above that of the notated measure and by William Rothstein as *supra* measure units that are perceived as if they were measures, because they exhibit a regular alternation of strong and weak "beats" analogous to that of single

---

4 Simha Arom, *African Polyphony and Polyrhythm* (Cambridge University Press, 1991).

5 Stephen Handel, "Using Polyrhythms to Study Rhythm," *Music Perception* 1 (1984): 465–84.

6 Jonathan Kramer, *The Time of Music: New Meanings, New Temporalities, New Listening Strategies.* (New York: Schirmer, 1988), p. 112.

7 Lloyd Miller, *Roots and Branches of Jazz* (Salt Lake City: Eastern Arts, 1987).

8 Fred Lerdahl and Ray Jackendoff, *A Generative Theory of Tonal Music* (Cambridge, Mass.: MIT Press, 1983), pp. 17–19 and 33.

measures.[9] This essay also adopts the view shared by Kramer and Lerdahl/ Jackendoff that rhythm should be grouped through patterns of relatively accented and unaccented timepoints, rather than through analogies to poetic feet.

Yeston defines *meter* as "an outgrowth of the interaction of two levels—two differently-rated strata, the faster of which provides the elements and the slower of which groups them."[10] Joel Lester similarly defines meter so that "pulses are grouped on a given level by accentual factors that occur at a slower pace than the pulse itself."[11] Yeston defines *rhythmic dissonance* as two levels that cannot be expressed as a simple multiplication or division of the other.[12] Since most of the polyrhythmic examples in this essay involve the metric organization of each of two dissonant layers, Yeston's definition of meter implies that these polyrhythms require at least four different strata; two consonant pairs must be dissonant to one another.

In discussing meter it is necessary to make a distinction between the terms *rhythm* and *meter*. Rhythm refers to both musical duration and accentuation. If this accentuation follows a regular pattern, the music is metered. Arom discusses the interaction between rhythm and meter:

> ... rhythm operates at two different levels in regularly accented music, whether monodic or polyphonic: the first derives from the distribution of beats into a given number of similar reference frames (or *measures*), which are defined by the regular repetition of an accented beat ...; the second is determined by the durations of sounds and silences. Western rhythm is thus two-sided. Rhythmic complexity is directly proportional to the extent of offsetting and ambiguity between the two levels.[13]

Arom describes the measure as a temporal matrix and a reference unit; as the basic level of rhythmic organization it provides a temporal reference for the musical durations, even if it is inaudible (as in highly syncopated music).[14]

In defining polyrhythm it is important to realize that a given polyrhythm may represent one of three distinct types.[15] A general definition of polyrhythm will

---

9 Kramer, p. 86; and William Rothstein, *Phrase Rhythm in Tonal Music* (New York: Schirmer, 1989), p. 40.
10 Yeston, p. 66.
11 Joel Lester, *The Rhythms of Tonal Music* (Carbondale: Southern Illinois University Press, 1986), p. 58.
12 Yeston, p. 76.
13 Arom, p. 204.
14 Ibid.
15 This division into three types is an extension of Krebs's two divisions of metric dissonance: my type A and type B are the same as his. It was necessary to add a type C in order to account for examples of gradually fluctuating tempi. (For his discussion of type A and type B dissonances, see Harald Krebs, "Some Extensions of the Concepts of Metrical Consonance and Dissonance," *Journal of Music Theory* 31 (1987), pp. 103–4.)

account for all three types of rhythmic dissonance between meters and/or quantifiable tempi.[16] These include the following:

> *Type A*: interaction of two or more rhythmic strings in which the grouping of regularly recurring attacks of each string is in a non-integer ratio (or one that cannot be reduced to an integer) to the other string(s); a special case of this occurs when a timespan is divided into two or more regular divisions (e.g. a bar of 4/4 divided into three's);

> *Type B*: a metric shift, in which two or more rhythmic strings express the same meter and tempo, but are displaced by a fixed duration; the various strands are "out-of-phase" with one another; and

> *Type C*: fluctuation of tempo against a steady tempo (or differently fluctuating tempi); this could also be called "polytempo," a specific case of polyrhythm.[17]

Any type A polyrhythm, consisting of two or more recurring patterns with a steady pulse, can be expressed as a ratio, as Figure 1 shows. This ratio can be reduced or enlarged proportionally (by multiplying or dividing the numerator and/or denominator), depending on the values of the beats under comparison. Yeston refers to the most reduced form (e.g. 2:3) as the "prime dissonant structure."[18] He also illustrates that the various proportionally-related streams of equally-spaced pulses produce a predictable, palindromic composite rhythm when the two rhythms sound together. For example, 2:3 creates the composite rhythm of 2112. Figure 1 shows the derivation of 2112 from the ratio 2:3, as well as several other examples of Type A polyrhythms. Figures 2 and 3 list some superparticular ratios and some prime ratios,[19] along with their composite rhythms.

---

16 "Tempo" is defined here as a certain number of beats per unit of time, or a specific (quantifiable) rate of pulse.

17 Arom calls this phenomenon "polymetric": "If we take 'metre' in its primary sense of *metrum* (the metre being the temporal reference unit), 'polymetric' would describe the simultaneous unfolding of several parts in a single work at different tempos *so as not to be reducible to a single metrum*" (Arom, p. 205, italics in original).

18 "A prime structure includes no other equal divisions of the time span except those of its constituent levels" (Yeston, p. 123).

19 These prime ratios are listed in Yeston, p. 123. Additional prime ratios included in Yeston are listed below:
> 5:19
> 7:13
> 7:17
> 7:19
> 11:13
> 11:17
> 11:19.

Figure 1: Some Examples of Composite Rhythms

x:y (x = y + 1)
List of composite rhythms:
> Numbers represent attack points;
> Value of number = length of timespan between attack points.

x:y	composite rhythm
3:2	2 1 1 2
4:3	3 1 2 2 1 3
5:4	4 1 3 2 2 3 1 4
6:5	5 1 4 2 3 3 2 4 1 5
7:6	6 1 5 2 4 3 3 4 2 5 1 6
8:7	7 1 6 2 5 3 4 4 3 5 2 6 1 7
9:8	8 1 7 2 6 3 5 4 4 5 3 6 2 7 1 8

Generalizations for superparticular ratios:
(1) every odd time-span in the composite rhythm produces a series: y, y-1, y-2 . . . 1; every even time-span produces the opposite series: 1, 2, 3 . . . y
(2) There are always an even number of attack points in the composite rhythm.
(3) There are always two equal parts to the palindromic arrangement of time-spans in the composite rhythm.
(4) Each consecutive ordered odd/even time-span value sums to x; the first and last time-span values = y; each consecutive ordered even/odd time-span value thereafter sums to y.

Generalizations for all ratios:
(1) Total number of attack points = x + y - 1.
(2) Time-spans create a palindrome.

Figure 2: Superparticular Ratios (Composite Rhythms)

List of composite rhythms:
        Numbers represent attack points;
        Value of number = length of timespan between attack points.

x:y	composite rhythm
2:3	2 1 1 2
2:5	2 2 1 1 2 2
2:7	2 2 2 1 1 2 2 2
2:11	2 2 2 2 2 1 1 2 2 2 2 2
2:13	2 2 2 2 2 2 1 1 2 2 2 2 2 2
2:17	2 2 2 2 2 2 2 2 1 1 2 2 2 2 2 2 2 2
2:19	2 2 2 2 2 2 2 2 2 1 1 2 2 2 2 2 2 2 2 2
3:5	3 2 1 3 1 2 3
3:7	3 3 1 2 3 2 1 3 3
3:11	3 3 3 2 1 3 3 3 1 2 3 3 3
3:13	3 3 3 3 1 2 3 3 3 2 1 3 3 3 3
3:17	3 3 3 3 3 2 1 3 3 3 3 3 1 2 3 3 3 3 3
3:19	3 3 3 3 3 3 1 2 3 3 3 3 3 2 1 3 3 3 3 3 3
5:7	5 2 3 4 1 5 1 4 3 2 5
5:11	5 5 1 4 5 2 3 5 3 2 5 4 1 5 5
5:13	5 5 3 2 5 5 1 4 5 4 1 5 5 2 3 5 5
5:17	5 5 5 2 3 5 5 4 1 5 5 5 1 4 5 5 3 2 5 5 5
7:11	7 4 3 7 1 6 5 2 7 2 5 6 1 7 3 4 7

Figure 3: Some Prime Ratios (Composite Rhythms)

II. Questions about the Perception of Polyrhythm

The process of transcribing and analyzing polyrhythmic passages led this author to a number of questions about the perception of polyrhythm, some of which will be addressed and some of which are left unanswered.

1. Can listeners really perceive polyrhythm, or do they actually focus only on one layer at a time? Is it possible to focus somewhere in between the layers, and therefore discern the tension and resolution *between* them?

2. Can two (or more) layers be truly equal, or is one layer inevitably primary? That is, in jazz, do listeners hear the rhythm section as the *main* grouping, while the soloist creates the dissonance? If they can be equal, at what point do they become equal?

3. Can different hierarchies of polyrhythmic relationships be perceived? That is, can we hear 7:4 at the same time as we hear 7:2? To put this another way, is it possible to discern hypermetric relationships, or a "hyper-polymeter"?

4. Can listeners perceive polyrhythmic motives at various structural levels, in a way analogous to motivic parallelisms in pitch?

Before discussing what most listeners can perceive, it must first be mentioned that some non-Western cultures are apparently better at perceiving many rhythmic layers at once. In a recent discussion with the author, a master drummer from Ghana, Abraham Kobena Adzenyah,[20] maintained that all master drummers are trained from childhood to hear all parts at once, not just one part at a time, or even the composite rhythm. Locke also makes a similar claim:

> ...rather than concentrating on their own parts, [African] musicians hear the whole polyrhythm...The challenge of performance lies more in perception than technique: can you hear the entire "musical mobile" without making a mistake in your own part?...creative performance depends upon a player's ever-renewing interpretation of his part within this kaleidoscopic musical context of shifting aural illusions.[21]

It is difficult for most Western listeners to perceive several layers all at once; one can focus on either one of the layers or on the composite rhythm in a single hearing, or one can shift from layer to layer. That means that in a two-part polyrhythm, there are essentially three possible streams to which the listener might

---

20 Adzenyah presented a workshop with Royal James Hartigan on the drum languages of West Africa and their relationship to jazz drumming at the 1991 annual meeting of the College Music Society in Chicago, Illinois.
21 Locke, p. 7.

attend: one of each of the conflicting layers, and the composite rhythm created between them. To add to the complexity, there are variations on how these three layers are heard, depending on whether, for example, the listener feels the quarter-note, half-note, full measure, or group of measures as the basic pulse in each stream. What can be perceived at all times, no matter where the focus, is the varying degree of tension created by all these complexities. The emotional effects of polyrhythm may vary (including uneasiness, humor, freedom), but this rhythmic device invariably creates a general perception of tension, an anticipation of resolution, and a sensation of forward momentum.

The hierarchical nature of rhythm and meter has been asserted by psychological as well as theoretical studies. For example, Handel lists the many advantages of hierarchical models of rhythms, one of which is the ability to predict and anticipate future elements:

> The multiple levels of the hierarchical tree allow us to vary the "grain" of our attention. At some times we attend to the rhythm among separated elements and at still other times we attend to higher level rhythms which act on groups of elements. In all cases however, the rhythm generates a trajectory, leading to expectancies concerning future events.[22]

III. Analysis

The analytical section opens with the music of Thelonious Monk, whose tunes were recorded earlier than the other two artists and whose examples are probably the least complicated. The first tune is "Bags Groove" (Example 1), which is played by Monk, but is composed by Milt Jackson;[23] it is a deceptively simple composition based on an ascending perfect fourth motive, with the accent on the top note. This accent usually falls on beat three, but as the motive is developed, the accent sometimes lands on beat one. As the upper set of brackets in Example 1 shows, this heavily accented third beat has the effect of displacing the downbeat of the 4/4 melody by two beats from the downbeat of the 4/4 played by the rhythm section: a type B polyrhythm. This displacement is "resolved" in measure 7, only to recur in measure 8.

The accented F5's and G♭5's form a clear neighbor-note figure (F5–G♭5–F5) that governs the voice leading of the tune. The prominent repetitions of F5 in measures 5–7 suggest smaller rhythmic groupings of three quarter-notes duration, as bracketed below the staff. These can be grouped into still smaller units of three eighth-notes

---

22 Handel, p. 468.
23 "Bags" is the nickname of vibraphonist Milt Jackson, best known as a member of the Modern Jazz Quartet and noted for his blues playing. Appropriately, "Bags Groove" is a blues.

Example 1: "Bag's Groove"—Tune by Milt Jackson; Solo by Monk
Transcribed from *Smithsonian Collection* by C. Folio

duration, as shown in the second row of brackets, beginning with the C5 in measure 5 and continuing through measure 10. [24]

Turning to the last eight bars of the improvisation (last two lines of Example 1), Monk creates a type A polyrhythmic passage out of the three-note motive, now transformed rhythmically into a triplet figure. [25] In the third bar, the motive is "squeezed" into a shorter timespan; it is repeated four times within three bars. Beginning in the third bar, the metric accents create a 3/4 against the basic 4/4 played by the rhythm section. [26] (To add to the complexity, two of the quarter-note beats in Monk's superimposed 3/4 meter are grouped into threes by the quarter-note triplet figures.) This 3/4 against 4/4 is an expression of the ratios 4:3 (at the level of the bar, with a composite rhythm in quarter-note durations of 312213, and 2:3 (at the level of the half note), with composite rhythm 2112. [27] Of the two proportions, 2:3 is the prime dissonant structure. The entrance of the E5 just before the last bar, interrupts the sense of 3/4. [28]

Many of Monk's tunes are polyrhythmic. One well-known example is "Straight No Chaser," which features 3/4 against 4/4 through constant repetition of the same

---

24 These groupings are asserted through phenomenal accents of various types: the first C in measure 5 is a point of initiation; the first F in the next group is accented through an upward leap; the following F anticipates the downbeat of the next bar – a cliché of jazz rhythmic style; the next F occurs after a leap and as part of pattern repetition. The groups of threes can be heard to continue through rests in measures 7 and 9, despite the absence of actual accents, because a pattern can be heard to continue until something else occurs strongly enough to negate it (see Lester, p. 16 and p. 77).

25 For an analysis of the force of motives as compositional determinants in jazz, see Gunther Schuller's "Sonny Rollins and the Challenge of Thematic Improvisation," *The Jazz Review* 1 (November 1968), reprinted in *Musings: The Musical Worlds of Gunther Schuller* (New York: Oxford University Press, 1986), pp. 86–97. Schuller mentions Monk (footnote, p. 93) as one of a handful of predecessors to Rollins in the art of motivic development in improvisation.

26 The groupings begin with the rests, only to keep this passage consistent with the tune. This excerpt clearly demonstrates the distinction between "metric" accents (on the rests) and "phenomenal" accents (on the F's and G's). A case could be made for hearing the groups of three's either way, whether the metric or phenomenal accents were used as grouping boundaries.

27 The ratio 4:3 describes four improvised 3/4 bars in the time of three of the rhythm section's 4/4 bars, while the ratio 2:3 describes two of the improvised 3/4 bars in the time of three half notes. Throughout the analyses, the denominator or second term of the ratio represents the pre-existing strata (or rhythm section) and the numerator or first term of the ratio represents the superimposed strata (or improvised soloist).

28 The last three bars exhibit other interesting subdivisions into groups of five. If we take the beginning of the pattern (the first-beat rest of the third bar from the end) as the first grouping boundary, then consider the phenomenal accents on the G of beat two of the next bar and the F in the last bar as initiating new groups, then a grouping of 5 + 5 quarter notes results. Furthermore, the syncopated E on the last eighth of the second bar from the end exactly bisects the last group of five, forming 5 + 5 eighth notes; although this E is a surprise, breaking up the previous pattern of threes (!), it has its own logic within the five-spans.

figure. Another such tune is "Played Twice," which abounds in rhythmic surprises (rhythm/contour analysis in Example 2).[29] Although it is a 16-bar tune whose form is AA¹BA² (4 + 4 + 4 + 4), the rhythmic groupings within each four-bar segment are irregular; each is grouped into some variation of 3 + 5 + 5 + 3 quarter notes (marked with brackets above Example 2):

1st 4 bars:	3 5 5 3
2nd 4 bars:	3 5 8 (8 = 5 + 3)
3rd 4 bars:	5 5 6 (5533 = rotation of 3553)[30]
last 4 bars:	3 5 5 3

The first 3553 is delineated by phenomenal accents on the G's at letter A, then a new motive appears at letter B which is repeated after five beats.[31] Letter A can be further divided into groups of three eighth notes, beginning with the three pick-up eighths, and forming a 3:2/3:4 pattern. The tune thus gets off to a rocky metric start (perhaps explaining the need for three cymbal strokes at the beginning).

The bridge (letter C) implies a 5/4 meter through pattern repetition (creating a 2:5/4:5 proportion). This meter has the effect of rotating the 3+5+5+3 grouping to become 5+5+3+3 (or actually 5+5+6). Each of the groups of five quarters is also bisected by a very strong dynamic accent on the last B♭ of each motivic figure.[32] All of this rhythmic activity occurs over a stationary F7 chord.

The last four bars initiate a recapitulation of the A section; however, Monk shocks his audience (at letter D) with a quickening harmonic rhythm (half-notes in

---

29 Because I was not able to acquire copyright permission for any of Monk's compositions, Examples 2 and 3 are in the form of rhythm and contour graphs. I refer to the *Real Book* for the only existing notated version of the tune, "Played Twice," as well as the aforementioned "Straight No Chaser."

30 This would be r_1, where $r_n(X)$ denotes the n-th rotation of X. See John Rahn, *Basic Atonal Theory* (New York: Longman, 1980), p. 113.

31 The downbeat of measure four (letter B), can also be heard, at first, as belonging with the first five quarter-note grouping as a "sixth beat"—a grouping elision that occurs several times in this very witty head.

32 It is interesting to compare various performances of "Played Twice." Takes 1, 2, and 3 of the quintet version are included on the compact disc, *Five by Five* (Riverside OJCCD–362–2/R–1150). On Take 3, Monk not only accents the B♭'s (last eighth note of each group in mm. 10, 11, and 13) more strongly than on Takes 1 and 2, but the rest of the band remains silent except for punctuations of the B♭'s. Here we see Monk "working out" a rhythmic idea in the recording session. When Monk records it four years later, in a quartet version, on the album *Always Know* (Columbia Records JG 35720, Lincoln Center, 1963), he introduces a major structural change: two beats are left out of m. 9 of Example 2. Thus the bridge begins two beats early, creating a 2/4 measure right before the bridge. Although this throws the 3553 pattern off balance, it makes the composition that much more interesting and unpredictable. The five-pattern in the bridge remains the same, with Monk giving the same strong accents to the B♭'s.

Example 2: Monk: "Played Twice"—A Rhythm/Contour Analysis
Transcribed from *Five by Five* by C. Folio

m. 16 and quarters in m. 17) and a shift into the tonally surprising D major. The first two quarter notes of the last bar create a V–I cadence (A7–D); the D chord on the second beat receives a strong accent, completing another 3553 pattern. The tune is then repeated (thus the title "Played Twice"?), giving the listener a second opportunity to make sense of the complex metric implications.

Yet another of Monk's tunes that features polyrhythm is "Criss Cross" (see linear reduction in Example 3). The four-bar introduction, beginning at letter A, sets up a grouping of three quarter-note durations against the 4/4 bar, expressing the 4:3 ratio. This grouping is created by the combination of accentuation through ascending leap, agogic length, and by the outlining of a rising chromatic step progression (marked with connecting beam in Example 3). When the tune begins

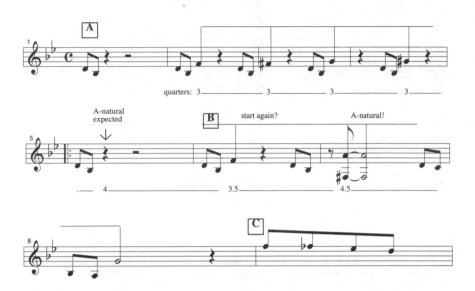

Example 3: Monk's "Criss Cross"—A Linear Analysis of the First Section of the Tune

at the double bar, the expectation is for the three-pattern to continue and for the line to proceed to A♮, but instead it takes some surprising detours. Rather than the 3 + 3 + 3 quarter-note grouping, Monk substitutes 3½ + 4½ + 3. Further, the tune appears to start the chromatic line again on F (letter B), but the next expected note, F♯, is transferred to an inner voice and is replaced by the originally expected A. The eighth-rest of silence before this F♯–A is a wonderful example of James Newton's observation that Monk "was a master of making space swing."[33] Monk's carefully planned silences are a hallmark of his style. At letter C, a second motivic idea appears, this time with a descending chromatic line, and a similarly unpredictable metric pattern.

Monk's improvisation on "Criss Cross" (rhythmic/contour analysis in Example 4) is motivically derived from the tune, treating the two motives polyrhythmically. The first example is a 2:3/4:3 passage based on the D5–B♭4 "pedal" motive from measure 1 of the tune. The polyrhythmic development of this motive features beginning-accented groupings, initiated by dynamic accents (and, in some cases, clusters), and phenomenal accents created by higher pitches. In measure 5, the second motive is taken from the tune (letter C in Example 3) in an augmented

---

33 Jazz flutist James Newton made this statement at his improvisation workshop, given at the 1991 National Flute Association Convention in Washington, D.C.

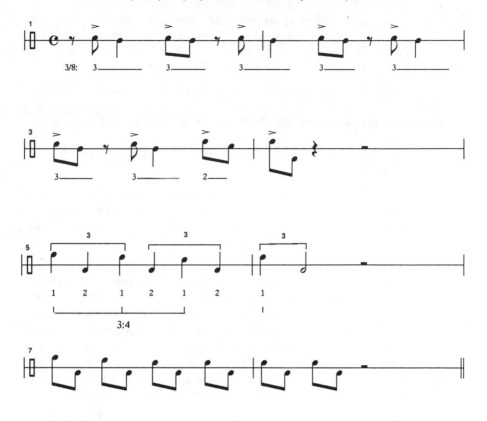

**Example 4: Monk's "Criss Cross"—Last A Section of Piano Solo;
A Rhythm/Contour Analysis
Transcribed from *Smithsonian Collection* by C. Folio**

rhythm. The top notes of these triplets are F6–F♭6–E♭6 and move in half-note triplets against the measure (3:4). Monk restates the second motive in its original eighth-note rhythm in measure 7, restoring the rhythmic equilibrium.

Ornette Coleman's album, *The Shape of Jazz To Come*, recorded May 22, 1959 in Los Angeles contains polyrhythms of a very different kind. One of the tunes from this album, "Congeniality," was transcribed and analyzed by Gunther Schuller.[34] In

---

34 This analysis appears in a collection of ten compositions by Coleman (MJQ 6), published by MJQ Music Inc. in 1961. The forward from this collection is reprinted in "Ornette Coleman's Compositions," *Musings*, pp. 80–85.

this analysis, Schuller describes a polyrhythm between the saxophone and bass that could be classified as a type B polyrhythm—Coleman starts a new phrase (measure 127) which is one beat off from the rhythm section. Schuller is not sure if this was intentional or if Coleman erred in his entrance. He further states:

> Yet this kind of polymetric displacement is the heart and soul of one of the primary antecedents of jazz, namely native African music, and is certainly not unknown in jazz improvisation. It is conceivable then that Mr. Coleman instinctively and deliberately made this choice, especially in as much as he likes to "turn phrases around on a different beat, thereby raising the freedom of my playing."[35]

"Lonely Woman," from the same album, is probably one of Coleman's most widely discussed compositions, inspiring analyses by Charles Hartman and Steven Block. When Schuller helped in the editing of this album, he made the following insightful comments about Coleman's style:

> Perhaps the most outstanding element in Ornette's musical conception is an utter and complete freedom. His musical inspiration operates in a world uncluttered by conventional barlines, conventional chord changes, and conventional ways of blowing or fingering a saxophone. Such practical "limitations" did not even have to be overcome in his music; they somehow never existed for him. Despite this—or more accurately, *because* of this—his playing has a deep inner logic. Not an obvious surface logic, it is based on subtleties of reaction, subtleties of timing and color that are, I think, quite new to jazz—at least they've never appeared in so pure and direct a form.[36]

The tune of "Lonely Woman" (Example 5) is a standard AABA form, but the description "standard" ends there. The tune of the A section is 15 bars of 4/4, played very freely,[37] and lasting 24 seconds, making the quarter note equal to an average of 150. But the bass and drums play at a faster tempo than the two horns and can be clocked at about 176, or approximately 1.17 times faster, and this in a double-time feel. The bass and drums play 17–18 bars to the horns' 15 bars in each A section, for a ratio of about 15:17.5. The ratio of tempi, 150:176, is close to 6:7 (6:7 = 150:175), suggesting a high-level 6 against 7—a type C polyrhythm. It is remarkable that all six A sections (both going in and going out) keep the proportion fairly consistent, differing in length only by a few seconds! Hartman points out that "it is usually the solo instruments that move fast against a slower

---

35 Schuller, *Musings*, p. 84.

36 Martin Williams, jacket notes to Ornette Coleman, *The Shape of Jazz To Come* (Atlantic 1317–2, 1959).

37 In fact the notation of this tune is a very "square" representation of what is actually played; the material is not in alignment with the notated meter, as the example suggests.

Example 5: Coleman's "Lonely Woman"—Tune

"Lonely Woman" By Ornette Coleman
Copyright © 1960 By MJQ Music, Inc. Used By Permission

Example 5 (cont.): Coleman's "Lonely Woman"—Tune

This transcription is an adaptation of two existing transcriptions, but with several additions and alterations: (1) *A Collection of Twenty-six Ornette Coleman Compositions* (New York: MJQ Music, 1968, p. 21) and (2) Steven Block, "Pitch-class Transformation in Free Jazz Music" (*Music Theory Spectrum* 12 [1990], p. 196).

moving accompaniment; 'Lonely Woman' turns the hierarchy upside down, exaggerating both tempi. The background seems desperately urgent, and the melody becomes still more eloquently mournful."[38]

As if the extreme rubato were not enough to disorient the listener rhythmically, the dynamic accents that Coleman and Don Cherry apply to the tune rarely suggest

---

38 Charles O. Hartman, *Jazz Text: Voice and Improvisation in Poetry, Jazz, and Song* (Princeton: Princeton University Press, 1991), p. 70.

a 4/4 pattern. The dynamic accents are marked in Example 5, with brackets denoting the rhythmic groups initiated by these accents; durations are measured in quarter-note units. The result of this metric ambiguity caused by irregular rhythmic grouping, combined with the rubato, is that "Coleman's tune moves as if it hardly lived within measures at all."[39] This irregularity is highlighted by the somewhat regular patterns of 3 + 1 (and 1 + 3) in the bass.

Coleman's improvised solo (Example 6) unfolds and builds in many subtle ways. It begins in the low register, climbing to the structural third scale degree (F5) in measure 12 after outlining a V7(♭9) over a tonic pedal point in D minor. Ornette expresses the dominant chord as a melodic diminution of A3–B♭3–C♯4 (circled in Example 6) over the first four bars, with successive notes of the motive separated by durations of thirteen and eight eighth-note units. The motive returns several times in decreasing numbers of eighth-note units: it appears in measures 6–7, at distances of three and two units; it is repeated an octave higher in measure 8, at distances of three and three units; and it continues up the chord in measures 10–11, at distances of two and two units. This compression of the motive gives the passage forward momentum. Compounding the tension created by this climbing V♭9, the meter becomes less and less clear in both the sax and the bass/drum layers: the clear 7+1 patterns in the bass (measured in eighth-note durations) in the first six bars give way to more erratic alternations between short and long, while Coleman's solo is far from a clear 4/4. At measure 15 (letter X), though, the two layers come together into a clear 4/4. One beat later, a cry of delight can be heard on the album from someone in the group.

In the last A section of the improvised solo (Example 7), Coleman frees himself completely from the meter, resulting in an extraordinary example of a type C polyrhythm. At measure 4, he begins to drag in relation to the steady tempo kept by the bass and drums, then accelerates to the point where he catches up again. The section is based on a simple two-note motive stated at the opening and consisting of a pitch contour of high to low and a rhythm contour of long to short (perhaps a reference to the 3 + 1 motive in the bass line of the tune). Rhythm contours, as introduced by Elizabeth West Marvin, "represent relative durations in much the same way that melodic contours represent relative pitch height, without a precise calibration of the intervals spanned."[40] In this example, the pitch contour of high/low matches the duration contour of long/short. The proportion of duration interval varies throughout the section, as does the pitch interval. The brackets in Example 7 outline this elastic motive, showing the various proportions of long to short in numbers of eighth notes (or sixteenth notes). Because of the higher pitch and agogic accent

---

39 Ibid., p. 63.

40 Elizabeth West Marvin, "The Perception of Rhythm in Non-Tonal Music: Rhythmic Contours in the Music of Edgard Varèse," *Music Theory Spectrum* 13 (1991): 64.

Example 6: Coleman's "Lonely Woman"—Beginning of Coleman's Solo
Transcribed from *The Shape of Jazz To Come* by C. Folio

Example 6 (cont.): Coleman's "Lonely Woman"—Beginning of Coleman's Solo

of the first note, this motive is beginning-accented; therefore, its repetition implies a constantly changing accentual stream above the steady 4/4 of bass and drums.

Eric Dolphy's rhythmic style continually evolved throughout his tragically short career. Early examples of his solos feature straight sixteenth-notes, played at break-neck speed, with little rhythmic variety. The turning point seems to be his collaboration with Coleman on the album *Free Jazz*, Dec. 21, 1960. The free group improvisation forced him to play without reference to harmonic changes or even a given meter or tempo—the tempo in *Free Jazz* varies from moment to moment. This experience seemed to free him, both rhythmically and harmonically.

Gary Giddens comments on Dolphy's stylistic change:

At least initially, [Dolphy] lacked the bebopper's ability to phrase with variety, to juggle the accents, and use space for emphasis. His mimetic gift for adopting vocal sounds, as well as technical devices like the tremolo and glissando, helped him to eventually dispel rhythmic monotony, but in his main body of work, there is a tendency to play long, ornate phrases in which the accents are placed on alternate beats with rotary precision. Among the

123

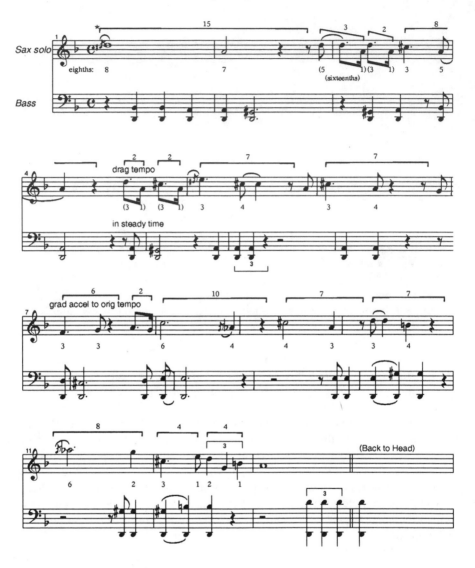

* Motive: pitch contour = <1,0>; rhythm contour = <1,0>

Example 7: Coleman's "Lonely Woman"—Last A Section of Solo
Transcribed from *The Shape of Jazz To Come* by C. Folio

Example 8: "Rally"—Tune by Ron Carter
Transcribed from *Magic* by C. Folio

"Rally" by Ron Carter
Prestige—BMI Permission granted by Fantasy Inc.

techniques aiding him in greater rhythmic/harmonic expressiveness was the emerging body of compositions making use of modes or free passages.[41]

An example of Dolphy's later style can be heard on the Ron Carter tune, "Rally" (Example 8), which was recorded after *Free Jazz* and after Dolphy joined John Coltrane's and George Russell's bands. The composition is in a standard 32-bar AABA form, but the B section is modal and is extended in each improvisation beyond the eight-bar limit. The freer B section provokes several polyrhythmic episodes in Dolphy's solo (given in Example 9) and also stimulates Dolphy's sense of humor. To keep track of the time, the drummer (Charlie Parsip) gives a clear "one" with a snare stroke on the downbeat of each measure; he also signals the end

41 Gary Giddens, jacket notes to Eric Dolphy and Ron Carter, *Magic* (Prestige P–24053, 1961).

of the B section with a "kick" on the fourth beat of the last bar (see lower line of Example 9). Dolphy creates a humorous polyrhythm at the beginning of this example, as he grunts through the bass clarinet and contradicts the 4/4 time with a simple three-note idea. This gets truncated into a two-note motive repeated in unpredictable timespans. At measure 9, he improvises a tune that resembles whole-tone version of "Pop Goes the Weasel."[42] The quotation creates three bars of 3/8 per 4/4 measure (or a 3:2/3:4 proportion), but begins to drag at measure 13. This variable tempo creates a series of shifting proportions—from 3:2 to 5:2, back to 3:2, finally synchronizing around measure 19 and returning to two beats per bar in measure 21. This passage thus combines type A and type C polyrhythms.

The three 3/8 bars within the 4/4 from measures 9–11 create a complex hierarchy that is graphed in Figure 4. Each square dot in the top two graphs represents the relative accentual weight of each beat (see Lerdahl/Jackendoff, p. 19 and Kramer, pp. 102–20, for similar types of graphs). The top graph represents the perceived meter (4/4 layer) and the middle graph weights the rhythms that Dolphy plays over the 4/4 meter (3/8 layer). In this 3/8 layer, there are nine eighth notes per 4/4 bar.[43] The resultant composite rhythm (bottom graph) combines the accentual weights of the two dissonant layers into a polymetric hierarchy. The numbers in the bottom graph represent composite rhythms at various levels of the hierarchy: 9:4 (441342243144); and 3:2 (6336, which equals 2112).

Although the process of graphing appears similar to Fourier analysis, in which sinusoidal wave forms are added together to form a complex wave, there are important differences. The most important difference is that rhythms are not sinusoidal, but consist of discrete points, making the polyrhythm graph much less complex than the graph of a complex wave form. A second important difference is in the perception. The resultant rhythm does not "fuse" in the same way that the complex wave form does to create a characteristic timbre. How this resultant rhythm actually *is* perceived is a topic for further investigation.

One of the most complex polyrhythms in jazz is found in Example 10, from Eric Dolphy's flute solo on "You Don't Know What Love Is." It is no coincidence that

---

42 Dolphy often quotes nursery rhymes or popular tunes within his polyrhythmic episodes, as if to convert the simple tune into something bizarre. Other examples include: "Softly, As in a Morning Sunrise" from the same album (also a quotation of "Pop Goes the Weasel"); "Hot House" (yet another "Pop Goes the Weasel") and "When Lights are Low" (a quotation from "Surrey With the Fringe On Top"), from *The Berlin Concerts*, (Inner City IC 3017, 1978); and "When Lights are Low" (a quotation from "Comin' Through the Rye") from *Copenhagen Concert* (Prestige 24027, 1961).

43 For convenience in aligning the graphs, the 4/4 layer spreads each measure over 18 segments, giving each quarter-note unit four and one-half segments. In the 3/8 layer, each eighth-note unit is represented by two segments. The quarter-note and eighth-note pulses are numbered under each of these layers accordingly. The composite rhythm here is a result of the interaction between a specific rhythm (played by Dolphy) and the already established feeling of 4/4 meter in the rhythm section.

Example 9: "Rally"—Dolphy's Solo in B Section
Transcribed from *Magic* by C. Folio

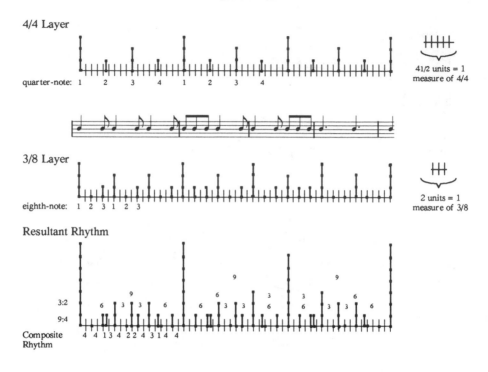

Figure 4: "Rally"—Graph of Polyrhythms (from mm. 9–13 of Ex. 9)

this solo is from *Last Date*, the last recorded album before his death, thus representing his most mature style. The proportion in this example of 7:4 has already occurred several times as a motivic element in the long, eleven-minute improvisation. At this point, late in the solo, Dolphy further subdivides seven into three's, so that seven 3/8 bars are implied over the 4/4 (thus, the time signature of 21/8 in the notated example);[44] in other words, four is divided by seven which is divided by three. It sounds as though Dolphy is playing in a different tempo of dotted-quarter = 186 (against the rhythm section tempo of quarter = 106). Within this tempo, Dolphy groups his rhythmic stream into hypermeasures of two, four, and eight, creating implied 6/8, 12/8, and pairs of 12/8 measures. The implied 12/8

---

44 Since the tempo of the tune is so slow and Dolphy's solo is quite fast, it was necessary to notate the solo in half-time. Two bars of 4/4 in the transcription equals one bar of the tune. This eleven-bar transcription thus represents only the first 5½ measures of the A section in the tune. Because of the slow tempo, the quarter note in the transcription is more likely to be perceived as the "beat" than the slower quarter-note pulse of the tune.

Example 10: "You Don't Know What Love Is"—Dolphy's Solo in 3A2
Transcribed from *Last Date* (Trip TLP–5506) by C. Folio

Example 11: 12/8 Patterns in Dolphy's Solo

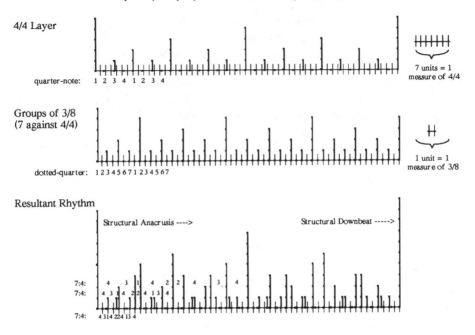

Figure 5: "You Don't Know What Love Is"—Graph of Polyrhythms
(from mm. 1–9 of Ex. 10)

bars are marked in Example 10 as beats 1–2–3–4 immediately below the flute solo. (Example 11 renotates Dolphy's solo in 12/8 supporting the hypermeasure grouping through repeated rhythmic patterns, marked by letters.) Perhaps not coincidentally, the length of the polyrhythmic passage (eight 4/4 bars), corresponds to the amount of time that it takes to bring all measures and hypermeasures of the two simultaneous meters into phase.[45]

Figure 5 graphs this passage from Example 10: the top graph represents 4/4 measures and hypermeasures played by the rhythm section; the middle graph shows the groups of seven 3/8 measures against this 4/4 and its hypermeasures (as played by Dolphy). There are twenty-one eighth notes in Dolphy's solo per 4/4 measure represented by the rhythm section. The bottom graph in Figure 5 combines the accentual weights of the top two layers. One can visualize from the graph the tremendous structural downbeat that is created at the beginning of the

---

45 Gretchen Horlacher develops the idea of metric strata going into and out of phase with one another (measured as "cycles") in her article, "The Rhythms of Reiteration: Formal Development in Stravinsky's Ostinati," *Music Theory Spectrum* 14 (1992): 171–87.

ninth measure, where Dolphy returns to the regular division of four beats to the bar in synchrony with the rhythm section. The numbers in the bottom graph illustrate the 7:4 composite rhythm (4314224134) at several hierarchical layers.

The rhythmic tension/release is paralleled in the realm of pitch. Most of the notes in this passage lie "outside" the notated chord changes and form polychords over the changes in the rhythm section. Also, a long-range motion can be heard from the prominent Bb5 at the beginning of the section (Example 10, mm. 1–2) to the resolution of the B5/B4, (enharmonically equivalent to Cb as the seventh of the Db7—m. 8), to Bb4/Bb5 of the Gm7 (downbeat of measure 9). This resolution occurs at the very moment that the polymeter reaches the point where it is back in phase. The cumulative effect of the passage is very complex, and all the more remarkable because it is improvised.

IV. Summary Remarks

The many types of polyrhythm discussed above reflect vast differences among the three artists. Monk's polyrhythms are of types A and B, are based on short motives derived from the tune, and feature space created by silence and simplicity. They are calculated to create surprise. Many of Monk's tunes themselves feature polyrhythm; the solos are primarily variations on the tune. Coleman's style of polyrhythm is characterized by rubato and fluctuating tempi, resulting in type C polyrhythm. The effect is of total freedom from the barline. The passages selected from Dolphy's solos are type A and type C polyrhythms, and are more complex than Monk's or Coleman's. The resulting effect of Dolphy's polyrhythmic style is a sense of tension combined with humor. The types of polyrhythms found in the above examples are not exclusive to jazz. It is hoped that such a study could also be applied to polyrhythm in other styles of music.

It seems appropriate to close with a comment on the topic of the analysis of jazz, a discipline that is just beginning to receive some attention. Some musicians erroneously object that to analyze jazz is to somehow detract from its "spontaneity." It is also believed that because jazz is spontaneous, it is not carefully constructed and is therefore not worthy of analysis. The growing number of analyses of jazz improvisations such as those by Lawrence Gushee, Barry Kernfeld, Steve Larson, Milton Lee Stewart, Steven Strunk, Jeff Pressing, and Steven Block,[46]

---

46 These and other analyses are discussed in Gary Potter's overview of various approaches in "Analyzing Improvised Jazz," *College Music Symposium* 30 (1990): 64–74; Lawrence Gushee, "Lester Young's 'Shoeshine Boy,'" *Report of the Twelfth Congress (Berkeley, 1977) of the International Musicological Society*, ed. Daniel Heartz and Bonnie Wade (Kassel: Barenreiter, 1981), pp. 151–69; Barry Dean Kernfeld, *Adderly, Coltrane, and David at the Twilight of Bebop: The Search for Melodic Coherence (1958–59)* (Ph.D. diss. Cornell University, 1981); Steve Larson, *Schenkerian Analysis of Modern Jazz* (Ph.D. diss., University

confirm the notion that much of the motivic and structural coherence so characteristic of "composed" music is present in this improvisational art form. As Larson points out, much jazz is "worked out," as is evidenced in the many examples of currently available alternate takes of jazz performances.[47] Recordings, of course, allow us to analyze jazz and also permit us the opportunity to return to it after we have gained more depth of understanding. This is especially important in hearing something as complex as polyrhythm. As Hartman puts it, "Listening to jazz on record, we relearn our complicated relation to time, over and over."[48]

of Michigan, 1987); Milton Lee Stewart, "Structural Development in the Jazz Improvisational Technique of Clifford Brown," *Jazzforschung/Jazz Research* 6/7 (1974/1975): 141–273; Steven Strunk, "Bebop Melodic Lines: Tonal Characteristics," *Annual Review of Jazz Studies* 3 (1985): 97–120; Steven Strunk, "The Harmony of Early Bop: A Layered Approach," *Journal of Jazz Studies* 6 (1979): 4–53; Jeff Pressing, "Cognitive Isomorphisms Between Pitch and Rhythm in World Musics: West Africa, the Balkans, and Western Tonality," *Studies in Music [University of Western Australia]* 17 (1983): 38–61; Jeff Pressing, "Pitch Class Set Structures in Contemporary Jazz," *Jazzforschung/Jazz Research* 14 (1982): 133–72; Steven Block, "Pitch-Class Transformation in Free Jazz," *Music Theory Spectrum* 12 (1990): 181–202.

47 Larson, p. 15.

48 Hartman, p. 74. Research for this paper was made possible in part through a summer research grant from Temple University. I would also like to thank Richard Cohn for his helpful criticisms and many insights into the analyses. This paper was originally presented at the 1991 annual meeting of the Society for Music Theory in Cincinnati, Ohio.

DISCOGRAPHY

1. Monk: "Blues Improvisation" (excerpt from "Bag's Groove"—composed by Milt Jackson).
    The Smithsonian Collection of Classic Jazz. Selected and annotated by Martin Williams.
    Recorded in New York, Dec. 24, 1954. Columbia Special Products P6 11871 (originally
    released on Prestige 24012). Personnel: Thelonious Monk, piano; Percy Heath, bass; Kenny
    Clarke, drums.

2. Monk: "Played Twice" (composed by Thelonious Monk).
    Five by Five. Produced by Orrin Keepnews. Recorded in New York, June 1–2, 1959. Riverside
    OJCCD–362–2 (R–1150). Notes by Orrin Keepnews. Personnel: Thelonious Monk, piano;
    Thad Jones, cornet; Charlie Rouse, tenor sax; Sam Jones, bass; Art Taylor, drums.

3. Monk: "Criss Cross" (composed by Thelonious Monk).
    The Smithsonian Collection of Classic Jazz. Recorded July 23, 1951. Originally released on
    Blue Note BLP 1509. Personnel: Thelonious Monk, piano; Edmond Gregory, alto sax; Milt
    Jackson, vibraphone; Al McKibbon, bass; Art Blakey, drums.

4. Coleman: "Lonely Woman" (composed by Ornette Coleman).
    The Shape of Jazz To Come. Produced by Nesuhi Ertegun. Recorded in Los Angeles, May 22,
    1959. Atlantic 1317–2. Notes by Martin Williams. Personnel: Ornette Coleman, alto sax; Don
    Cherry, cornet; Charlie Haden, bass; Billy Higgins, drums.

5. Dolphy: "Rally" (composed by Ron Carter).
    Magic. Produced by Esmond Edward. Recorded June 20, 1961. Prestige P–24053. Notes by
    Gary Giddens. Personnel: Eric Dolphy, bass clar.; Ron Carter, cello/bass; Mal Waldron, piano;
    George Duvivier, bass; Charlie Parsip, drums.

6. Dolphy: "You Don't Know What Love Is" (composed by Don Raye and Gene DePaul).
    Last Date: 1964. Recorded June 2, 1964 in Hilversum, Holland. Trip Jazz TLP–5506
    (originally released as Limelight LS–86013). Personnel: Eric Dolphy, flute; Misja Mengelberg,
    piano; Jacques Schols, bass; Han Bennink, drums.

A Generalization of Contour Theory to Diverse Musical Spaces: Analytical Applications to the Music of Dallapiccola and Stockhausen

Elizabeth West Marvin

In recent years, music theorists have begun systematically to isolate and discuss one aspect of musical structure that has long been a concern of composers and ethnomusicologists: musical contour.[1] Ernst Toch and Arnold Schoenberg were among the first composers to address the subject of contour in music-theoretical writings after 1945.[2] In the field of ethnomusicology, Mieczyslaw Kolinski, Charles Adams, and composer-musicologist Charles Seeger developed and published systems for the analysis of contour in the 1960s and 70s.[3] More recently, composer-theorists such as Robert Morris, Larry Polansky, James Tenney, and Robert Cogan have again brought to the attention of music analysts the role of musical contour as a structural element in compositional designs.[4] This paper

1 The groundbreaking publication in the field of recent contour theories is Robert Morris's *Composition with Pitch-Classes: A Theory of Compositional Design* (New Haven: Yale University Press, 1987). Applications of contour theories to the analysis of music by Schoenberg (op. 19/4 and op. 47, respectively) may be found in Morris's "New Directions in the Theory and Analysis of Musical Contour," *Music Theory Spectrum* 15 (1993): 205–28, and in Michael Friedmann, "A Methodology for the Discussion of Contour: Its Application to Schoenberg's Music" *Journal of Music Theory* 29 (1985): 223–48. Elizabeth West Marvin and Paul A. Laprade explore contour relationships in Anton Webern's op. 10/1 in "Relating Musical Contours: Extensions of a Theory for Contour" *Journal of Music Theory* 31 (1987): 225–67. My work, both in "Relating Musical Contours..." and in "The Perception of Rhythm in Non-Tonal Music: Rhythmic Contours in the Music of Edgard Varèse," *Music Theory Spectrum* 13 (1991): 61–78, is deeply influenced by and indebted to Morris's work. An early version of the present paper was read at the 1990 annual meeting of the Society for Music Theory (Oakland, California).

2 See Ernst Toch, *The Shaping Forces in Music* (New York: Criterion Music Corp., 1948; rpt. New York: Dover Publications, 1977), pp. 78–101; and Arnold Schoenberg, *Fundamentals of Musical Composition*, ed. Gerald Strang and Leonard Stein (London: Faber and Faber Ltd., 1967), pp. 113–15.

3 See Mieczyslaw Kolinski, "The Structure of Melodic Movement: A New Method of Analysis," in *Studies in Ethnomusicology* 2 (1965): 96–120; Charles Adams, "Melodic Contour Typology," *Ethnomusicology* 20 (1976): 179–215; and Charles Seeger, "On the Moods of a Music-Logic," *Journal of the American Musicological Society* 13 (1960): 224–61. Kolinsky's methods are also discussed in Marcia Herndon's "Analysis: The Herding of Sacred Cows?" *Ethnomusicology* 18 (1974): 219–62.

4 In addition to Morris's work, cited above, other relevant publications include: Larry Polansky

begins by sketching some strengths and weaknesses of selected contour theories, then it outlines and illustrates applications of a contour theory that can partition segments into equivalence classes, make comparisons using clearly-defined equivalence and similarity relations, and be generalized to various musical spaces, allowing comparisons across these spaces. Finally, several analytical examples show the fruitfulness of an approach to analysis of recent music that considers various musical features—not only pitch, but also dynamics, duration, timbre, and so on—as elements that may be ordered by sequential time, register, or other means, to form musical contours.[5]

Figure 1 shows contour graphs as they appear in Arnold Schoenberg's *Fundamentals of Musical Composition*. In reference to these graphs, Schoenberg discusses several general features of melodic contours, noting that

> melodies proceed in waves, a fact which can readily be observed here. The amplitude of these waves varies. A melody seldom moves long in one direction. Though the student was advised to avoid repeating the culmination point, the climax, the graphs show that many a good melody does so. The student had better not attempt it.[6]

Although Schoenberg frequently cites melodic contour as an important structural element in composition, his examples do not attempt to categorize contours into discrete types. Ernst Toch's *The Shaping Forces in Music* leans more in this direction. Toch refers to melodic contour as the "wave line," illustrated graphically in Figure 2, and defined as a melody's "'ups and downs' not confined to stepwise motion but showing a variety of intervals."[7] Further, he categorizes particular features of melodic contours, illustrating these with examples drawn from a diverse repertoire and with occasional contour graphs. Examples 1a and 1b reproduce Toch's examples of "melodic elasticity" and the "wind-up." A contour that shows melodic elasticity is one in which a series of small steps in one direction is followed by a leap in the opposite direction, or

---

and Richard Bassein, "Possible and Impossible Melodies: Some Formal Aspects of Contour," *Journal of Music Theory* 36 (1992): 259–84; and James Tenney's two-part *META + HODOS and META Meta + Hodos*, 2nd ed. (Oakland, Cal.: Frog Peak Music, 1988). Finally, Robert Cogan's work, in *New Images of Musical Sound* (Cambridge, Mass.: Harvard University Press, 1984) and elsewhere in this volume, uses spectrographic images of sounding music to chart and analyze contour, among other musical features. See also his *Sonic Design: The Nature of Sound and Music* (Englewood Cliffs, NJ: Prentice-Hall, Inc., 1976), co-authored with Pozzi Escot, for graphic analyses of musical contours.

5 The analytical examples are not intended to represent complete analyses, but only to demonstrate the analytical possibilities available within the theoretical framework of a generalized contour theory.

6 Schoenberg, p. 103. The contour graphs in Figure 1 are reproduced from Schoenberg's Example 99, p. 114.

7 Toch, p. 78. The diagrams in Figure 2 are from Toch, pp. 80 and 93.

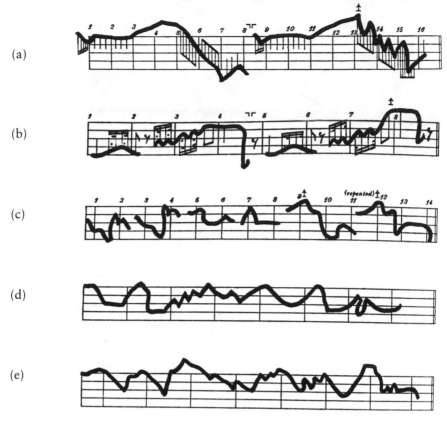

**Figure 1: Arnold Schoenberg's Contour Graphs of Compositions by Mozart
from *Fundamentals of Musical Composition***

© 1967 Reprinted by Permission of Faber and Faber Ltd

(a) Menuetto from String Quartet, K. 575—III (mm. 1–16)
(b) Andante from Symphony, K. 543—II (mm. 1–8)
(c) Cherubino's aria, "Non so più cosa son" from *The Marriage of Figaro*
    (mm. 2–15)
(d) Allegro grazioso from Piano Sonata, K. 333—I (mm. 1–8)
(e) Allegro from Piano Sonata, K. 281—III (mm. 1–8)

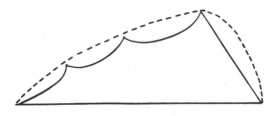

Figure 2: Ernst Toch's Contour Graphs

© Copyright 1948. Reprinted from *The Shaping Forces in Music* by Permission.
Courtesy of the Estate of Ernst Toch and Dover Publications, Inc.

alternatively a leap in one direction is followed by stepwise motion in the other.[8] The wind-up begins with "a group of short, quick notes, anything from a turn . . . to an independent, characteristic motif."[9] In these examples, the wind-up melodies are followed by an upward leap and stepwise descent, also demonstrating their melodic elasticity.

In Toch's discussion of wave forms, the author demonstrates his understanding of musical contour as a concept that may be generalized from pitch to a temporal domain:

What constitutes "stepwise progression" in the linear component, namely a series of small *line divisions*, corresponds in the rhythmical component to a

---

8   Ibid., p. 86. The melodies illustrating melodic elasticity in Example 1a are Toch's Examples 149, 152, 162, and 163, which appear on pp. 86–89.
9   Ibid., p. 95. The melodies illustrating the wind-up in Example 1b are drawn from Toch, pp. 96–97, and represent his Examples 190, 196, and 197.

(a) Melodic elasticity:

(b) Wind-up:

Examples 1a–b: Toch's Melodic Types

Reproduced from *The Shaping Forces in Music*

series of small *time divisions*—fast progression, short notes. What constitutes the "skip" in the linear component, namely the fusion of a few small tone divisions into one big tone division, corresponds in the rhythmical component to the fusion of a few small time divisions into one big time division—slow progression, long notes.[10]

For James Tenney, this generalized view of musical contour, which encompasses not only pitch but many other parameters, is central. Several of Tenney's contour graphs, called "parametric profiles," are illustrated in Figure 3; their vertical axes are labelled "some parametric scale." As he describes these profiles,

the horizontal axis . . . represents time, and the vertical axis represents an ordinal scale of values in one of the various parameters . . . For example, if the vertical ordinate is pitch, such a plot will show melodic contour . . . If the vertical axis is made to represent loudness, one might plot the time-envelope of the attack and decay of a simple element, or the dynamic shape of some large clang or sequence.[11]

The ordinal scale of values on the vertical axis is defined as a "'rank ordering' of relative magnitudes of some attribute, an ordering which involves the distinctions 'greater than' and 'less than', but does not purport to show how much greater or how much less one point on the scale may be than another point."[12] Tenney's ordinal scales of values resemble the "sequential dimensions" posited by Morris to define musical contours in *Composition with Pitch-Classes*. According to Morris, a "sequential dimension of order n is a basic musical attribute whose points (or states) are listed in order corresponding to the numbers 0 to n-1."[13] Yet there are important differences. First, when Tenney quantifies these attributes for application to musical analysis, the scales chosen represent absolute, calibrated values rather than relative ones; thus, for example, semitones are tallied for the pitch parameter and small rhythmic note-values are tallied for the time parameter.[14] In Tenney's applications,

---

10 Ibid., p. 98.
11 Tenney, p. 33. The terms "clang" and "sequence" are defined as follows (p. 23): "I propose the word *clang*—to be understood to refer to any sound or sound-configuration which is perceived as a primary musical unit—a singular aural gestalt . . . Finally, some term is needed to designate a succession of clangs which is set apart from other successions in some way, so that it has some degree of unity and singularity, thus constituting a musical gestalt on a larger perceptual level or temporal scale . . . For this larger unit I shall use the word *sequence* . . . ." Figure 3 reproduces Tenney's Figures 3, 4, and 5, which appear on p. 34.
12 Ibid., p. 84.
13 Morris, *Composition with Pitch-Classes*, p. 282.
14 See, for example, James Tenney with Larry Polansky, *Hierarchical Temporal Gestalt Perception in Music: A "Metric Space" Model* (Toronto, Ontario: York University Press, 1978), pp. 1–20, and "Temporal Gestalt Perception in Music: A Metric Space Model," *Journal of Music Theory* 24 (1980): 205–41.

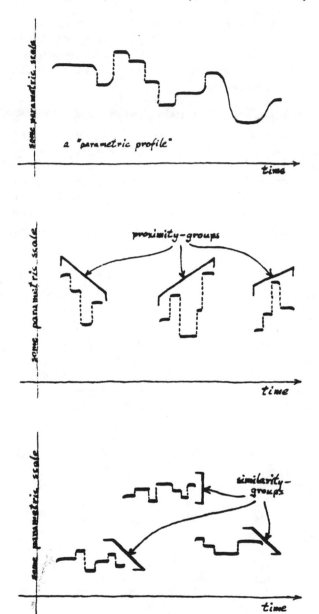

Figure 3: James Tenney's Contour Graphs from *META + HODOS*

these parameters are then weighted and combined to determine musical segmentations, rather than to compare contours across differing musical dimensions. Another difference between the two theories is demonstrated by the graphs of Figure 3, in which the horizontal axis always represents time; Morris's generalization of contour theory removes this limitation.

Extensive categorizations of contours into distinct types occur in the ethnomusicological literature. Charles Adams's 1976 study, "Melodic Contour Typology," gives a critical summary of methodologies employed by various ethnomusicologists, including symbolic narration, word-list typology, and graphic diagrams, among others.[15] The most influential proponent of graphic diagram analysis is Mieczyslaw Kolinski, whose graphic technique is illustrated in Figure 4. Here, melodic structure is seen as a concatenation of a number of distinct contour types—shown by alternating hollow and filled-in points on his contour graphs—into larger complexes. Kolinski's analysis of the Kwakiutl song shows, for example, one contour type beginning at the number two and extending for six pitches, denoted on the diagram by six filled-in points. The last three of those points overlap with a new four-note contour type, denoted by hollow points, extending from the number three. Each of the points represents a pitch of the melody; the pitch names and number of semitones between pitches are specified in the left and right margins. Each contour segment is numbered in the diagram and formal units are assigned alphabetical designations. Kolinski defines six "categories of movement complexes: standing, hanging, tangential, overlapping, distant, and including"; these may rise or fall, widen or narrow.[16] Figure 5 shows several examples of contours categorized according to this typology.

One strength of Kolinski's system is the graphic clarity with which equivalence among contour subsegments is shown. Note in Figure 4, for instance, that the final segment denoted in hollow points, beginning at the number seven, is of the same contour type as the segment beginning at the number three. These segments are graphed identically, even though the intervallic contents of these contours differ. While equivalent subsegments are clearly identified by Kolinski, his theory provides no formal method for comparing contours that are similar but not equivalent. Further, his methodology is limited to melodic contour analysis,

---

15 Adams, passim.

16 Kolinski, pp. 100–03. These terms are defined on these pages as follows: "In a standing complex the lower level, in a hanging complex the upper level of both recurrent movements is the same . . . In a tangential complex the opposite pitch levels of the two recurrent movements are the same . . . If the ranges of the two recurrent movements overlap, one may speak of rising overlapping or falling overlapping complexes . . . If the ranges of the two recurrent movements lie beyond each other, one may speak of rising distant or falling distant complexes. If the range of one recurrent movement lies within that of the other one, one may speak of widening including or narrowing including complexes." Figure 4 is drawn from Kolinski, p. 114; Figure 5 is from pp. 100–01.

Song of the Kwakiutl Indians (recorded by Franz Boas)
♩ = 120. Orig. + 3 st.

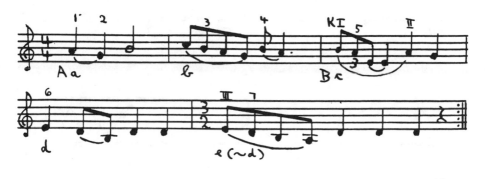

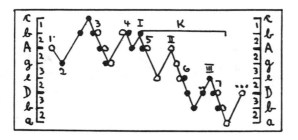

Figure 4: Mieczyslaw Kolinski's Contour Graphs

graphed with pitch on the vertical axis and sequential time on the horizontal.

Adams's contour typology differs from previous theories in that it may be used to categorize a melody of any length into one of only fifteen discrete contour types of two to four elements. His graphs represent not every pitch of a given melody, but rather only the initial, final, highest, and lowest pitches, based on the perceptual salience of these contour "markers." Figure 6 shows the fifteen melodic contour types resulting from Adams's approach.[17] The three columns represent the

---

17 Figure 6 is reproduced from Adams's Table 5, p. 199. Readers may notice some similarity between Adams's approach to contour analysis and the recent work of Morris in "New Directions," cited above. Both theories recognize the perceptual salience of the first, last, highest, and lowest elements of a contour. Morris's work has richer analytical applications,

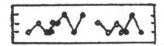

**Widening Standing
Complexes**

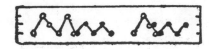

**Narrowing Standing
Complexes**

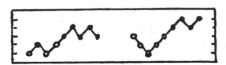

**Widening Hanging
Complexes**

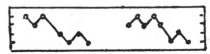

**Narrowing Hanging
Complexes**

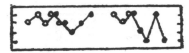

**Rising Distant
Complexes**

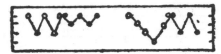

**Falling Distant
Complexes**

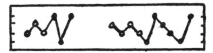

**Widening Including
Complexes**

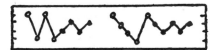

**Narrowing Including
Complexes**

Figure 5: Kolinski's Complexes of Recurrent Movements

however, since it is based upon a recursive reductive algorithm that produces distinct hierarchical levels of contour analysis. Other distinguishing features of Morris's recent work, such as its inclusion of simulaneities and its ability to model contours in various musical dimensions, are discussed in more detail in the body of this essay.

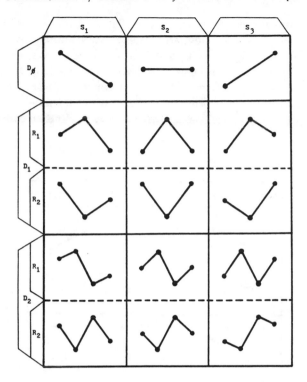

Figure 6: Adams's Melodic Contour Typology

Reprinted from *Ethnomusicology*, the Journal of the Society for Ethnomusicology
[Vol. 20 (1976): 199], by Permission of the Author.

"slope" (descending, level, or ascending), while the rows represent "deviations" from the inital and final pitches by the highest and lowest pitches. D_0 means that the highest and lowest pitches are also the initial and final; D_1 means that one of the extreme pitches is also the initial or final; D_2 means that both extremes are distinct from the initial and final. Contours labeled R_1 and R_2 are "reciprocals" (inversions) in Adams's typology, and simply reverse the patterns of downs and ups. One obvious advantage of this analytical system is that melodies or segments of virtually any length may be compared, so long as the extremes are not repeated. By delineating only the extremes of the melody or phrase, however, important contour information about relationships among melodic subsegments is lost.

One of the first systems of contour typology to be broadly generalized by its author to a number of different musical domains was proposed by Charles Seeger. In his 1960 "On the Moods of a Music-Logic," Seeger proposed twelve contour types for segments of three and four elements. Figure 7, reproduced from Adams's discussion of Seeger's work, summarizes these types graphically, with Seeger's alphabetical labels placed in the central columns.[18] Seeger's twelve moods actually encompass more contours than Figure 7 implies, since types B, D, E, and F [both large- and small-case] may occur in several variant forms, as Adams's diagrams, reproduced in Figure 8, make clear. All of the variants for mood D are shown in Figure 8; each variant expresses the pattern <+ + ->, but in each case the extent of the minus differs.[19]

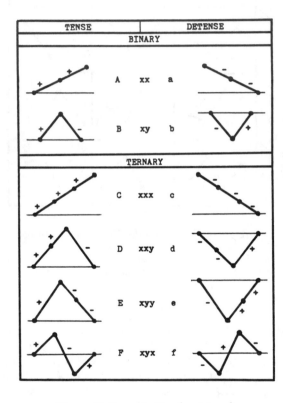

Figure 7: Seeger's Twelve Moods

---

18 Figure 7 is reproduced from Adams's Table 2, p. 193.

19 Figure 8 is reproduced from Adams's discussion of Seeger's work; see Adams, p. 192 (Example 12). These five contours, renotated numerically with 0 representing the lowest contour pitch and (n-1) the highest are: D_1 = < 0 1 2 0 >, D_2 = < 1 2 3 0 >, D_3 = < 0 2 3 1 >, D_4 = < 0 1 2 1 >, and D_5 = < 0 1 3 2 >. Each represents a different c-space segment class, as defined by Marvin and Laprade: rc4-1/6, c4-6, c4-4, rc4-1/4, and c4-2, respectively.

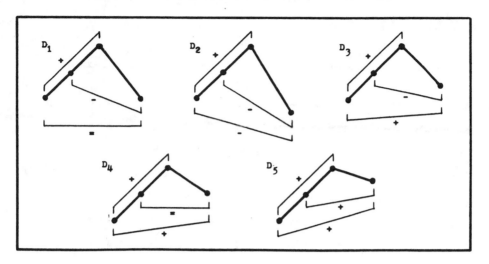

Figure 8: Variant Forms of Seeger's Contour D, < + + - >

Seeger's conception from his very first definition is a broad one; he states, for example

> Pitch may rise, dynamics become louder, tempo faster, proportion increasingly divided. I shall refer to this direction of variance as *tension* and shall indicate it by the sign plus (+). Pitch may fall, dynamics may become softer, tempo slower, proportion less divided. I shall refer to this direction of variance as *detension* and shall indicate it by the sign minus (-).[20]

Figure 9a shows Seeger's realization of the twelve moods as dynamic progressions and as dynamic levels, and Figure 9b as tempo progressions and levels. Seeger's examples are unique among those surveyed here in that elements of his moods are not restricted to discrete states or levels (such as *piano* or Allegro), but also include spans between states (like crescendo or accelerando), which he terms "progressions."

Recent work by Larry Polansky and Richard Bassein and by Robert Morris continue to develop contour theory, but in different directions from those to be discussed here.[21] Polansky and Bassein use "ternary (base 3) numbers to describe

---

20 Seeger, p. 236. Figure 9a is a reproduction of Seeger's Example 7, p. 242; Figure 9b is Seeger's Example 8, p. 245.

21 Polansky and Bassein, "Possible and Impossible Melodies: Some Formal Aspects of Contour," and Morris, "New Directions in the Theory and Analysis of Musical Contours," cited above.

(a) Dynamic contours:

PROGRESSIONS	LEVELS
in minimal and medial extension	in medial and maximal extension

Binary

A ·——═·══· a ·══·══·   ♪ ♪   A m* mf f   a m mp p

B ·══·══· b ·══·══·   ♪ o   B m mf m   b m mp m

Ternary

C ·——══·══· c ·════·——·   ♪♪♪   C m mf f ff   c m mp p pp

D ·——══·══· d ·════·——·   ♪♪o   D m mf f m   d m mp p m

E ·══·══·══· e ·══·══·══·   ♪oo   E m f mf m   e m p mp m

F ·══·══·══· f ·══·══·══·   ♪o♪   F m mf mp m   f m mp mp m

*m = a theoretical level between mp and mf

(b) Tempo contours:

PROGRESSIONS	LEVELS
in medial and minimal extension	in medial and maximal extension

Binary

A	*ac. ac.*	a	*dec. dec.*	A	*M* *	*pm*	*f*		a	*M*	*mm*	*s*	
B	*ac. dec.*	b	*dec. ac.*	B	*M*	*pm*	*M*		b	*M*	*mm*	*M*	

Ternary

C	*ac. ac. ac.*	c	*dec. dec. dec.*	C	*M*	*pm*	*f*	*F*	c	*M*	*mm*	*s*	*S*
D	*ac. ac. dec.*	d	*dec. dec. ac.*	D	*M*	*pm*	*f*	*M*	d	*M*	*mm*	*s*	*M*
E	*ac. dec. dec.*	e	*dec. ac. ac.*	E	*M*	*f*	*pm*	*M*	e	*M*	*s*	*mm*	*M*
F	*ac. dec. ac.*	f	*dec. ac. dec.*	F	*M*	*pm*	*mm*	*M*	f	*M*	*mm*	*pm*	*M*

*M = Moderato; *pm* = piu mosso; *f* = faster; *F.* = still faster; *mm* = meno mosso; *s* = slower; *S* = still slower.

Figures 9a–b: Seeger's Contours Expressed as Progressions and Levels

Reprinted from *Journal of the American Musicological Society* [Vol. 13 (1960): 242, 245] by Permission.

contour, [where] 0 means 'is less than,' 1 means 'is equal to,' and 2 means ' is greater than.' "[22] From the upper right-hand triangle of a matrix that displays the magnitude (less than, equal to, or greater than) of each contour element in relation to each of the other elements, these authors derive a multi-digit number that completely describes what they call the "combinatorial" contour. Not all base 3 numbers of a given number of digits generate "possible" contours, however, which is the subject of the authors' further commentary. Polansky and Bassein explicitly state that theirs is a generalized view of contour (not limited to melodic pitch contours), and they give one example that illustrates their analytical technique at the highest hierarchical level, by diagramming four-element contours representing the pitch contour, intensity contour, and temporal density contour of Ruggles's *Portals*.[23]

Morris formalizes a hierarchical model of contour relationships using a contour reduction algorithm that successively prunes pitches that are not the first, last, maximum, or minimum elements of a given contour. The number of times the algorithm must be invoked to reduce a contour to its prime is its "depth"; the depth is a rough measure of a contour's complexity. Morris's analysis of Schoenberg's Op. 19, no. 4 reveals the interaction of pitch-class set analysis with contour analysis at differing hierarchical levels. He further generalizes the theory to include simultaneities and presents a table of 53 prime classes, incorporating contours with simultaneities as well as purely linear contours. Finally, Morris revisits Polansky and Bassein's impossible contours, using the prime classes with simultaneities as a way to model such contours.

With so many ways to categorize contour types, what criteria might the analyst use to choose among these varying systems? First, although graphing provides a clear visual representation of melodic contour, graphs are somewhat cumbersome to construct, compare, and reproduce. Numerical representation—as in Morris's contour pitches or Friedmann's contour class—conveys at least as much information, is more compact and easier to reproduce and discuss, and can easily be converted to graphic form if necessary.[24] Further, contour graphs of the Schoenberg or Adams type provide no vehicle for precise discussion of relationships among a contour's component parts, or for measuring similarity among contours, as numerical representation does. Numerical representation of contour elements has enabled Marvin and Laprade to generate a table of contour equivalence classes, which lists a prime form representative for all contours of up to six distinct elements, as well as similarity functions to measure the degree of similarity among contours.[25] More recently, Polansky and Bassein and Morris have

---

22 Polansky and Bassein, p. 263.

23 Ibid., p. 273.

24 Morris defines contour pitches on p. 26 of *Composition with Pitch-Classes*; Friedmann defines the contour class on p. 227 of "A Methodology."

25 Morris defines the COM-matrix and uses it to define contour equivalence on p. 28 of *Composition with Pitch-Classes*. Marvin and Laprade's listing of contour-space segment-

generated equivalence class lists for musical contours: for "ternary combinatorial contours" in the first case, and for basic and secondary "prime classes" in the second.[26] Finally, flexibility in assigning to the vertical axis other musical elements such as timbre, dynamic, duration, and so on, is important in the analysis of recent repertories, where contours of tone color, loudness, etc. are found. A graphic representation whose horizontal axis always represents time restricts the analyst from considering registral or other possible modes of ordering.[27] Thus, a sequential succession of time points on a contour graph's horizontal axis may be considered just one possible sequential dimension of many that may be used to order musical contours.

It is this assumption that lies at the foundation of Morris's generalized definition of contour. Thus, a contour is "a set of points in one sequential dimension ordered by any other sequential dimension," and "a sequential dimension of order n is a basic musical attribute whose points (or states) are listed in order corresponding to the number 0 to n-1."[28] In the most commonly-understood meaning of the term contour—that is, melodic contour—the two sequential dimensions are contour space, extending from low to high, and sequential time, extending from early to late. A further generalization is proposed here: to expand the concept of "points" in these definitions to include also "spans" in various musical spaces. Thus in the temporal dimension, contours could be formed of durational spans, numbered from short to long, and ordered by register, sequential time, or other means.[29] In

---

classes of cardinalities 2 through 6 appears in the appendix of "Relating Musical Contours," pp. 257–62. Their similarity relationships are defined on pp. 234–45. Michael Friedmann also defines equivalence classes for contours by different means, using the CASV and CCV (p. 234), in "A Methodology for the Discussion of Contour"; see also his "A Response: My Contour, Their Contour," in *Journal of Music Theory* 31 (1987): 268–73.

26 See Polansky and Bassein, pp. 267–69; Morris, in "New Directions," presents basic and secondary prime classes on pp. 220–21.

27 Registral orderings of twelve-tone rows in the music of Elliott Carter are considered in the Mead essay that opens Part II of this volume; registral orderings of dynamic and durational contours in the music of Karlheinz Stockhausen are illustrated Examples 3 and 7 following.

28 Morris, *Composition with Pitch-Classes*, pp. 282–84.

29 My "The Perception of Rhythm in Non-Tonal Music," cited above, presents analytical applications. David Lewin expanded upon the ideas presented in that article in his keynote address to the Society for Music Theory (Cincinnati, 1991), subsequently published as "Some Problems and Resources of Music Theory" in *Journal of Music Theory Pedagogy* 5 (1991): 111–32. Lewin distinguishes among equivalent duration contours by means of "grouped partial summing." This analytical tool sums the durations of rhythmic values that occur in adjacent order positions of a duration contour, then determines the duration segment class of the resulting "summed" contour. Partial summing can in fact assist performers in negotiating rhythmically-difficult passages, as Lewin convincingly demonstrates in a passage from Stockhausen.

Lewin's most recent book, *Musical Form and Transformation: 4 Analytic Essays* (New Haven: Yale University Press, 1993) intersects with this study in the spheres of repertoire the authors have chosen to analyze, though our analytical methodology is very

the pitch dimension, spans might measure the distance between elements in a contour, numbered from narrow to wide, without precisely calibrating the pitch-space distance. In yet another musical dimension, contours comprised of dynamic spans might, like Seeger's "progressions" of Figure 8, measure the distance spanned between varying dynamics—*pp* to *mp* occupying a narrower span than *pp* to *ff*, for example. A generalized definition of musical contour enables analysts to make structural comparisons between contours in different musical spaces.

Examples 2 and 3 illustrate the methods by which contours, comprised of points or spans in various musical spaces, are identified and compared. The opening of Dallapiccola's "Fregi," given in Example 2a expresses the melodic contour < 5 4 1 2 3 0 >, ordered in sequential time, with 5 representing the highest contour pitch and 0 the lowest.[30] (The "contour-interval" analysis given in this example will be discussed in the context of a more formal definition of pitch-span space below.) Measure 14 of the first movement of Stockhausen's *Klavierstücke*, No. 2, given as Example 2b, illustrates an instance of a single contour segment type, < 3 2 0 1 >, expressed both as a dynamic contour and as a melodic contour. If the listener were to segment the melody of the uppermost voice only, by virtue of its pitch proximity in the upper register, the resulting contour would express < 3 2 0 1 >, both in terms of relative pitch height and relative dynamic (< *fff ff pp p* > = < 3 2 0 1 >). Another way to show this one-to-one correspondence would be to order the dynamic contour of this upper voice by register, rather than by sequential time. Ordered by register, low to high, the dynamic contour is < *pp p ff fff* > or < 0 1 2 3 >; that is, the higher the pitch, the louder the dynamic.

In contrast, Example 3, drawn from the concluding measures of this movement, shows an inverse linear correspondence between dynamics and register. The melodic contour of just measures 59–60 alone, ordered in sequential time, is < 2 0 3 1 4 >. The dynamic contour (soft to loud), also ordered in sequential time, produces the inversely-related succession < 2 4 1 3 0 >. In inversely-related segments such as these, elements in corresponding order positions sum to (n-1), where n equals the cardinality of the segment; in this case, corresponding elements sum to 4. If the dynamic contour of mm. 59–60 is ordered in register, it expresses the succession < *fff f mf p pp* > or < 4 3 2 1 0 >; in other words, the higher the pitch, the softer the dynamic.

A correspondance between durational and dynamic contours also occurs in the final measures of the movement, as measures 60–61 of Example 3 show.

---

different. Lewin provides readers with a concise introduction to his transformational theories via "Simbolo," from Dallapiccola's *Quaderno musicale di Annalibera* (pp. 2–15). His second chapter, "Making and Using a Pcset Network . . ." focuses on Stockhausen's *Klavierstück III* (pp. 16–67).

30 Morris defines contour pitches as "the (pitch) elements of c-space," where c-space is "a pitch-space consisting of elements arranged from low to high disregarding the exact intervals between the elements" (*Composition with Pitch-Classes*, p. 340).

(a) Dallapiccola, "Fregi" from *Quaderno musicale di Annalibera*, mm. 1–3:

Contour-pitch representation:
   < 5 4 1 2 3 0 > in contour-space, ordered in sequential time
"Contour-interval" representation:
   Friedmann's CIS: < -1, -3, +1, +1, -3 >
   Marvin's ps-space segment: < 4 3 1 0 2 >

(b) Stockhausen, *Klavierstücke*, No. 2, Mvt. I, m. 14:

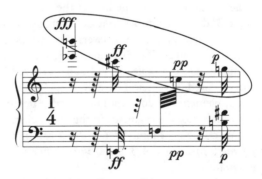

< 3 2 0 1 > expressed as both a melodic and dynamic contour, ordered in s-time
< 0 1 2 3 > expressed as a dynamic contour, ordered by register

Examples 2a–b: Contours in Various Musical Spaces

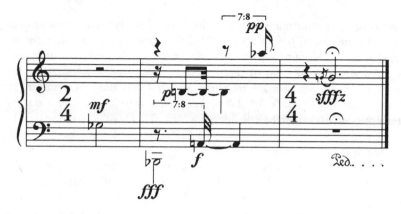

Stockhausen *Klavierstücke* Nr. 2, Movement 1

Measures 59–60:
Contour pitches (low to high) ordered by sequential time: < 2 0 3 1 4 >*
Dynamics (soft to loud) ordered by sequential time:

$$< mf\,fff\,p\,f\,pp > = < 2\ 4\ 1\ 3\ 0 >*$$

Dynamics (soft to loud) ordered by register (low to high):

$$< fff\,f\,mf\,p\,pp > = < 4\ 3\ 2\ 1\ 0 >$$

(*In inversely-related segments such as these, elements in corresponding order
positions sum to (n-1), in this case 4.)

Measures 60–61:
m. 60: dynamics ordered by sequential time: < 3 1 2 0 > . . . followed by < 4 >.
m. 60: durations ordered by register:**   < 3 1 2 0 > . . . followed by < 4 >.

(**E.g.: the longest note in the bass, next-to-shortest in the tenor, next-to-longest
in the alto, and shortest in the soprano)

**Example 3: Contour Correspondences Across Musical Spaces in
Stockhausen, *Klavierstücke* , No. 2, Mvt. I, mm. 59–61**

Considering the penultimate measure alone, the first dynamic contour ordered in sequential time is < *fff p f pp* > or < 3 1 2 0 >; this is followed after the rest by a single-element "contour"—a still louder final pitch (*sfffz*), which might be considered < 4 > in relation to the preceding contour. Considering the length of each pitch in the penultimate measure, ordered this time by register, the first durational contour is also < 3 1 2 0 >. Again, this is followed after a rest by a still longer note, which might be considered < 4 >. This inverse relationship between dynamic and duration is fairly easy to hear; that is, the loudest note is the longest, the softest is the shortest, etc.[31]

Examples 4a and 4b show < 2 0 1 3 > expressed in duration space and dynamic space, ordered in sequential time. Some problems arise in contour analysis when examining passages such as these, which are partly monophonic and partly chordal. A consideration of the dynamic contour of Example 4a, for instance, presents some problems because of the multi-dynamic first and last chords. One approach might be to acknowledge that in some musical contexts, the louder elements "mask" the softer ones; thus the loudest dynamic of each sonority might be used analytically to represent the entire. This may not represent an accurate dynamic contour in other contexts, however, such as the representation of a chord that is primarily soft, but which has single loud or accented soprano or bass note, for example. On the other hand, this procedure—assigning a chord its contour-segment number based upon the element of greatest magnitude—does make intuitive sense for durational contours, given a texture that is partly monophonic and partly chordal. That is, given a chord with a simultaneous attack but differing durations among its elements (as in the final chord of Example 4a), the chord's perceived duration might be based upon the longest-sounding pitch of the chord. The earlier release of chordal elements might be heard as a change in the chord's timbre, but not affect its perceived duration. Thus the duration contour of Example 4a would remain < 2 0 1 3 >, in spite of the fact that selected chordal members of the final sonority are shorter in duration than the initial chord.

An alternative approach to the question of multi-dynamic chords might be to take the mean value of the elements in the chord, measured along the same

---

31 Linear and inverse linear relationships among melodic, dynamic, and durational contours such as those demonstrated in Examples 2 and 3 are certainly audible. What is unclear is the extent to which listeners are able to perceive contours ordered by sequential dimensions other than register and sequential time, and the extent to which listeners can perceive contours in all possible musical spaces. This ability probably varies widely with musical experience and training, but little empirical data exists to demonstrate this. For the purposes of this study then, contour analysis will be derived primarily from score notation (with some transcription for the excerpt from Stockhausen's *Kontakte*), with the understanding that the score notation may not always model the perceived acoustic signal because of dynamic or timbral masking, auditory streaming, etc. In general, analytical choices and segmentation have been guided here by the ear as well as the eye.

(a) < 2 0 1 3 > expressed in duration-space:
Stockhausen, *Klavierstücke*, No. 2, Mvt. I, mm. 9–11

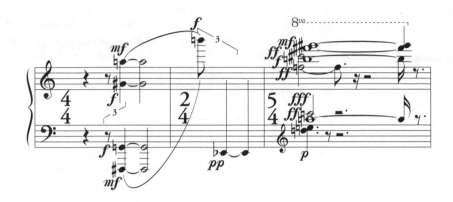

(b) < 2 0 1 3 > expressed in dynamic-space:
Stockhausen, *Klavierstücke*, No. 2, Mvt. I, mm. 30–31

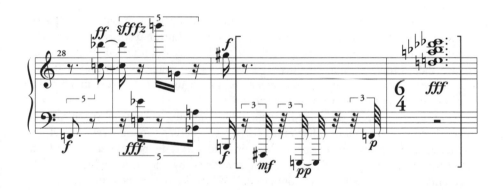

Stockhausen *Klavierstücke* Nr. 2, Movement 1
© Copyright 1954 by Universal Edition (London) Ltd., London   © Copyright renewed
All Rights Reserved   Used by permission of European American Music Distributors Corporation,
sole U.S. and Canadian agent for Universal Edition (London) Ltd., London

Examples 4a–b: Expressions of < 2 0 1 3 >

sequential dimension as the entire segment. This would represent the "average loudness" of the chord in relation to the other elements of the segment. Using this model, the dynamic contour of Example 4a would be < 1 2 0 3 >; the average of the first chord's dynamics, < *mf f f mf* >, would be slightly softer than the second *forte* pitch, and the averaged dynamics of the final chord would be the loudest of the contour. This too seems counter-intuitive, since the density, register, and spacing of the initial chord would result in a sonority that sounds louder than the single *forte* pitch that follows it. The method to be employed here will therefore be an "additive" one, in which the values for the elements in a multi-dynamic chord will be summed. This sum reflects the fact that a chord of three *forte* pitches will sound louder than a single *forte* pitch, because of the density of the chord. Thus, to return to Example 4a, the dynamics represented here, < *pp p mf f ff fff* >, will be represented respectively by the integers < 0 1 2 3 4 5 >. If each chord is represented by the sum of its dynamic values, the dynamic contour of this excerpt, ordered in sequential time, would be < 10 3 0 26 >. (By way of illustration, the first chord's < *mf f f mf* > dynamics are expressed numerically as < 3 2 2 3 >, which sum to 10, and so on.) Marvin and Laprade define a translation operation by which contour segments may be renumbered "from 0 for the lowest c-pitch to (n-1) for the highest."[32] Thus < 10 3 0 26 > may be translated to the dynamic contour < 2 1 0 3 >. Similarly, Example 4b's dynamic contour < 2 0 1 18 > would translate to < 2 0 1 3 >.

Further formalization of methods for contour analysis in music that is partly monophonic and partly chordal remains a topic for additional study. One possible generalization might state that simultaneities in spaces comprised of points are to use the "additive" method illustrated in dynamic space above, and that that simultaneities in spaces comprised of spans are to use the "largest magnitude" method illustrated in duration space above.

Theories previously developed for melodic contours in contour space may be generalized to contours in other musical spaces, whether those spaces are defined by sequential points or by spans. Marvin and Laprade present a prime form algorithm and several measurements of similarity by means of which contour segments may be classified and compared.[33] While discussion of similarity among contours is beyond the scope of this paper, the concept of equivalence classes— defined by operations on Morris's comparison matrix (COM-matrix)—will be used in the analyses following. In Example 5, two contours from the Stockhausen piano piece under consideration are presented, one in which dynamics are ordered by register and one in which dynamics are ordered by sequential time. Two sub-segments, < 3 4 2 5 > and < 1 2 0 4 >, are bracketed. Figure 10a shows comparison

---

32 Marvin and Laprade, p. 255. See also pp. 228 and 245 for discussions of the translation operation.

33 The similarity relations are defined in Marvin and Laprade, pp. 234–45 (see note 25).

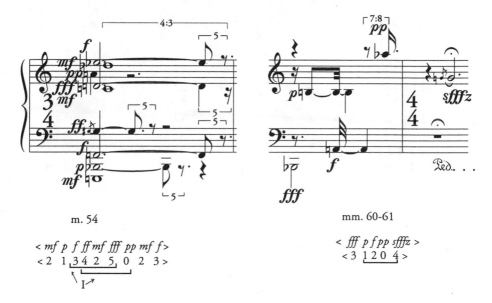

m. 54

mm. 60-61

< mf p f ff mf fff pp mf f>
<2 1 3 4 2 5, 0 2 3>
         I

< fff p f pp sfffz >
<3 1 2 0 4>

Stockhausen *Klavierstücke* Nr. 2, Movement 1
© Copyright 1954 by Universal Edition (London) Ltd., London   © Copyright renewed
All Rights Reserved   Used by permission of European American Music Distributors Corporation,
sole U.S. and Canadian agent for Universal Edition (London) Ltd., London

Example 5: Contour Equivalence in Stockhausen, *Klavierstücke*, No. 2, Mvt. I, mm. 54 and 60–61

matrices for each. The COM-matrix, as defined by Morris, is a two-dimensional array that displays the results of the comparison function, returning "+" if b is greater than a, "-" if b is less than a, and "0" if the values are the same.[34] These subsegments are indeed equivalent, since they produce the same matrix. Further, if the two segments are renumbered, via translation, from 0 to (n-1); both become < 1 2 0 3 >.

The dynamic contour drawn from measure 54, when translated, also contains an overlapping statement of this segment's inversion, < 2 1 3 0 >. The inversion of a segment S, of n distinct elements, is found by subtracting each element from (n - 1). Thus, in inversionally-related contours, two elements in the same order position will sum to (n-1), as was previously illustrated in Example 3. In effect, this results

---

34 Morris, *Composition with Pitch-Classes*, p. 28.

(a) Equivalence:

	3	4	2	5
3	0	+	-	+
4	-	0	-	+
2	+	+	0	+
5	-	-	-	0

< 3 4 2 5 >
= < 1 2 0 3 > by translation

	1	2	0	4
1	0	+	-	+
2	-	0	-	+
0	+	+	0	+
4	-	-	-	0

< 1 2 0 4 >
= < 1 2 0 3 > by translation

(b) Inversion:

Subsegment < 4 2 5 0 > is the inversion of < 3 4 2 5 > by translation, since
< 2 1 3 0 > is the inversion of < 1 2 0 3 >.

< *f ff mf fff* >
< 1   2   0   3 >

< 2   1   3   0 >
< *ff mf fff pp* >

Inversion may be found by subtracting each element from (n-1). If (n-1) is odd, this results in a "swap" between the lowest and highest number, next-to-lowest and next-to-highest, etc. If (n-1) is even, elements swap but (n-1)/2 retains its position.

COM-matrices: Each entry swaps "+" for "-" (and vice versa) in inversionally-related contours.

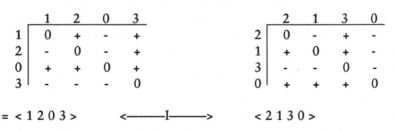

	1	2	0	3
1	0	+	-	+
2	-	0	-	+
0	+	+	0	+
3	-	-	-	0

= < 1 2 0 3 >

	2	1	3	0
2	0	-	+	-
1	+	0	+	-
3	-	-	0	-
0	+	+	+	0

< 2 1 3 0 >

<————I————>

Figures 10a–b: Contour Equivalence and Inversion Defined

in the elements "swapping" positions within the segment. In Figure 10b, for example, the loudest and softest dynamics swap, and the next-to-loudest and next-to-softest swap. If (n-1) is an even value, one element—(n-1)/2—will retain its position. In their COM-matrices, inversionally-related segments swap "+" for "-" (and vice versa) in each position. By extending standard terminology for ordered segments to contour segments, the retrograde or retrograde inversion of a segment S—R(S) or RI(S)—may be found by listing the elements of S or I(S) in reverse order. Segments related by translation, inversion, retrograde, and retrograde-inversion belong to the same contour segment class.

Sequential dimensions, as defined by Morris, encompass more than just dynamic, registral, or temporal continua. They extend even to timbral spaces, and may be used to define such contours as noise content ordered by loudness, location ordered by contour pitches, or envelope ordered by vowel color.[35] As these categories suggest, contour-based methodology seems a promising vehicle for analysis of electronic music. One way to proceed in analyzing this repertoire is to transcribe various musical elements in terms of sequential dimensions. Transcription of microtonal or other nonequally-tempered passages might be facilitated by melodic contour notation. Nonmetric and nonbeat-based rhythms might be notated as durational contours. Figure 11 shows a short excerpt from Stockhausen's *Kontakte*, with the composer's score of the electronic sounds at the top of the example and my analysis of selected melodic and rhythmic contours (identified alphabetically) below. The melodic and duration contours notated numerically beneath the score are not derived solely from the score, but also from my hearing of the excerpt. The graphic score does roughly show duration in section IXC by spacing of "barlines" and in IXD by space between points.

The excerpt opens with Contour A, < 1 0 2 >, realized in both contour and duration space. The following contour, marked B, belongs to the same segment class in both spaces; its duration contour is identical, and its melodic contour is an inversion of A. This segment, < 1 0 2 >, together with its inversion, retrograde, and retrograde inversion appears as a subsegment in every contour of cardinality 3 or higher in the excerpt, with the exception of Contours C and J (which are uni-directional). These latter two, which are inversionally related in contour space and equivalent in duration space, appear at the end of the two subsections marked by the composer in the score, and may play a "cadential" role. The retrograde-inversion of Contour A, < 0 2 1 >, is the dynamic contour notated by Stockhausen across the bottom of the score: *pp, ff, mf*. A criticism might be raised that three-element contours can belong to one of only two possible segment classes, < 0 1 2 > or < 0 2 1 >—once retrograde, inversion, and retrograde inversion are invoked as equivalence criteria—and that therefore the relationships among Contours A, B, C, and J in this excerpt are of little significance. The fact remains,

---

35 Morris, *Composition with Pitch-Classes*, pp. 281–85.

(a) Score excerpt (Sections IXC and IXC):

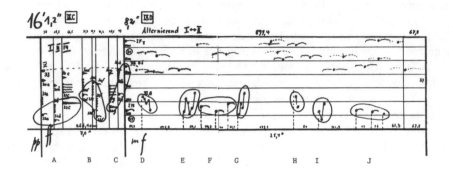

(b) Analysis of Rhythmic and Melodic Contours for Segments A–J

Duration Contours:

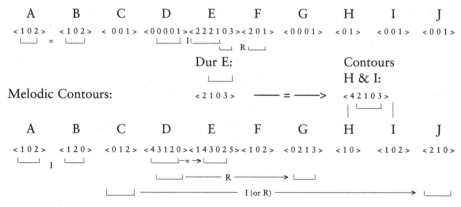

Note also:

Contour A is an equivalent segment in duration space and (melodic) contour space.

Duration subseg E, < 2 1 0 3 >, appears as a subseg of the combined H & I melodic contour.

Figures 11a–b: Melodic and Rhythmic Contours in Stockhausen's *Kontakte*

however, that the passage begins and ends with contours clearly segmented into three-element groups, and that their contour relations are clearly audible. Further, the contour labelled A almost always occurs in the same form, as < 1 0 2 >, when it is stated alone (not as a subsegment of a larger contour); the only exceptions are one statement each of the inversion < 1 2 0 > and retrograde < 2 0 1 >. Likewise, Contour C, < 0 1 2 > recurs only once and only in inversion (though this is equivalent to the retrograde, since < 0 1 2 > is inversionally symmetrical).

In the excerpt's second part, significant relationships occur among larger contours. Note, for example, that contours D and E share duration-space subsegments that are inversionally-related. Further, they share the melodic contour subsegment, < 3 2 0 1 >. Some four-note subsegments occur in both duration space and contour space. The last four elements of melodic contour D, for example, form < 3 1 2 0 >; its retrograde appears as the duration contour of segment G. Similarly, the final three elements of segment E's duration contour, < 1 0 3 >, appear again in duration space as segment F. In addition, segment E's final four durations, < 2 1 0 3 >, are echoed as a melodic contour formed of segments H and I. Again, this analysis is not intended to be exhaustive, but merely to demonstrate a possible application of contour theory to the electronic medium. Indeed, contour theory has potential for modelling structure among many musical dimensions in electronic compositions. If, like Morris, the analyst considers such dimensions as envelope (short to long), noise content (pure to noisy), and timbre (dull to bright) as sequential dimensions, contour notation may be used to analyze and compare even the colors of electronic sounds.[36]

To illustrate additional analytical applications of contours formed of spans, pitch-span space (ps-space) is defined more fomally here as a type of space consisting of spans between pitches, numbered in order from narrow to wide, beginning with 0 up to (n-1). Unlike intervals in pitch space, which also measure

---

36 Morris, *Composition with Pitch-Classes*, p. 282. I must admit here that the transcription of timbral contours is not an easy task. These analytical applications I leave to those who work more regularly with electronic music and are better able to categorize and make fine discriminations among timbres, envelopes, noise contents, and so on. Other approaches to timbre analysis in terms of sequential dimensions may be found in Wayne Slawson's work, most recently "Circling the Sound-Color Square: A New Set of Invariant Operations," delivered at the 1989 national meeting of the Society for Music Theory. Other work of interest includes Cogan, *New Images of Musical Sound* (cited above), David L. Wessel, "Timbre Space as a Musical Control Structure," *Computer Music Journal* 3 (1979), pp. 45–52; Kaija Saariaho, "Timbre and Harmony: Interpolations of Timbral Structures," *Contemporary Music Review* 2 (1987), pp. 93–133; and Fred Lerdahl, "Timbral Hierarchies," in the same issue, pp. 135–60. Wessel describes a two-dimensional model with one axis representing "dull" to "bright," and the other "less bite" to "more bite." Saariaho uses a sound-noise axis. Lerdahl discusses a vibrato dimension and a "harmonicity" dimension (its prototype has entirely natural harmonics), which are combined in a two-dimensional array. These models seem appropriate dimensions for contour analysis.

spans, ps-space contours are not calibrated by an equally-spaced means of measurement. Thus, spans in ps-space represent relative registral distance in ps-space in much the same way that duration contours represent relative temporal distance, or length, in duration space. Ps-space segments (ps-segs) are contours made up of ordered sets of spans in ps-space. Any ordered, contiguous subgrouping of a given ps-seg is termed a ps-subsegment (or ps-subseg), and may be renumbered from 0 to (n-1) via the translation operation defined previously. Subsegments that are non-contiguous in sequential time or in register may be considered analytically only if strongly associated by some other musical feature, such as timbre.

Pitch-span contours address the same analytical issue as Friedmann's "contour interval successions," or CIS. They both provide a way of comparing distances between contour pitches, although pitch-span contours carry slightly more information. Referring briefly back to Example 2a, this melodic contour, < 5 4 1 2 3 0 > would result in a CIS of < -1, -3, +1, +1, -3 >. Since Friedmann's contour intervals are "infinitely expandable or contractable in pitch space,"[37] they do not account for the fact that the -1 between the first two elements (a major seventh in pitch space) is quite a bit larger than the +1 between the fourth and fifth elements (a major second in pitch space). The pitch-span succession for this melody, ordered in sequential time, would assign 0 to the narrowest span and (n-1) to the widest, resulting in the succession < 4 3 1 0 2 >. It would accurately reflect the relative intervallic size between contour pitches in contour space, without the precise calibrations that characterize intervals between pitches in pitch space. Unlike the CIS, a ps-space contour cannot be derived from the integer representation of the contour pitches in the segment, but must be determined directly from the musical source by score analysis or by ear.

Example 6 provides an illustration where pitch-span contours are ordered in register, rather than in time, resulting in a precise method for describing chordal spacing. The first three chords, labelled X, show a pitch-space expansion of pitch-class set {1, 2, 4, 7}. Each successive chord encompasses a wider range; yet all are equivalent ps-space contours that can be represented as ps-seg < 0 1 2 >, a spacing that features successively-larger spans from bottom to top.[38] By way of contrast, the three chords labelled Y are pitch-space expansions of the same pitch-class set, this time realized as ps-seg < 1 2 0 >. Example 6b shows additional members of segment Y's ps-space segment class < 1 2 0 >, giving one possible realization each of I-, R-, and RI-related spacings.

Two final excerpts from Stockhausen's *Klavierstücke*, No. 2, first movement, demonstrate contour equivalences across duration, dynamic, and pitch-span

---

37 Friedmann, p. 230.

38 Morris calls this type of spacing "inverse overtone spacing," one of six spacing types defined in *Composition with Pitch-Classes*, pp. 54–55. He notes that spacing types are somewhat related to the idea of contour-classes in c-space. While his six spacing types are not equivalence

(a) Equivalent Spacings in Ps-Space:

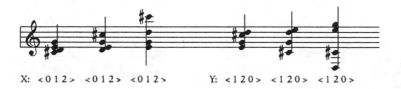

X: <0 1 2> <0 1 2> <0 1 2>   Y: <1 2 0> <1 2 0> <1 2 0>

(b) Representative Ps-Space Segment Class Members with Y < 1 2 0 >:

I(Y): < 1 0 2 >   R(Y): < 0 2 1 >   RI(Y): < 2 0 1 >

Examples 6a–b: Ps-Space Segments

spaces. This movement is articulated into five large sections by the statement of a sustained multi-dynamic chord and/or by complete measures of silence. Example 7 juxtaposes two of these multi-dynamic chords for comparison. Although the chords share few common contour subsegments (see, for example, the shared segment marked C), contour analysis reveals some remarkable structural features within each individual chord. For example, in the measure 11 chord, the spacing of its outer extremes is identical: a major second followed by a perfect fourth. The distribution of the inner voices prevent the chord from forming a perfect pitch-space symmetry, but if the pattern of spacing is divided in two, as shown numerically by the ps-segments at the bottom of the example, the pitch-span contour of the lower half is the inverse of the upper: < 0 2 1 2 > and < 2 0 1 0 >, after translation. (Contours in Examples 7 and 8 marked "ps" are pitch-span contours, those marked "dur" are duration contours, those marked "dyn" are dynamic

---

classes, he observes that it is possible to define criteria for spacing-types that would form equivalence classes. Paul Laprade has expanded upon these spacing types and illustrated their analytical applications in "The 'Shapes' of Boulez's *Sonatina for Flute and Piano* (1946)," presented at the 1990 annual meeting of the Society for Music Theory. Richard Hermann, in his "Issues of Gesture, Form, and Pitch Structure in Debussy's Music" (paper delivered at the 1989 annual meeting of the Society for Music Theory) develops formal intervals similar in conception to ps-space contours, but applies them to spans in formal analysis. His "Theories of Chordal Shape . . ." in this volume examines chord spacing in Berio's *Sequenza IV for Piano*.

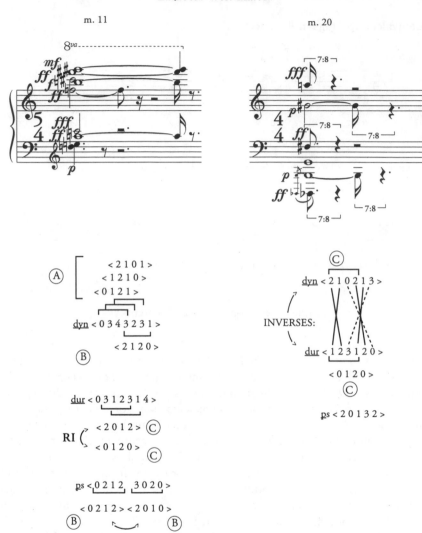

Stockhausen *Klavierstücke* Nr. 2, Movement 1

Example 7: Contour Analysis of Stockhausen's Multi-Dynamic Chords in
***Klavierstücke*, No. 2, Mvt. I, mm. 11 and 20**

contours, and those marked "c" are melodic contours.) Segment < 0 2 1 2 >, marked contour B in the example, appears in retrograde in the pattern of dynamics as well. Put simply, the upper four dynamics retrograde the order of the bottom four pitch spans. A more striking structural link between musical spaces occurs in the measure 20 chord; its entire dynamic contour is the exact inversion of its durational contour. Thus the softer the dynamic, the longer the rhythmic value, and vice versa.[39]

One final aural association that benefits from contour analysis is that between measures 17–18 and measures 32–33, given in Example 8. These passages sound like they might be inversionally-related. Closer analysis reveals that they are not inverses, but they are linked in other ways. First, the melodic contour of the upper line of the first passage, < 1 3 2 0 >, is the inversion of the other passage's bracketed dynamic contour, < *mf pp p fff* > or < 2 0 1 3 >. In addition, the durational contour of the first passage is identical to the melodic contour of the second. That is, the shortest element of the first contour corresponds with the lowest element of the second, the longest element of the first corresponds with the highest element of the second, and so on.[40]

The paper closes with a discussion of the interaction between ps-space contours and row structure in "Accenti," from *Quaderno musicale di Annalibera*, by Luigi Dallapiccola. The chord succession given in Example 9 represents each of the verticalities in the movement. Frequently, one note changes in the course of a sustained chord; these are shown as noteheads with "ties" attached to all but the pitch that changes. Figure 12a diagrams the movement's form: an A–B–A', in which the concluding A' section also divides into a smaller a–b–a'. Formal divisions are characterized primarily by changes in rhythmic patterning and chordal spacing.

The composition's texture consists primarily of five-note chords, all statements of set classes 5–26 [0, 2, 4, 5, 8] and 5–27 [0, 1, 3, 5, 8]. This arrangement is not simply a result of consecutive ordered pitch classes (pcs) from the work's row, as Figure 12b illustrates. The first five notes of the opening row, $T_{10}P$, form set class 5–27.[41] But it is only with the replacement of pc 3 with pc 2, the final note of the

---

39 This analysis assumes that the grace notes at the bottom of the chord are considered a physical necessity for striking the entire chord and are not considered "longer" because of them, and that the score contains a typographical error: that B1 should be a tied half note value rather than a tied whole note (note its parallel alignment with the G♯4 above).

40 In duration contours that contain rests, the duration of an element is determined by the onset of the next element. It is this "inter-onset interval" that is represented in the duration contour (see Marvin, "The Perception of Rhythm," p. 67). In this example, then, < 1 0 2 3 > represents the rhythm < triplet 32nd plus triplet eighth rest, triplet sixteenth plus triplet 32nd rest, triplet sixteenth tied to a sixteenth, dotted half >.

41 Set classes are identified using "Forte numbers"; see Allen Forte, *The Structure of Atonal Music* (New Haven: Yale University Press, 1973). Rows are identified using "fixed do" numbering; that is, C = 0 throughout.

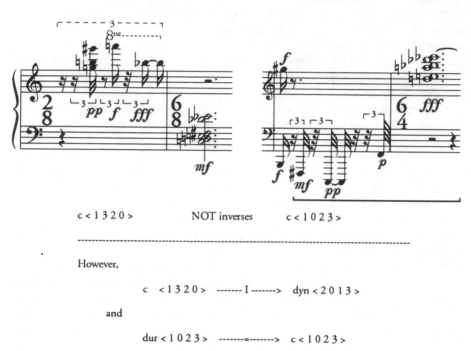

mm. 17-18   mm. 32-33

c < 1 3 2 0 >   NOT inverses   c < 1 0 2 3 >

However,

c < 1 3 2 0 >   ------- I -------->   dyn < 2 0 1 3 >

and

dur < 1 0 2 3 >   --------=-------->   c < 1 0 2 3 >

**Example 8: Analysis of "Inversionally-Related" Contours in Stockhausen,
Klavierstücke, No. 2, Mvt. I, mm. 17–18 and 32–33**

A SECTION: mm. 1–4

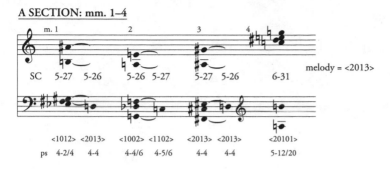

B SECTION: mm. 5–8

A' SECTION: mm. 9–16

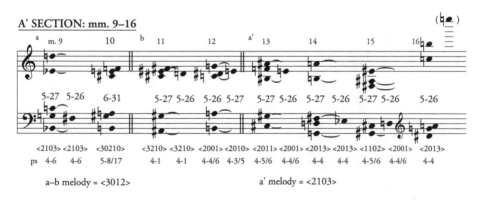

**Example 9: Ps-Space Segments in Dallapiccola's "Accenti"
from *Quaderno musicale di Annalibera***

(a) Formal design:

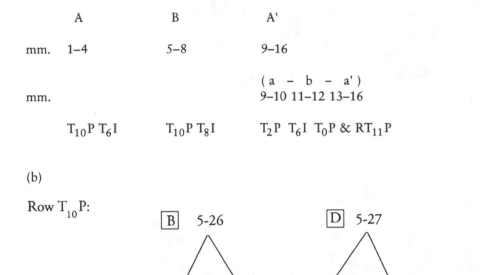

	A	B	A'
mm.	1–4	5–8	9–16

mm.

$$(a \ - \ b \ - \ a')$$
9–10 11–12 13–16

$T_{10}P \ T_6I$ $T_{10}P \ T_8I$ $T_2P \ T_6I \ T_0P \ \& \ RT_{11}P$

(b)

Row $T_{10}P$:

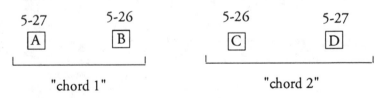

Order of presentation:

Figures 12a–b: Form and Row Structure in Dallapiccola's "Accenti"

first hexachord, that 5–26 is formed. The verticality formed by the second hexa chord in measure 2 is initially "missing" pc 0, which cannot be present if the 5–26 sonority is to be maintained. With the replacement of pc 1 by pc 0, 5–27 is formed. Thus, the pattern set up in the first measures is: 5–27, change one note to 5–26; then, a new chord maintains 5–26, change one note to return to 5–27. As Example 9 shows, only two chords break this alternation between pentachords: that which closes the A section in measure 4, and that which closes A-prime's first subdivision in measure 10. These cadential exceptions are six-note chords, both members of set class 6–31 [0, 1, 4, 5, 7, 9]. Indeed, the music that ends each of the three primary formal divisions is "marked" somehow: in measure 4, by the six-note chord, and in measures 8 and 16 by the single *sff* pitch, notated in Example 9 in parentheses, a departure from the prevailing pentachordal texture.

The pitch-span contours of the movement's five-note chords represent only a few distinct spacings, and certain spacings are linked to the formal structure. Each spacing belongs to one of four pitch-span segment classes—c4–1, c4–4, c4–5, and c4–6 on Marvin and Laprade's table of contour segment classes—or to some "repeated-span" contour that can be derived from these ps-segclasses by the internal repetition of a span. Figure 13a gives the contour segment classes of cardinality 4 for reference;[42] Figure 13b illustrates the way in which contours with an internal repetition are categorized. The COM-matrix is examined for "extra" zeros in the upper right-hand triangle (which appear in addition to the zeros of the main diagonal); then two matrices are generated that would replace these zeros entirely with pluses or with minuses. Figure 13b illustrates with the ps-segment < 1 0 0 2 >, found commonly in the Dallapiccola movement; this segment generates a matrix with one extra zero in the upper right-hand triangle. Its contour segment class label is derived from segments < 2 0 1 3 > and < 2 1 0 3 >, shown with their related matrices: ps-segclasses 4–4 and 4–6. Because the three matrices differ by so few positions, these contours (c4–4, c4–6, and c4–4/6) are considered highly similar, forming a transitive triple.

Returning to Example 9, note that ps-space contour < 2 0 1 3 > represents the most common chord spacing found, occurring in measures 1 (second chord), 3, 5, 14, and 16. With just one exception this pitch-span contour is reserved for chords in the A and A' sections; it occurs three times in A and five times in A'. The exception occurs only on the first beat of the B section, as a transition to the new section. Note in measure 3, that the pitch change (C♯ to D♮) and the attendant set-class change, does not change the chord spacing from < 2 0 1 3 >—likewise in measure 14. In addition to its prominence as a pitch-span segment, < 2 0 1 3 > also occurs as the melodic contour of the uppermost pitches of the A section. Further, its retrograde, < 3 1 0 2 >, is the melodic contour of the soprano line melody of the B section. Although the A' section's melody does not express this contour, its two

---

42 Marvin and Laprade, p. 257.

(a) Contour Segment Classes of Cardinality 4:

c4–1	< 0 1 2 3 >	c4–5	< 0 3 1 2 >
c4–2	< 0 1 3 2 >	c4–6	< 0 3 2 1 >
c4–3	< 0 2 1 3 >	c4–7	< 1 0 3 2 >
c4–4	< 0 2 3 1 >	c4–8	< 1 3 0 2 >

(b) Repeated-Span Contour:

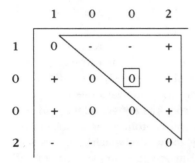

Two Related Matrices:

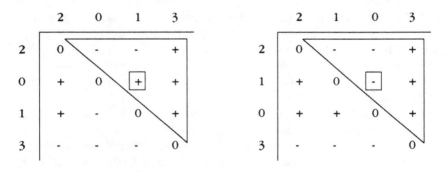

< 2 0 1 3 >   < 2 1 0 3 >

To calculate prime form: To calculate prime form:

    I: < 1 3 2 0 >   I: < 1 2 3 0 >

    R: < 0 2 3 1 > = ps 4–4   R: < 0 3 2 1 > = ps 4–6

Therefore, < 1 0 0 2 > = ps 4–4/6

Figures 13a–b: Repeated-Span Contours

halves express retrograde-related melodic contours as well: mm. 9–12 state < 3 0 1 2 >, while mm. 13–16 state < 2 1 0 3 >. To summarize, the two most common contours in this piece are expressed not only as chord spacings, but as melodies: < 2 0 1 3 > and its retrograde are the melodic contours of the upper line in the A and B sections, while < 3 0 1 2 > and its retrograde are the contours of the melodies in the two halves of the A' section.

Repetition of a particular row does not guarantee identity of chord spacing. Both the A and B sections begin with $T_{10}P$, as Figure 12 shows. Comparing each consecutive chord in mm. 5–6 with its pitch-class equivalent in measures 1–2 reveals that no two chords so aligned share the same spacing in spite of their pitch-class identity. This, along with rhythmic change, helps contribute to the aural dissimilarity of the A and B sections. In other words, in spite of the fact that these measures begin with the same row, partitioned the same way, a primary factor in creating a formal boundary here is the spacing of the chords. Likewise, measures 3 and 11–12, drawn from section A and the small-b section of A', express the same row: T_6I. The two begin with the same partition and thus identical pitch classes, but their spacing is quite dissimilar, distinguishing between their formal functions.

Before leaving this example, it should be pointed out that in at least one case, the disjunction between formal divisions is somewhat softened by identity of pitch spacing. Note that the final chord of the B section (mm. 7–8) and the first of the A' section (m. 9) belong to different set classes, but to the same ps-space segment class, 4–6, < 2 1 0 3 >. In spite of the ps-space contour repetition, this formal boundary is clear because of the single-note *sff* pitch between chords and because of the change in register and rhythmic pattern. Finally, two instances of retrograde-related spacings occur in "Accenti," both with repeated-span segments: ps < 1 0 0 2 > appears in mm. 2 and 5–6, while its retrograde appears in mm. 12, 13, and 15. Similarly, in mm. 2 and 10 ps < 1 1 0 2 > appears, while < 2 0 1 1 > is stated in m. 13.

To conclude, analyses that focus on identification of, and relationships among, pitch-class sets or rows may reveal much about a work's underlying structure, but they reveal little about the ways in which those pitch-class structures are articulated musically as pitches, expressed in register, in time, in intensity, and so forth. A generalized theory of musical contour may help to fill in this analytical "gap" and to work in conjunction with pitch-class analysis to provide a more complete model of musical structure.

The Beatles as Composers:
The Genesis of Abbey Road, Side Two

Walter Everett

In June, 1969, Paul McCartney called George Martin and asked if he would produce a new LP for the Beatles. The year preceding the phone call had been a difficult one for the band: Apple, the corporation that handled their business interests, was losing vast amounts of money through disastrous mismanagement. The group hired an accountant whose abrasiveness led to a lost opportunity for the Beatles to buy up large blocks of shares in companies that owned sizeable portions of their performing and songwriting royalties—the shares went to other buyers in February–May, 1969.[1] McCartney's relentlessness in having the group realize the details of his "head" arrangements led to friction; due to the tension of recording sessions, two of the quartet had quit the group for several days each (Ringo Starr in August, 1968, and George Harrison in January, 1969). Growing differences in artistic goals led to a number of solo projects.[2] Perhaps least encouraging for their future as artists, an entire month's worth of incomplete recordings—the "Get Back" project of January, 1969, intended as a set of live recordings without studio

---

1 The accountant, Allen Klein, was hired by three Beatles against the wishes of McCartney. Further exacerbating tensions between himself and the group, McCartney bought tens of thousands of shares in Northern Songs without the others' knowledge. Due to a court case that was settled in April, 1969, all of the Beatles' performance royalties from recordings were frozen for a number of weeks. Regarding the sales of 23% of Dick James Music and 90% of NEMS Enterprises, see Allen J. Wiener, *The Beatles: A Recording History* (Jefferson, N.C.: McFarland & Company, Inc., 1986), pp. 131–52; Peter Brown and Steven Gaines, *The Love You Make: An Insider's Story of the Beatles* (New York: McGraw-Hill Book Company, 1983), pp. 334, 343 and 348.

2 Individual projects of 1969 included John Lennon's inauguration of the Plastic Ono Band, his release of two singles and three albums, and other public events including avant-garde concert performances, underground film presentations, and "bed-ins" for peace in Amsterdam and Montreal. McCartney and Harrison produced records for a half dozen other artists and the latter released a solo album of electronic music; Starr had a film role in *The Magic Christian*. Shortly before the September 26, 1969, release of *Abbey Road*, Lennon announced to his partner that he was finished with the group; the split became irrevocable with McCartney's public announcement of his intentions to leave the band in April, 1970. Regarding the members' personal animosity, see Lennon's December, 1970, *Rolling Stone* interview with Jann Wenner ["Lennon Remembers"], rpt. in *The Ballad of John and Yoko*, ed. Jonathan Cott and Christine Doudna (Garden City, N.Y.: Rolling Stone Press, 1982), p. 106; McCartney's

gimmickry—lay on the shelf, with no agreed-upon plan for release.[3] So when asked to produce a record for a band that seemed to have lost its direction, Martin dictated that the LP would have to be a polished studio album "like the old days," rather than recordings of unfocused performances of half-finished compositions like those of January. Given these circumstances, it is somewhat remarkable that *Abbey Road*, principally recorded in July and August of 1969 and destined to be the group's last LP, is universally regarded as a coherent demonstration of inspired composition, impeccable vocal and instrumental ensemble, and cleverly colorful engineering.

Before particulars of Side Two are addressed, it would be useful to examine the general procedures for the composition and recording of the LP. *Abbey Road* is the only Beatle album made entirely with eight-track equipment.[4] In July and August, the group and its producer would typically meet in EMI Studios (on Abbey Road, St. John's Wood, hence the album title) to hear a first demonstration of a new song by its composer. Afternoon-through-evening rehearsals would then begin, with the composer leading the others through the essential parts and chord changes. At a certain point, the tapes would begin rolling, and any number of takes of the song's basic structure would be recorded until it was decided that a "best" one had been achieved. This recording of the basic tracks would usually consist of McCartney's

interview with Kurt Loder, *Rolling Stone* 482 (September 11, 1986): 100; and Brown and Gaines, *The Love You Make*, p. 361. For details on Lennon's 1969 activities, see Wiener, *A Recording History*, pp. 140–50, and Jonathan Cott, "John Lennon: How He Became Who He Was," in *The Ballad of John and Yoko*, pp. 35–37.

3   During the "Get Back" sessions, the Beatles' hopes for building their own recording studio fell through when Martin and engineer Glyn Johns declared the group's equipment to be rubbish and ordered workable mixing consoles to be borrowed from EMI immediately. In February–May, the Beatles worked on material that was to be included on *Abbey Road* in eleven recording sessions, only three of which involved Martin (who had produced every new recording released by the Beatles since October, 1962). See Mark Lewisohn, *The Beatles Recording Sessions: The Official Abbey Road Studio Session Notes*, 1962–1970 (New York: Harmony Books, 1988), pp. 164–65, 170–76. Material from the "Get Back" sessions was finally produced by Phil Spector in March–April, 1970, and released under the film title, *Let It Be* (Apple PCS 7096; May, 1970).

4   The Beatles had their first taste of eight-track consoles and tape machines at Trident Studios in July, 1968, for work on "Hey Jude." Most of their recordings, dating from the October, 1963, tapings of "I Want to Hold Your Hand" and "This Boy," were done on four-track tape. (Their first two LPs and first four singles had been performed virtually live on two-track tape, with minimal overdubs.) The advent of four-track tape enabled a change in the Beatles' compositional methods, especially with the LP *Help!* (recorded February–June, 1965) and subsequent work, wherein much of the composition and arranging was decided upon after the laying-down of basic tracks. Conversely, the Beatles' interest in ever more complex timbres and arrangements contributed to a spiraling boom in recording technology in the late 1960's. See Lewisohn, *Recording Sessions*, pp. 36, 54, 146 and 152. See also George Martin with Jeremy Hornsby, *All You Need Is Ears* (New York: St. Martin's Press, 1979), pp. 72, 108–10, 117–18, 134, 142–43 and 145–55.

Hofner or Rickenbacker bass, Starr's Ludwig drum kit, and electric and/or acoustic guitars played by Lennon and/or Harrison, one instrument per track; if McCartney played piano on the basic tracks (which he had done often since 1966), then another would play bass at the same time (as Harrison did on "Golden Slumbers"/"Carry That Weight," with the same six-string Fender bass he used on the "White" album in 1968) or McCartney would subsequently dub a bass line (as with "You Never Give Me Your Money"). During this initial recording, the composer would sing the main vocal part so as to guide the performance, but this part would eventually be erased from the tape, giving way to the superimposition of polished lead and backing vocals. (In a sense, the process is rather like Mozart's habit of writing a *particella* draft for an opera or concerto—the structural solo and bass lines would often be committed to paper first, after which time the inner parts would be composed and assigned instrumentation.) Following the completion of the basic tracks, Martin and the Beatles would put their heads together and arrange the remaining parts over a period of days or weeks, filling up the eight tracks with vocals, new parts for guitar, keyboard and/or percussion, any orchestral parts, and effects. The tone colors of vocals and instruments would often be manipulated during the recording, leading to hours of experimentation. Martin summarizes his working relationship with the Beatles with candor:

> There were no clear lines of demarcation. It was more a question of being a good team than of isolating individuals as being producer, arranger or songwriter. When I arranged, I worked closely with John, Paul or whoever it was, and they arranged with me . . .
>
> A two-way swing developed in our relationship. On the one hand, as the style emerged and the recording techniques developed, so my control—over what the finished product sounded like—increased. Yet at the same time, my need for changing the pure music became less and less. As I could see their talent growing, I could recognise that an idea coming from them was better than an idea coming from me, though it would still be up to me to decide which was the better approach. In a sense, I made a sort of tactical withdrawal, recognising that theirs was the greater talent.[5]

Once the recording had been completed, the eight tracks would be mixed for the stereo master. During that process, Martin, the Beatles, and their team of engineers further altered the colors of individual tracks and the relationships between them by adjusting the volume, deciding upon a frequency band equalization, opting for band-pass filtering, sending to any of several echo devices, limiting or compressing the amplitude, and deciding upon the amount of the signal to be sent to each of the two stereo channels; all for each of the eight tracks.[6]

---

5 Martin with Hornsby, *All You Need*, pp. 167, 259.
6 See Dave Harries, "Recording Equipment," in *Making Music*, ed. George Martin (New York:

For the new album, McCartney and Martin wanted to have a series of interconnected songs, but Lennon dissented. It was decided that to satisfy both Beatles, Side One would consist of six separate songs, and much of Side Two would be a medley. Lennon could very well have considered this medley to be emblematic of his and McCartney's artistic differences when he told an interviewer two years later, "by the time the Beatles were at their peak, we were cutting each other down to size, we were limiting our capacity to write and perform by having to fit it into some kind of format and that's why it caused trouble."[7]

The album's second side (presently marketed as tracks 7–17 of the compact disc) consists for the most part of a medley of complete songs and fragments that cohere by virtue of tonal organization and thematic recapitulation. It is introduced by one fully independent song and a second composition that, as a prelude, prepares the beginning of the medley proper. The side ends with a brief ditty, "Her Majesty," which is included only by virtue of McCartney's approval of an accidental splice by a tape operator.[8] Figure 1 lists the songs and their composers for the whole of Side Two; those songs in the medley that were recorded without a break are joined by a "plus" sign (+); those joined in post-production by either a crossfade or a hard tape edit are marked by a virgule (/). Because they represent strong, original contributions by each of the three composing Beatles, the first three songs of the side will be considered as closely as space allows. A deeper-level analysis of the entire medley concludes the essay.

"Here Comes the Sun" reflects both the brightness of the spring day on which it was written and the blossoming confidence of the composer, who learned his craft in the shadows of Lennon and McCartney. Harrison says that the song "was written on a very nice sunny day in Eric Clapton's garden. We'd been through real hell with business, and it was all very heavy. Being in Eric's garden felt like playing hooky from school. I found some sort of release and the song just came."[9] Figure 2 diagrams the genesis of the recording of "Here Comes the Sun." Each rectangle represents the contents of one of the tape's eight tracks. These are numbered

---

Quill, 1983), pp. 242–44. Harries worked as a technical engineer for Martin on many Beatle recordings in 1966–69.

7 Interview of Oct., 1971, *The Beatles Tapes from the David Wigg Interviews* (released in the U.K. as Polydor 2683 068; July, 1976). McCartney unilaterally set the formats for both major Beatle projects of 1967, *Sgt. Pepper's Lonely Hearts Club Band* and *Magical Mystery Tour*.

8 Engineer John Kurlander explains the survival of "Her Majesty" in Lewisohn, *Recording Sessions*, p. 183.

9 "George Harrison on Abbey Road," *Rolling Stone* 44 (October 18, 1969): 8. Harrison provides more detail on the song's having been inspired by his escape from meetings with bankers and lawyers concerning contracts and shares in his interview of early November, 1969 (not March, 1969, as stated in the album's notes), in *The Beatles Tapes*. Harrison also mentions here that "I finished [the song] later when I was on holiday in Sardinia"; that holiday was taken in June, 1969.

7. "Here Comes the Sun" (Harrison)
8. "Because" (Lennon)

Medley:
9. "You Never Give Me Your Money" (McCartney) /
10. "Sun King" (Lennon) +
11. "Mean Mr. Mustard" (Lennon) /
12. "Polythene Pam" (Lennon) +
13. "She Came In Through the Bathroom Window" (McCartney) /
14. "Golden Slumbers" (McCartney) +
15. "Carry That Weight" (McCartney) /
16. "The End" (McCartney)

17. "Her Majesty" (McCartney)

Figure 1: Side Two of *Abbey Road* (Tracks 7–17 of CD)

First Generation

July 7: Basic Tracks, Take 13	July 7: SI onto Take 13	July 8: SI onto Take 13
(1) Bass (PMcC)		
(2) Drums (RS)		
(3) Acoustic Gtr 1 (GH)		
(4) Guide Vocal (GH)		Lead Vocal (GH)
	(5) Acoustic Gtr 2 (GH)	
		(6) Bkg Vocals (PMcC, GH)
		(7) Bkg Vocals (PMcC, GH)

Figure 2: "Here Comes the Sun"

176

Second Generation

July 8: Tape reduction, Take 13 to Take 15	July 16: SI onto Take 15
(1) Ac Gtrs 1,2; 50% bass, drums, lead vocal	
(2) Bkg vocals; 50% bass, drums, lead vocal	
	(3) Handclaps (m 32, fourth time, to m 37)
	(4) Harmonium (mm 24–26, second time)

Jul. 8: rough mono remix
for Harrison to study

Aug. 4: rough stereo remix
for Harrison to study

Aug. 6, 11: SI onto Take 15	Aug. 15: SI onto Take 15; Martin conducts orchestra	Aug. 19: SI onto Take 15
(1) [see July 8]		
(2) [see July 8]		
(3) [see July 16]		
(4) [see July 16]		
(5) Acoustic Gtr 3 (GH)		
	(6) 4 vlas, 4 vclli, 1 stg bass	
	(7) 2 pic, 2 fl, 2 alto fl, 2 cl	
		(8) Moog (GH)

Figure 2 (cont.): "Here Comes the Sun"

Third Generation

Aug. 19: Stereo remix 1 from Take 15 (tape runs at 51 cps instead of 50 cps, raising pitch c. 1/3 semitone)	Aug. 20: Master tape
(1) Guitars 1, 2, Harmonium, Moog; 60% woodwinds; 50% bass, drums, ld voc, gtr 3, strings; 0— 50% backing vocals	LEFT
Handclaps; 40% woodwinds; 50% bass, drums, ld voc, gtr 3, strings; 50–100% backing vocals	RIGHT

Figure 2 (cont.): "Here Comes the Sun"

(1 through 8) for their first use; blank spaces retain the contents of previous sessions. The table indicates that basic tracks of bass, drums and acoustic guitar were recorded on July 7, and a second acoustic guitar was superimposed the same day (the abbreviation "SI" denotes superimposition). Vocals were added on the following day, after which the seven tracks were mixed down to two channels in order to allow for further overdubs. Several of these dubs preceded the recording of Martin's orchestral score on August 15, and the song's final touches—Harrison playing his Moog synthesizer—were added on the 19th, the day before the compilation of the master tape for the entire album.[10] This song apparently features no contribution from Lennon, who was recuperating from a car accident during the recording of the basic tracks and subsequent vocals.

Example 1 presents a reduced score of "Here Comes the Sun." Measures 1–8 constitute an instrumental introduction that closes on V^7. An introductory chorus (mm. 9–13) and guitar break (m. 14) prepare the verse–chorus combination (mm. 15–30), which is heard twice. A contrasting middle section (mm. 30b–32) is heard six times with varied instrumentation, and a four-measure retransition

---

10 The track numbers given in Figures 2–4 are hypothetical. Percentages indicate that during mixing, the signal from a given track was split and portions were sent to each channel to allow for varied placements in the stereo image; for example, in "Here Comes the Sun," the bass, drums, lead vocal and strings are heard in the center, the woodwinds are heard just left of center, and the backing vocals appear sometimes on the extreme right, sometimes in the center. Figures 2–4 derive from information in Lewisohn, Recording Sessions, pp. 176–80, 183–85, 187 and 190–91; and from listening to both the basic tracks (as heard on the "bootleg," *Return to Abbey Road*) and to the LP's final mix.

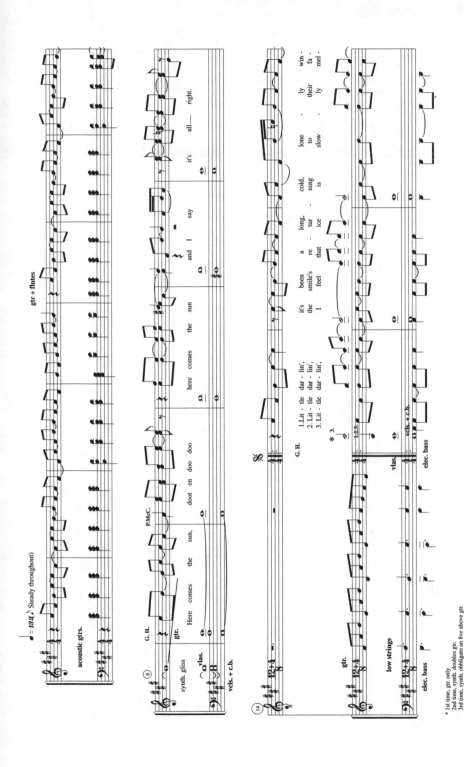

Example 1: "Here Comes the Sun" (George Harrison, Spring, 1969)

Example 1 (cont.): "Here Comes the Sun" (George Harrison, Spring, 1969)

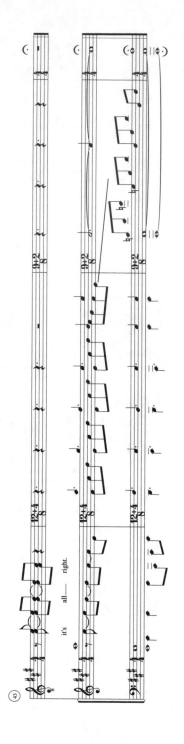

Example 1 (cont.): "Here Comes the Sun" (George Harrison, Spring, 1969)

(mm. 33–36) achieves the V[7] in preparation for the third verse and chorus (mm. 15–28 once again); the song concludes with a coda (mm. 37–46). The middle section, featuring the repeated text, "Sun, sun, sun, here it comes," takes on the quality of a mantra. This hearing is certainly in keeping with the composer's philosophy, as he devoted nine weeks in early 1968 to transcendental meditation in Rishikesh, India.[11] As summarized in Example 2, the voice leading of this middle section (mm. 31–32) consists of a series of upper-neighbor chords (marked "N") that fall in fourths, from C to G to D to A (quoting Lennon/McCartney's retransition from "A Day in the Life," 1967), with a structural gentleness that enhances the suggestion of a meditative state. Harrison's meditation becomes truly transcendental when the dominant harmony of measure 33 reveals that the root of the A major chord of measure 32, heard six times as a point of tonal arrival, truly functions as an upper neighbor to the third of V harmony (hence the exclamation point in the sketch). The composer's enlightenment is seemingly celebrated in measures 33–36 by the retransition's radiant unfolding of V[7] harmony, culminating on the exuberant seventh, D6.[12]

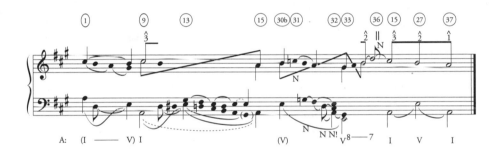

Example 2: "Here Comes the Sun"

---

11 Harrison and Lennon meditated under the guidance of Maharishi Mahesh Yogi in Rishikesh, February 16–April 19, 1968. In speaking about meditation and chanting in November, 1969, Harrison conjures a mystical joy like that which he had perhaps hoped to express a few months earlier in "Here Comes the Sun": "music is such a powerful force . . . it's really the same end as meditation; the response that comes from it is in the form of bliss" (*The Beatles Tapes*).

12 Dramatic retransitions prolonging V7 were a hallmark of early Beatles recordings (as in "Twist and Shout" [February, 1963]; "I Want to Hold Your Hand" and "This Boy" [October, 1963]; "Yes It Is" [February, 1965] and "Day Tripper" [October, 1965]), but they declined in numbers in later recordings. An unmistakable exception to this decline was the powerful V9 in the retransition of Lennon's B-side, "Revolution" (July, 1968).

"Here Comes the Sun" is a fine example of growth in rhythmic complexity. The song is introduced by increasing syncopation in the vocal parts (a characteristic of Harrison's earlier compositions, particularly "If I Needed Someone" [October, 1965] and "I Want to Tell You" [June, 1966]). The stress of weak parts of beats is emphasized by cross-rhythms in the guitar break (m. 14), where two measures' length of common time is accented so as to produce a pattern in eighths of 12 + 4 (as notated in Ex. 1), free enough to suggest joyous abandon. Following the first verse/chorus, this break is extended by two 4/4 measures (mm. 29–30a), but the second verse/chorus is extended by only one 4/4 measure (m. 29). These aspects of asymmetry prepare the middle section's constantly changing meter, which is built upon the irregular accent pattern of the eighths of the guitar break (m. 14), but the cascading fourths create a new metrical grouping. A regular 4/4 pattern in the retransition then aids the listener in predicting the verse's return. The coda brings together the vocal syncopations from the chorus (mm. 37–41), the cross-rhythms of the guitar break (m. 42) and a unique rehearing of the ending of the chorus (m. 43). Finally, the coda juxtaposes for one time only the guitar break (m. 44) with a rehearing of the middle section (mm. 45–46), where the A major chord finally proves itself to be a steadfast harmony.

Dominated at first by layers of acoustic guitar and low strings, "Here Comes the Sun" represents the brightening sun in the middle section by the Moog synthesizer motive that rises in register, becomes progressively purified in timbre, and culminates in a V^7-prolonging retransition highlighted by brilliant frequencies in piccolos and well-placed cymbal crashes.[13] The middle section features a patch probably based on a sawtooth wave, realized as the motive sounds in four different

---

13 *Abbey Road* contains the only appearances of a modular synthesizer on a Beatles record. Harrison obtained it in late 1968 (it is heard on his solo LP, *Electronic Sound*, released in the U.K. as Zapple 02; May, 1969). Photographs in *The Beatles Monthly Book* 74 (September, 1969) show it to resemble closely (or to be) a Moog Mk 3C synthesizer, with two five-octave keyboards, a ribbon controller (played by McCartney in his solo on "Maxwell's Silver Hammer"), various modules including voltage-controlled oscillators, noise generator, ADSR envelope generators, two 904A voltage-controlled low-pass filters, and three 902 voltage-controlled amplifiers.

Each Moog module (itself equipped with potentiometers and/or switches to regulate its effect) is capable of altering an incoming voltage. The resulting controlled voltage can then be applied (by a patch cord) to another module, controlling the effect of that oscillator, filter or amplifier on a second incoming signal. Thus an oscillator might generate, from the incoming power supply, one of several basic waveforms: a single frequency (approaching a theoretically pure sine wave), or a pre-set combination of harmonic partials above a fundamental frequency (producing various timbres such as the flute-like triangle wave, the clarinet-like square wave, or the buzz-like sawtooth wave), or combinations of non-harmonic frequencies (as with random noise generators, as that added to Lennon's "I Want You (She's So Heavy)," on Side One of *Abbey Road*). A patch (a combination of patch cords) might determine that one of several filters, such as a low-pass filter (which produces a controllable reduction of partials above a dial-regulated or voltage-controlled frequency) or a band-pass filter (which allows the

registers; with each higher octave, the edge of the sawtooth seems dulled a bit (approaching the purity of a sine wave), but not so much that its last appearance, which concludes on A5 in measure 32, doesn't lead perfectly to the bright attack of the piccolos on G♯5 in measure 33.[14] A second patch (seemingly based on a triangle wave and featuring a light portamento) was used in two other passages that exemplify on a larger scale the rising octaves of the middle section: in the second verse, the Moog doubles the solo guitar line at the unison and in the third verse (these two verses straddle the "enlightening" middle section and retransition), the Moog adds an obbligato line an octave above. The high-register triangle wave (which heavily emphasizes the fundamental) joins the family of flutes and piccolos. Figure 2 indicates that the Moog performances completed the composition and recording of "Here Comes the Sun," following even the orchestral overdubs (which are normally a song's final addition). Martin's touch with the woodwinds was complimented perfectly by Harrison's final superimpositions, all working together to reflect the sun's increasing brilliance.

On *The Wedding Album*, which preserves the sounds of the events surrounding the March, 1969, wedding of John Lennon and Yoko Ono, Lennon can be heard

---

portion of a signal between two pre-set frequencies to pass unaltered while upper and lower frequencies are progressively filtered) might be applied to the output of an oscillator, the result of which is fed to an amplifier. The voltages of either the filter or the amplifier might be controlled in turn by an envelope generator (which may control the speed and intensity of a tone's attack, decay, sustain and release). Other modules may have special effects, such as reverberation or regeneration (the resonant emphasis of a particular frequency). For further information on analog synthesis contemporaneous with the production of *Abbey Road*, see Hubert S. Howe, Jr., *Electronic Music Synthesis: Concepts, Facilities, Techniques* (New York: W. W. Norton & Company, Inc., 1975), pp. 69–138.

Considering the group's and its engineer's experimentation with oscillators, filtering and amplification modifications, the synthesizer had become the logical next step in a progression of keyboard instruments through Hammond organ, electric piano, harmonium, Mellotron (first used in "Strawberry Fields Forever" in November, 1966) and Clavioline (used in "Baby You're a Rich Man," May, 1967). The Beatles' use of the Moog follows that of Paul Beaver (1967) and Walter Carlos (1968), but preceeds most appearances in rock music (by groups such as Emerson, Lake and Palmer; Yes, etc.).

14 The synthesizer's tone quality blends so well with that of the winds, that with their entry in the last hearing of mm. 30b–32, the flutes (just left of center in the stereo image) seem to pull the Moog from left to center (without panning), suggesting the sun approaching an "overhead" location for the bright retransition. In conversations with the writer on July 19–20, 1991, Martin Sweidel offered two possible causes for the apparent change in timbre of the sawtooth wave: first, that a low-pass filter might have had a successively stronger effect on high partials the higher the octave; second, that this early equipment might have had noticeably non-linear features. (Because all partials are present in the sawtooth wave, this signal is highly prone to distortion in both circuitry and acoustic resonance.) Sweidel also suggests that both the glissandi and the occasional vibrato might have been controlled by the ribbon, while the basic frequency was simultaneously regulated from the equal-tempered keyboard.

picking arpeggiations on acoustic guitar. The arpeggiations were later to become the accompaniment to "Because," a composition that in its final form is dominated by the "hot" hollow-body electric sound of Lennon's Epiphone Casino guitar, doubled by an electric harpsichord played by Martin.[15] While the lead vocal and guitar arpeggiation can be assumed to be Lennon's own, the two backing vocal parts were arranged and taught by rote (the Beatles do not read music) by Martin, his only such contribution to a Beatles recording. Aside from singing backing vocals, McCartney plays bass and Harrison plays the Moog, apparently with three different patches. The first patch, an expertly-programmed sawtooth wave modified in emulation of a horn, doubles the guitar part at the song's climax in measures 31–34. (The patch probably added some noise alongside the sawtooth, with both sources led to voltage-controlled low-pass filters regulated by separate envelope generators. This would have allowed the noise to have a faster attack and decay than the slower-to-open, long-sustaining sawtooth would have. It may also have had a bit of regeneration to simulate the horn's natural resonance around 500 Hertz, and a touch of reverberation.) The second and third patches sound simultaneously in the song's conclusion; on the left channel, an envelope generator with a slow attack regulates a low-pass filter, causing the upper partials to open up in sequence on each note, and a simple triangle-like wave is heard on the right channel). There is no percussion, although Starr kept a steady beat on his hi-hat during the recording of the basic tracks.[16] The full score is recreated here as Example 3.

"Because" was the first Beatle recording since "Yes It Is" (February, 1965) to feature three-part vocal harmony throughout.[17] On "Yes It Is" and on "This Boy" before it (both Lennon compositions, as is "Because"), McCartney, Lennon and Harrison arranged their own vocal parts. With "Because," for some reason, it was Martin's task to compose McCartney's and Harrison's parts. The producer's general impression about bringing Lennon's ideas to completion might well apply here:

---

15 The guitar playing heard on *The Wedding Album* (Apple SMAX 3361) was taped in Amsterdam on March 26, 1969; it amounts to the following progression in C (not the eventual C♯) minor, played with the same figuration as heard in the final version: I–V6–VII° $\frac{4}{3}$/V–V6–I. (Despite the C♯ minor model in Beethoven's "Moonlight Sonata," as discussed below, this Amsterdam recording suggests that Lennon originally thought of "Because" in C minor. Lennon did not have perfect pitch; it is therefore somewhat possible that his Amsterdam guitar was tuned low, and that his picking pattern was in C♯ but sounded transposed to C minor, or that for the final recording a capo enabled a C minor finger pattern to sound in C♯ minor. The part is equally playable in C minor and in C♯ minor.) The arpeggiation on the Casino is very much like that heard on "I Want You (She's So Heavy)" (recorded in February and April, 1969, for *Abbey Road*).

16 The microphone for the hi-hat was fed via a pre-mix fader to headphones only; the signal was not sent to tape machines. Lewisohn, *Recording Sessions*, p. 184.

17 Harrison discussed his fondness for the three-part harmonies of "Because" with Wigg in November, 1969, for *The Beatles Tapes*.

Example 3: "Because" (John Lennon, Mid-1969)

Example 3 (cont.): "Because" (John Lennon, Mid-1969)

Example 3 (cont.): "Because" (John Lennon, Mid-1969)

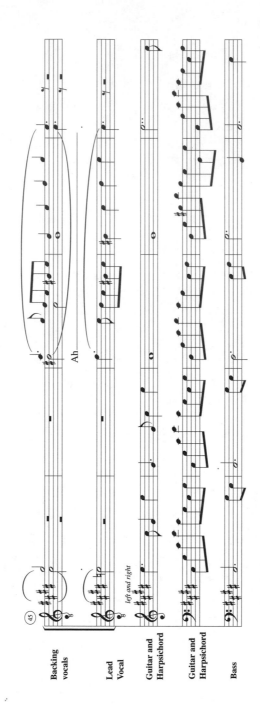

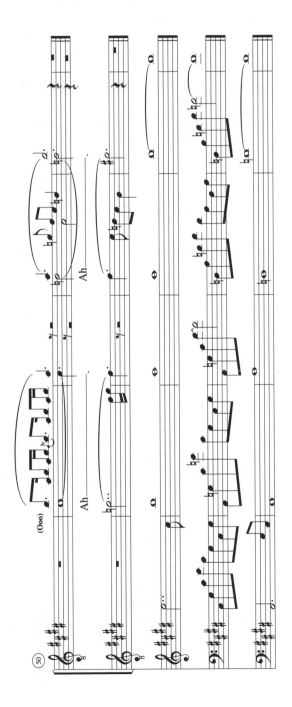

Example 3 (cont.): "Because" (John Lennon, Mid-1969)

rtney was always definite in his ideas, and it is true to say that
ive thoughts in The Beatles came from him. John Lennon, on the
d, lacked the dogged persistence for thinking out detail, and one
search for his ideas. But his songs were so inherently full of
atm... here that the construction of their recordings became almost like an
archaeological dig, and equally rewarding.[18]

In fact Martin remembered arranging Lennon's part as much as McCartney's for
"Because" : "When we worked out those harmonies, I would sort of go down to
the piano and say 'Right. John, you sing this. Paul, you sing this.' And Paul would
then say 'Well, can I sing such-and-such?' You know, that was the way we worked
it out."[19] This does not ring completely true, because Lennon's and Harrison's
parts occasionally exchange positions, creating the impression that Harrison's part
was arranged around Lennon's structural line. As shown in Figure 3, the three-part
vocals were recorded three times, and so the end result is a nine-man choir, three
on a part. The full sound compliments the exaggerated sustain of Martin's electric
harpsichord and the long notes of McCartney's bass.

"Because" is notable for its unresolved, circular harmonic structure; vaguely
reminiscent of a slow movement from a Corelli or Handel sonata (perhaps because
of the harpsichord?), this song ends on VII°$^4_3$ of what follows, which in this case is
McCartney's "You Never Give Me Your Money."[20] As shown in Example 4, this
VII°-type harmony had ended the first verse—see measure 20—but with a highly
ambiguous function. Because one would expect ♮II (m. 19) to lead to V, a hearing
of V$\flat^7_5$ with lowered seventh scale degree may be considered in measure 20; f♮
would then be heard as a chromatic passing tone—all in all, an unlikely function.

---

18 Martin, "Record Production," *Making Music*, p. 267.

19 Paul Lawrence interviews George Martin, *Audio* 62/5 (May, 1978): 56. A single take of one
set of "Because" vocals can be heard on the unauthorized recording, *Ultra Rare Trax, Vols. 5
& 6*, with Lennon singing on the left, McCartney in the center, and Harrison on the right.
According to Lewisohn, two tape tracks were devoted to a second and third take of the vocals
(this corroborates Martin's frequently-articulated memory of the nine-man chorus), and two
more tracks were given to the Moog (this is confirmed by ear in the song's conclusion). With
these, the three backing tracks and the first set of vocals, then, all eight tracks would be full (as
shown in Figure 3), with one track given to each of the three takes of vocals. The only
explanations that come to mind for the *Ultra Rare Trax* recording, which would have
necessitated at least two (and likely three) tracks for this one take, are that at some point the
original tracks were "bounced down" (mixed into a second generation) to accommodate more
superimpositions (which fact should not have escaped Lewisohn, who normally documents
such procedures very carefully), or that the "bootleg" presents a rehearsal not preserved on the
working tape (highly unlikely, given the polished vocal performance that is identical to the final
product). Apparently the documents cannot rectify this incongruity.

20 McCartney's "For No One" (recorded in May, 1966), featuring both a clavichord and a
pianoforte, ends on V4–3, but does not resolve into the next song, "Doctor Robert," on
Revolver.

First Generation

Aug. 1: Basic Tracks, Take 16	Aug. 1: SI onto Take 16	Aug. 4: SI onto Take 16	Aug. 5: SI onto Take 16
(1) Elec Hpsi (GM)			
(2) Elec Gtr (JL)			
(3) Bass (PMcC)			
(4) Guide Vocal (JL)	Vocals (PMcC, JL, GH)		
(Pre-mix): hi-hat to headphones		(5) Vocals (PMcC, JL, GH)	
		(6) Vocals (PMcC, JL, GH)	
			(7) Moog 1 (GH)
			(8) Moog 2 (GH)

Second Generation

Aug. 12: Stereo remix 2 from Take 16	Aug. 20: Master tape
(1) Electric Harpsichord, Moog 1; 50% bass, vocals	LEFT
(2) Electric guitar, Moog 2; 50% bass, vocals	RIGHT

Figure 3: "Because"

Part I

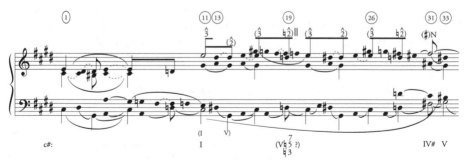

Example 4: "Because"

Part II

Example 4 (cont.): "Because"

The true nature of this chord is revealed after the second verse, in measure 30, as VII°$^4_2$ of a structural IV. Following this, the listener would probably then retrospectively hear the cadence of measure 20 as an interrupted motion to a dominant preparation. The chord's other appearance, in measure 44, is wrapped in yet a new guise, due to a restructuring of hypermeasures as newly interpreted by the chorus.[21] (Because the vocal parts were arranged by Martin, this restructuring following the third verse may be his creation, although the process is very similar to a technique of reinterpreting hypermeasures with which Lennon had experimented in the similarly "circular" "Sexy Sadie," recorded in July, 1968, for *The Beatles*.) Phrases were initially arranged in groups of 4 + 4 + 2 measures (as in mm. 11–20 and, eliding with the following phrase, 21–31). The final verse (beginning in m. 35) melts into a coda without a definite cadence and is grouped, by virtue of choral downbeats, as 4 + 4 + 4 (!) + 4 + 4 (the final measure extended by a measure-long fermata), even though the instrumental tracks continue with the identical parts articulating the original hypermeasures. So this time, the harmony heard once as a strangely altered V and twice as VII°^{7} (once to F♯ and once to A) is neither. It is a contrapuntal entity that neighbors the tonic and has a common tone with it. As in measure 30, the chord in measure 44 occurs within the phrase, so the potential cadential third-progression of measures 45–50 (as suggested in

---

21 "Hypermeasure" is Edward T. Cone's term for a multi-measure, large-scale metrical grouping. See Cone, *Musical Form and Musical Performance* (New York: W. W. Norton & Company, Inc., 1968), pp. 40 ff. The out-of-phase nature of the metrical structures and tonal groupings in the conclusion of "Because" has antecedents in the traditional repertoire; what seems unique in "Because" is the shift from one hypermetrical interpretation to another within the same piece. See Fred Lerdahl and Ray Jackendoff, *A Generative Theory of Tonal Music* (Cambridge, Mass.: The MIT Press, 1983), p. 30; and William Rothstein, *Phrase Rhythm in Tonal Music* (New York: Schirmer Books, 1989), p. 29.

Ex. 4) is clouded in ambiguity. Because of the phrase configuration, this linear progression cannot be heard as a structural gesture.[22]

"Because" is typical for the Beatles only in that it is inspired by sources outside of rock music. The song is Lennon's recomposition of the first movement of the "Moonlight" Sonata, and there are a few points of similarity between the song and its model.[23] Both arpeggiate triads and seventh chords in C♯ minor in the baritone range of a keyboard instrument at a slow tempo, move through the submediant to the Neapolitan, and approach VII°[7] of IV via a common tone. Lennon says, "Yoko was playing 'Moonlight Sonata' on the piano. She was classically trained. I said, 'Can you play those chords backwards?' and wrote 'Because' around them."[24] If one considers that in Beethoven, the opening "Moonlight" arpeggiations appear in an ascending manner only, one might guess that Ono was instructed to reverse that direction; the resulting "circular" ascending and descending arpeggiations that characterize nearly every measure of "Because," then, can be related to a hearing of Beethoven with both forwards and backwards "chords."

Thus far, the adjective "circular" has been applied to both the harmonic structure and the surface figuration. The notion of circularity is at the heart of the poetic text, as in the play on words upon which the first verse is built: a second meaning of the word "turn" follows the word "round." The second verse reinterprets "blows" following "wind," and the third verse provides a double meaning for "blue" with "cry." The punning process itself involves a sort of a twisting, circular thinking. Circularity is also inherent in the constant shifts back-and-forth in the poet's perspective: each verse alternates an external appearance with its effect upon the composer's psyche. On the structural dominant in measure 33, Lennon makes his strongest point; he surprises the listener by extending the circle from the universal "all" not to the first-person "me," but to the second-person "you." This statement, about the universality of love, has a fully mystical quality only slightly less strongly suggested by the spiritual reactions to the world, the wind, and the sky in the three verses.[25] A final clue to the circularity of

---

22 The group's recasting of a compositional feature in numerous contexts was perhaps first realized to this extent in "She Loves You" (recorded for the Beatles' fourth single in July, 1963), a joint Lennon–McCartney composition that highlights many varied relationships between pitch-classes G and E. Following a full development of the "double-tonic" G/E contrast, the three singers' final tonic chord in G major contains both a G and an E—against the advice of Martin. See this writer's "Voice Leading and Harmony as Expressive Devices in the Early Music of the Beatles: 'She Loves You'," *College Music Symposium* 32 (1992): 19–37.

23 Of over 200 compositions, "Because" is the Beatles' only song in C♯ minor.

24 G. Barry Golson, ed., *The Playboy Interviews with John Lennon and Yoko Ono* (New York: Berkley Books, 1981), p. 201. The interviews from which this quote were taken were conducted September 8–28, 1980. Also during these conversations, Lennon gives Ono general credit as his inspiration: "She's the teacher and I'm the pupil" (p. 113).

25 "John has experiences, and recreates in us, a small mystical experience . . . . Causality is released and there is no before and after: *because* that flat supertonic is a moment of revelation, it needs

the relationships between Lennon and his outside world as expressed in "Because" can be heard in one of Lennon's last compositions, "Watching the Wheels" (recorded in the autumn of 1980 for the LP, *Double Fantasy*). Here the composer explains his years of daydreaming while watching cars roll by his Dakota apartment. Lennon says of "Watching the Wheels": "the whole universe is a wheel, right? Wheels go round and round. They're my own wheels, mainly. But you know, watching meself is like watching everybody else." [26]

Just as Harrison's "Here Comes the Sun" expresses a release from the woes of Beatle business, that same tension inspired McCartney's "You Never Give Me Your Money." Figure 4 summarizes the recording of this song. Basic tracks recorded in the spring were given a new vocal on July 1 (the first day expressly devoted to the new album), and some aborted work was done on July 30. McCartney revised bass and piano tracks on July 31, presumably due to a re-thinking of the section that begins in measure 25 (see Ex. 5); the piano part in this passage became quite different between the basic tracks and the eventual overdub. On August 21, the end of the song's stereo mix was merged with a four-track mix of tape loops of sound effects (made by McCartney on his home machines), and the result was crossfaded into the beginning of "Sun King." Despite the role of *musique concrète* in Lennon's previous tape compositions "Tomorrow Never Knows" (which features a live studio mix of a number of tape loops onto basic tracks, produced on April 7, 1966), "I Am the Walrus" (wherein a September 29, 1967, radio broadcast of *King Lear* was fed, live, into the final mono mix) and "Revolution 9" (recorded in May–June, 1968), and despite Lennon's experimental work with Yoko Ono, McCartney was perhaps the true avant-garde adventurer in the Beatles. He first brought the loops to the studio that were used in "Tomorrow

---

no resolution." Wilfrid Mellers, *The Music of the Beatles: Twilight of the Gods* (New York: Schirmer Books, 1973), p. 118. In the art of Lennon and Ono, the wind and the sky were special: their first collaboration (1967) was called "Half a Wind Show"; in Double Fantasy (August–September, 1980, released as Geffen GHS 2001); October, 1980), he refers to her as "the other half of the sky." The line "head in the clouds" from "Lucy in the Sky With Diamonds" (March, 1967) is made into a visual image on the cover of Lennon's LP, *Imagine* (July, 1971, released as Apple SW 3379; September, 1971). For insight into Lennon's value of the state of daydreaming and into the mystical roles of wind and sky in his spirituality, see this writer's "Fantastic Remembrance in John Lennon's 'Strawberry Fields Forever' and 'Julia'," *Musical Quarterly* 72 (1986), p. 380.

26 Jonathan Cott, "The Last *Rolling Stone* Interview" [December 5, 1980], in *The Ballad of John & Yoko*, ed. Cott and Doudna, p. 191. The relationship in Lennon's mind between fantasy and circularity is expressed again in his 1980 memories of his composition, "I'm Only Sleeping" (recorded April–May, 1966): "it's got backwards guitars, too. That's me—dreaming my life away." Golson, ed., *The Playboy Interviews*, p. 208. The line "dreaming my life away" is a quote from "Watching the Wheels." Perhaps "Because" could have borrowed the Beethoven subtitle, "quasi una Fantasia," as well as the "backwards chords."

Never Knows," it was he who conceived of the aleatoric orchestral passages in "A Day in the Life" (recorded on February 10, 1967), and it was his idea to have Stockhausen's likeness on the cover of *Sgt. Pepper's Lonely Hearts Club Band* (photographed March 30, 1967).[27]

First Generation

May 6: Basic tracks, Take 30 (26 mm. longer than final mix)	July 1: SI onto Take 30	July 11: SI onto Take 30	July 15: SI onto Take 30
(1) Piano (PMcC)			
(2) Drums (RS)			
(3) Leslie Gtr (GH)			
(4) Distorted Gtr (JL)			
(5) Guide Vocal (PMcC)	Lead Vocal (PMcC)		
		(6) Bass (PMcC)	
			(7) Backing vocals (PMcC, GH, JL), Tambourine

Experimental Mixes for Study

July 30: Reduction Mix (Take 30 into Take 40; Duration still 5:43)	July 30: Stereo mix of Take 40	July 30: SI onto Take 40	July 30: Rough test: Crossfade mix of medley for study
	LEFT		
	RIGHT		
		Vocal (PMcC)	

Figure 4: "You Never Give Me Your Money"

---

27 McCartney listened to a great deal of Cage, Berio, and Stockhausen in 1966–67. Perhaps it was McCartney's boldness with tape loops that encouraged Martin to revive his expertise with sound effects (which he developed in the late 1950's) for the effects that were to pepper Beatles records from "Yellow Submarine" (June, 1966) onwards. At the end of "You Never Give Me Your Money," McCartney's bell tape loop is heard twice; the second hearing also includes cicadas, birds, etc. A cricket lives for 27 seconds into "Sun King." McCartney's home electronic music activities are discussed in two items in *The Beatles Monthly Book* 33 (April, 1966): Neil Aspinall's "Neil's Column," p. 6, and Frederick James's "Beatles Talk," p. 12.

Further Work with Take 30

July 31: SI onto Take 30
(1) Piano (PMcC) (mm. 25 ff.)
(2) [see May 6]
(3) [see May 6]
(4) [see May 6]
(5) [see July 1]
(6) bass (PMcC)
(7) [see July 15]

Crossfade to "Sun King":

McCartney's homemade tape loops
E7 bell, birds, bubbles, crickets, cicadas

Aug. 5: Take 5 of 4-track mix of sound
effects of loops; bell loop heard twice

Second generation: *Third generation:*

Aug. 13: Stereo Mix 23 from Take 30; pans, ADT, reverberation, compr./lim., EQ	Aug. 14: Stereo crossfade remix 11 with sound effects	Aug. 20: Master tape	Aug. 21: Stereo crossfade remix 12 of takes with Stereo Mix 23
Pianos; 50% Gtr (GH), bass; 25% Gtr (JL); 0–50% vocals, tamb	LEFT	LEFT	LEFT
Drums; 50% Gtr (GH), bass; 75% Gtr (JL); 50–100% vocals, tamb	RIGHT	RIGHT	RIGHT

crossfade of "You
Never Give Me Your
Money" / "Sun King"
inserted into master

Figure 4 (cont.): "You Never Give Me Your Money"

Example 5: "You Never Give Me Your Money" (Paul McCartney, Spring 1969)

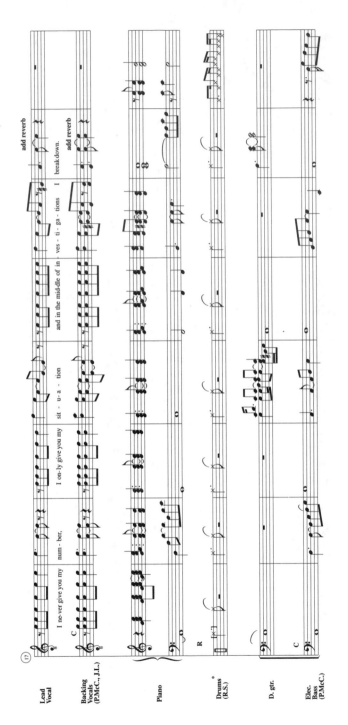

*Drums: lines for cymbals (1. crash, 2. ride, 3. hi-hat)

spaces for skins (1.snare, 2.tenor tom, 3.floor tom, 4.bass drum)

Example 5 (cont.): "You Never Give Me Your Money" (Paul McCartney, Spring 1969)

Example 5 (cont.): "You Never Give Me Your Money" (Paul McCartney, Spring 1969)

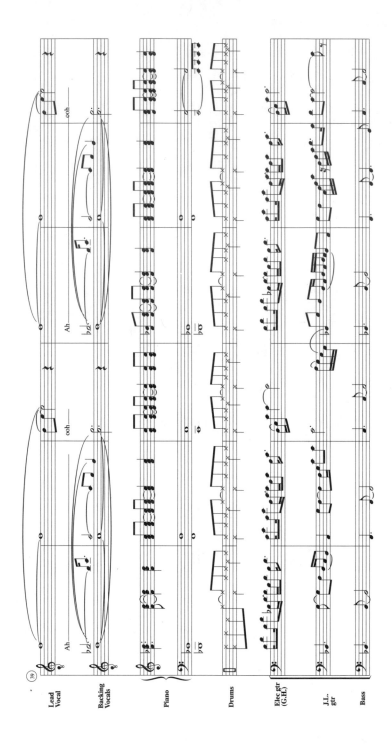

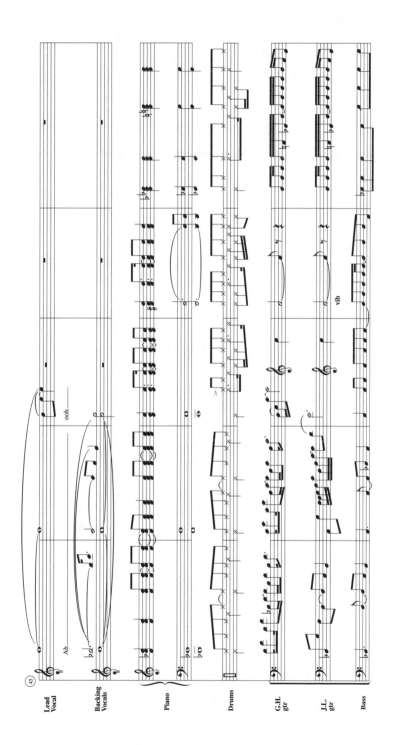

Example 5 (cont.): "You Never Give Me Your Money" (Paul McCartney, Spring 1969)

Piano

Drums

G.H.
gtr

J.L.
gtr

Bass

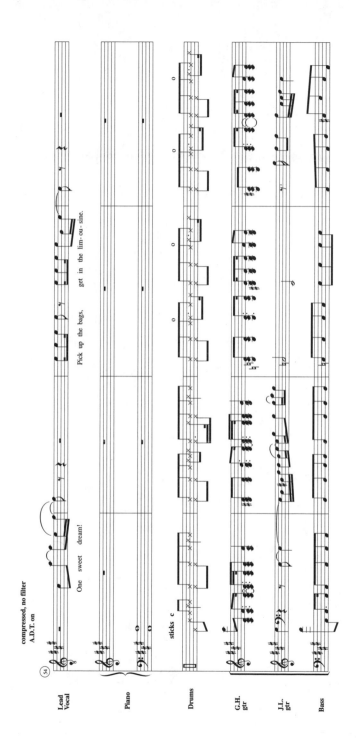

Example 5 (cont.): "You Never Give Me Your Money" (Paul McCartney, Spring 1969)

Example 5 (cont.): "You Never Give Me Your Money" (Paul McCartney, Spring 1969)

Example 5 (cont.): "You Never Give Me Your Money" (Paul McCartney, Spring 1969)

* at splice in bell loop, add cicadas, m. 83.

Example 5 (cont.): "You Never Give Me Your Money" (Paul McCartney, Spring 1969)

Example 5 (cont.): "You Never Give Me Your Money" (Paul McCartney, Spring 1969)

The Beatles' interest in electronic effects also shows in the timbres of "Money." Harrison's guitar is wired through the amplifier and the revolving Leslie speaker of a Hammond organ for a bell-like tone (a favorite effect first used in "Tomorrow Never Knows," for Lennon's voice as well as Harrison's backwards guitar; aside from the havoc wreaked upon upper partials, the Leslie effect combines a tremolo with a Doppler-produced vibrato). Lennon's guitar timbre is also manipulated, apparently through "pre-amp" distortion, achieved by overloading his amplifier with a high-gain setting on the instrument. (Because the piano can be heard acoustically leaking onto the microphone in front of Lennon's guitar amplifier, the distortion could not have been achieved by plugging the guitar directly into the console and thus overloading the board—as had been done for the "Revolution" single, July, 1968—nor was it achieved by adding complex partials with a "fuzz box," used by the Beatles since McCartney's second bass part for "Think for Yourself," November, 1965.) Additionally, in the mixing process, limiters, compressors and filters cut the dynamic range and the outer-range partials of McCartney's vocal and piano beginning in measure 25; the piano sounds as if it might have been recorded at half-speed, a favorite trick of Martin's, presumably so as to evoke a barrelhouse style by calling to mind the honky-tonk piano. During the mixing session, McCartney's vocal in measures 12–15 was also treated to Artificial Double Tracking ("ADT"), a technique that achieves a tape-derived out-of-phase choral effect from a single performance; this color emphasizes the phoniness of the "funny paper" mentioned in measure 12. A touch of tape echo is added to the singer's cadence in measure 23, portraying a "break down" and preparing for the ringing colors of Harrison's guitar, which enters in measure 28 and is faded up high in the mix in measure 33.[28]

"You Never Give Me Your Money" is McCartney's first multi-section through-composed song (Lennon's earlier "Happiness is a Warm Gun" [September, 1968] was the Beatles' first example of such a structure). The sections are numbered below the sketch in Example 6. Part One (mm. 1–24) is a passage heard first on instruments only, then with a single vocal line and finally with three vocal parts, all bemoaning the Beatles' business hassles. Example 6 shows how the passage is based on a 5–8 sequence with sevenths, prolonging primary tone E5 in A minor. A dominant function in measure 24 tonicizes C major for Part Two (mm. 25–32), a repeated phrase based on a descending sixth-progression with parallel thirds below.[29] The

---

28 Limiting, compressing and ADT helped create the "sound" of Revolver (April–June, 1966; Parlophone PCS 7009; August, 1966), *Sgt. Pepper's Lonely Hearts Club Band* (December, 1966–April, 1967; Parlophone PCS 7027; June, 1967) and *Magical Mystery Tour* (April–May, August–October, 1967; Parlophone SMMT-1; December, 1967). For details, see Martin with Hornsby, *All You Need*, pp. 143, 155; Martin in *Audio* (1978): 58 and 60; Harries, "Recording Equipment," p. 244; Lewisohn, *Recording Sessions*, pp. 70, 72; and Howe, *Electronic Music Synthesis*, pp. 65–67.

29 A polyphonic vocal line based on parallel thirds is also featured in Lennon's "Mean Mr.

Part I

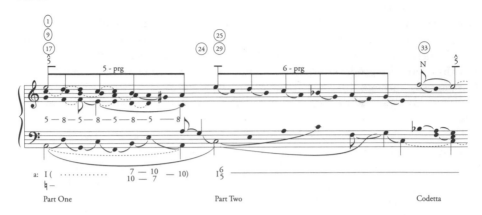

Part II

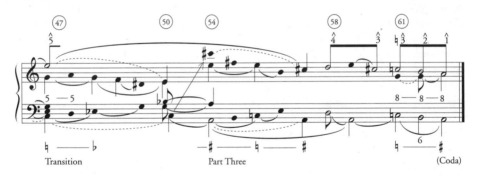

Example 6: "You Never Give Me Your Money"

evocation of nostalgia by the honky-tonk piano and the haze of the filtered colors may also have a "flashback" effect, as the singer remembers a time when he had "nowhere to go." A codetta to Part Two (mm. 33–47) prolongs C major with neighbor functions, B♭ falling to F, which falls to C; the B♭ refers back to Part Two's

Mustard" (part of the Side Two medley), but no particular significance should be attached to this similarity, as McCartney had used this structure many times since one of his earliest compositions, "Love of the Loved" (recorded by the Beatles in January, 1962), memorably in the verse of "Hello Goodbye" (October–November, 1967).

tonicization of IV in measures 26 and 30.[30] The lack of harmonic progression and the suddenly slow harmonic rhythm in new three-measure groupings, heard five times (a pattern that is akin to the gentle middle of "Here Comes the Sun"), characterize the singer's freedom from care. The special "magic feeling" is emphasized by Starr's ride and crash cymbals and by Harrison's ringing Leslie-treated guitar (with triad arpeggiations descending in fourths, which also may recall the middle section of "Sun").

Measures 48–54 constitute a dramatic transition to Part Three. The transition contains three phases: the first (m. 47, fourth beat, to m. 50) introduces both guitars in unison, supported with mixture from the blues-related pentatonic minor scale (spelled C–E♭–F–G–B♭; see E♭ in m. 49), all prolonging primary tone E5. The E♭ of measure 49 prepares the second phase of the transition (mm. 50–53, third beat), wherein an octatonic system (C–C♯–E♭–E♮–F–G–A–B♭) develops B♭ a bit further in a move from C7 to A. Here, tonal centers of C and A battle for primacy in a three-part guitar flourish that alternates major triads and major-minor seventh chords (continuing a pattern begun in the pentatonic-minor colored m. 49) , the roots of which articulate a diminished-seventh cycle, C–E♭–G♭–A, on the downbeats. The third phase (mm. 53–54) supports a chromatic ascent to C♯6 in Harrison's guitar, at which point the A pentatonic system declares victory over that of C.[31]

The transcendence of the motion back to A highlights the text, "one sweet dream, pick up the bags, get in the limousine," which Tim Riley hears as a

---

30 As shown in the lower staff of Example 6, mm. 33–35, the root motions from B♭ to F and from F to C (conveying no harmonic motion) support resolutions of inner-voice neighbors B♭ to A and F to E, respectively. These gentle falling motions, along with the pair of anticipatory oblique voicings (F to F and C to C, respectively), create what will be referred to here as a "double-plagal" cadence.

31 In addition to the earlier "Dear Prudence," *Abbey Road* features Harrison's highest guitar work, probably due more to a growing aural imagination than to increasing technical facility—he had long played lower strings in very high positions. Referring to Harrison's most-used guitars, the C♯6 is at the top of the neck of his Futurama (played for the Beatles in 1960–61), his fireglow twelve-string Rickenbacker (1964–66), his blue Stratocaster (1965–69) and his rosewood Telecaster (1969). The D6 could be sounded (without bending) on Harrison's three Gretsch models (1961–63, 1963–65, 1965–69), his sunburst Casino (1965–67), his red Gibson SG (1966–69), and his Les Paul (1968–69). The Gibson Les Paul is his electric guitar that is probably heard most on *Abbey Road*. Harrison's Beatle-career peaks ascend from G5 in "Everybody's Trying to Be My Baby" (October, 1964) through A5 of "Run for Your Life" (October, 1965) and "Good Morning Good Morning" (February, 1967) to C♯6 in "Octopus's Garden" (April, 1969; *Abbey Road*, Side One) and "You Never Give Me Your Money" (May, 1969); and to D6 "Dear Prudence" (August, 1968) and "Come Together" (July, 1969; *Abbey Road*, Side One). This general ascent does not include the E7 natural harmonic that Harrison played on "Nowhere Man" (October, 1965), but it would be decidedly confirmed were one to consider the line of Leslie-enhanced harmonics that concludes "Oh! Darling": F♯7–C♯7–B6–F♯6–C♯6–A5 (April, 1969; *Abbey Road*, Side One).

suggestion of "the sweeping rush of early fame"—again, McCartney reliving his past.[32] Part Three (mm. 54–68) transposes the first phase of the transition, now heard in A (with pentatonic mixture) (and now with the same boogie guitar chords on A and B—with complete upper neighbors on the highest-sounding string—with which Harrison opened "Eight Days a Week"—in the days of early fame, October, 1964), and then transposes the falling fourths from the Part Two codetta. A measure in slow triple meter (m. 60) heralds the structural close, 3̂–2̂–1̂ (mm. 60–61) in parallel octaves. This close is confirmed by a soulful falsetto an octave above (mm. 66–67).

The coda (mm. 69–88), "one, two, three, four, five, six, seven; all good children go to heaven," sounds like a youth's bedtime prayer (have McCartney's memories reverted that far?) and—with its ten-fold repetition—like another mantra.[33] The coda's ringing guitar figure recalls that of the Part Two codetta (and therefore the contemplative middle section of "Here Comes the Sun").

As bass player and possessor of the Beatles' highest vocal range, McCartney was usually in a good position to demonstrate his gift for melody and countermelody, and his command of consonance and dissonance. A number of his two-part ad-libs captured in the film, *Let It Be* (January, 1969) testify to his natural talent for counterpoint; on *Abbey Road*, his most elegant polyphony appears on his "Maxwell's Silver Hammer" and Harrison's "Something," both on Side One.

Even for a gifted contrapuntist, the power of monophony has great value in rock music. John Covach has a theory that rock musicians may adopt a learned, contrapuntal style when performing on the keyboard (Billy Joel often exemplifies this), while music dominated by electric guitars thrives on the unified energy of parallel fifths and octaves (The Who and Led Zeppelin come to mind).[34] "You Never Give Me Your Money" begins with a piano-oriented linear intervallic pattern and ends with guitar-based structural parallel fifths and octaves, and the transition from one instrumentation to the other is a gradual one that follows a shift in harmonic systems. The "regression" from a learned style to parallel octaves follows the increasing freedom from authority expressed in the poetic text. McCartney's piano, which carries the opening, begins to fade from centerstage when it is overshadowed by the bass; the piano has a lesser role in measures 33–54 and then disappears.

---

32 Tim Riley, *Tell Me Why* (New York: Alfred A. Knopf, 1988), p. 328.

33 Beginning with "Ticket to Ride" (February, 1965) the Beatles appended several songs with highly repetitive codas; notable examples include the "Maori finale" of "Hello Goodbye" (October, 1967) and especially the trance-inducing ending of "Hey Jude" (July–August, 1968), which is based on the ♭VII–IV–I "double-plagal" pattern discussed in note 30 above. (The "Maori finale" to "Hello Goodbye" was likely so named by one of the principals; it has been referred to thus by fans since so labelled—without explanation—in Mal Evans and Neil Aspinall, "How the Magical E.P.s Were Made," *The Beatles Monthly Book* 54 (January, 1968): 11.)

34 Covach discussed this notion with the writer in November, 1989.

Harrison's guitar takes over gradually; it enters as a rhythm instrument in measure 28 and then dominates the song after its boost of volume in measure 33. This boost is accompanied by the guitarist's switch in measure 33 from the mellow "rhythm" pick-up at the neck to the bright "lead" pick-up at the bridge. As Example 6 shows, Parts One and Two exemplify standard practice in the major-minor system, and the listener might even guess that Part Two is to function as a divider in approaching the dominant of A minor.[35] The neighbor harmonies of the codetta are functional, but here is planted the seed of subtonic harmony (on B♭, which was first heard in Part Two as a chromatic intensification of IV and then in the codetta as the root of the double-plagal IV of IV). This is the chord that is to bring the composer away from the strong tension involving V and I, and into the blues-derived pentatonic scale. Giving further credence to Covach's observation, guitars adorn the transition with the new pentatonic materials. While the harmonic materials are altered in the transition, there is still a strong element of surface counterpoint in the outer parts of the transition as well as its transposition at the beginning of Part Three. It is also revealed here that the C major passage is to play no harmonic role; it is heard in retrospect as preparation for the C of the A pentatonic-minor conclusion, and so is labelled in Example 6 as an inversion of the tonic harmony.

The pentatonic system does not know the harmony of the major-minor system; triads are usually all major (as in the A major, B major, C major and E major chords that open Part Three), because they are simply heard as doublings, in natural overtones, of the pentatonic "roots." These do not normally have harmonic/contrapuntal relationships between them, other than the powerful but primitive passing functions (such as "I"–"II♯"–"III") and neighbor functions (such as "I"–"♭VII"–"I"). As David Lewin has discovered in Debussy, parallel motion is not always a product of voice leading—it does not always represent more than one voice at work.[36] Therefore, the song can end with $\hat{3}$–$\hat{2}$–$\hat{1}$ in parallel octaves (a doubled single voice) in the outer "parts ." A vestige of counterpoint remains with the inner-voice neighbor G4 in the passing chord which "supports" $\hat{2}$.

---

35 Actually, I–III–V–I in minor is not a common structure in rock music. It was used by the Beatles only in McCartney's "Another Girl" (February, 1965), Lennon's "Wait" (June and November, 1965) and McCartney's "Your Mother Should Know" (August–September, 1967).

36 Lewin, "Some Instances of Parallel Voice-Leading in Debussy," *19th Century Music* 11 (1987): 59–72. Edward T. Cone expresses a similar hearing in an accompanied vocal repertoire that is perhaps more germane to the topic at hand: "The instrumental part may consist of a single line doubling the voice. The troubadours may well have accompanied themselves, or had themselves accompanied, in this way. Hardly more independent is the instrumental part that, while consisting of simple chords rather than pure melodic doubling, is essentially nothing more than an amplification of the vocal line, as in the accompaniments devised by balladeers for performance on lute, guitar, harp, or the like." *The Composer's Voice* (Berkeley: University of California Press, 1974), p. 58. See also Peter Westergaard, *An Introduction to Tonal Theory* (New York: W. W. Norton & Company, Inc., 1975), p. 77.

The coda (mm. 69 ff.; see Ex. 5) alternates C major triads with A major-minor seventh chords, reminding the listener of the transition's octatonic passage involving C7 and A7 chords; the chord tones in the coda are, again, overtone doublings of non-functional roots a third apart, but McCartney sings G-as-octatonic-neighbor-to-A while Lennon sings B♯-as-octatonic-neighbor-to-C♯, as if counterpoint were an issue. Harrison's voice, however, freezes G♮ as a pentatonic member of both chords; the G never really resolves, but remains above the A harmony. In fact, the C major chord is heard as its consonant support. The song's opening chord is, of course, A–C–E–G, and it was a common Beatle effect to end a piece with a dissonant sonority that relates to the work's opening.[37] "All good children go to heaven," even those innocents who create a structural close by singing in octaves with the bass.

One might be tempted to hear a coherent structure in A major articulated by the first three songs of Side Two, especially since "Because" resolves into "You Never Give Me Your Money." This grouping is overridden, however, by the virtually seamless medley that begins with the third song, and by the fact that Part One of "You Never Give Me Your Money" receives an unexpected recapitulation in "Carry That Weight"—lending new structural significance to this third song of the side. It remains now to examine, if only briefly, the nature of the large structure of the medley, from "You Never Give Me Your Money" through "The End."

The concept of the medley seems to have been a joint creation of Martin and McCartney, probably during the month of June, 1969. Both claim credit for the notion: McCartney says, "I wanted to do something bigger, a kind of operatic moment . . . . We wanted to dabble and I had a bit of fun making some of the songs fit together, with the key changes. That was nice, it worked out well."[38] Martin says: "I wanted to try and make side two a continual work. That was Paul and [me] getting together . . . I was trying to get Paul to write stuff that . . . referred back to something else. Bring some form into the thing."[39] Most of the medley songs had

---

37 "A Hard Day's Night" (April, 1964) is a good example of a coda's "frozen" subtonic element that is related to the introduction: this song (in G pentatonic) opens with a strident chord on Harrison's twelve-string Rickenbacker, D3–F3–A3–C4–G4 (thirdless V⁷ function colored by an anticipation of tonic); the song's coda consists of Harrison's alternation of G4 and F4 over C4 and A3 pedals (tonic harmony with non-resolving subtonic neighbors). The song's verse emphasizes the tonic/subtonic relationship.

38 Lewisohn, *Recording Sessions*, p. 14.

39 Martin, interviewed by Chris Hodenfield, *Rolling Stone* 217 (July 15, 1976): 87. Martin has also implied an involvement with the composition as well as the concept: "the segues were my idea, to have a continuous piece of music. Wherever possible we would design a song that way." Lewisohn, *Recording Sessions*, p. 192. In a contemporaneous source, albeit a "fanzine," credit for the concept was given entirely to McCartney. See Frederick James, "In the Studio," *The Beatles Monthly Book* 74 (September, 1969): 10. McCartney's affinity for larger structures is evident in his LP, *Band on the Run* (September, 1973; Apple SO 3415; December, 1973) and

already been composed before Martin was asked to produce a new album: "Mean Mr Mustard" and "Polythene Pam" had been conceived in India (in early 1968). At the time of the filming of *Let It Be* (January, 1969), "She Came In Through the Bathroom Window" was nearly complete and "Sun King" was in a rudimentary form. "You Never Give Me Your Money" was written in the Spring of 1969 and first taped in early May. All of these songs had originally been performed in the same keys as the final versions, and the only change in any of them that might have been made with an ear cocked toward overall unity was Lennon's decision to change the name of Mr. Mustard's sister, Shirley, to Pam. The medley's remaining songs tell a different story. Following the McCartney/Martin phone conversation, recordings for *Abbey Road* began on July 1 with "You Never Give Me Your Money" overdubs; the next day, basic tracks for "Golden Slumbers"/"Carry That Weight" were taped; sessions for "The End" began on July 23. These last two tapings include a number of very clear references to previously-recorded medley songs.

Example 7 presents a deep-level analysis of the medley's tonal structure, showing less detail for the older compositions and more for "Golden Slumbers," "Carry That Weight" and "The End." Lennon's "Mean Mr. Mustard" and "Polythene Pam" are chiefly concerned with inner voices in the V prolongation in A, but McCartney recaptures the upper voice with the now-notorious G♮-in-the-context-of-A, to portray the sudden entry of "She Came in Through the Bathroom Window." The strong instrumental retransition to A that announces "Window" (recorded with the basic tracks of both "Pam" and "Window" on July 25) is based upon descents heard in Lennon's "Mustard" and "Pam"; the two preparatory motions are marked in Example 7 as "α" and the retransition as "α!," which refers to the completion of the line in its return to A. One might guess that McCartney was thinking primarily about this retransition when he spoke of "making some of the songs fit together, with the key changes." One aspect of "Pam" resurfaces in "The End": the former ends with an instrumental jam in which the "neighbor-to-the-neighbor" function, the "double-plagal" ♮VII–IV–I, is the basis of eleven guitar variations; in "The End," the choral section and the famous solos (wherein McCartney, Harrison and Lennon trade lead guitar improvisations) are built upon fourteen hearings of the neighbor relationship I–IV(–I).

More to the point is McCartney's recomposition of "You Never Give Me Your Money" in "Golden Slumbers" and "Carry That Weight." As did "Money," "Slumbers" opens with an A minor seventh chord on the piano (with a new voicing) and begins its structure with falling fifths in the bass (bracketed in Example 7 and marked "β"). The bracket labelled "γ" marks a quotation from the

---

even more so in his eight-movement "Liverpool Oratorio" (EMI CDS 7 54371 2), a concert work for orchestra, chorus, boys' choir and soloists (co-written with Carl Davis) that received its première in June, 1991.

Part I

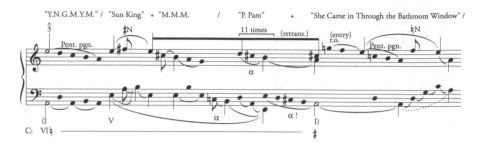

Part II

Part III

Example 7: Side Two Medley

structure of Part Two of "Money," and those marked "δ" indicate three different passages in "Slumbers" and "Weight" that recompose the C–B–A bass line from the coda of "Money." In the last version, "δ3," Harrison's guitar quotes the "Money" coda. Of course, the arrival point in "Weight" marked "recap."

(introduced by the "δ" motive) is a complete rehearing of the foreground diminution of Part One of "Money." [40]

McCartney's twist is that "Money" is now heard in the context of C major. Robert Gauldin has discussed the relationships between the tonal areas of C and A in *Abbey Road* in terms of Wagnerian "double-tonic" juxtapositions, and many examples of C–A relationships can be seen throughout Example 7, as well as in other *Abbey Road* compositions.[41] The medley's most telling juxtaposition of A and C comes in "The End," at the moment the tonicized A major moves to II of C. In Example 7, this point is marked with the text, "and in the end"; the full score of the passage is given as Example 8. The final cadence of the medley (followed only by a brief plagal coda that refers back to Part Three of "Money") sets the text, "and in the end the love you take is equal to the love you make," so that both a tonal and a metric modulation occur precisely on the word "equal," the word that separates the two halves of the equation.[42]

Despite the extremely varied circumstances of composition for the various medley songs (and also the fact that most of the basic composition was complete

---

40 Given that "Slumbers" was composed while McCartney was visiting Liverpool (in May or June, 1969?), previous to the group's return to the studio in July, it is highly unlikely that Martin had much input into that composition. "Weight," on the other hand, sounds very much to this listener as if it could have been composed in the studio with help from all on hand, and Martin might very well have suggested the return of the "δ" motive, if not the recapitulation of the "Money" theme. It seems likely that Martin and McCartney made a joint decision about the hard edit joining "Carry That Weight" and "The End."

41 Robert Gauldin, "Beethoven, Tristan, and The Beatles," *College Music Symposium* 30 (1990): 142–52. Robert Bailey credits Guido Adler with the embrace of fluctuating tonal centers in Wagner's *Tristan* Prelude and discusses the alternating pair, A and C, as a "double-tonic complex" in the whole of Act I of the same work. Robert Bailey, ed., *Wagner: Prelude and Transfiguration from Tristan and Isolde*, Norton Critical Scores (New York: W. W. Norton & Company, Inc., 1985), pp. 116–17, 121–25, 134–38. The double-tonic complex is also operative in early Beatle compositions, "She Loves You" (1963), "Not a Second Time" (1963) and "Girl" (1965) among them.

42 Lennon found this line of verse to be "a very cosmic, philosophical line," one of his few public compliments for McCartney's poetry (Golson, ed., *The Playboy Interviews*, p. 213). The text is certainly in sympathy with Lennon's essential line in the middle of "Because." Due to an altered tape speed, the intonation in this portion of "The End" is unnervingly more than a quarter-tone sharp; McCartney belatedly corrected this error by performing a medley of "Golden Slumbers" / "Carry That Weight" / "The End," all well in tune, during his 1989–90 world tour. One live recording can be heard on the tour album, *Tripping the Live Fantastic* (Capitol CDP 7 94778 2; November, 1990). What has been referred to as a "metric modulation," as in the work of Elliott Carter, is perhaps more properly understood as a modulation of tempos that pivots on sub-metrical relationships. Thus, simple groupings of eighths (Ex. 8, m. 6), while retaining their individual durations, are regrouped as compound triplets (m. 7, a move encouraged by the vocal syncopations in mm. 3 and 5) and the new beat duration is in turn divided once again into two simple eighths (m. 8), resulting in a tempo one-third slower than the original.

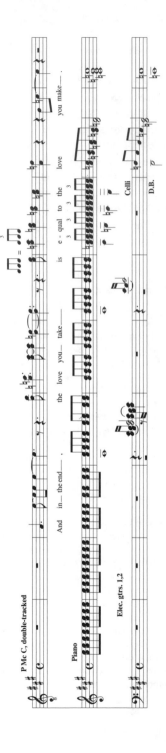

Example 8: "The End" (Paul McCartney, July, 1969)

before the concept of the medley was voiced), one searches for an overarching theme in this group of songs that were chosen and joined in a very conscious manner. The juxtaposition of A and C seems to be a central concern, and certainly a clue exists in "Golden Slumbers," wherein a desire to find a way home is sung in A minor, and the consequence of the return, a lullaby, is set in C major; A contains tension and C, repose. Much of the poetic text of the medley deals with selfishness and self-gratification—the financial complaints in "You Never Give Me Your Money ," the miserliness of Mr. Mustard, the holding back of the pillow in "Carry That Weight," the desire that some second person will visit the singer's dreams (perhaps the "one sweet dream" of "Money"?) in "The End"; these are all set in the context of the tonal center of A. Generosity is expressed in the comfort offered in "Golden Slumbers"; in "Carry That Weight," the group can be heard to admonish the singer to stop being so selfish (recall McCartney's preoccupation with his personal financial difficulties); these are the points where C is central. A great compromise in the "negotiations" is finally achieved in the equation of "The End"—apparently McCartney has understood the repeated C major choruses, because he comes to the earth-shaking realization that there is only as much self-gratifying love ("the love you take"), that of A major, as there is of the generous kind ("the love you make"), that of C major. While not an unusual theme for the Beatles (and certainly one of central importance to Lennon, as in "The Word" [November, 1965] and "All You Need Is Love" [June, 1967]), it seems rewarding to hear this uplifting message as a very personal final gift from McCartney to his mates, as well as from the Beatles to the world.[43]

43 The writer is pleased to thank the Horace H. Rackham School of Graduate Studies for awarding a Rackham Faculty Fellowship to make this research possible. Portions of this essay were presented to the City University Music Analysis Conference, London (September, 1991).

DISCOGRAPHY

The Beatles. *Abbey Road*. First pressings: Apple PCS 7088 (released in U.K., September 26, 1969), Apple SO 383 (released in U.S., October 1, 1969). Digital remastering for compact disc: Parlophone 7 46446 2 (released October 20, 1987).

──────. *The Beatles Tapes from the David Wigg Interviews*. Polydor 2683 068 (released in U.K., July 30, 1976).

──────. *Watching Rainbows*. "Audifon L–7." Unauthorized release (probably late 1970's).

──────. *The Beatles Live at Abbey Road Studios*. "ARS Z–9083." Unauthorized release (early 1984).

──────. *Return to Abbey Road*. "NW–8." Unauthorized release (late 1985).

──────. *Ultra Rare Trax Vol. 5 & 6*. "Swinging Pig Records: TR 2191 S." Unauthorized release (1988).

John Ono Lennon and Yoko Ono Lennon. *The Wedding Album*, Apple SMAX 3361 (released first in U.S., October 20, 1969).

Structural Factors in the Microcanonic Compositions of György Ligeti[1]

Jane Piper Clendinning

Introduction to the Microcanonic Compositions

After his arrival in the West in 1956, György Ligeti began to develop a new compositional technique that he called "micropolyphony"—a kind of counterpoint in which multiple musical lines are combined to form a dense polyphonic texture. In Ligeti's micropolyphonic compositions, the listener's ear is drawn to the overall texture, rather than the interplay of individual lines as in traditional contrapuntal contexts. Ligeti comments:

> Both *Atmosphères* and *Lontano* have a dense canonic structure. But you cannot actually hear the polyphony, the canon. You hear a kind of impenetrable texture, something like a very densely woven cobweb . . . The polyphonic structure does not actually come through, you cannot hear it; it remains hidden in a microscopic, under-water world, to us inaudible. I call it micropolyphony (such a beautiful word!). All in all, you cannot hear my music as it appears on paper. Of course, while actually composing each piece I worked on what we hear, as we hear it.[2]

In developing his micropolyphony, Ligeti drew upon his knowledge of tonal and modal contrapuntal techniques and on his study of twentieth-century serial counterpoint (particularly the music of Anton Webern and Boulez's *Structures Ia*), but his method is not dependent on tonal, modal, or serial systems.[3] However, he

---

1 The research material in this essay is a condensed and revised version of material appearing in the author's dissertation, *Contrapuntal Techniques in the Music of György Ligeti* (Ph.D. diss., Yale University, 1989). Portions of this essay were presented as a paper at the 1988 Society for Music Theory National Conference in Baltimore, Md.

2 Peter Varnai, "Beszélgetések Ligeti Györggyel" (1978), tr. Gabor J. Schabert in *Ligeti in Conversation* (London: Eulenberg Books, 1983), pp. 14–15.

3 There are numerous references to the influence of past masters of counterpoint on Ligeti's style in Péter Várnai's interview with Ligeti. See particularly pp. 14–15, 30, 35–36, 49–51, and 71. Ligeti's analysis of Boulez's *Structures Ia* is published in his article "Pierre Boulez," in *Die Reihe* 4: *Young Composers* (Bryn Mawr: Theodore Presser, 1960), pp. 36–62.

did adapt techniques traditionally associated with counterpoint such as canon, imitation, and compound melody in combining melodic strands into his micropolyphonic fabric. In his compositions, as in traditional counterpoint, the contrapuntal lines interact to form harmonies.

Many of the micropolyphonic compositions composed after 1965 belong to a particular subcategory of micropolyphony that I have labeled *microcanon*, defined as a polyphonic texture formed from a pitch succession set canonically in many voices at short time intervals. Although the original ordering of the pitches is strictly maintained in all canonic voices, the durations of pitches in each canonic strand are adjusted by the composer to control the flow and registral shape of the piece more precisely and to create the desired vertical alignments. The performance instructions in each of the microcanonic compositions indicate that the tones are to enter imperceptibly, with no audible accents except the rare ones indicated in the score. The varying metrical placement of each canon tone in the various voice parts, the rarity of pitches entering on the notated beats, and the required method of articulation result in an absence of a perceptible beat or meter. The microcanon is typically set at the unison, restricting the operable range to that of the original pitch succession.[4] The canonic voices may begin simultaneously, then diverge to start the canon or begin with staggered entrances. In some canonic sections, the canon is accompanied by sustained pitches or a second canon.

Ligeti's compositions written in the years 1965–68 include a group of pieces in which microcanon is the primary feature of construction: the Kyrie from the Requiem (1963–65), *Lux aeterna* (1966), *Lontano* (1967), and the ninth movement of the *Ten Pieces for Wind Quintet* (1968). Later compositions that include microcanon or a recognizable extension of it in combination with other techniques form a second grouping: *Ramifications* (1968–69), the *Chamber Concerto* (1969–70), the "Selbstportrait" movement of *Three Pieces for Two Pianos* (1976), the *Drei Phantasien* (1982), and the *Magyar Etüdök* (1983).[5] Although there have been a number of studies considering one or another of the microcanonic compositions, most of the analytical literature on these works has been limited in scope to consideration of a single piece, and, in some cases, to a single aspect of one piece.[6] The limitations in scope of many of the previous studies

---

4 In most of the microcanonic pieces, the pitch succession is set in canon at the unison, but in *Lontano*, with the availability of orchestral resources, entire canonic textures are sometimes doubled at one or more octave multiples.

5 All of the microcanonic compositions listed and many of Ligeti's other contrapuntally-based compositions dating between 1965 and 1984 are considered in detail in Clendinning, *Contrapuntal Techniques*. The reader is referred to that source for more extensive analytical information on the compositions discussed in this article.

6 The studies of *Lux aeterna* and *Lontano* by Jonathan W. Bernard are notable exceptions: Jonathan W. Bernard, "Inaudible Structures, Audible Music: Ligeti's Problem and his Solution," *Music Analysis* 6 (1987): 207–36; and "Voice Leading as a Spatial

have caused the authors to overlook important aspects of the compositions[7] and have precluded the development of a generalized view of Ligeti's microcanonic technique.[8] Examination of these compositions as a group enables the analyst to draw conclusions on the basis of all the evidence that is available.

Microcanonic procedures are employed in substantial portions of each of the compositions in the first group, but the technique is explored in a slightly different way in each piece. The Kyrie from the Requiem, the earliest of the compositions included in this category, anticipates many of the procedures developed more fully in the later compositions, but differs significantly from them in its large-scale construction and diverges slightly in aspects of small-scale structure.[9] Ligeti views the Requiem and the choral composition that followed, *Lux aeterna*, which sets an

---

Function in the Music of Ligeti," in *Music Analysis* 13 (1994): 227–53. In each of his articles aspects of the microcanonic compositions are considered in conjunction with other works by Ligeti.

Among the studies limited to a single composition are those of *Lontano* by Reiprich and Rollin and that of *Lux aeterna* by Jarvlepp: Bruce Reiprich, "Transformation of Coloration and Density in György Ligeti's *Lontano*," *Perspectives of New Music* 16 (1978): 167–80; Robert Leon Rollin, "Ligeti's *Lontano*: Traditional Canonic Technique in a New Guise," *Music Review* 41 (1980): 289–96; Rollin, "The Genesis of Canonic Sound Mass in Ligeti's *Lontano*," *Indiana Theory Review* 2/2 (1978–9): 23–33; Rollin "The Process of Textural Change and the Organization of Pitch in Ligeti's *Lontano*" (D.M.A. Thesis, Cornell University, 1973); Jan Jarvlepp, "Pitch and Texture Analysis of Ligeti's *Lux aeterna*," *ex tempore* 2/1 (1982): 16–32.

The rather interesting study of *Lux aeterna* by Robert Cogan approaches that composition through spectrum analysis. See Robert Cogan, "György Ligeti: *Lux aeterna*," in *New Images of Musical Sound* (Cambridge, Mass.: Harvard University Press, 1984), pp. 39–43.

There are two published analytical studies of the *Ten Pieces for Wind Quintet*: Monika Lichtenfeld, "*Zehn Stücke für Bläserquintett* von György Ligeti," *Melos* 39 (1972): 326–33; and Charles D. Morrison, "Stepwise Continuity as a Structural Determinant in György Ligeti's *Ten Pieces for Wind Quintet*," *Perspectives of New Music* 24 (1985): 158–82. Neither author discusses the ninth movement in detail.

7 In the studies of *Lontano* by Reiprich and Rollin, the failure to recognize the intimate connections between the canon melodies of *Lontano* and *Lux aeterna* led both of these authors to concentrate on the "connections" between "canon melody fragments" in *Lontano* that are simply segments of a continuous canon melody (see note 11 for details regarding the connections between these two compositions).

8 For example, Jarvlepp noticed the prevalence of "neighbor" motion, but was unable to determine whether "this is coincidental or a deliberate compositional device" (Jarvlepp, p. 19).

9 In the Kyrie, two contrasting types of pitch successions are set in canon in up to twenty parts (five voice-part groups with four parts each). The two distinct types of lines interact throughout the movement, forming a continuous contrapuntal texture resistant to division into the clear sections typical of the later microcanonic pieces. The construction of the pitch successions and the implementation of canonic settings within voice-part groups are similar in the Kyrie and later microcanonic compositions. Although the Requiem is a landmark work in Ligeti's output, the work as a whole has received little attention in the analytical literature. For a detailed study of the Kyrie movement, see Clendinning, pp. 124–9.

associated text, as the end of one stylistic period and the beginning of another.[10] In many ways, *Lux aeterna* can be considered the archetypical microcanonic composition—the canonic sections and the means by which they are combined are relatively straightforward. *Lontano*, the orchestral piece that follows *Lux aeterna*, presents more of an analytical challenge in comparison to the preceding composition because of its complex orchestration and its length. Ligeti often refers to these two compositions as a pair, with good reason—in addition to similarities in construction and concept, the pitch successions set in canon in *Lontano* are derived from those of *Lux aeterna*.[11] The ninth of the *Ten Pieces for Wind Quintet*, one of ten miniatures each featuring a different combination of compositional techniques and instrumentation, is like an abbreviated single section of the longer vocal and orchestral compositions that preceded it. Despite slight variations in the implementation of microcanonic compositional techniques within this group of compositions, the basic elements of that technique and the resulting large and small structures are similar in each of these pieces.

Ligeti's micropolyphonic composition differ from traditional counterpoint in that the fine details and, in many cases, the individual lines are not readily noticed by the listener. In listening to Ligeti's micropolyphonic compositions, some individual linear details stand out, but the strongest impression is created at a higher level of the structure by the harmonies and registral gestures formed by the individual lines. Ligeti states this concisely: "polyphony is what is written, harmony is what is heard."[12]

---

10 Ursula Stürzbecher, "György Ligeti" in *Werkstattgespräche mit Komponisten* (Cologne: Musikverlag Gerig, 1971), p. 45; Pierre Michel, "Entretiens avec György Ligeti" in *György Ligeti: Compositeur d'aujourd'hui* (Paris: Minerve, 1985), p. 174.

11 Treated section by section, the relationship between the canon melodies of *Lux aeterna* and *Lontano* is as follows: The succession of 31 pitches that is set in canon in the first section (mm. 1–37) of *Lux aeterna* appears complete in section 1 (mm. 1–41) of *Lontano*, transposed up 3 semitones. The first 28 pitches of the first canon from the second section (mm. 39–88) of *Lux aeterna* are transposed down 4 semitones to form the pitch succession of the first canon in *Lontano* section 3 (mm. 122–65). The last six pitches from the end of this *Lux aeterna* pitch succession do not appear in the *Lontano* canons. The pitch interval succession formed by the initial 14 pitches of the first canon from *Lux aeterna* section 2 is inverted beginning on G4 (G above middle C) to form the second canon in *Lontano* section 3. The pitch succession from *Lontano* section 2 (mm. 56–110) is derived from several *Lux aeterna* pitch successions: the initial 10 pitches are a transposition down three semitones of the succession in *Lux aeterna* section 2 canon 2; pitches 10 to 20 are the initial 11 pitches of the succession from of *Lux aeterna* section 3 (mm. 90–126) transposed up 13 semitones; three pitches are inserted; then pitches 24 to 36 of the *Lontano* succession follow the *Lux aeterna* section 3 succession as before, beginning with pitch 12 and continuing to pitch 24 of the *Lux aeterna* succession. At that point, the succession from *Lontano* diverges from the *Lux aeterna* succession and begins to circle through a group of pitches, gradually dropping out pitches one at a time. For charts illustrating these correspondences and additional information see Clendinning, pp. 209–12 and 86–152.

12 György Ligeti, Program notes on *Lontano* (Wergo recording WER 60 095 [LP], 1984). In this essay, I will use the term *harmony* as Ligeti does, to refer to the vertical combinations created

Ligeti's emphasis on the harmonic aspect of these compositions raises an obvious question: if the harmonies and registral shaping are to be the most noticeable features of the microcanonic compositions, why did the composer write such carefully controlled canonic structures? He responds:

> The canon allowed me to write melodically a certain succession that I wanted to render simultaneously, vertically. Thus, the canon is a medium of gradually developing a simultaneity. I use canons so dense that one hears, not the polyphonic fabric, but a vertical homogeneity which changes unceasingly.[13]

And adds:

> The canon offers the possibility of composing a fabric of melodic strands according to well-defined rules of construction ... If you asked me "why the canon?," I would respond for horizontal/vertical unity.[14]

Ligeti's technique of microcanon fulfills his expressed need for a compositional method that provides internal structure and coherence, building upon canonic procedures of past masters of counterpoint whom he admires, yet moves beyond the techniques of previous generations to develop new contrapuntal methods and explore novel sonic possibilities.

Analytical Approach

This essay concerns the relationship between the canonic construction and the resulting structures of the microcanonic compositions on three levels: 1) the *microstructure*, 2) the *audible surface*, and 3) the *macrostructure*. The term *microstructure* refers to the smallest-scale elements of the musical structure—the note-to-note construction of linear strands and the interaction of simultaneously sounding lines in forming individual harmonies. Although the details of this level

---

by pitches that sound at the same time. His use of the term harmony does not imply such tonal constructs as the reduction of the many possible vertical combinations to a few prototypes by invoking the concepts of octave equivalence and the invertible triad and seventh chord, or harmonic function determined by the prevalent scale or key; nor does it imply a simultaneous attack of the pitches in the harmony (pitches could have entered at different times, but continue to sound forming a harmony).

13 "Le canon me permet d'écrire mélodiquement une certaine succession que je veux rendre simultanée, verticale. Le canon est ainsi un moyen de développer graduellement une simultanéité. J'utilise des canons tellement denses que l'on n'entend pas le tissu polyphonique, mais une homogénéité verticale qui change sans cesse" (Michel, *György Ligeti*, p. 163).

14 "Le canon offre la possibilité de composer une toile de fils mélodiques selon des règles de construction assez bien définies ... Si vous me demandez: "pourquoi le canon?", je vous répondrai pour l'unité horizontal/vertical" (Ibid., p. 152, my translation).

are not readily audible, they are essential to the coherence of the structure of the composition because the audible larger structures of the piece are built from them. The role of the small-scale construction of pitch successions and the combination of the lines in canon in the creation of particular pervasive harmonies will also be examined.

The shaping of complete lines and the action of lines and harmonies in the formation of phrases and sections belong to the middle level—the *audible surface*. At this level, the small-scale harmonic, linear, and rhythmic aspects of the composition unite to create the registral/temporal shapings typical of these compositions. In the longer microcanonic compositions, discrete sections are combined to make a large-scale form or *macrostructure*.

A close analysis of the first section of *Lux aeterna* introduces the analytical method and relevant terminology; here the interaction of linear, harmonic, registral, and pacing aspects show typical means of shaping sections in the microcanonic compositions as a group. Structural elements shared by the microcanonic compositions are then examined by topic with examples from other sections of various microcanonic compositions.

Examination of a Typical Microcanonic Section:
The Opening of *Lux aeterna*

The opening of *Lux aeterna* illustrates basic features of the microcanonic construction and the means by which sections are shaped. The macrostructure of *Lux aeterna* consists of three large canonic sections linked by *sectional connectors* made of sustained harmonies (Figure 1). Each connector begins as the preceding canonic section nears completion and ends after the following canonic section begins over it. The connectors in this work are distinguished from the canonic sections by the simultaneous entry of the pitches that make up the connector, which contrasts with the staggered entries of pitches in the canonic portions, as well as by timbre, range, or both. In each case, the connections are smoothed by duplication in the connector of the pitches or pitch classes with which the adjacent canons begin and end. The first and last sections of *Lux aeterna* are built from a single line set in canon, with the second featuring two distinct canons I have labeled Canon A and Canon B. All three sections include sustained pitches or simultaneities that are independent of the canon, whose placement is indicated in Figure 1.

The first section extends from the beginning of the composition to m. 37. In this section, a 31-tone pitch succession (shown in Example 1)[15] is set against itself in canon

---

15 In this essay, *tone* will be used to refer to a pitch in a specific order position in a particular pitch succession. The order positions, numbered beginning with 1, are indicated on the examples showing canon pitch successions.

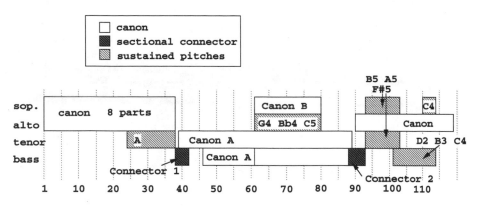

Figure 1: Macrostructure, *Lux aeterna*

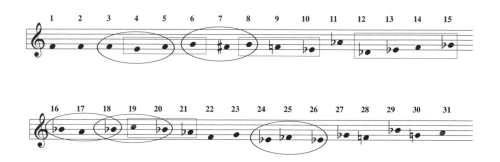

Example 1: Canon Melody, *Lux aeterna*, Section 1, mm. 1–37

at the unison at short time intervals in the eight voices of the soprano and alto parts (see Example 2). The tones of the succession are sounded in the order shown in Example 1 in each voice, without repetition with the exception of the last tone, which is repeated until all voices have finished the canon.[16] The individual voices do not move through the line at the same rate. After all voices complete the first tone of the canon (by m. 5), some sound each tone briefly before moving to the next while

---

16 Since the three-fold repetition of the first pitch (F4) is consistent in all of the statements of the pitch succession, that repeated pitch has been counted as three ordered tones. The last tone of the canon line is not repeated a consistent number of times in the presentation of the canon in various voices, and has been represented as a single canon tone.

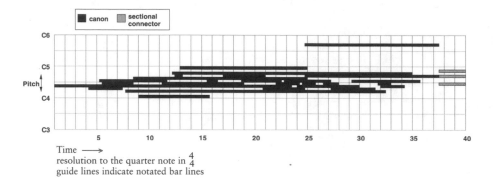

Figure 2: Range Graph, *Lux aeterna*, Section 1

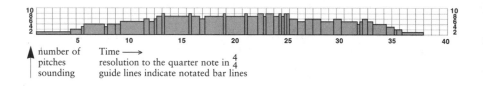

Figure 5: Pitch Count Graph, *Lux aeterna*, Section 1

others linger on each tone, with the resulting variation between voices in the duration of canon tones causing an increase from one or two canon tones sounding at the same time in mm. 1–4 to four to six in mm. 6–13.

Many aspects of the music combine to create the audible shaping of the beginning and end of this section. The section begins with an opening gesture typical of these pieces—a registral expansion and an acceleration of activity. To the listener, the spread in range covered from a single pitch to a span of eleven semitones [11] (by m. 13) is perhaps the most noticeable manifestation of the expansion.[17] The registral expansion is illustrated in Figure 2 by a *range graph*. In the

---

17 I will indicate harmonic (vertical) pitch intervals and interval stacks by integers in square brackets, each of which indicates the number of semitones of a harmonic interval (for example, [11] for a span of 11 semitones and [3][2] for minor third/major second), with the intervals listed from the lowest to the highest. Since registral placement is important in Ligeti's musical

236

Structural Factors in the Microcanonic Compositions of György Ligeti

LUX AETERNA

Example 2: *Lux aeterna* (Peters Edition No. 5934) mm. 1–8

range graphs, the divisions on the y-axis of the graph represent a semitone of the chromatic scale. The Acoustical Society of America pitch designations for C's (pitch class integer 0) are given along the left side of the graph.[18] Horizontal dotted lines are provided between pitch classes 0 and 1 and between 6 and 7 to serve as guide lines. The divisions on the x-axis of the graph represent a durational unit (usually the notated beat unit from the meter signature of the composition) as indicated in the labeling of the graph.[19] Groups of durational units corresponding to bar lines in the score are indicated by vertical dotted guide lines. All pitches sounding in any part within a particular durational unit are shaded, showing the registral distribution of pitches sounding in relation to time.[20]

The expansion of range at the beginning of *Lux aeterna* is reinforced both by an acceleration in the pacing of activity and by increasing complexity of the harmonies. *Pacing* can be defined as a measure of audible "motion" in a passage of music. Two types of motion are identifiable in the microcanonic compositions: *structural motion,* in which the music seems to be moving forward at a faster or slower rate than previously; and *surface motion,* in which there is more or less activity, without there necessarily being an associated change in the forward motion. The two types of motion are affected by distinct but interrelated means. The level of surface activity is affected by the number of events that occur in a span

---

structures, intervals rather than interval classes will be designated unless otherwise noted. This method of indicating vertical distances between two pitches follows the practice of Jonathan W. Bernard in *The Music of Edgard Varèse* (New Haven: Yale University Press, 1987), p. ix.

18 The Acoustical Society of America pitch designations (middle C = C4; the C one octave above middle C is C5; B a half step below middle C is B3; etc.) will be used throughout for labeling of pitches.

19 In the range graphs, as in the other graphic tools that will be employed in this analytical approach, the graph represents information accurately only to the resolution of the time unit that is selected. The goal in selecting the time units for these graphs was to choose those that provide sufficient reduction of information to be useful in analysis without unacceptable loss of detail. In that the measure beginnings are not metrically accented, the selection of measures as the unit in which to represent the counts is arbitrary. The graphs differ slightly in detail if other groupings of the same length are examined.

20 Many scholars, including Uve Urban, Pozzi Escot, and Jonathan Bernard, have found this type of graph useful for examination of registral/temporal relationships in Ligeti's compositions. See Uve Urban, "Serielle Technik und barocker Geist in Ligitis Cembalo-Stuck *Continuum*," *Musik und Bildung* 5 (1973): 63–70; Pozzi Escot, "Charm'd Magic Casements," in *Contiguous Lines: Issues and Ideas in the Music of the '60's and '70's*, ed. Thomas DeLio (Lanham, Md.: University Press of America, 1985), pp. 31–56; and Jonathan Bernard, "Inaudible Structures" and "Voice Leading."

The graphics in this essay were developed using a Macintosh computer and the MacDraw II graphics program published by Claris Corporation, with the analytical information entered by hand for each illustration. For general information regarding the use of graphic illustrations for analysis and recent developments in computer graphics generated automatically from a score input file, see Alexander Brinkman and Martha Mesiti, "Graphic Modeling of Musical Structure," *Computers in Music Research* 3 (1991): 1–42.

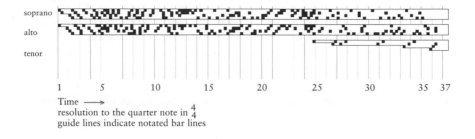

Figure 3: Entrance Graph, *Lux aeterna*, Section 1

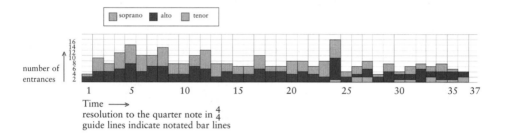

Figure 4: Entrance Graph Summary, *Lux aeterna*, Section 1

of time. Changes in the rate of events can be accessed in these pieces by locating and counting the number of articulations and rearticulations of pitches and comparing the counts in various parts of the section or composition. The placement of the entrances of tones in particular voice-leading strands are illustrated in an entrance graph (Figure 3). In this graph, each unit on the *x*-axis represents a time unit as indicated on the graph's legend (usually a quarter note duration). Each voice part is represented on a separate horizontal strip, with strips ordered according to voice-part groups. A square is shaded in each voice part strip for each time unit in which a tone is attacked in that voice part. For ease in locating trends in the fluctuation of the number of entrances, the total number of entrances in measure have also been represented in a bar graph (Figure 4) aligned under the entrance graph, with the contributions of the various voice-part groups indicated by shading. The grouping into measures reduces the accuracy of the information presented for any particular point, but provides an average to indicate larger trends.

The sense of structural motion is created not so much by the amount of activity but by the nature of the activity. Audible changes of pitch, in which the music seems to "move" to new harmonies, contribute more to a sense of forward motion than do rearticulations of a fixed pitch or set of pitches, even though the rate at which tones sound is not changed. Structural motion in this music is analogous to the harmonic rhythm, or the rate of harmonic change, in tonal contexts. The range spanned, the degree of registral filling, and the number of distinct pitches sounding in a span of time are all visible on the range graph, Figure 2. However, the information regarding the number of distinct pitches sounding at a point in time and the rate of harmonic change is easier to evaluate directly with the registral information removed. In the pitch count graph, Fig. 5 (aligned under the range graph Fig. 2 to which it is related) the number of pitches sounding in a time unit are represented in a bar graph, with the perimeter lines of the bars indicating a change in pitch content. Since the intervallic combinations making up the harmonies are non-functional, not implying a resolution, harmonies cannot be classified based on their functional "distance" from a consonant sonority. I will refer to harmonies as ranging from simple to complex based on the number of distinct pitches included in the vertical segment, with harmonies with fewer pitch elements "simpler" and those with more pitch elements "complex."

As Figure 2 shows, the harmonic component in the opening of this section has changed from a unison—perhaps the most stable of harmonies—in mm. 1–3 through a chromatically-filled span of three semitones in mm. 5–7 to a simultaneous Db4–Eb4–F4–Gb4–Ab4–Bb4–C5 diatonic collection in mm. 13–15. By m. 13, the number of pitches sounding (Figure 5) has increased gradually from one to seven, and remains at seven or eight until m. 25. (The counts of eight in the middle section are due to the temporal overlapping of a departing pitch with one that is entering the texture.) Although the number of entrances in a time unit fluctuates throughout the section, the count is generally high at the beginning, decreasing after m. 13 to remain relatively stable in the middle of the section. To the listener, the motion from the opening gesture to the midsection to the closing is so gradual that the midsection is distinguishable simply by its relative lack of registral expansion or contraction. The midsection is characterized by static registral outer boundaries (Eb4 and C5, a span of [9]) and shifting internal filling, with all but two or three of the pitches encompassed in the span sounding at any given time.

The section ends with one of two closing gestures typical of the microcanonic composition–contraction accompanied by deceleration of pacing. The closing of the section is signalled by the entrance of the final tone of the canon with an octave doubling (A5), the only deviation from the presentation of the canon pitch succession at the unison, reinforced by the entrance of the tenor section on A4 in m. 24. The dramatic entrance of the A5 and of the tenor section is prepared by a flurry of activity in the preceding measure, which has the greatest number of entrances and the most rapid harmonic changes of the entire section. The separation of the A5 from the rest of the canon by an unfilled registral span emphasizes the role of this pitch as an octave doubling.[21] At this point, the range span excluding the octave doubling of the final A of the canon shrinks to a span of [7] (E♭4 to B♭4) in mm. 25–32, then the range shrinks gradually (mm. 32–35) as the individual voices gradually reach the end of the canon pitch succession and repeat the final tone. As the canon winds down, the number of pitches sounding at once decreases and there are fewer entrances in the three voice part groups than there were in two voice part groups in the previous subsections. Finally, as the last voices reach the final tone, the harmony thins to the octave A's, closing the section on a sustained stable interval.

All of the structural elements contributing to the sense of sectional shaping that have been discussed so far are a part of the audible surface—the middle level. These result from the microstructure of the composition, in particular, the note-to-note construction of the pitch succession and the harmonies resulting from the canon. The pitch succession of this section is primarily conjunct, with an emphasis on two patterns made of pitch intervals [1] and/or [2] (I will refer to these small intervals traditionally called the half step and the whole step, respectively, as "steps"). The first pattern, the *returning step formation* (circled on Example 1), looks like "upper or lower neighbor" patterns of tonal music with the pitch interval of [1] or [2] ascending or descending followed by the same pitch interval in the opposite direction to return to the initial pitch, but the visual similarity does not correspond to a functional one in this non-tonal context. The initial and final pitch in the returning step formation are not "prolonged."[22] Because of the type of texture used in the microcanonic compositions, repetition of a pitch can cause it to be emphasized, but does not necessarily do so if the repeated pitch is buried in the middle of the texture.[23] When set in canon, the returning step formations keep the

---

21 For Ligeti's comments on his use of octave doublings as a cadential gesture at the end of sections see the Várnai interview, pp. 28–31 and 44.

22 Joseph Straus argues forcefully in his article "The Problem of Prolongation in Post-Tonal Music" *Journal of Music Theory* 31 (1987): 1–21, for restrictions of use of the term "prolongation" for contexts that meet four conditions which he specifies: 1) the "consonance-dissonance condition"—there must be "a consistent, pitch-defined basis for determining structural weight"; 2) the "scale-degree condition"—there must be "a consistent hierarchy of consonant harmonies"; 3) the "embellishment condition"—there must be "a consistent set of relationships between tones of lesser and greater structural weight"; and 4) the "harmony/voice-leading condition"—there must be "a clear distinction between the vertical and horizontal dimensions" (pp. 2–6 with discussion following). In Ligeti's microcanonic compositions, the first three conditions are not met—there is no consistent hierarchy of relationships between the pitches and there is no opposition of consonant and dissonant elements. There are emphasized pitches and harmonies in these compositions, but their importance is established in the local context by duration, repetition, or registral or timbral isolation.

23 For example, the initial pitch of the first section of *Lux aeterna*, F4, is emphasized by its entry alone, and remains sounding in at least one voice part for most of the section. However, it does not continue to be as noticeable in the middle portion of the section when it is subsumed in a fuller texture.

initial and final tone of the three tone pattern sounding and restrict the range spanned by the canon at the beginning and end of the section.

The other common pattern, the *unidirectional step formation* (boxed on Example 1), consists of an ascending or descending stepwise succession of pitches that look like fragments of traditional scales (tonal, modal, whole-tone, octatonic, and others) but frequently do not correspond to a segment of any familiar scale. Although unidirectional step formations appear "scale-like," they may in some cases more accurately be considered arpeggiations of harmonies, since prominent harmonic structures in these compositions are made of [1]'s and [2]'s.[24] Unidirectional step formations, when set in canon, correspond to the expanded range and gradual changes in harmonies in the middle of the section.[25]

General Characteristics of the Microcanonic Compositions

Harmony

For the compositional techniques in Ligeti's microcanonic compositions to be classified technically as "counterpoint," the combination of melodic lines should "be brought into agreement through some deliberated principles, such as those of harmony."[26] Ligeti's canons do form harmonies in a consistent fashion, but not according to the functional tonal practices of eighteenth- or nineteenth-century counterpoint. The listener perceives little or no sense of harmonic "progression" or "function" in the microcanonic compositions—one simultaneity develops into the next through the action of the canon. However, Ligeti does have the means for creating relative harmonic stability and instability: first, by the consistent use of particular trichords as contextually-established stable sonorities, suitable for cadences and starting points of sections; and secondly, by variation of the complexity of the simultaneities in the process of the composition.

---

24 Straus's fourth criterion for "prolongation" in post-tonal music (see note 22) requires that there be a clear distinction between the vertical and horizontal dimension (Straus, "Problem," pp. 5–7). In the microcanonic compositions, the function of a particular pitch as a part of a line (horizontal relationship) and as a part of a harmony (vertical relationship) is unambiguous because of the canonic construction of these compositions. However, because of the type of harmonic materials featured in these compositions, intervals [1] and [2] are not exclusively voice-leading intervals—they may also be a component of a harmony. Straus's fourth condition for prolongation is also not met in the microcanonic compositions.

25 For detailed analysis of the relationship of the construction of this canon melody (and those in other sections of *Lux aeterna*) to specific locations in the registral shape see Bernard, "Voice Leading."

26 Claude V. Palisca, "Kontrapunkt," *Die Musik in Geschichte und Gegenwart*, ed. Friedrich Blume (Basel: Bärenreiter und Kassel, 1958): 1522. The quotation cited is from the English typescript from which the *Musik in Geschichte und Gegenwart* article "Kontrapunkt" was translated (personal copy), p. 1.

The harmonies most commonly employed in exposed positions as sectional connectors and at the beginnings and ending of sections are the trichords that Ligeti refers to as the "typical Ligeti signals"—a stack of a minor third and a major second and a stack of two major seconds ([3][2] or [2][3] and [2][2]).[27] For example, this microcanonic section of *Lux aeterna* is connected to the next by a sustained F♯4 A4 B4 [3][2] (visible at the end of the range graph, Figure 2), a "Ligeti signal" harmony. Although Ligeti does not mention combinations of a whole step and a half step ([1][2] or [2][1]) in his discussion of the "Ligeti signals", these harmonies are likewise emphasized as sectional connectors and as cadential harmonies in the microcanonic compositions from this time period. They can be thought of as resulting from interlocking the [2]'s and [3]'s of a "Ligeti signal" trichord rather than stacking them.[28] Ligeti also typically employs intervals that are acoustically stable, such as the perfect octave and the unison, at cadential points.

In addition to their prominent placement of the "signals" as sectional connectors and at the beginning and ends of sections, the composite harmonies throughout most of the midportion of the first section of *Lux aeterna* can be broken down into overlapping representatives of Ligeti's signature trichords. These harmonies are most obvious as the "stripes" in the middle of the section on the range graph, which are formed of a series of [2]'s, but also can be thought of as the internal components of chromatically-filled intervals. Ligeti describes his harmonic practice as follows:

> . . . no direct succession or linking of harmonies takes place here; there is instead a gradual metamorphosis of intervallic constellations, this is to say, certain harmonic formations merge and develop into others, as it were— within one harmonic formation the precognition of the next harmonic constellation appears and then prevails, gradually clouding the first until only traces of it remain and the new formation has completely evolved. This is achieved technically by polyphonic means: the imaginary harmonies are the result of the complex interweaving of the parts, whereas the gradual clouding and renewed crystallization are the result of the discrete changes in the separate parts.[29]

The internal construction of harmonies from [2]'s and [3]'s is made audible both by the way in which harmonies are introduced—often growing from a clear [2][3],

---

27 Várnai, pp. 28–29.

28 The relationship between a trichord and a second trichord formed from the interlocked intervals of the first is discussed in detail in Bernard, *Varèse*, pp. 74ff. He refers to the second trichord in this relationship as a *first-order derivative* of the initial trichord, created by an *infolding* of the initial trichord, and proves that each trichord has only one interlocked or *infolded* form. To my knowledge, the other trichordal relationships described by Bernard are not systematically employed in Ligeti's music.

29 Ligeti, Program notes for *Lontano*, p. 22.

[3][2], or an interlocked version of them—and by the changes of harmonies throughout, which thin to reveal internal "signal" harmonies. The prominence of these harmonies in the microcanonic compositions (and other Ligeti compositions from the time period) suggests that they were not created by accident—the canons are designed to achieve these harmonies.

Canon Pitch Successions

In each of the canonic sections of *Lux aeterna* and the other microcanonic compositions from this period, the exact pitches and ordering of tones are strictly maintained in each of the replications of the pitch succession, thereby preserving the intervallic sequence and contour of the original. Thus, the shaping of the pitch succession corresponds to the overall shaping of the canonic texture. The pitch successions are structured with few internal repetitions of sequences of directed pitch intervals longer than the two interval returning step pattern. Motivic activity in a traditional sense is not emphasized in these compositions because of the lengthy durations assigned to many of the canon tones and the immersion of the individual lines in the canonic texture.

There are two basic types of canon pitch successions: conjunct and wedge-shaped. All of the canonic lines from *Lontano* and *Lux aeterna*, including that of Example 1, and the "Kyrie eleison" lines from the Kyrie of the Requiem are primarily composed of the former type. In these pitch successions, most of the adjacent pitch intervals are either [1]'s or [2]'s. The two patterns identified previously—the returning and unidirectional step formations—predominate. The returning step formations are most common at the beginning or ending of the canon pitch succession, where they act to restrict the range encompassed by the line. Unidirectional step formations are typical in the middle of a line, where they expand the range covered by the canon. In this group of pitch successions, directed interval successions other than the returning step and unidirectional step formations follow melodic principles typical of species practice—for example, skips are filled in by stepwise contrary motion.

The other type of canon pitch succession, a wedge-shaped line, occurs in the "Christe eleison" group from the *Requiem* and the ninth of the *Ten Pieces for Wind Quintet*. The canonic line from the ninth of the *Ten Pieces*, shown in Example 3, begins with a repeated E♭6, the alternately ascends and descends chromatically, moving to a D6 and D♭6 in the lower strand and an E6, F6, G♭6, and G6 in the upper strand. The C6 that would have come next in the lower strand seems to have been transposed up an octave to C7, appearing in order position 16. Although the size of the intervals between adjacent pitches in the succession increase, these lines, like those of the first type, are constructed from stepwise motion—in this case in two alternating, diverging strands. The action of the wedge-shaped line in musical space is evident in the range graph for this composition (Figure 6). As in the

Example 3: Canon Melody, *Ten Pieces for Wind Quintet* No. 9

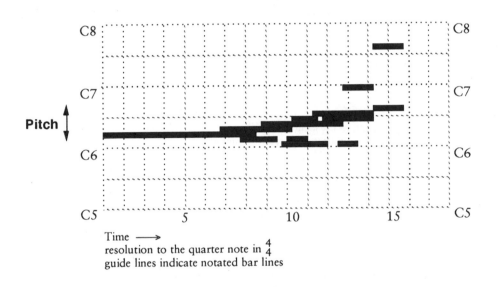

Figure 6: Range Graph, *Ten Pieces for Wind Quintet* No. 9

compositions with conjunct-type canon pitch succession construction, the shaping of the line corresponds to the overall shaping of the canonic texture.

Although the opening of the movement is static as far as pitch is concerned, the nine rearticulations of the initial pitch with the players breathing (audibly, if desired) between canon tone changes, create subtle rhythmic motion as the frequency of rearticulations of the tone entrances increases over the first seven measures. The locations of entrances of tones for each instrumental part are represented in Figure 7 by shaded squares. This acceleration in the rate of

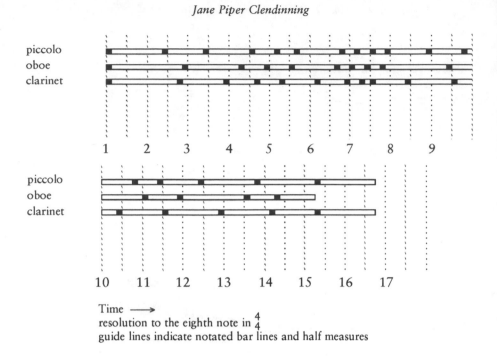

piccolo
oboe
clarinet

1 2 3 4 5 6 7 8 9

piccolo
oboe
clarinet

10 11 12 13 14 15 16 17

Time ⟶
resolution to the eighth note in $\frac{4}{4}$
guide lines indicate notated bar lines and half measures

Figure 7: Entrance Graph, *Ten Pieces for Wind Quintet* No. 9

rearticulation introduces the opening of the wedge from the unison E♭6 to a sustained symmetrical structure (C♯6 F♯6 G6 C7 [5][1][5]) in mm. 13–14. The composition ends with its range at the widest span, culminating in a resting point on a stable interval, an octave (A♭6 and A♭7), which enters in both the piccolo and the clarinet in the first simultaneous attack after that with which the movement began.

Sectional Shaping

The primary elements contributing to the audible sectional shaping are range, pacing, and harmonic complexity. The two most common registral shapes for the microcanonic components of sections are those of the two passages of music previously examined: expansion/contraction, as in the first section of *Lux aeterna*, and an expansion that ends at its widest point, as in the ninth of the *Ten Pieces*. These shapes are accompanied by a harmonic motion from a stable interval, usually a unison, to another stable interval, often a unison, octave, or dyad from a "Ligeti signal"—a [2] or a [3].

246

The interaction of pacing, harmonic complexity, and range in the shaping of sections can be examined in two sections built from a single canonic line—the second section of *Lux aeterna* and the third section of *Lontano*. The relationship between the canon pitch successions of the two sections is as follows: the first 28 tones of the first pitch succession from the second section of *Lux aeterna*, canon A (shown in Example 4), appears transposed down four semitones as the first pitch succession, canon A, of the third section of *Lontano*; the pitch interval succession formed by the initial 14 pitches of canon A from *Lux aeterna* section 2 is inverted beginning on G4 to form the pitch succession of canon B in *Lontano* section 3.

In the second section of *Lux aeterna*, the primary canon of the second section, canon A, follows the registral expansion/contraction pattern of previous canons (range graph, Figure 8), but starts relatively high in the range and ends low (the first tone of the canon, F♯4, is the highest; the last, E3, next to the lowest). This section divides into two parts, mm. 39–60 and mm. 60–88, based the number of pitches sounding (pitch count graph, Figure 9) and the entrance rate (entrance rate graph and entrance graph summary, Figures 10 and 11). The number of pitches sounding and the rate of entrances generally increase from the beginning of the section to mm. 50–52, with a slight decrease preparing the entry of the basses in m. 46. There is a marked decrease in the number of pitches sounding and in the entrance rate prior to the soprano and alto entries in m. 61, the end of the first subsection and the beginning of the second.

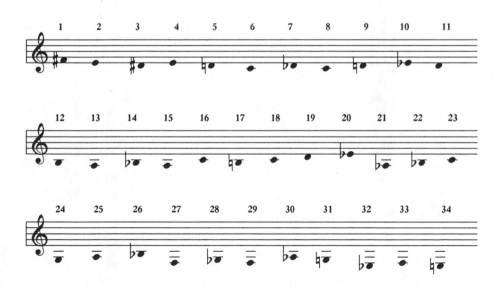

Example 4: Canon Melody A, *Lux aeterna*, Section 2

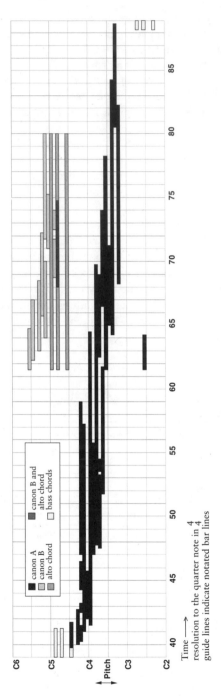

Figure 8: Range Graph, *Lux aeterna*, Section 2

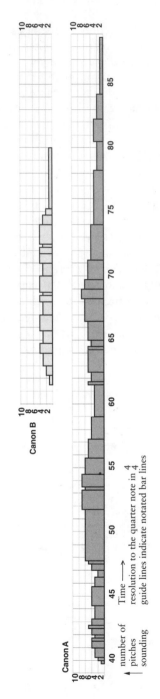

Figure 9: Pitch Count Graph, *Lux aeterna*, Section 2

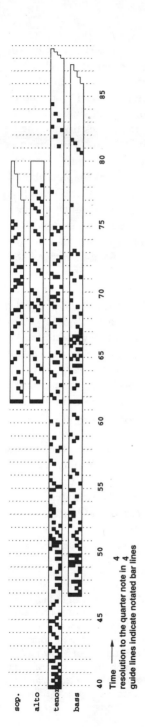

Figure 10: Entrance Graph, *Lux aeterna*, Section 2

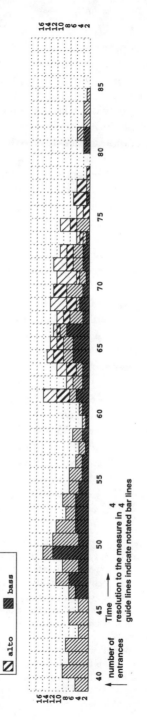

Figure 11: Entrance Graph Summary, *Lux aeterna*, Section 2

The soprano and alto parts enter simultaneously, the former with a new canon (canon B) and the latter with a chord. The alto parts cycle through the pitches C5, B♭4, and G4—[3][2]—in such a way that at any given time, all three pitches are sounding in one or another of the four alto voices. The attack of the first tone of canon B coincides with the entrance of all of the basses simultaneously on the next tone of canon A—all of which are octaves of G. Some of the basses double the G of their canon at an octave—the only tone of canon A that is dropped an octave—registrally balancing the entrance of the altos and sopranos (range graph, Figure 8).[30] The soprano's "miniature" canon follows the sectional shaping plan of registral expansion/contraction of the longer canons. The second subsection, like the first, has a gradual increase then decrease in pitch count and entrance rate (see graphs 9, 10, and 11). Both canons begin and end with a unison.

The harmonic microstructure is built of combinations of Ligeti signals as in the first section of the composition. The harmonies in mm. 54–65 and mm. 68–80 illustrate Ligeti's description of his harmonic practice. Measure 54 begins with a A♭3 A3 B♭3 B3 C4 D4 E♭4 sonority ([1][1][1][1][2][1]). By the third quarter of the measure, the A3 drops out, leaving a [2][1][1][2][1]. The departure of the B3 by the end of m. 55 and the D4 by the second quarter of m. 57 reveals a [2][2][3] (A♭3 B♭3 C4 E♭4) which had been present in the harmony since m. 51, but was hidden by the other pitches sounding with it. With the departure of the E♭4 at the end of m. 58, the harmony becomes a [2][2] which sounds for two and a half measures. A♭3 is replaced by G3 in m. 61, making a [3][2] (G3 B♭3 C4), which continues to sound until m. 65 but is obscured by the addition of A3 in m. 62, F3 in m. 64, and F♯3 in m. 65. The harmonic process in mm. 68–80 is similar to that of mm. 54–65, revealing a [2][2] (E♭3 F3 G3) in mm. 74–78.

Although the third section of *Lontano* sounds quite different from the second section of *Lux aeterna*, both are constructed similarly to other microcanonic sections with an expansion/contraction registral shaping (the graphs for *Lontano* are Figs. 12, 13, and 14).[31] The non-canonic harmonies with which this section begins (D3 F3 G3 and octave duplication of the outer pitches of that harmony) are

---

30 There is not a precise intervallic inversional relationship here: the soprano canon enters on G5, [19] above C4, the top pitch of canon A at that point; the G2 in the basses is [17] below the C4. However, the aural effect of the entry of the basses in the previously unused lower register is that of a "counterweight" to the entry of the sopranos.

31 For *Lontano*, only the entrance graph summary has been provided, rather than in individual instrumental "strips" as on the previous entrance graphs, because the number of instrumental parts make a graph of the previously employed format unwieldy. As in previous entrance graph sets, the "compression" of the information in the entrance graph summary allows the changes in the overall number of entrances to be represented more clearly, but does not allow relative durations of pitches in individual parts to be determined from the graph. In the entrance graph and in the pitch count graph, octave doublings of canon tones have been counted separately, yielding a count of the number of different pitches sounding or entering in a time unit. The number of instruments playing any given pitch in not tabulated in this graph.

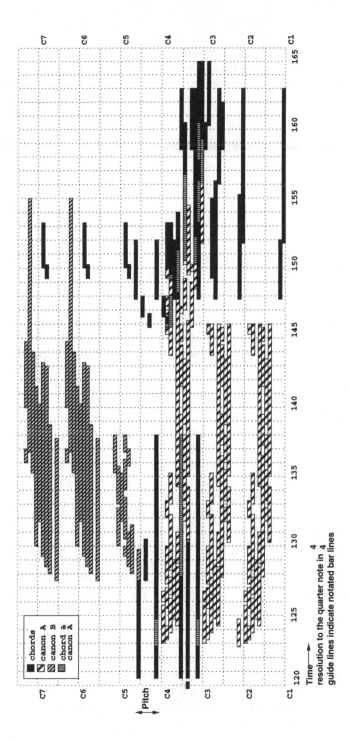

Figure 12: Range Graph, *Lontano*, Section 3

Ligeti's signature sonority [3][2] (range graph, Figure 12). Canon A enters in four parts m. 122, occupying the lower portion of the range; canon B enters in eight parts m. 127, filling the upper range. With the availability of orchestral resources, both canons are reinforced by octave doublings—canon A at the octave and double octave below, and canon B at an octave above throughout and at the octave below for part of the canonic setting. Canon A begins with a rapid introduction of the first ten tones of the canon, but its entrance rate stabilizes by m. 124 prior to the entrance of canon B (entrance graph, Figure 14). The initial tones of canon B are introduced more slowly than those of canon A, with some tones sounding in one or more of the canonic voices for as long as ten measures.

The overall registral shaping of the opening of this section is an expansion, but the expansion here takes place at a faster rate and in a shorter span of time than in previously examined sections. From the chordal introduction, the range grows to cover three octaves by m. 125 and almost six by m. 130 with the entrance of canon B (range graph, Figure 12). As in previous sections, the mid-section is characterized by relatively constant outer registral boundaries. The registral expansion is accompanied by an abrupt increase in the number of pitches sounding from m. 122 to m. 125, followed by a second dramatic increase in the number of pitches in mm. 127–136 with the entry of canon B (pitch count graph, Figure 13). In mm. 124 to 144, the number of pitches sounding in canon A is relatively constant, but the total number of pitches sounding decreases from m. 135 to m. 145, corresponding to a drop in the number of pitches sounded in canon B.

The contraction phase begins in m. 140 as the number of pitches sounding in canon B decreases and the harmonies thin in route to the conclusion of the canon on octave D3's and as the last of the sustained pitches introduced in the transition from section 1 finally die out. From the disappearance of the octave doublings of canon A in m. 145 to the end of the composition, as the number of parts performing the canons decreases, the number of sustained pitches increases, as sustained pitches begin to dominate the texture. As canon B fades out in mm. 145–154, there are two very audible entrances of sustained pitches—the first in m. 147 with octave D's and A's (making open perfect fourths, fifths, and octaves), the second with octave B♭'s that move to B's. The A canon, which can be traced on the score to m. 160, disappears into the sustained pitches five measures previously from the listener's perspective. Unlike many of the other "contraction" subsections, this one does not close to an octave or dyad and ends with two and a half octaves of range still open. The section, and the entire composition, is brought to a close by the slowing and eventual disappearance of the canon and by the braking action of the accumulated sustained pitches. The final sonority of the composition is B2 C♯3 D3 [2][1], the interlocked signal trichord, which has appeared often in the other compositions of this group.

The setting of the canon A pitch succession in *Lontano* is similar to that of the corresponding pitch succession in the second section of *Lux aeterna* in several

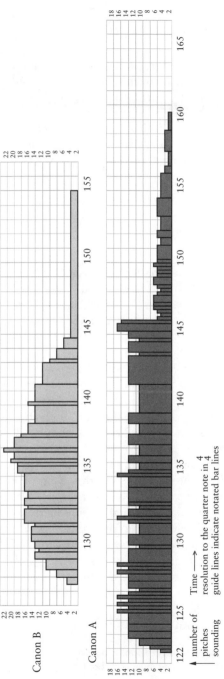

Figure 13: Pitch Count Graph, *Lontano*, Section 3

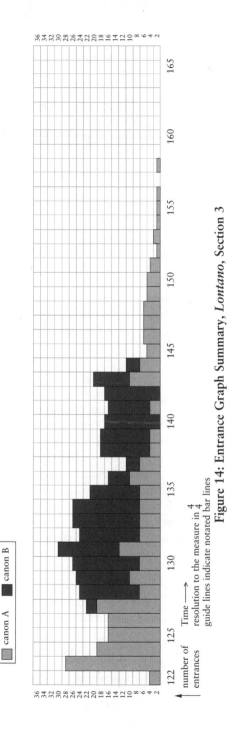

Figure 14: Entrance Graph Summary, *Lontano*, Section 3

respects. The range graph of canon A in *Lux aeterna* to about m. 60 parallels that of the portion of the range graph in *Lontano* that represents the presentation of canon A in one octave to about m. 147 (range graphs Figs. 8 and 12). The entrance graph summaries for the A and B canons are similar for the two sections, with a "two hump" shaping (see Figs. 11 and 14). The decrease in entrance rate at the end of the section in *Lontano* is more abrupt than the corresponding point in *Lux aeterna* because of the cessation of canon tone doublings at the end of m. 145. Although the canon pitch succession A is set in the individual canons similarly in the two compositions, the employment of doublings in *Lontano* and the differences in the sustained pitch components and in the canon pitch successions B of the two sections ensure that the composite texture and the resulting aural effect in each of the compositions are different.

Aspects of the Macrostructure

In *Lux aeterna* and *Lontano*, three distinct sections are joined together by sectional connectors to create the overall form of the composition The connectors in *Lux aeterna* are simply sustained trichords—the first a "Ligeti signal" (discussed earlier), the second a "signal" trichord that expands outward by semitones to form a [3][4] prior to the beginning of the third section. The connectors between the sections of *Lontano* also consist of sustained pitches, in this case contrasting with the canons in the surrounding sections.[32]

Although the connectors between the sections are relatively straightforward, the means by which the sections themselves interact to form a unified composition is much more complex. The larger-scale form of these pieces is not based on repetition of sections, variation techniques, or other traditional means of creating coherence between sections of a work, but there is a strong sense of connected-ness in *Lux aeterna* and *Lontano*. The coherence of the macrostructure of each composition, the sense of overreaching connectedness uniting the internal sections into a single large composition, is created by the same aspects that shape the internal sections—range, pacing, and harmonic complexity—but on a larger scale.

In both compositions, the range spanned within the individual sections increases as the piece progresses, accompanied by changes during the course of the composition in the complexity of the harmonies and the pace of activity. The pitch extremes and variations in the number and type of canons and sustained pitch elements present in each section can serve as indicators of the large-scale registral and pacing gestures within these two compositions.[33] In *Lux aeterna* the widest

---

32 Discussed in detail in Clendinning, *Contrapuntal Techniques*, pp. 140–46.

33 Of course, the number of semitones spanned and the number of distinct compositional elements in a section are only rough indicators of the sense of registral expansion and increase or decrease in activity experienced in listening to *Lux aeterna* and *Lontano*. However,

range spanned in the first section is D♭4 to A5 [20], in the second G2 to G5 [36], and in the third D2 to B5 [45]. Although each section has its own expansion/contraction registral shaping, the overall gesture is a gradual expansion, mostly in the lower range, of over two octaves. The initial section features canon alone, the second two canons and sustained tones, and the third one canon and sustained tones, forming a pattern of growth followed by a decline in the number of compositional elements at the level of the macrostructure that parallels a typical sectional shaping. As in *Lux aeterna*, the range spanned in the sections of *Lontano* increases in the course of the piece with a relatively consistent upper extreme and expansion into lower registers.[34] In general, the number of compositional elements increases from section to section, with one canon and sustained pitches in the first two sections (but with more sustained pitch activity independent of the canon in the second) and two canons and sustained pitches in the final section. In both compositions, the closing of range in the final section also acts to close the structure as a whole.

As in the individual sections, range, pacing, and harmonies are not the only elements contributing to the sense of shape and coherence. Among the more subtle sources of continuity at work at the level of the macrostructure as well as the audible surface are: the unity of sound quality throughout a composition; the persistent application of canonic technique; the consistency in construction of the canon pitch successions and of the harmonic components; and the similarity in shaping of individual sections.

Microcanon and Later Compositions

The microcanonic techniques first explored by Ligeti in the four compositions from 1965–68 reappear in various guises in compositions from 1968 through the 1980s. Although the manifestations of microcanon in these later compositions retain many of the salient features identified above, they also reveal a wealth of compositional possibilities available through extensions of the basic microcanonic techniques by the incorporation of new ideas, combination with other techniques explored in earlier compositions, changes in the compositional "rules" to introduce new freedoms or new constraints, or some combination of those categories.

The contrapuntal ideas explored in these four early compositions have

---

consideration of the details of the use of range and pacing in the microstructure of either composition would require previous discussing of the audible surface of each of the three sections, which exceeds the scope of this essay. For a detailed discussion of the role of symmetry and spatial relationships in the large-scale registral shaping of *Lux aeterna* see Bernard, "Voice Leading."

34 The extremes in the first section are E4 and C7 (doubled an octave higher by the string harmonics part of the time), the second G♭1 and C7, and the third C♯1 and E7.

influenced Ligeti's output beyond the employment of microcanon proper in the later works. The two basic sectional shapes—gradual expansion and internal filling followed by contraction and thinning of texture and gradual expansion with the section ending at its widest span—are common in subsequent compositions.[35] The method of melody construction, heavily dependent on step motion, is a basis for the voice-leading of individual strands in the compound melody of the pattern-meccanico compositions written shortly after *Lux aeterna* and *Lontano*.[36] The Ligeti signal harmonies, not present in the Kyrie, the first of the microcanonic compositions, became an important aspect of Ligeti's compositional technique.[37] The carefully crafted, complex interaction of line and harmony evident in the microcanonic compositions is also typical of Ligeti's later contrapuntal writing. With these four compositions from the mid-1960s, Ligeti began the development of a new type of counterpoint, a process of exploration that has continued throughout the 1980s.

---

35 *Continuum* for harpsichord (1968) is one of many examples of the use of these sectional shapes in a non-microcanonic composition. See Clendinning, *Contrapuntal Techniques*, 186–205, and Urban, "Serielle Technik," pp. 63–71.

36 These compositions, which include *Continuum, Coulée* (1968), *Ramifications* (1968–69), and portions of the Second String Quartet (1968), the "Selbstportrait" movement of the *Three Movements for Two Pianos* (1976), and the *Drei Phantasien nach Friedrich Hölderlin* (1982), form a subcategory of Ligeti's micropolyphonic compositions that he refers to as *meccanico* or "machine-like." In the compositions that I have labeled *pattern-meccanico*, the linear strands of the counterpoint are formed from incessant repetition of melodic segments, or patterns, which undergo gradual changes in pitch content. Patterns in some sections of works also form internal voice-leading strands as a sort of compound melody. See Clendinning, *Contrapuntal Techniques*, pp. 167–75 and "The Pattern-Meccanico Compositions of György Ligeti," *Perspectives of New Music* 31 (1993): 192–234.

37 In Clendinning, *Contrapuntal Techniques*, chapters 3 and 4, these harmonies are shown to be important in a variety of contrapuntally-based compositions dating from the late 1960s to the 1980s.

III
Insights from Other Disciplines

Theory, Analysis, and the "Problem" of Minimal Music

Jonathan W. Bernard

> Sculpture involving unitary forms, being bound together as it is with a kind
> of energy provided by the gestalt, often elicits the complaint among critics
> that such works are beyond analysis.   Robert Morris[1]

"There's hardly anything there." "Nothing happens." Minimal music, a direct
offshoot of minimalism in the plastic arts (of which Morris's "unitary form"
sculpture is one manifestation), poses similar challenges to critics, theorists, and
analysts of music.[2] Remarks such as those above, which respond both to the
extremely restricted nature of the materials and to their deployment over (usually)
considerable stretches of time, can also be taken as *aesthetic* responses to the
perceived difficulty of constructing theoretical/analytical systems that would
engage minimal music successfully yet still be complex enough to prove interesting
by contemporary standards of the discipline. Theorists have come to expect music,
especially twentieth-century music, to present an intricate surface that can be
penetrated only through the application of sophisticated analytical tools. Out of a
presented richness emerges, through abstraction and generalization, a relatively
simple framework which is taken to represent "what is really going on" in the
music, not so much despite the fact that it is not directly or immediately perceivable
as *because* it is not directly or immediately perceivable. At the same time, many
such analyses leave the way open, implicitly or explicitly, for alternative, equally
valid interpretations—even interpretations based on the same theoretical premises.
Thus to the "deep structure" itself is attributed as well a certain richness,
potentially inexhaustible in nature.

Minimal music threatens to frustrate such strategies on both levels. First,
instead of richness, one encounters sparseness at the surface. The number of

---

1 Robert Morris, "Notes on Sculpture," in *Minimal Art: A Critical Anthology*, ed. Gregory
   Battcock (New York: Dutton, 1968), pp. 222–35.
2 The evidence attesting to the aesthetic reliance of minimal music upon minimal art is exposed
   in detail in my article, "The Minimalist Aesthetic in the Plastic Arts and in Music,"
   Perspectives of New Music 31 (1993): 86–132; as such, it is a useful companion piece to the
   present essay.

distinguishable elements, by comparison to Western music both previous to and contemporaneous with the minimal, has been severely reduced. Second, the well-publicized effort on the part of minimalist composers to be as "accessible" as possible unmistakably implies that their music has no secrets, hence no layers of meaning either. The *literalist* quality of minimalism attempts to exclude the possibility of interpretation—to assert, in other words, that there is only one "right way" to hear the music. This is more or less an automatic outcome of the (projected) failure of abstraction to find anything to work on, hence to yield anything worth knowing.

Morris, in the epigraph that opens this essay, attributes the phrase "beyond analysis" to outside observers (critics) and thus implies that the quality it denotes was achieved accidentally by the minimalist sculptors, as a by-product of other artistic aims. In fact, however, it was deliberately sought. "I'm interested in the inscrutability and the mysteriousness of the thing," said sculptor Tony Smith, referring to qualities that he tried to incorporate into his own work.[3] And Frank Stella, by his own testimony, was quite happy with what he had achieved in his metallic pinstripe paintings of 1960: "... a real aggressive kind of controlling surface, something that would sort of seize the surface ... I also felt, maybe in a slightly perverse way, that it would probably also be fairly repellent. I liked the idea ... that these would be very hard paintings to penetrate."[4] In both cases, the viewer's desire to get beyond the surface—to analyze, in other words—would eventually fade in the face of the dawning realization that these works of art in fact consisted of nothing *but* surface. Stella again: "My painting is based on the fact that only what can be seen there *is* there ... What you see is what you see."[5] In an attempt to place their work beyond the reach of analytic technique as "normally" construed, minimal artists also adopted the stratagem of redefinition. For example, Donald Judd asserts, in an essay first published in 1965, that "half or more of the best new work in the last few years has been neither painting nor sculpture," and that its creators have rejected both yet maintain a relationship of some sort to one or the other (or both). Judd dubs this work with a new term that is also the title of his essay: "Specific Objects."[6]

The aesthetic connections between minimal art and minimal music are sufficiently numerous and pervasive to lead one to believe that the minimalist composers have striven for similar results. Steve Reich, in "Music as a Gradual Process" (1968)—perhaps the best known of his writings—articulated his interest

---

3 Samuel Wagstaff, "Talking to Tony Smith," in Battcock, pp. 381–86.

4 Stella, interviewed in 1970; quoted in Anna C. Chave, "Minimalism and the Rhetoric of Power," *Arts Magazine* 64/5 (January, 1990): 44–63.

5 Bruce Glaser, "Questions to Stella and Judd" (interview), in Battcock, pp. 148–64.

6 Donald Judd, "Specific Objects," *Arts Yearbook* 8 (1965); rpt. in Donald Judd, *Complete Writings 1959–1975* (Halifax: Nova Scotia College of Art and Design/New York: New York University Press, 1975), pp. 181–89.

in "perceptible processes" and his desire "to be able to hear the process happening throughout the sounding music."[7] But what, exactly, *are* these processes? Evidently they are not compositional, since Reich distinguishes his "perceptible processes" from those of John Cage, for example—"compositional ones that could not be heard when the music was performed"—thereby implying that the compositional process, not necessarily connected to the audible music, has no relevance to the listening experience. Yet later in his essay Reich expresses his desire to arrive at "a compositional process and a sounding music that are one and the same thing."[8] All that is really clear about these processes is that in their unrelenting audibility they are meant to palliate whatever urge the listener might feel to discover "something more" about structure. If the process *is* the structure, and if it sits plainly exposed on the surface of the music, why inquire further? Thus is the inscrutability of the work safeguarded, as if to say: "Pay no attention to that man behind the curtain."

In this essay, the implications of the minimalist compositional stance as an obstacle to theory and analysis are examined in detail, and some possible routes to a solution are proposed, by way of models from the visual arts, using analysis of specific pieces and passages as a vehicle.

First of all, what *is* minimal music? Although the adjective "minimal" came into general use by the mid-1970s and eventually supplanted various alternatives, such as "repetitive," "systemic," or "solid state," there was never any firm agreement about how broadly or how narrowly it was to be construed. No list of "typical characteristics" can serve as a foolproof test of what is minimal and what is not.[9] Given, however, that minimalism in the visual arts is customarily taken to encompass a very wide range of work—wide enough that some of the artists included aim at divergent, even contradictory results—one might favor the broader interpretation on the musical side as well, taking in not only the familiar triumvirate of Reich, Terry Riley, and Philip Glass but also La Monte Young, John Adams, and even certain other composers such as Alvin Lucier, Pauline Oliveros, and Frederic Rzewski, not all of whose works fit the minimalist mold under even the loosest of definitions. A chronological broadening also makes sense: much of what Glass and Reich, in particular, have written in recent years can be regarded as still essentially minimalist, the opinions of certain critics notwithstanding.[10]

---

7 Reich, "Music as a Gradual Process" (1968), in *Writings about Music* (Halifax: Nova Scotia College of Art and Design/New York: New York University Press, 1974), pp. 9–11.

8 Ibid., p. 10.

9 See, however, "The Minimalist Aesthetic," pp. 96–106 passim, for some perhaps not entirely useless generalizations.

10 See, for example, John Rockwell, *All-American Music: Composition in the Late Twentieth Century* (New York: Knopf, 1983), especially Chapter 9; K. Robert Schwarz, "Steve Reich: Music as a Gradual Process," Part II, *Perspectives of New Music* 20 (1981/82): 225–86 (especially 244–50).

Admittedly, for both composers *something* changed—in Glass's case, it was sometime around *Einstein on the Beach* (1975–76); for Reich, it happened after *Drumming* (1971)—but, as will become clear below, in neither case should a technical adjustment be taken to signal a substantive change. This is true for Reich even though in the past couple of decades he has occasionally gotten away from minimalism, as in *Tehillim* (1981); more recent pieces, such as *The Desert Music* (1982–84) and *Different Trains* (1988), show a continued fidelity to the minimalist aesthetic. Glass's history is somewhat different and will be discussed later.[11]

What minimal music is *not* is at least as important, in particular as a prelude to engagement of more directly analytical questions. In this connection, several myths are well worth dispelling.

Minimal music is not *static*. To hear it as static is to take at face value, and therefore rather superficially, the facts of extensive use of literal repetition and of the stringent limits placed upon the total repertoire of material. Of course, in a piece like Reich's *Piano Phase* (1967) there is a great deal of direct repetition of figures, far more than in much other, contemporaneous music. But beyond this local level there is a steady sequence of changes; in fact, the entire work could be said to be dedicated to the process of change. Moreover, the larger pattern that is established after a few phase shifts effectively instills in the listener an *expectation* that further shifts will occur, each after an inexactly specified yet not indeterminate number of repetitions of a new configuration. The periodic accumulation of tension associated with such expectation and its corresponding release upon fulfillment, taken together, are anything but static. Even in a work like La Monte Young's *The Well-Tuned Piano* (1964–), in which things take a long (sometimes very long) time to happen, and of which a typical performance can last for over five hours without a break, there is directionality and progression. Young's detailed notes to the published recording identify sections by exact timings and by titles that, functioning as they do as labels for the harmonic and thematic materials in use, reveal clearly teleological motivations.[12]

The static hearing of minimal music is, admittedly, widespread among critics. One, for example, has written of its "restricted harmonic palette, usually modal and static" and has asserted that "not much happens in minimal music."[13]

---

11 Some European composers' work has been called minimalist as well; the characterization seems less than compelling, however, in such cases as Michael Nyman and Louis Andriessen, perhaps because they acquired the style at second hand. As for Arvo Pärt, he should not be considered a minimalist at all, since the intensely expressive character of his work is diametrically opposed to the reigning aesthetic.

12 La Monte Young, *The Well-Tuned Piano*, recording of performance at 6 Harrison Street, New York, October 25, 1981; issued with booklet of essays and notes (Gramavision 18–8701-2, 5 CDs, 1987).

13 Robert Carl, "The Politics of Definition in New Music," *College Music Symposium* 29 (1989): 101–14.

Deprived of access to sufficiently large resources—so seems to run the argument—this music is reduced to aimless fluctuation. But a restricted harmonic palette no more mandates stasis than the unbroken 3/4 time of a waltz imposes rhythmic rigidity and sameness throughout. There are, after all, other ways available in both cases to promote variation and progression. Analysts ignore at their peril minimalist composers' intense interest in strictly controlling listeners' sense of the passage of time.

Minimal music is also not *non-Western* in any meaningful sense. That composers like Reich, Riley, and Glass, through their study of African, Indian, and Far Eastern musics, have essentially divorced themselves from the Western tradition and have thereby placed their music out of the reach of "traditional" criticism or analysis is not a claim that withstands scrutiny. It is, in fact, rather insulting to the non-Western musics themselves, for the idea that such musics are separable from their respective cultural contexts, and are therefore ultimately available to any non-native willing to undergo long immersion and exposure, is really a Western idea, and a chauvinistic one to boot. This is not to dismiss Reich's adoption of African drumming patterns, for instance, as mere exoticism—like, say, Mozart's "Turkish" music in *Die Entführung aus dem Serail*—but only to point out that even if they had wanted to, none of the minimalists could have become non-Western composers. In fact, they seem to have wanted something else. As Reich has put it: "My interest was in the rhythmic structure of the music. I didn't want to *sound* Balinese or African. I wanted to *think* Balinese or African. Which meant that I would sound like myself while expanding my ideas about how to rhythmically structure my pieces." [14] In other words, Reich never had any intention of surrendering his individuality to the exigencies of a foreign musical culture. All he meant to effect was a fruitful collision between his own sensibility and other ways of thinking about musical materials in order to jolt himself out of what he had come to see as his own culturally induced rut. Accordingly, there is no particularly compelling reason to expect the various analytical methodologies developed for non-Western music to have relevance to (thoroughly Western) minimal music.

Finally, although minimal music exhibits certain totalitarian tendencies (the "one right way to hear it" mentioned above), it is undoubtedly wrong to accuse minimalist composers of attempting specifically to hypnotize their listeners, to distract them from some alleged lack of substance by aural tricks designed to confound ordinarily attentive ears. Initially, in the mid-1960s, critics apparently suspected something along these lines, to judge from the early popularity of such descriptors as "trance music." The possibility that composers' principal aim in such music was the creation of aural illusions may have led some critics to posit an

---

14 Reich, "Non-Western Music and the Western Composer," *Analyse Musicale* 11 (1988): 46–50.

analogy between their efforts and op art, a form of painting related to minimalism that at first struck some as important but eventually proved rather frivolous and shallow for having concentrated on achieving a "dazzling hypnotic effect" in preference to more substantial artistic accomplishment.[15]

The misconceptions enumerated above have probably had something to do with the demonstrably low level of interest in pursuing analysis of minimal music. The implications of the direct link to minimal art, even if not previously well understood, have also proved a discouragement. In minimalist painting and sculpture, the drastic reduction in the number of elements effectively forces the viewer to focus on *arrangement*, meaning the preplanned conception of the work as a whole, rather than the more traditional *composition*, which implies an involvement with parts whose shape, size, color, and relative location have been adjusted and re-adjusted by the artist as the creative act progresses. Taking their cue from this shift in orientation, minimalist composers often make it a losing proposition for the listener to do more than *just barely* focus on differences between chords and motives, for instance—only to the threshhold necessary for apprehending the temporal process. Thus, one cannot grasp the nature of patterns or structural frameworks in such music by studying the elements themselves for regularities or features held in common; rather, it would seem, one must learn to ignore the elements insofar as that can be managed. Faced with this potentially formidable obstacle, some have concluded that analysis of minimal music, beyond mere description, is impossible.[16] Others, however, have made attempts of varying effectiveness, two of which are particularly worth discussing in detail.[17]

---

15 See E. C. Goossen, "Two Exhibitions," in Battcock, pp. 165–74, as well as Stella's and Judd's withering criticism of Victor Vasarely in Glaser, "Questions to Stella and Judd," pp. 149–51, 155. Brian Dennis has commented on the analogy between minimal music and op art and has drawn similar conclusions: "Such effects [as those of op art] are never so great in repetitive music; in any case, most composers deny that this is their aim" ("Repetitive and Systemic Music," *The Musical Times* 115 [1974]: 1036–38). K. Robert Schwarz, on the other hand, sees in Reich's *Come Out* "the aural equivalent of op art" for the way in which it compels the listener to "fixate upon various transitory patterns which arise out of the phasing process," and that in fact "it is the presence of these dazzling, constantly shifting figures that make the early tape pieces interesting to hear over and over again" ("Steve Reich: Music as a Gradual Process," Part I, *Perspectives of New Music* 19 [1980/81]: 373–92).

16 Dan Warburton, in "A Working Terminology for Minimal Music" (*Intégral* 2 [1988]: 135–59), states that: "Given a music as consciously 'self-explanatory' as minimalism, it is up to the student to determine to what extent his/her observations will remain merely descriptions" (p. 138). Warburton has obviously already made that decision for himself: most of his article is given over to consideration of the merits of various extant descriptive labels and proposals for new ones of his own.

17 Some others are: Wesley York, "Form and Process," *Sonus* 1/2 (1981): 28–50; rpt. in *Contiguous Lines: Issues and Ideas in the Music of the '60s and '70s,* ed. Thomas DeLio (Lanham, Md.: University Press of America, 1985), pp. 81–106 (on Glass's *Two Pages* [1968]); Jonathan D. Kramer, *The Time of Music* (New York: Schirmer Books, 1988), pp. 389–94 (on Rzewski's

Paul Epstein, in his fine analysis of Reich's *Piano Phase*, explores insightfully the ramifications of the phasing process, including such matters as the qualitative differences between the odd- and even-numbered phases and the overall (retrograde-) symmetrical design.[18] Epstein also devotes considerable attention to the perceptually distinguishable stages in the transitional passages. His account, as a phenomenological exercise, is quite valuable in itself; of even more interest, however, is his report that Reich's phase shifting, though realized by human performers in real time, produces the same distinguishable stages when realized by computer. This observation belies Reich's claim, expressed in "Music as a Gradual Process" and often reiterated since, that among the "unintended by-products" or "mysteries" of a process which would keep a piece unpredictable, hence interesting, are the "slight irregularities in performance."[19] Real, *structural* unpredictability, if it is to exist at all, must come from some other source.

The most ambitious, and in many respects the most successful published attempt so far at analysis of the minimal repertoire is a recent study by Richard Cohn dealing with two of Reich's phase-shifting pieces, *Phase Patterns* (1970) and *Violin Phase* (1967).[20] Using beat-class methodology, Cohn models rhythm in Reich's music, in a way both rigorous and ingenious, analogously to pitch class in earlier post-tonal music; he shows that these rhythmic structures have the same sort of richness, in terms both of their overall symmetry and local unpredictability. He concludes that "by freezing pitch, Reich did not abolish the old modes of hearing, but simply displaced them, transferring them from one domain to another"—at

---

Les Moutons de Panurge [1969]); Daniel Warburton, "Aspects of Organization in the *Sextet* of Steve Reich" (Ph.D. diss., University of Rochester, 1987); Timothy A. Johnson, "Harmony in the Music of John Adams: From *Phrygian Gates* to *Nixon in China*" (Ph.D. diss., S.U.N.Y. at Buffalo, 1991); Johnson, "Harmonic Vocabulary in the Music of John Adams: A Hierarchical Approach," *Journal of Music Theory* 37 (1993): 117–56.

18 Paul Epstein, "Pattern Structure and Process in Steve Reich's *Piano Phase*," *The Musical Quarterly* 72 (1986): 494–502. Other, briefer comments of theoretical interest on this work are to be found in Dennis, "Repetitive and Systemic Music," and Robert Morris, "Generalizing Rotational Arrays," *Journal of Music Theory* 32 (1988): 75–132 (see 91–94).

19 Reich, "Music as a Gradual Process," pp. 10–11. Boulez makes the same point, by implication, in his critique of the work of minimalist composers, whom he describes as "making use of certain phenomena previously little used, such as phase shifting—that is, technological phenomena, but realized, if you will, by hand, in order to preserve for them an imperfect aspect." ("From the Domaine Musical to IRCAM: Pierre Boulez in Conversation with Pierre-Michel Menger," trans. Jonathan W. Bernard, *Perspectives of New Music* 28 [1990]: 6-19.) A more plausible explanation than Reich himself has offered for his lack of interest in electronically aided composition or performance is, simply, a growing preference for the sonic qualities of acoustic instruments; note that since 1973 he has even abandoned the electric organ.

20 Richard Cohn, "Teleology, Craft, Tradition, and Analysis in a Minimalist Context: Transpositional Combination of Beat-Class Sets in Steve Reich's Phase-Shifting Music," *Perspectives of New Music* 30 (1992): 146–77.   •

least in the phase-shifting pieces. Still, Cohn's analyses leave the unsettling impression that there may be less here than meets the eye. Reich's work has often been denigrated as little more than child's play, and Cohn does help redress the critical balance by showing that Reich has indeed engaged in careful calculation to obtain his results. Nevertheless, formalization in this instance poses its own set of problems, for in the very act of getting to Reich's processes Cohn has—perhaps unavoidably—focused a great deal of attention on Reich's *elements*. The ironic outcome of this approach may be to make the music seem inadequate to what is being asserted about it. Cohn's comparison of the contrapuntal potential of a Bach fugue subject to the phase-shifting potential of Reich's "materials" actually serves to emphasize this problem: compared to a Bach fugue, after all, a phase-shifting pattern that works itself out even in a moderately interesting way is a relatively simple system. It would appear that rhythmic analysis of this music can be pushed only so far along these lines, where the complexities of earlier music—tonal or post-tonal—are taken as the standard for artistic achievement.

What, then, is to be done? Will we end up confronted with Hobson's choice, forced either to declare the music beyond analysis owing to the inadequacies of theory or to dismiss the music as unworthy owing to its inability to stand up to analysis? Fortunately, there is another alternative. It demands, however, that the prospective investigator be willing, not to abandon quantitatively oriented methods, but to deemphasize them somewhat in favor of taking seriously the connections between minimal music and minimal art and treating them, rather than simply as an avenue for metaphorical comparison, as a way of "seeing" the music, or *as if* one could see it. This is not tantamount to expecting that it will be possible to convert a piece of music somehow into an *actual* painting or sculpture. Minimalism in music is not parasitic; no composer, it seems safe to say, has ever generated a minimal piece by taking over the salient features of some particular work from the plastic arts and transmuting them into aural terms, so any analyst who tried to carry out the reverse process would probably find it just as impossible. But one important fact to be noted is that art theorists and critics do not *measure* for the most part; the precise physical dimensions of a work are generally confined to catalogue descriptions, and have about the same kind and degree of interest as would the number of pages in a score to musicians. Thus an analytic approach to minimal music might prove more viable if it were less exclusively bound up with exactitudes. It is important to remember that the elements of a minimal work are often not all that interesting, being as they are nearly nonexistent. The adjustment of perspective to allow for what is *not* to be said about a work, as much as for what is to be said, will be crucial to surmounting the obstacles to such an approach.

As an example of what the connection to visual art might have to tell us about minimal music, consider again, for a moment, *Piano Phase*. It is significant that no published analysis treats more than the first and longest cycle of phases in this work (including the three cited above).[21] Analysts have, perhaps understandably, concentrated more upon the work as an example of the phasing technique; once this has been explained, it is clear that the remaining two cycles operate in the same fashion, although they are progressively shorter. One implication of this omission, however, is that the rest of the piece is actually uninteresting. To think of the piece in visual terms, by contrast, opens up valuable new perspectives. A fruitful point of contact would be certain wall drawings of Sol LeWitt, an artist with whom Reich is known to have an affinity.[22] One in particular, at the Museum für Gegenwartskunst in Basel, sticks in my mind.[23] The pencilled design, radiating from a central, symmetrical point, delineates regions that alternate regularly between relative sparseness and relative density, very much like the alternating stretches of rhythmic synchrony and rhythmically out-of-phase transition that characterize the form of Reich's piece. Furthermore, in viewing the LeWitt, one's eye is drawn in an inwardly spiraling motion—or, perhaps, a series of progressively smaller concentric circles; in Reich's piece, the ear is led on an analogous journey through the three sections. The analogy is not perfect: the number of phases traversed in the shorter journeys does not decrease in the drawing as it does in the piece, and the bases for symmetry are different in the two works. But, for reasons discussed above, the chances that the structures of two works in two different media would coincide exactly are essentially nil.[24]

There are many other ways in which the difficulties of analyzing minimal music might productively be addressed, several of which are illustrated in the next section of this essay in forms ranging from "thought analyses" to actual analytical samples. My intention here is to set forth a broad range of possibilities without claiming to have been comprehensive or exhaustive—or, for that matter, to have said all that there is to say about the piece or passage in question.

I. Alvin Lucier, *I am sitting in a room* (1969)

For this work, as for the many other minimalist tape pieces, one might do best to construct a literal visual representation, using the spectrographic method pioneered

---

21 See note 18.

22 Emily Wasserman, "An Interview with Composer Steve Reich," *Artforum* 10/9 (1972): 44–48.

23 Sol LeWitt, Wall Drawing No. 179, *Circles, Grids, and Arcs from Four Corners and Four Sides* (1973). Black pencil.

24 In the course of my visit to the Basel museum, I returned several times to the LeWitt and found on each occasion that my eye was caught first by the periphery of his drawing, then drawn gradually into the center along a spiral path. The drawing is quite large—overpoweringly and deliberately so, in fact, for the size of the room in which it has been installed—and for this reason cannot be taken in at a single glance. Sheer size is a quality that it shares with many other minimal works, a quality that imposes a temporal dimension upon the viewer's experience.

by Robert Cogan, to produce a picture of the sound of the speaking voice at various stages of the transformation.[25] These stages range from the "natural" voice at the beginning to the sound of its complete absorption into the acoustics of the room at the end.[26] Such a "conversion" would yield a series of distinct steps, akin to those of serial (visual) art, each characterized by a different range of bandwidths, dominant frequencies, and densities. Although the information yielded by these spectrographs is in part quantifiable—as Cogan's own analyses show—it is not "readable" in the same way as are, for example, the directions for performance provided by a conventional score; thus we are forced to consider process without much distraction from the elements, which are not very distinct in these pictures. Judging from the way the music sounds, one might predict a fairly rapid progression away from the normal voice characteristics, with an ever slower rate of change as the piece approaches its end; if such a progression could be graphed, it would look more or less like a hyperbola, with zero on the vertical axis representing complete absorption into the acoustics of the room, and with time represented on the horizontal axis.[27] It would be interesting to compare the two commercially issued recordings in terms both of general pattern and specific details.[28] How much difference, for instance, does the free choice of room for recording actually make?

This example is all the more apropos here because, as it happens, the work already has a "visual analogue": that is, Mary Lucier's series of Polaroid snapshots that was directly inspired by her husband's music. Although these photographs in themselves make a rather poor analysis of *I am sitting in a room* (unsurprisingly, since they were never intended as such), they do help explain how easily the idea

---

25 See Robert Cogan, *New Images of Musical Sound* (Cambridge, Mass.: Harvard University Press, 1984).

26 The "score" for this work is simply a set of written instructions. A performance consists of reading a given text aloud (self-referential, in that it describes what will happen as the work unfolds) and recording it on tape, then playing it back into the room and recording that sound on a second tape recorder, then playing that recorded recording back again into the room and recording it on the first tape recorder, and so on for an indefinite number of repetitions. The segments are then spliced together (or dubbed onto a new tape) in the order in which they were recorded. For further information, see Alvin Lucier and Douglas Simon, *Chambers* (Middletown, Conn.: Wesleyan University Press, 1980), pp. 29–39. See also my discussion of this piece in "The Minimalist Aesthetic," pp. 101, 121.

27 On the other hand, my impression might not be borne out at all, if Lucier himself is correct: "The rate of transformation isn't constant . . . For the first few generations it moves at a seemingly constant pace, then, in one or two generations, the movement speeds up, then slows down again. It seems to operate on its own set of rules. It's very mysterious." (Lucier and Simon, p. 39.)

28 The recordings are: Source Records Number Three, issued with the periodical *Source: Music of the Avant Garde* 4 (issue no. 7, 1970), 15 generations on one side of a 10-inch LP (total duration 15'); Lovely Music VR–1013 (1981), 32 generations on two sides of a 12-inch LP (total duration 45').

and realization of Alvin Lucier's piece can be conceived of in the visual domain. By taking a photo of the first photo (of the chair in the room in which her husband sat when he made his original recording), then taking a photo of the photo of the photo, and so on, Mary Lucier introduced a slight error of size at each copy, so that the image gradually enlarged and moved off the picture: "There was a dark shadow behind the lamp which grew on each reproduction, until finally the fifty-second one is completely black; the shadow behind the lamp grew until it took up the whole image." This outcome is not to be regarded as analogous to imperfections in the duplication of sound introduced and magnified by concatenated recordings of recordings; Alvin Lucier himself asserts that the equipment he used produced practically no distortion and "did a marvelous job of maintaining [the tape matter]."[29] But it *could* be regarded as analogous to the "disappearance" of the voice into the acoustics of the room, and the corresponding expansion of that acoustical presence to surround us, the listeners, as if we had become engulfed by the voice and, from that vantage point, were no longer able to understand it.

II. Glass, *Music in Twelve Parts* (1971–74): Part 5

Glass has described *Music in Twelve Parts* as "a modular work, one of the first such compositions, with twelve distinct parts which can be performed separately in one long sequence, or in any combination or variation."[30] The meaning of this statement is not precisely clear, but it seems to indicate that each of the twelve parts

---

29 Lucier and Simon, pp. 34, 39. Some of Mary Lucier's photos are reproduced on the sleeve of the Lovely Music recording of *I am sitting in a room*.

30 From Glass's liner notes to his recording of *Music in Twelve Parts* (Virgin 91311-2, 3 CDs, 1988). That Glass would refer to this piece as "one of the first" modular works shows all the more clearly the extent of his indebtedness to minimal art. In making this statement, quite evidently he has not taken into consideration certain other, earlier musical works that could be described as modular, such as Earle Brown's *Folio* (1952) or Karlheinz Stockhausen's *Klavierstück XI* (1956), or even Pierre Boulez's Third Piano Sonata (1956–63)—not, however, out of carelessness, but because the aesthetic as well as the music-technical basis of those earlier works is so different. Moment form, as exhibited in *Klavierstück XI*, does not involve a preplanned trajectory through the material; as the performer, one is directed to set one's own course, and to do it spontaneously. Further, there are many more such spontaneous choices to be made in the course of Stockhausen's relatively brief piece than there are pre-arranged choices in the three-hour duration of *Music in Twelve Parts*. Both the kind and degree of control, in short, that Glass is exerting have the effect of severely constraining the result by comparison to the Stockhausen. The same sort of spontaneity—an aspect of the abstract-expressionist aesthetic that is fundamentally inimical to minimalism —is evident in Brown's *Folio*, where the range of choices in performance is even greater than in the Stockhausen owing to the notation chosen for the individual pieces, some of them displaying neither recognizable musical symbols nor guide to interpretation. See my discussion of abstract expressionism and aleatory, and of

may be regarded as an independent unit whose musical integrity is not damaged by being performed by itself or out of order with the others or as part of a group of fewer than twelve. In this respect, the work as a whole echoes many modular works in painting and sculpture whose components retain their artistic validity when exhibited independently or in various different spatial arrangements.[31]

Part 5 of this piece, at first glance, seems transparent in its simplicity: the principal pitch materials are a pair of notes a whole step apart; the supporting harmonies are not differentiated in any clear-cut fashion.[32] What do vary are the rhythm of what will here be termed the *cycle* of these two notes and their associated sung syllables, the rhythm of each larger *unit* which these cycles constitute, and the number of repetitions that each unit receives. A *segment* comprises the unit together with its succeeding repetitions; these are marked throughout the following analysis by timings taken from the (to date only) commercially issued recording.[33]

From the chart given as Example 1, it is evident that the form of Part 5 consists of two large rhythmically defined motions, of similar though not identical contour. The first begins with a single small unit of two equal durations repeated many times, whose size increases modestly over the next several segments before being reduced to two equal durations again (at 2:09), this time twice the length of those in the initial unit. Immediately thereafter, the unit length increases greatly to the first maximum (between 4:17 and 5:31) before shrinking again. Already at 5:31, however, the repeated eighths resemble the opening (though the interjected dotted-eighth pairs prevent an exact duplication); then, at 6:35, the unit is the same as it was at 0:23, except that the component cycles are in reverse order. When this resemblance continues at 7:05 (compare to 0:58), we receive the impression that the second large motion is firmly under way, its beginning having been dovetailed over the course of a minute or so with the end of the first motion. The second motion continues from there much as the first did, with slight enlargement of the unit (7:42, 8:20), reduction to a pair of equal values (9:12), followed by massive enlargement through the segments beginning at 10:00, 10:51, 11:56, and 13:27. What starts out to be the third presentation (at 14:48) of the unit first heard at 13:27 is truncated at 15:18 as the dotted-quarter pairs are reiterated from that

---

"constrained chance" in such works as Terry Riley's *In C*, in "The Minimalist Aesthetic," pp. 87–91 and 96–97 respectively.

31 For example, Carl Andre's *Equivalents I–VIII*, as discussed and illustrated in "The Minimalist Aesthetic," pp. 99–101 and Example 9.

32 These harmonies are supplied by sustained notes in winds and keyboards and by a (keyboard) bass line moving in constant sixteenths.

33 The timings are given in the format minutes:seconds. As is the case with almost all of Glass's works, no study score is available of this piece. The transcription in Example 1 below is my own; no guarantees can be made that the notation coincides exactly with Glass's score, although I do believe that in itself the transcription is quite accurate.

♩ = MM 104 approx

Segment No.	Time	Unit	Cycles/ Unit	Beats/ Unit	Units/ Segmt.	Cycles/ Segmt.	Beats/ Segmt.
1	0:00	*(notation)*	1	1	41	41	41
2	0:23	*(notation)*	2	3	20	40	60
3	0:58	*(notation)*	2	3	19	38	57
4	1:31	*(notation)*	3	6	11	33	66
5	2:09	*(notation)*	1	2	32	32	64
6	2:48	*(notation)*	5	9	7	35	63
7	3:23	*(notation)*	10	18	5	50	90
8	4:17	*(notation)*	18	27	5	90	135
9	5:31	*(notation)*	8	9	7	56	63
10	6:07	*(notation)*	4	4.5	11	44	49.5
11	6:35	*(notation)*	2	3	18	36	54
12	7:05	*(notation)*	2	3	22	44	66
13	7:42	*(notation)*	2	4.5	15	30	67.5
14	8:20	*(notation)*	3	9	10	30	90
15	9:12	*(notation)*	1	4	21	21	84

Example 1: Glass, *Music in Twelve Parts* (1971–74): Part 5, Rhythmic Plan

Music composed by Philip Glass
Copyright 1974 Dunvagen Music Publishers, Inc.   Used by permission

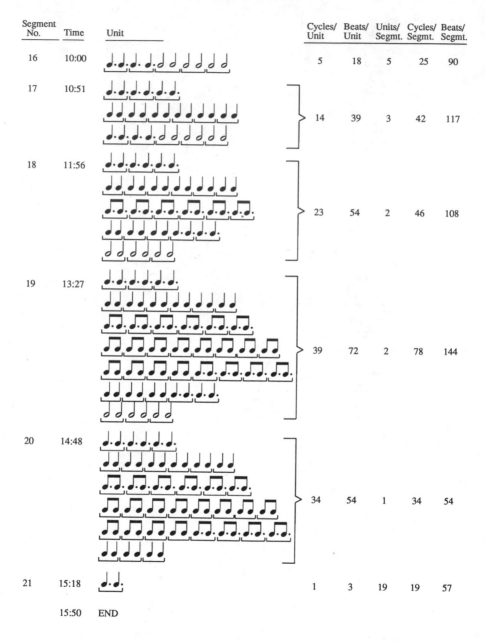

Segment No.	Time	Unit		Cycles/ Unit	Beats/ Unit	Units/ Segmt.	Cycles/ Segmt.	Beats/ Segmt.
16	10:00			5	18	5	25	90
17	10:51			14	39	3	42	117
18	11:56			23	54	2	46	108
19	13:27			39	72	2	78	144
20	14:48			34	54	1	34	54
21	15:18			1	3	19	19	57
	15:50	END						

Example 1 (cont.): Glass, *Music in Twelve Parts* (1971–74): Part 5, Rhythmic Plan

point to the end of Part 5, where they become the basis for the initially reigning triple meter of Part 6.

The trouble with the foregoing description is that it lends the impression of segments that are rigidly and absolutely differentiated from one another. Two conditions conspire to keep the listening experience from being as simple as it appears it should by all rights be. One is the blurring of boundaries between segments; the other is the multiple ways in which the passage of time may be defined and kept track of. Paradoxically, it is the very simplicity of the "raw materials" that makes the eventual listening experience so complicated.

As far as boundaries are concerned, it should be obvious even at the very beginning that the first segment might as easily consist of 42 units as 41, since the second segment begins with the same pair of eighths. In fact, the notational alternative chosen, which also affects the third segment, seems preferable only because it avoids the necessity of supplying a fragmentary unit of two quarters before the fourth segment begins. On the other hand, to tolerate this single fragment would allow more explicit representation of the connections between the second and eleventh and the third and twelfth segments, since no reversal would take place anymore. In any case, the presumed need for a clear representation of *elements* on paper has already distorted the connection between that representation and the listening experience. Scanning the makeup of other adjacent units in the chart, the reader will notice further ambiguities in partitioning, ambiguities which become more pronounced as the units lengthen. For example, there is no way of hearing that the first unit of segment 8 (beginning at 4:17) is actually not the sixth repetition of segment 7 until 4:25, where pairs of eighths begin.

Why would Glass have sought such an effect? One's first impression is that it makes more difficult the business of following the progress of the piece. Actually, however, it does the opposite: as suggested above in the discussion of putative connections between op art and the rhythmic devices of minimal music, this is not *trompe l'oreille*, but rather a deemphasis of parts in favor of the whole.[34] In fact, there are many other such blurrings, beyond those produced by overlaps of identical components. Moving from the second to the third segment, for instance, we certainly perceive a qualitative difference, but it is not so stark as the quantitative difference in notation seems to convey. What comes across to the ear is that the second cycle in each unit has been smoothed out. It doesn't come across as a whole new rhythm mainly because nothing else changes: neither the pitches, nor the timbre, nor the dynamics, nor the tempo. This sameness has the effect, not of training one's attention solely on rhythm, as if it were "the only thing that mattered" to musical succession, but rather of denying that the change *in itself* has any special importance.

---

34 See also my comments on Glass's *Music in Fifths* (1969) in "The Minimalist Aesthetic" (p. 105). Although the effects obtained in *Music in Twelve Parts* are a good deal more intricate and subtle than in the earlier piece, the underlying aim appears to be substantially the same.

These observations lead us directly to more general consideration of the nature of time in this piece. Several factors affect our sense of its passage: one, the relative lengths of the units; two, the number of cycles each contains; three, the number of repetitions of the unit making up each segment. None of these factors, of course, engages absolute or clock time in more than an indirect way, though not surprisingly the number of beats per unit exhibits a close correlation to number of cycles per unit. More interesting is the rough tendency of the number of unit repetitions per segment to vary inversely with the number of cycles per unit; this result may suggest some sort of compensatory relationship between the two. The remaining totals tabulated reveal only an approximate correspondence between cycles/segment, beats/segment, and the other measures of activity.

These data aside, however, it may be worth considering the possibility that the peaks in the series of cycles/unit, and the corresponding troughs in the repetitions/segment, are at least as important for what they reveal of a qualitative difference between the larger units (those of at least four cycles) and the shorter ones. The longer ones do something that the shorter ones don't: they embed sub-units that can sound like repeated units in their own right, thus embodying two levels of repetition. And the longest units of all (Nos. 8, 17, 18, and 19) have yet another property: they progress through repetitions of cycles that are made up of increasingly shorter values, reaching their minimum duration with paired eighths and moving back to longer values in such a way as to complete a circle upon beginning repetition of the whole unit. In its general design, this motion echoes the organization of the two larger motions that constitute the entire Part 5.

What visual analogue does such a piece suggest? One could imagine a mosaic work, vaguely grid-like in design perhaps, in which the indivisible component tile, like the cycle of Glass's piece, was everywhere so perfectly obvious to the eye that it quickly ceased to have any interest as such. One could then overlook these components and concentrate upon larger, "holistic" matters (to use one of the minimalist artists' favorite words), which would, however, present a good deal of ambiguity. A large two-part division would provide a minimal structure, but even the division between parts would not be perfectly well defined, and all other plausible groupings of tiles would overlap and blur together somewhat. Certain larger regions of the work would seem to have substructures of their own. A fine-grained, essentially uniform background would correspond to the accompanying wind and keyboard parts. The work of several artists provides useful points of reference, particularly Agnes Martin's mosaic-like grids, Larry Poons's fields of tiny lozenges, and Jackie Winsor's knot "sculptures."

III. Reich, *Music for 18 Musicians* (1974–76)

The obvious correspondent for this piece in the visual domain is the serial genre, in which the components (somewhat distinct from those of modular works) tend to be arranged for viewing in a prescribed order.[35] The form of this work, which comprises eleven sections each based on a different chord, flanked at the opening and conclusion by a fairly rapid presentation of the entire eleven-chord series, even suggests a mode of "viewing": the listener scans the series once quickly, then goes back to the beginning to study each component closely in its turn, then scans quickly once more.

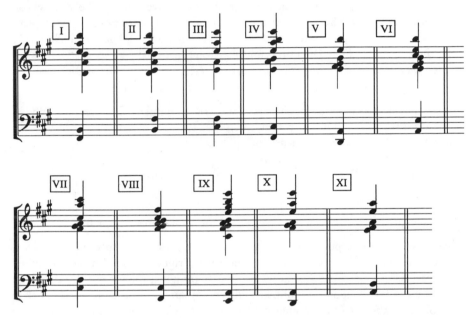

Example 2: Reich, *Music for 18 Musicians* (1974–76):
Introductory Chord Sequence

This sample analysis treats the eleven-chord opening (Example 2) by itself—not as a substitute for examining the entire work, which would most certainly prove

---

35 In fact, the distinction is not clear-cut, partly because no general agreement on terminology was ever reached among critics, but also, presumably, because the works themselves often cannot be so unambiguously classified.

rewarding (especially if the entire score were readily available for study), but in the interest of considering what impact the idea of "series" in visual art might have upon "harmonic progression" in the musical sense.[36] It goes without saying that this sequence of chords does not display any common-practice functional qualities; K. Robert Schwarz, for one, finds little to say about it other than that "many of the eleven chords are merely inversions or revoicings of the previous sonority, and there is no modulation."[37] Actually, only one chord (the second) so duplicates its predecessor; and closer examination reveals other interesting features that Schwarz apparently overlooked. To model what is going on here, an attempt will be made to emulate the methodical working through of possibilities often exhibited in the work of one of the premier serialists of the minimal movement, Sol LeWitt, whose titles often summarize his organizational principles: "All Variations of Incomplete Open Cubes"; "Squares with a Different Line Direction in Each Half Square"; "Bands of Color in Four Directions and All Combinations"; etc.

By way of preliminary observation, there are four important "rules" consistently followed throughout the entire sequence of chords:

1. The universal set of pitch classes is strictly limited to those naturally occurring in a three-sharp signature.
2. Every chord contains at least four pitch classes.
3. A and F♯ are found in every chord.
4. Either C♯ or D is present in every chord, but never both.

One further rule is:

5. The presence of E is a necessary condition to the presence of B.

There is only one exception to this fifth rule, and it occurs for a specific reason that will become apparent below. The first and fourth rules mandate that the number of pitch classes in a chord can never be greater than six; the second through fifth rules impose limits upon the number and type of subsets of the universal set that may occur as chords. Other regularities become apparent if the pitch-class contents of each chord are viewed a kind of partial scale, an incomplete version of the universal set.

To begin, the common elements A and F♯ can be fixed as endpoints for such a partial scale, supplemented by one of the C♯–D pair (arbitrarily, on this occasion, D) and with the upper portion of the entire span filled in with the E to arrive at the minimum allowable number of pitch classes:

---

36 Example 2 is taken from Schwarz's summary of the chordal sequence provided in "Steve Reich: Music as a Gradual Process," Part II, p. 247, and has been checked against a copy of the composer's hand-copied score (Introduction and Sections I–VII only) found in the University of California Library system.

37 Schwarz, "Steve Reich," Part II, p. 246.

A   D   E   F♯   (I)

Next, the remaining gap between A and D is filled in to the extent possible:

A   B   D   E   F♯   (II)

Now start over again with A and F♯, this time adding the member of the C♯–D pair not used the first time around and again filling in the upper portion of the span:

A   C♯   E   F♯   (III)

Next, analogously to (II), fill in the B:

A   B   C♯   E   F♯   (IV)

Return to the first five-note chord (II) and add one more note, the only one still available for this chord:

A   B   D   E   F♯   G♯   (V)

Now return to the second five-note chord (IV) and do the same as in (V):

A   B   C♯   E   F♯   G♯   (VI)

Begin again with A and F♯, but now that the upper limit of the scale has been expanded to G♯, include this pitch class also, as well as one from the C♯–D pair (since this makes four, add no other elements for the time being):

A   C♯   F♯   G♯   (VII)

Now add B, in analogy to the move from (III) to (IV):

A   B   C♯   F♯   G♯   (VIII)

Next, reintroduce E, obtaining the same result as at (VI), but by a different route:

A   B   C♯   E   F♯   G♯   (IX)

Shift the C♯ to D to produce the alternate form of the "complete" six-note scale, comparable to (V) in relation to (VI), but at the same time remove the B:

A   D   E   F♯   G♯   (X)

Finally, remove the G♯:

A   D   E   F♯   (XI)

This (XI) turns out to be the same as (I). Accordingly, to give the sequence circular implications, but not the same literal beginning and end, a revoiced form of (II) is substituted at position (I):

A   B   D   E   F♯   (I, final form)

With this last adjustment, the entire sequence has been "generated."

As an algorithm, of course, the preceding is not terribly rigorous. Particularly unsatisfactory is the recourse to successive *subtraction* of elements to obtain (X) and (XI), since such a procedure has played no role up to this point. And such matters as spacing, doubling, and vertical order are not engaged at all by this account. To put matters in appropriate perspective, however, it bears keeping in mind that in serial works of visual art, the range of possibilities is always governed by some set—perhaps quite arbitrarily selected—of initial conditions. There are three important limits on these powers of governance, though: (1) they do not control every aspect of the material—for instance, in a LeWitt line drawing, the width of the lines is not precisely specified, although it tends to be about the same throughout the work; (2) they do not necessarily require that the working through of possibilities be accomplished in any particular sequence; and (3) the serial strategies growing out of them often do not even exhaust the entire range of possibilities. As to the first, one could take the state of being "about the same" to correspond to the general conditions of, say, spacing in Reich's chords: the lowest two pitches always a fourth or fifth apart; a relatively wide gap separating them from the middle range, where notes tend to be more closely spaced; and an upper group of three pitches in which again wider spacings tend to dominate. As far as (temporal) order is concerned, although there may not seem to be anything absolutely *inevitable* about the order of Reich's chords, it is undeniably interesting that three "nested" sequences each consisting of a four-, a five-, and a six-member chord are given, that a fourth such sequence is implied in retrograde, and that an "exceptional chord" (VIII, the only one that violates Rule 5) is used to strengthen the analogy between the pairs (III),(IV) and (VII),(VIII).[38] And concerning the third limit, of all the possibilities admitted by the five rules given above, only two chords fail to appear.

Seen from this angle, Reich's selection of chords certainly has something of the "systematic" about it, in the LeWittian sense. Moreover, this interpretation of the chordal sequence shows it to be nonhierarchical in the same way that works of serial art generally are. The series is not really a "progression," in the tonal-hierarchical sense, because it lacks organic qualities; the order is imposed from without.

IV. Glass, *Satyagraha* (1980): Act I, Scene 1 ("The Kuru Field of Justice")

Glass himself has attested to a major stylistic shift in his work during the mid-1970s, one that had a large impact upon what may still be his most famous

---

38 Notice also that the choice of lowest part for both pairs of chords is the same (C♯3–F♯2), further reinforcing the analogy.

piece, *Einstein on the Beach*. This shift was brought about principally by reinvolvement, for the first time since his student days, with harmony, specifically root-movement harmony, and his integration of it with an already well-developed rhythmic practice in a way that, as he says, is meant to be "functional" in the sense of its employment in eighteenth- and nineteenth-century Western music.[39] For this reason, evidently, Glass does not regard *Einstein* as a minimalist work, though he is content to apply that label to all his previous music from 1965 through *Music in Twelve Parts*.[40]

In some of Glass's more recent music, although the minimalist appellation may no longer be perfectly appropriate, neither is it completely inappropriate. This is so because his work has begun to resemble another art form, to which minimalism was closely allied from its beginnings: namely, pop art. The principal difference between the two has always been that pop art deals in images that are readily recognizable from the world of commercial art and photography—including, specifically, advertising—whereas minimal art tends to a much simpler and more "neutral" look, such as the geometrical solids that Morris called "unitary forms," or Judd's wall-mounted boxes. Otherwise, however, the presentation is strikingly similar: bright, uniform colors, with an emphasis on surface rather than depth; a certain aloofness, or at least as nearly complete a removal as possible of expression in the conventional sense (including that of 1950s abstract-expressionist art); and, often, a modular/serial mode, in which the panels or other units arranged for viewing one after the other (though not always in an absolutely prescribed order) convey a sensation of gradual change or slight, barely perceptible variation over time.

It is not so much the simple fact of occurrence of triads and other recognizable chords from older practice as their employment in certain ways that suggests an analogy between pop art's incorporation of commercial images and Glass's borrowings from commercial (pop) music. In neither case, of course, is the practice of the source actually duplicated. We do not mistake Andy Warhol's soup cans or Brillo boxes for advertisements of these products, at least not for very long; by the same token, the first scene of *Satyagraha* does not sound very much like pop music, although the conventions of pop are certainly evident here.[41]

Let us see, however, how Glass himself describes the opening of his opera. His notation of the first four measures (Example 3)—the harmonic basis for the entire 18:46 of the first scene—is accompanied by the following commentary:

---

39 Philip Glass, *Music by Philip Glass* (New York: Harper & Row, 1987), pp. 59–62.
40 See liner notes to Virgin recording of *Music in Twelve Parts*, cited in note 30.
41 The same can be said of Glass's venture into collaborative songwriting, *Songs from Liquid Days* (1985): the point is not to write pop songs, but to draw on the power of "hooks" and other highly formulaic gestures endemic to pop practice and put it to work to serve artistic ends that are, after all, not identical to those of Top 40 radio or MTV, whatever else one might think of them. See also note 44.

Example 3: Glass, *Satyagraha* (1980): Act I, Scene 1 ("The Kuru Field of Justice"), mm. 1–4

By Philip Glass   HarperCollins Publishers
© Copyright 1987 by Dunvagen Music Publishers, Inc.   Used by permission

For *Satyagraha* I concentrated on only one [combination of harmonic and rhythmic structure], using it in all seven scenes of the opera. Listeners familiar with Baroque music will recognize it as the chaconne, a form in which a harmonic pattern with changing rhythmic and melodic material is repeated throughout a piece, making it a specific kind of variation form. The fifth movement of Bach's D-minor partita for unaccompanied violin is an example that will be familiar to many people . . .

An interesting feature of this progression is that it is the same as one often heard in flamenco guitar music. This particular form of Spanish folk music was introduced into Spain by gypsies who, it is believed, originated in India. There are very few harmonic practices shared by East and West since harmonic practice hardly ever turns up at all in Eastern music. This particular pattern is one of the few I know of that is common in the West and may have had its origin in the East.[42]

Glass is certainly no ethnomusicologist, but he is no naive musician either. It seems incredible that he would not be aware of the banal quality of this material, or that his use of it would fail to suggest to him a "debased" origin. The unabashed parallel fifths (and, eventually, octaves) evoke, not Bach, but Bacharach; likewise, the leaden way in which the variations proceed ensures that the whole thing will never get off the ground. Glass evidently does not intend his variations to transcend the repeating four-measure module and create a new structure; the procedure he adopts is simply (as he calls it) "additive," and it can function perfectly well while leaving the original module "virtually unchanged," as by his own account it does in Act II, Scene 2.[43]

---

42 Glass, pp. 115–16.
43 Glass, p. 116. Glass may have adopted this term from Curt Sachs, who discusses "additive" rhythm as an aspect of "oriental" rhythmic practice. See Curt Sachs, *Rhythm and Tempo: A Study in Music History* (New York: Norton, 1953), pp. 90–95.

The best possible construction that could be placed on Glass's explanation *cum* rationale is that he was in fact consciously thinking of Bach and flamenco when he wrote *Satyagraha* but that other models, unconsciously emulated, eventually proved more influential in shaping the final product, perhaps without his becoming aware of how much the balance had shifted.[44] A more cynical interpretation would hold that he invokes older Western and Eastern practice as a kind of smokescreen, that actually he had the true character of his material well in mind and deliberately exploited it, subjected it in fact to monstrous amplification and extension much as Warhol does with his (seemingly) endlessly repeated silkscreened images of such pop icons as Marilyn Monroe and Elvis Presley. Glass's variation procedure seems to owe all too much to such works, in which the background color may change from panel to panel or a kind of overlaid "wash" may provide some textural variation without ever substantially altering the image, which remains blatantly (and, sooner or later, boringly) apparent throughout.[45]

Whether one opts for the charitable or the cynical view, it is worth noting that the facts of Glass's background argue forcefully for the conclusion that he would have made his decisions about the use of such materials from a point of view strongly formed by immersion in the visual arts. Many of Glass's comrades during his years as an up-and-comer in New York were from the worlds of painting, sculpture, theatre, film, and dance. Through his first wife, JoAnne Akalaitis, he was associated with Mabou Mines, an experimental theatre/mixed-media group originally formed by Americans living in Paris in the mid-1960s whose base of operations eventually shifted to New York. As is well known, he established close friendships and working relationships with Richard Serra, Sol LeWitt, and Lucinda Childs, among others. The musicians with whom he eventually formed the Philip Glass Ensemble were misfits like himself, people who had moved downtown either in a spirit of rebellion against the rigidities of the musical "establishment" or because they felt genuinely isolated in the world of music and were looking for some way to connect with the other arts—or both.

---

44 The progression I–VII–VI–V♮ in the minor mode (in parallel triads) appears, for instance: as the introductory vamp in "Walk, Don't Run" (recorded by The Ventures, 1960); as the verse and instrumental break in "Runaway" (Del Shannon, 1961); as the verse in "Don't Let Me Be Misunderstood" (The Animals, 1965); as the verse in the first part of "Good Vibrations" (The Beach Boys, 1966); and as the verse in "Happy Together" (The Turtles, 1967). Many other examples exist.

45 Wim Mertens, on the other hand, asserts that the individual harmonies in such passages "are used in a way that takes them outside the tonal functionalism of the classical system"; they do not form progressions precisely because, juxtaposed in simple parallel, they fail to connect. (*American Minimal Music*, trans. J. Hautekiet [London: Kahn and Averill/New York: Alexander Broude, 1983], p. 79.) This is an interesting argument, but ultimately I cannot find it convincing when it is obvious that Glass is consciously invoking common practice or (even if unconsciously) making use of more recent commercial practice, any more than I can look at a Warhol soup can as an abstract image.

Example 4: Glass, *Satyagraha*: from Act I, Scene 1

Music composed by Philip Glass
Copyright 1982 by Dunvagen Music Publishers, Inc. Used by permission

By contrast, Glass's formal musical training, though extensive, appears to have exerted a relatively slight impact on his development as an artist. Five years at Juilliard did not prepare him to appreciate the contemporary scene in Paris as defined by Pierre Boulez and the Domaine Musical, which Glass later described as "a wasteland, dominated by these maniacs, these creeps, who were trying to make everyone write this crazy creepy music."[46] He has repeatedly emphasized the importance of his studies with Nadia Boulanger as a part of his musical formation,

---

46 Quoted, from an imprecisely identified interview, by John Rockwell in *All-American Music*, p. 111.

but he seems to have a curious love–hate relationship with those memories. At one point in his autobiography he recalls the glee with which he flouted the traditional prohibition of parallel fifths by writing a piece that consisted of nothing else; one can imagine that he might have derived even more such perverse satisfaction from the opening scene of *Satyagraha*, since here the parallels are joined to "functional harmony," or at least a recognizable simulacrum thereof. Glass's "return" to harmony may be even more significant for the evidence it presents of a desire to escape the criteria of conventional criticism; note that the explicit embrace of commercial images by Warhol and others was, among other things, a way of frustrating critical attacks on their interest in the marketability of their product. The nature of Glass's chaconne theme fits this conjecture, as does its subsequent treatment, which is very often awkward from a traditional point of view (see Example 4).[47] After studying passages of this kind, it is difficult not to be reminded of Clement Greenberg's remarks about pop art, which he acknowledges "partakes of the trend to openness and clarity" but does not "challenge taste on more than a superficial level" and for that reason is "not . . . an authentically new episode in the evolution of contemporary art."[48]

In an earlier article, I cast some doubt on the proposition that minimal music would endure—and, therefore, stand up to analysis—skeptical that, to paraphrase Gertrude Stein, there was really enough there there. The preliminary results reported above cannot be regarded as having decided this issue one way or the other, giving as they do only a hint of what actual analytical method might be for minimal music; yet they do justify at least some confidence that strategies can be devised which engage the general problems of this repertoire and affirm its unique aesthetic basis without effectively condescending to it. Even the section on *Satyagraha*, negative though it is in its judgment, takes the music—and the creative impulse behind it—seriously.

One matter remaining to be addressed concerns the eventual extent and limits of minimalism in music. Those familiar with John Adams's personal history, for example, will realize that he lacks the intimate contact with artists and their works in the visual realm that the older minimalists have experienced. At what point will it be reasonable to surmise that contemporary compositional practice has grown so far out of minimalism as to have in fact departed from it? After all, in the visual arts themselves this has already long since happened. In general, from the mid-1970s onward there has occurred a notable diversification and "enrichment"

---

47 Example 4 is my own transcription of a single variation (comprising two statements of the chaconne bass) near the end of Act I, Scene 1; it is taken from the recording of *Satyagraha* (CBS I3M 39672, 3LPs, 1985).

48 Clement Greenberg, "Post-Painterly Abstraction," in *The Great Decade of American Abstraction: Modernist Art 1960–1970*, ed. E. A. Carmean, Jr. (Houston: Houston Museum of Fine Arts, 1974), pp. 72–74.

of the harmonic content of minimal music; this has had the perhaps predictable result of encouraging the renascence of more familiar types of pitch-hierarchical models in some recent analytical work.

I would, however, counsel caution. The so-called "return to harmony" or even "return to tonality," much remarked upon by critics, is (at least in the case of Reich and Adams) really an *appropriation* of harmony for purposes that are essentially new and not yet at all well understood. To assume that composers, by retrieving such superficially familiar sonorities as triads and major-minor seventh chords, have also taken on, whether intending to or not, the hierarchical nature of common-practice tonality (if not its specific structures) may be assuming far too much. The surface is still remarkably shiny, bland, and—by the standards of music written earlier in this century—featureless; it is still concealing by denying that it has any depth. Post-minimalist or not, this music still seems to owe a lot to minimalism—and to the extent that it does, it will likely remain impenetrable without the mediation of the visual models of minimalism.

The Question of Climax in Ruth Crawford's String Quartet, Mvt. 3

Ellie M. Hisama

Ruth Crawford's strikingly original conception for the slow movement of her String Quartet (1931) is established in its opening bars. They draw the listener into an unfamiliar sound-world, one in which the voices twist over, then under one another, come together and veer apart, creeping up all the while. As Example 1 shows, about three-quarters of the way through the work, the voices crescendo to *fff*, attack triple-stops, and snap apart—that is, the piece reaches a climax. The voices then swiftly descend and return to the soft and slow quality of the opening to conclude the movement.

The presence of the climax suggests a significant critical question about the piece: as a remnant of earlier musical procedures, it seems incompatible with the work's otherwise wholly modernist technique and aesthetic. In other words, the climax just doesn't seem to fit the piece.[1]

While musing over the various possibilities with which I could explore the question of climax in the work, I wondered whether feminist theory might prove useful to such a study. Over the past two decades feminism has transformed entire disciplines; I hoped it could bring crucial insights to music theory as well.[2]

Crawford's String Quartet seemed a promising piece to begin forging an

---

1 Judith Tick has discovered that the third movement's climax over mm. 68 through 75 was not present in the 1931 version but was added several years later. The version included as Example 1 was published in 1941. Her findings appear in "The Evolution of Ruth Crawford's String Quartet 1931," a paper presented at the 1987 national meeting of the American Musicological Society, New Orleans, Louisiana.

2 Many feminist theorists have argued against the standard academic writing style that takes on a disembodied voice of authority. Instead, as in my discussion here, the first-person narrative and an explicit subjective position is often crucial to a feminist stance. I hope it will become apparent that I hear the piece in the way I am suggesting because of the construction of my own identity. Recent examples of this style of writing include bell hooks, *Yearning: Race, Gender, and Cultural Politics* (Boston: South End Press, 1990); Trinh T. Minh-ha, *Woman, Native, Other: Writing Postcoloniality and Feminism* (Bloomington: Indiana University Press, 1989); Michele Wallace, *Invisibility Blues: From Pop to Theory* (London: Verso, 1990); and Patricia J. Williams, *The Alchemy of Race and Rights* (Cambridge, Mass.: Harvard University Press, 1991).

III
The dotted ties indicate that the first tone of each new bow is not to be attacked; the bowing should be as little audible as possible throughout.
The crescendi and decrescendi should be equally gradual.
Andante (♩= 116)
sempre legatissimo
sempre simile
5
10
15
20

Example 1: Ruth Crawford, String Quartet, Mvt. 3 (1931)

© 1941 Merion Music, Inc. Used By Permission Of The Publisher

Example 1 (cont.): Ruth Crawford, String Quartet, Mvt. 3 (1931)

Example 1 (cont.): Ruth Crawford, String Quartet, Mvt. 3 (1931)

* The half notes in measures 85-88 should be faster than the quarter notes in measure 77.

Example 1 (cont.): Ruth Crawford, String Quartet, Mvt. 3 (1931)

example of what feminist music theory might be.[3] The work has always struck me as an inappropriate specimen to slide under the microscope of set theory, a frequently used mode of music analysis for post-tonal music, for it is not composed of a few set classes which a set theorist would locate and trace through their various manifestations. Consequently, I developed another method to analyze the Quartet's third movement. What I hope to demonstrate by applying this model to the composition is that close readings of musical structure and formalist music theory may address, and in fact grow out of, a feminist consciousness.

In attempting to reconcile feminism with music theory, I want to commit myself to close readings of musical structure for two reasons. The first is personal; I enjoy doing it. The second is more global. If we are to build a feminist community of music scholars which includes those trained as music theorists, we need to leave open as many ways of reading as possible. Although some feminists reject rational and formalist approaches as masculinist, I do not find it necessary or desirable to stop analyzing music from codified principles—in short, to designate formalism as the Other in feminist music analysis.[4] I want to claim instead that hearing pieces of music *as feminists* may lead us to reject our traditional analytical tools and encourage us to develop new ones, which may be formalist as a particular piece warrants. Because some works might exceed our received ways of hearing, theorizing, and critiquing, I believe they deserve consideration through alternative theoretical models.

In the fall of 1929, Ruth Crawford moved to New York in order to continue her musical education. Only 28, she was extraordinarily fortunate to have already earned the admiration and support of colleagues who could wield a good deal of influence. With the aid of Henry Cowell, she was provided a room in the home of music patron Blanche Walton and the opportunity to study composition with Charles Seeger, who had been Cowell's own mentor. Walton provided Crawford both financial and emotional support, and the composer Marion Bauer, whom she met at the MacDowell Colony, became her mentor. In 1930, the Guggenheim

---

3   Joseph N. Straus discusses some of the issues encountered in bringing feminism to music theory in his book *The Music of Ruth Crawford Seeger* (Cambridge: Cambridge University Press, forthcoming) and in "Structural Issues in the Music of Ruth Crawford Seeger," a paper presented in the colloquium series of the Group for Gender Studies in Music, Harvard University, March, 1990. Suzanne G. Cusick, Marion A. Guck, Marianne Kielian-Gilbert, and Susan McClary have offered dazzling insights into this fledgling area of research in their essays that appear in *Perspectives of New Music* 32 (1994): 8–85.

4   One such writer who has questioned the compatibility of rationalism and formalism with feminism is Mary Daly, *Beyond God the Father: Toward a Philosophy of Women's Liberation* (Boston: Beacon Press, 1973).

Foundation awarded her a year-long fellowship in composition, its first to a woman.[5]

Yet Ruth Crawford was no stranger to the many barriers that resulted from sexist opinions about women composers. Charles Seeger was initially reluctant to accept her as a student because he believed women to be incapable of composing; the director of the Guggenheim Foundation did not want even to consider her application on the simple grounds of her sex.[6] Crawford's diary entry from February 22, 1930 records a memory of being shut out:

> The musicologists meet. It is decided that I may sit in the next room and hear [Joseph] Yasser [a visiting musicologist] about his new supra scale. Then when I come out for this purpose, I find someone has closed the doors. Blanche is irate, so am I. Men are selfish, says Blanche. You just have to accept the fact. Perhaps, I wonder, their selfishness is one reason why they accomplish more than women . . . I walk past the closed door to my room, and when I pass I turn my head toward the closed door and quietly but forcibly say, "Damn you," then go on in my room and read Yasser's article. Later, my chair close to the door, I hear some of the discussion.[7]

I have chosen to lead into my analysis with this image because it powerfully illustrates Crawford's status as a composer. Living in the Walton home, she had much easier access to musical resources than most composers of her time, male *or* female, but as a woman, she was still kept from entering the drawing room on the occasion of Yasser's visit and was reduced to pressing her ear to the door in order to pick up whatever scraps of information she could.

While much of Crawford's music is obviously a product of her rigorous training

---

5 Biographical information on Crawford is provided in Matilda Gaume, *Ruth Crawford Seeger: Memoirs, Memories, Music* (Metuchen, N.J.: Scarecrow Press, 1986). Judith Tick's new biography is entitled *Ruth Crawford Seeger, An American Woman's Life in Music* (New York: Oxford University Press, forthcoming).

6 Seeger recalls how Henry Cowell convinced him to give Crawford composition lessons despite his negative view of women composers in Ray Wilding-White, "Remembering Ruth Crawford Seeger: An Interview with Charles and Peggy Seeger," *American Music* 6 (1988): 446. Dane Rudhyar recalls his efforts to persuade the director of the Guggenheim Foundation, Henry Allen Moe, to review Crawford's application in Gaume, *Ruth Crawford Seeger*, p. 41.

7 Gaume, *Ruth Crawford Seeger*, p. 196. Contrary to what Crawford had apparently been told, Yasser's supra scale was not the only topic discussed that day. In a 1972 interview, Charles Seeger mentioned that the New York Musicological Society had been founded at the meeting, and stated that he had purposefully excluded Crawford from this important event because he wanted to avoid the incipient criticism that musicology was "women's work." (She was permitted to attend subsequent meetings to organize the Society.) Charles Seeger's remarks appear in *Reminiscences of an American Musicologist*, interviewers Adelaide G. Tusler and Ann Briegleb, Oral History Program, University of California at Los Angeles, 1972. I would like to thank Taylor Greer for passing on this information.

in musical modernism, I shall argue that her compositions also reflect her gender. I do not mean this in a biological or essentialist sense. Rather, I mean that as a woman, Ruth Crawford often found herself pushed to the outside of professional circles and that the structure of this string quartet movement mirrors her social, gender-based exclusion. As a result of this gender-based exclusion, her compositions became a site of resistance, speaking in what the literary theorist Elaine Showalter calls a "double-voiced discourse." [8] Because I am grounding my argument in the social exclusion and double participation that some women experience, rather than in their biology, I am not arguing that *all* women composers create such artistic spaces. Nor am I claiming anything like "every woman is destined to write music that is somehow different from the music men write and that is somehow similar to music written by other women." Such a generalization assumes that women and men are monolithic groups, which I do not believe, and disregards historical context and individual experience, factors which I consider crucial to my reading of Crawford's work. [9]

The groundwork for my argument that links Crawford's string quartet movement to her gender is a theory offered by the anthropologist Edwin Ardener, who has suggested that women in a society operate both within a dominant group and in a space outside it. From his studies in Cameroon, he argues that Bakweri women, who are "muted" both socially and linguistically, express their views of the world not through direct expository speech but through the encoded realms of art, myth, or ritual. [10] Although some feminist theorists romantically urge us to celebrate such spaces as pure realms of female culture, unsullied by the dominant male culture, it is important to acknowledge that many of these models are not autonomous. As Showalter observes, because of the widespread influence and authority of the dominant male-generated model, and the necessity that women present their concerns in a form acceptable to men in order simply to be heard, a muted group's perceptions of the world and forms of self-expression are often transmitted through the dominant order. [11]

---

8 Elaine Showalter, "Feminist Criticism in the Wilderness," in *The New Feminist Criticism: Essays on Women, Literature, and Theory,* ed. Elaine Showalter (New York: Pantheon Books, 1985), p. 263.

9 Some of Rose Rosengard Subotnik's work may illuminate my argument about the relationship between this quartet movement and Crawford's subject position. She reflects upon what she understands to be structural parallelisms between a person's life and work in *Developing Variations: Style and Ideology in Western Music* (Minneapolis: University of Minnesota Press, 1991).

10 Edwin Ardener, "Belief and the Problem of Women" in *Perceiving Women,* ed. Shirley Ardener (New York: John Wiley & Sons, 1975), pp. 1–18, and his "The 'Problem' Revisited" in the same volume, pp. 19–28. The term "muted group" was suggested by Charlotte Hardman.

11 Showalter, "Feminist Criticism in the Wilderness," pp. 261–63. Sandra M. Gilbert and Susan Gubar suggest that nineteenth-century writing by European and American women, including Jane Austen, Mary Shelley, Emily Brontë, and Emily Dickinson, generally displayed a normal

Using Ardener's theoretical framework, I shall claim that while Crawford's Quartet movement *seems* to work its way up to a traditional climax, it actually creates a musical space within which another procedure subverts the climax.[12] Because this undercurrent is much less obvious than the loudly trumpeted moment of climax, I shall introduce an analytical model to account for its presence. Consequently, rather than having to conclude that the movement's promise of a new musical vision is spoiled by an unimaginative narrative strategy, we may alternatively understand it as challenging or even parodying a nineteenth-century climax and might contemplate the possibility that the foiling of the climax is in some way related to Crawford's experience as a woman.[13] Her composition, then, would be not just revolutionary but also distinctly feminist in undercutting a dominant, masculinist musical narrative by including a second narrative wholly independent of the first.[14]

---

surface design but often concealed other less accessible and acceptable levels of meaning. They present this argument in *The Madwoman in the Attic: The Woman Writer and the Nineteenth-Century Literary Imagination* (New Haven: Yale University Press, 1979, 2nd edn. 1984).

More explicit expressions of women's feelings of exclusion and invisibility in male-dominated social spaces have recently appeared in collections intended to provide a forum for such writings. Three such books are *This Bridge Called My Back: Writings by Radical Women of Color*, ed. Cherríe Moraga and Gloria Anzaldúa (Watertown, Mass.: Persephone Press, 1981; 2nd edn. Latham, N.Y.: Kitchen Table, Women of Color Press, 1983); *All the Women Are White, All the Blacks are Men, But Some of Us Are Brave: Black Women's Studies*, ed. Gloria T. Hull, Patricia Bell Scott, and Barbara Smith (Old Westbury, N.Y.: The Feminist Press, 1982); and *The Forbidden Stitch: An Asian American Women's Anthology*, ed. Shirley Geok-lin Lim and Mayumi Tsutakawa (Corvallis, Ore.: Calyx Books, 1989). Mitsuye Yamada describes her double invisibility as a Japanese-American woman in "Invisibility is an Unnatural Disaster: Reflections of an Asian American Woman" in *This Bridge*, pp. 35–40; Barbara Smith writes of her exclusion as a Black lesbian in "Toward a Black Feminist Criticism," in *But Some of Us Are Brave*, pp. 157–75.

12 Susan McClary has suggested reading musical climaxes in sexual terms in "Getting Down Off the Beanstalk: The Presence of a Woman's Voice in Janika Vandervelde's *Genesis II*," in *Feminine Endings: Music, Gender, and Sexuality* (Minneapolis: University of Minnesota Press, 1991), pp. 112–31. Although I intend the traditional musical sense of "climax" in my discussion, another reading of the movement might usefully link it to sexuality.

13 I mean "parody" in the sense proposed by Linda Hutcheon in her *A Theory of Parody: The Teaching of Twentieth-Century Art Forms* (New York: Methuen, 1985). In her examination of parody in twentieth-century painting, music, literature, and architecture, she suggests that modern parody does not necessarily ridicule, but possesses a range of intentions, including playfulness and irony as well as scorn.

14 I do not know whether Crawford intended the movement to enact the specific feminist strategy I am suggesting here, or even whether she considered traditional musical climaxes to be a male domain. Although what she set out to do certainly interests me, the analysis I offer here does not depend upon compositional intent. Rather, my reading emerges from my knowledge of Crawford's strong feelings about the inequity of women compared to men, and my own identity as an Asian-American woman who occupies social spaces analogous to the two musical spaces I perceive in this piece.

The Quartet's third movement opens by establishing its unusual musical processes: instead of the instruments keeping their distance, marking off their registral territory, they snuggle together a semitone apart and often pack themselves within the space of a minor third as they creep up toward the downbeat of m. 75, the point at which they break apart. The viola and cello are tossed up into registers alien to their usual tessitura, effecting unusual tone qualities; voices rub against each other at the space of a semitone; instruments shift pitch in turn. The movement rejects the predominant Classical string quartet model in which the first violin takes on the role of leader over harmonic support provided by the second violin, viola, and cello. Instead, the instruments work cooperatively, sharing in the same musical tasks.[15]

Yet in contrast to these innovative musical strategies, the movement takes on a traditional narrative shape. As Figure 1 graphically demonstrates, the voices collectively inch upward. They also gradually get louder. The four horizontally directed lines in this figure represent each instrument's path through the piece.[16]

In m. 65 (sonority change 53 in Figure 1) the violins begin a game of one-upmanship which brings all instruments to the pinnacle of the piece and to its subsequent collapse. Ten measures later, the movement becomes very loud, shifts from legato bowing to attacks via triple-stops in all instruments, and sprawls across four octaves. In a traditional musical narrative, this moment would serve as the climax.

My analytical model, however, reveals a second narrative, which depends on the following paradigm. Think of the instruments as four strands of sound that are woven together throughout the piece. Each strand occupies a characteristic register, one not located in absolute pitch space but defined relative to the other strands'

---

15 In her own analysis of this movement, which she sent to Edgard Varèse in 1948, Crawford describes a melodic line extending through the piece whose tones are distributed among the four instruments. For example, the melodic line in mm. 12–15 is made up of the viola's D♯–F♯–violin 2's A–B♭–cello's G♯–B. Crawford's analyses of the Quartet's third and fourth movements are available in the Library of Congress, Seeger Collection.

Marion A. Guck has suggested that instead of conceiving of musical elements as competing with each other, we might alternatively read them as working cooperatively. In my reading, I use both models in describing different stretches of the music. Guck describes these possibilities for perceiving music in "The Model of Domination and Competition in Musical Analysis," a paper presented at "Feminist Theory and Music," University of Minnesota, Minneapolis, June, 1991. The relationship of competition to gender is also discussed in *Competition: A Feminist Taboo?*, ed. Valerie Miner and Helen E. Longino (New York: The Feminist Press, 1987).

16 I have assigned middle C the value of 0 on the *y*-axis and have measured pitches in semitones. For the double- and triple-stops, the graph displays the highest voice for the violins and the lowest voice for the viola and cello. My thanks to Tim Campbell for his suggestions on the graph. Margaret E. Thomas offers other types of graphic analyses in *The String Quartet of Ruth Crawford: Analysis With a View Toward Charles Seeger's Theory of Dissonant Counterpoint* (M.A. thesis, University of Washington, 1991).

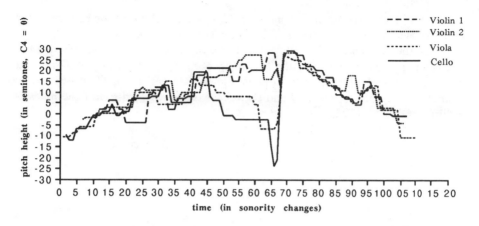

Figure 1: Voice Leading Graph, Crawford String Quartet, Mvt. 3

registral position. The reference state is that in which the sound-strands do not cross; that is, when the first violin occupies the highest register, the second violin the second highest register, the viola the third highest register, and the cello the lowest register. As the instrumental voices begin to twist and weave together, the pattern becomes more intricate. We can think of the piece as moving through varying patterns whose intricacy we can measure. The lowest possible measurement will indicate the state in which no strands cross; the highest possible measurement will indicate the greatest degree of "twist" possible for the four sound-strands.[17]

A closer look at the first three notes of the movement will introduce the mechanics of the analysis. The viola enters on a barely audible C♯3, quickly crescendos and dies away. As it swells a second time to *p*, the cello enters a semitone above it, *ppp*, and similarly pulsates between *p* and *ppp* in turn, alternating with the viola in dynamic prominence. The cello then moves underneath the viola in m. 5 to sound the pitch a semitone below the viola's

---

17 In their treatise on composition, *Tradition and Experiment in the New Music*, Seeger and Crawford use the term "twist" to indicate a single musical line consisting of at least three pitches whose contour goes up and then down, or down and then up. In contrast, I use "twist" to describe the pattern of all four voices at any given moment. This treatise appears in Charles Seeger, *Studies in Musicology II, 1929–1979*, ed. Ann M. Pescatello (Berkeley: University of California Press, 1994). I would like to thank Joseph Straus for alerting me to this reference. Taylor A. Greer commented upon this treatise in "Of Neumes and New Music: Charles Seeger's Theory of Music Form," presented at the 1992 national meeting of the Society for Music Theory (Kansas City, Kansas).

sustained C♯3. With the cello's move to C♮3 in m. 5, the two instruments swap registral places. The cello becomes the lower voice, the viola the higher.[18]

Using the conventions introduced in Example 2, we can explore this registral exchange in greater detail. At the beginning of m. 5, the cello is higher than the viola; at the end of m. 5, the viola is higher than the cello. (Throughout the examples, the notes of violin 2 and the cello have downward stems; the notes of violin 1 and the viola have upward stems.)

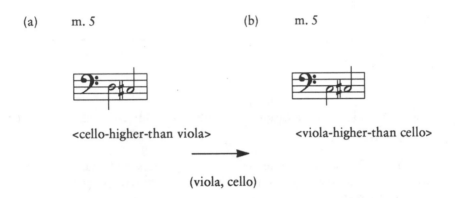

(a)   m. 5

<cello-higher-than viola>

(b)   m. 5

<viola-higher-than cello>

(viola, cello)

Examples 2a–b: Permutational Notation for Registral Exchange between Viola and Cello

The change from Example 2a to Example 2b is labelled with the permutation symbol (viola, cello) that denotes an interchange between the viola and cello. This interchange transforms Example 2a, <cello-higher-than-viola>, into Example 2b, <viola-higher-than-cello>. Example 3 illustrates an abbreviation of this terminology; by calling the viola "instrument 3" and the cello "instrument 4," the two situations may be notated as <4–3> and <3–4>.

The first situation, <4–3>, is thus transformed into the second, <3–4>, by the permutation (34), which simply means that instruments 3 and 4 exchange registral

---

18 The following section of theory is derived from Daniel Harrison's recent work on permutations in "Some Group Properties of Triple Counterpoint and Their Influence on Compositions by J. S. Bach," *Journal of Music Theory* 32 (1988): 23–49. Permutations are an example of transformational theory, an area that David Lewin has explored in *Generalized Musical Intervals and Transformations* (New Haven: Yale University Press, 1989). Henry Klumpenhouwer lucidly engages Harrison's and Lewin's work in *A Generalized Theory for Atonal Voice Leading* (Ph.D. diss., Harvard University, 1991). I am grateful to Shaugn O'Donnell for his expert advice on preparing my musical examples.

(a)   m. 5   (b)   m. 5

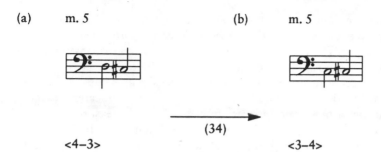

(34)

<4–3>   <3–4>

**Examples 3a–b: Numerical Notation for Registral Exchange
in a Two-Voice Sonority**

roles. Regarding the movement of the voices as an exchange helps us to chart the crossing of each sound-strand.

Example 4 applies this permutational notation to the sonorities of m. 25, two examples of the four-voice sonority patterns that predominate in the piece.

(a)   m. 25   (b)   m. 25

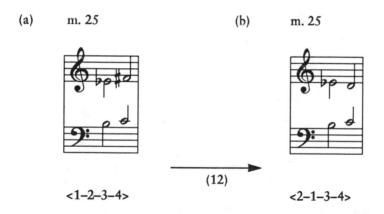

(12)

<1–2–3–4>   <2–1–3–4>

**Examples 4a–b: Numerical Notation for Registral Exchange
in a Four-Voice Sonority**

The only instrument to change pitch in m. 25 is violin 1, which moves from F♯4 to D4. The registral disposition of the first sonority of Example 4 is represented as <1–2–3–4>. That is, instrument 1 is in the highest register, instrument 2 in

297

the second highest register, and so forth. The second sonority is represented as <2–1–3–4>; instrument 2 is now in the highest register and instrument 1 is in the second highest register. The permutational notation (12) shows that instruments 1 and 2 have switched places, and the others remain in relative position.

Appendix A is a score reduction that displays all the simultaneities of the piece using two staves. The first set of numbers below each system indicates measures; when more than one simultaneity appears in a measure, its measure number is followed by a letter (e.g., 8a, 8b). The second set of numbers indicates simultaneities, to which I shall subsequently refer as "sonorities." Appendix B lists all the strand patterns of more than two strands in Appendix A, using numerical notation. Its first three columns list the measure number, sonority, and the strand pattern(s) for that measure. The fourth column lists the permutations that connect successive strand patterns. The number in the fifth column measures the "degree of twist" of the sound-strands at any given moment. The numbers in the sixth and seventh columns, "Max" and "N", will be discussed shortly.

To measure the degree of twist, I have borrowed Milton Babbitt's idea of order inversions which he introduced to investigate a completely different musical relationship.[19] In my application, a degree of twist equal to 0 occurs when the instrumental strands do not cross; as Example 5 illustrates, their registral disposition is <1–2–3–4>.

<1–2–3–4>

Example 5: Degree of Twist = 0 in a Four-Voice Sonority

The degree of twist for any other strand pattern is defined as the number of times an instrument is "out of sequence" as compared with the reference pattern.

---

19 Babbitt employs order inversions to investigate properties of twelve-tone row forms in "Twelve-Tone Invariants as Compositional Determinants," *Musical Quarterly* 46 (1960): 246–59.

For example, given the pattern <2–1–3–4> of Example 4, we can calculate its degree of twist to be 1, for as Example 6 illustrates, it contains just one reordering of <1–2–3–4>.

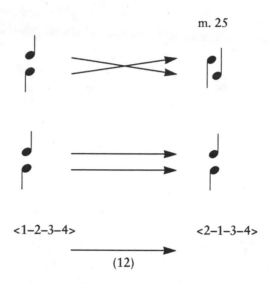

m. 25

<1–2–3–4>   <2–1–3–4>

(12)

Example 6: Degree of Twist = 1 in a Four-Voice Sonority

Example 7 demonstrates a degree of twist equal to 5 for the strand pattern <3–4–2–1>. It contains five reorderings (or five twists) of the basic no-twist pattern.

Measuring the degree of twist for each sound-strand pattern throughout the piece enables us to describe the progression of these patterns. Although perceiving the exact degree at any one moment would require the musical ability to recognize each instrument's placement in relation to all the others—not an easy task, to be sure—many listeners do have the ability to hear that these strands are being continually woven and unwoven into configurations of varying intricacy, and to discern an increase or decrease in the degree of twist which the numbers reflect.[20]

---

20 A performance can certainly encourage this hearing. To consider one example, the recording by the Composers Quartet (Nonesuch H–71280, 1973) strives to keep each instrument's timbre indistinguishable from the others', making it more difficult to hear the twisting of voices from this performance than from one that preserves a separate identity for each instrument. The Composers Quartet's performance is based on a paradigm that Robert P. Morgan characterizes in the liner notes as a "sound mass" from which each voice emerges and recedes in turn.

m. 75c

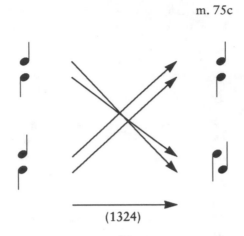

(1324)

Example 7: Degree of Twist = 5 in a Four-Voice Sonority

In order to characterize the twining activity throughout the piece, Example 1 is annotated with the degree of twist for each sonority of three or more voices. The first three-instrument grouping occurs with the second violin's entrance in m. 13. Here, the degree of twist registers 0. It gradually reaches 2 in m. 18 through a progression of 0–0–1–2–2.

At m. 19, the first violin enters, bringing the total of voices to four, and the degree of twist collapses back to 0. (Appendix B lists this moment as a *three-voice* strand pattern, $\frac{<2\text{–}3\text{–}4>}{(1)}$, in order to suggest that instrument 1 is doubling instrument 2, having not yet asserted its first-violin identity.) On beat 3 of m. 19, the cello's change to C♯4 increases the degree to 1; in m. 20, the second violin's move to E♭4 effects an increase to 2; and in m. 24, the cello's subsequent drop to B3 brings the degree back down to 0. To summarize, the opening gesture of the three instruments (mm. 13–19) begins with no degree of twist, increases to 1, then 2, then drops back down to 0; it immediately repeats this sequence in mm. 19–24. (The drop from degree 2 to 1 in m. 21 is relatively brief, and does not affect the overall profile.)

Note that this twisting activity of the voices is quite different from the overall upward registral climb toward the moment of climax and release. Within the dimension of voice-weaving, an increase is followed immediately by a decrease.

In Figure 1, the degree of twist at any given moment is not the number of points of intersection between the lines tracing each instrument's path, but is the number of "disorderings" a registral arrangement has from the <1–2–3–4> prototype.

The musical movement, then, is not simply a vector pointed toward m. 75; rather, it rocks back and forth.[21]

Measure 24 initiates a steady increase in twist, from 0 to the maximum degree of 6 in m. 32, where the cello reaches G4. The degree of twist then immediately decreases, 6–4–3–3–2–2, returning to degree 0 at m. 39.

The permutations, listed in Appendix B, help to articulate the increasing and decreasing degrees of twist. From mm. 13b–15, the rising degree numbers correspond to no change, symbolized by (), or change measured in two-element permutations, or 2-cycles. The return to degree 0 at m. 19a takes place over a 3-cycle, (243). From mm. 19a–22, the numbers correspond to 2-cycles, while the approach to degree 0 at m. 24 corresponds to a 3-cycle. Furthermore, a 3-cycle over mm. 30–32 accompanies the move from degree 4 to 6, and a 3-cycle also marks the return at m. 39a to degree 0. To summarize this section of the piece, 3-cycles accompany movement to degrees 0 or 6; 2-cycles and ()-cycles are used to move between other degrees of twist.

Attending to the permutations thus makes it easier to hear the continual transformation of strand patterns. I would like to suggest two additional listening strategies. The first is to listen for prominent melodic leaps. For example, at m. 24 the cello drops a fourth from E4 to B3, bringing the degree-of-twist progression back to 0. At mm. 31–32, the cello also signals the move to degree 6, the greatest degree of twist, with its distinct tritone ascent from C♯4 to G4. The second listening strategy is to trace the path of a single strand. For instance, over mm. 24–32 the cello moves up from the lowest registral position to the highest while the degree of twist increases from 0 to 6.[22]

Returning in m. 39 to the musical narrative, we hear the degree of twist drop to 0, then increase to 1, 3, and then to 4, yielding the value of 4 three times over mm. 45–47. While the twisting activity pauses in these three measures, each

---

21 Some readers may assume that when I use the terms "increase" and "decrease" to describe segments of twist numbers, I am suggesting that an increase in the degree of twist parallels an increase of "tension" in the sound-strand weaving, and that each cycle of increase followed by decrease imitates the long-range narrative. However, I want to avoid giving the impression that the sound-strand activity simply mirrors the traditional musical narrative. The equation of greater degree of twist with greater tension is incompatible with my metaphor: a high degree of twist for any strand pattern in the cloth would not be considered a more "tense" moment in the weave. Regarding the degree of twist as a measurement of tension or stress that is alleviated would also be inconsistent with my argument that this hidden dimension subverts the dominant, traditional narrative. To do so would therefore diminish the feminist content of my argument, one aspect of which I consider to be the refusal of this second musical space merely to reflect the first, to borrow Virginia Woolf's metaphor of a looking-glass to describe women's expected roles in relation to men in *A Room of One's Own* (San Diego: Harcourt Brace Jovanovich, 1989), p. 35.

22 In mm. 13–15, the cello similarly moves from the lowest register to the highest register while the degree of twist increases from 0 to its local maximum of 2.

instrument abandons its climb upward: the viola sustains its E4 throughout; in m. 45 the first violin dives 10 semitones, from C5 to D4; in m. 46 the cello drops 8 semitones from C♯5 to F4; and in m. 47, the second violin falls 9 semitones from D♯5 to F♯4. (Figure 1 shows the similar downward motion of the three instruments over sonorities 31–33.) This stretch of music thus exemplifies a local correspondence between the upward ascent and the steady twining activity of the sound-strands; both are temporarily abandoned. (This moment does not, to me, indicate mutual recognition or reinforcement between the two spaces; indeed, points of coincidence might be expected of two forces operating independently of one another.)

To move out of degree 4, the first violin ascends a fourth at m. 49 from D4 to G4, and the degree drops to 1.[23] This drop is accompanied by permutation (1342), the first 4-cycle to occur in the piece. The degree of twist then increases to 2 and swiftly reaches the maximum degree 6 at m. 56a with another 4-cycle. Degree 6 is displaced on the next beat by 4, which in turn decreases to 2 at m. 58b. With the assistance of the 3-cycle (234), the degree of twist returns to 0 at m. 59. Figure 1 shows this passage in which the violins begin to split off registrally from the viola and cello over sonorities 44 to 65 (mm. 59–75).

After the strand pattern reaches degree 0 at m. 59, it returns this value for four measures until the second violin ascends in mm. 62–63 by a major third, F♯5 to A♯5, a move that shifts the degree to 1. The value of 1 is returned seven times before violin 1 plays its first double-stop in m. 68. In other words, the sound-strands cease their continual to-and-fro motion and grind to a halt. But in striking contrast, it is at this moment of relative repose, when the continual shifting of patterns pauses for quite a long time, that the tension of the piece starts to build more quickly, soon to become unbearable.[24]

When the double- and triple-stops commence in m. 68, we cannot continue to calculate their degree-of-twist values as we did for the three- and four-strand patterns. The model can be generalized in the following way to accommodate this increase in the number of registral voices in a sound-strand pattern from four to five, six, seven, eight, or twelve as needed.

Example 8 represents the sonority at m. 70b as <3–1–4–2–7–5–6–8>. The strand patterns are ordered, as before, from high to low, but the first violin's double-stop notes are designated 1 and 2, the second violin's notes 3 and 4, etc. Since the sonority contains five reorderings of <1–2–3–4–5–6–7–8>, it would be assigned a degree of twist of 5.

The overall increase in degree of twist in Appendix B for mm. 68–75a from 2

---

23 The first violin's ascent by a fourth in m. 49, bringing the degree down from 4 to a local low of 1, mirrors the cello's earlier drop of fourth in m. 24, which brought the degree down from 2 to 0.

24 What I wish to emphasize in mm. 59–67 is the slowing and stopping of the twisting activity, not the relatively low degree of twist. The moment of relative repose occurs because the weaving stops, not because it has reached degrees 0 and 1.

m. 70b

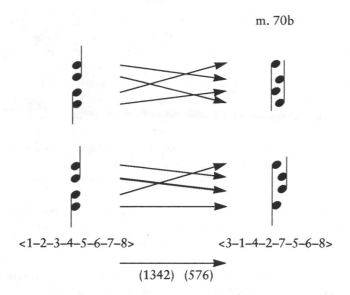

<1–2–3–4–5–6–7–8>   <3–1–4–2–7–5–6–8>

(1342) (576)

Example 8: Degree of Twist = 5 in an Eight-Voice Sonority

to 9 is a bit misleading because with an increase in the number of registral voices, the maximum possible degree of twist increases proportionally. The sixth column in Appendix B contains the maximum possible degree of twist for each expanded strand pattern. A three-voice sonority has maximum degree of 3 (e.g., <4–3–2>); a four-voice sonority has a maximum degree of 6 (e.g., <4–3–2–1>). A five-voice sonority has a maximum degree of 9; a six-voice sonority has a maximum degree of 13, and so forth.[25]

A sonority's degree of twist divided by its maximum possible degree of twist gives a more accurate figure for comparing the degrees of twist among sonorities of different sizes. The seventh column in Appendix B lists these relative values as N (=Degree of Twist ÷ Maximum Degree of Twist). For mm. 68–74, the values range from .08 to .25. In contrast to the heightening intensity of this passage as it progresses toward the climax, the degree of twist stays within a relatively small

---

25 Although the maximum degree of twist for a five-voice strand (e.g., <5–4–3–2–1>) would be 10, the maximum number for the sonority in m. 68 is 9. Since a double-stop played by violin 1 would always be notated numerically as <1–2> and never as <2–1>, to count <2–1> as a twist would inflate the Max number. The 10 twists that would be possible for five distinct instrumental voices is thus decreased by one when two of the voices are played by a single instrument, bringing the maximum number down to 9. The same reasoning applies when calculating the Max numbers for all the other double- and triple-stops in the passage. I am indebted to Jeffrey Stadelman for alerting me to this feature of Max numbers.

range. The climax sonority of m. 75 registers degree 9, which appears on first glance to be a local high, but with a maximum degree of 46 for a twelve-note sonority, its N-value is merely .20, remaining well within the small range already established. The highest N-value for mm. 68–75 is .83 at m. 75c, which is less than the N-value of 1 obtained at m. 32 and m. 56a. The events on the surface of the music are therefore not reinforced at the level of voice-twisting activity; the weaving of the sound-strands has slowed considerably, in contrast to the bells and whistles going off that signal a climax. This disjunction between the two dimensions continues after the moment of climax. During the release of surface tension, the twisting again commences—the sonority on the last beat of m. 75 registers 17 out of a maximum 24, or .71, a prominent increase from .20 of m. 75's downbeat sonority.

Calculating the degree of twist for the slurred eighth- and sixteenth-note figures that connect the climax sonority to the octachord in m. 75 beautifully illustrates the twisting activity. If we count the four beginning pitches and four end pitches of the slurred figures in m. 75 as each constituting a strand pattern, we can measure the degree of twist for these figures before and after their two-and-a-half octave sweep. Appendix B lists the beginning pitches in m. 75b as pattern <2–1–3–4> with degree of twist 1, and lists the end pitches in m. 75c as pattern <3–4–2–1> with a degree of twist 5. The increase from 1 to 5 suggests that over the second and third beats of m. 75, the strands plait rapidly from a nearly untwisted state into an highly twisted pattern.[26]

As Example 1 shows for m. 77 to the end of the piece, the steady increase and decrease of the degree of twist is mostly absent. Now the patterns shift much more rapidly, beat to beat, in what seems an almost random fashion in contrast to the instruments' steady collective descent after their triple-stop attacks: they sink downward, moving as relentlessly to the piece's nadir as they did to its peak.

By tracing these twists systematically through the quartet movement, then, we are able to perceive a musical space through which an alternative narrative is written, one that proceeds alongside the more prominent narrative of the music's surface that drives toward the climax. My analysis recognizes Crawford's experience as a modernist and as a woman while it attempts to make sense of the composition's structure and aesthetic; as I have argued, her gender animates her work in a way not readily evident but which can be made audible, in this case, through formalist analysis.

In a 1976 interview, Charles Seeger acknowledged his former prejudice against women composers:

---

26 My thanks to Anton Vishio for his ideas on how to apply my model to the inner pitches of m. 75.

I was very snooty in those days about women composers and had come more or less to the conclusion that the great tradition of European music, say from 1200 to about 1930, had been created mostly by men and that it was a bit absurd to expect women to fit themselves into a groove which was so definitely flavored with machismo (and, of course, the early music of the twentieth century and the late music of the nineteenth century was machismo with a capital M).[27]

My reading of his wife's string quartet movement suggests how a woman composer did manage to situate herself simultaneously "within the groove" and outside it, to flow with the mainstream and to run a countercurrent underneath it. Rather than refusing to answer the compositional call to machismo, I believe that Ruth Crawford did reply and in the dominant discourse—but she answered deviously, to borrow a phrase from Teresa de Lauretis.[28] Thus she managed to speak the language of the "great tradition" while also maintaining a space of resistance in her art.

I hope that, like Crawford, we will begin to carve out new spaces from which we might consider musical structure. If we are to bring the compelling questions of feminist critical theory to music analysis, we need more music theories than the few now in currency to engage effectively the works that speak to us, in order that we may speak back—as feminists.[29]

---

27 Ray Wilding-White, "Remembering Ruth Crawford Seeger," p. 445. Seeger's designation of 1930 as the year that concluded men's dominance in European music composition may have had something to do with the fact that Crawford composed most of her mature works in the early 1930s: she wrote the String Quartet in 1931; the four *Diaphonic Suites*, *Piano Study in Mixed Accents*, and *Two Chants for Women's Chorus* in 1930; *Rat Riddles* over 1930–32; and her songs *Chinaman, Laundryman* and *Sacco, Vanzetti* in 1932. Matilda Gaume lists Crawford's oeuvre in "Ruth Crawford Seeger," in *Women Making Music: The Western Art Tradition, 1150–1950*, ed. Jane Bowers and Judith Tick (Urbana: University of Illinois Press, 1986), p. 387. Seeger discusses the question of difference between the music of men composers and women composers further in his essay "Ruth Crawford," in *American Composers on American Music: A Symposium*, ed. Henry Cowell (New York: Frederick Ungar, 1933; rpt. Stanford: Stanford University Press, 1962), pp. 116–17.

28 Teresa de Lauretis, *Alice Doesn't: Feminism, Semiotics, Cinema* (Bloomington: Indiana University Press, 1984), p. 7.

29 This essay developed from a paper I wrote for a seminar at Harvard University, Spring 1990. I am grateful to David Lewin for his careful reading of several versions and for his many beneficial suggestions. It was originally presented at "Feminist Theory and Music," a conference held at the University of Minnesota, Minneapolis, in June, 1991, and was given in a different form in a colloquium at Wesleyan University, in November, 1992. For their invigorating and thoughtful commentary, I would like to thank Elizabeth West Marvin and Richard Hermann, Joel Lester, John Rahn, Philip Rupprecht, Joseph N. Straus, Catherine Torpey, and especially Anton J. Vishio, who has been extraordinarily helpful throughout the process of writing this essay.

Ellie M. Hisama

Appendix A

List of Simultaneities

Appendix B

Table

Meas.	Sonority	Strand Pattern [hi-mid-lo]	Permutation	Degree of Twist	Max	N = Degree/Max
13b	7	<2-3-4>		0	3	0
			()			
14a	8	<2-3-4>		0	3	0
			(34)			
14b	9	<2-4-3>		1	3	.33
			(24)			
15	10	<4-2-3>		2	3	.67
			(243)			
18	11	<3-4-2>		2	3	.67
			(243)			
19a	12	<2-3-4> (1)		0	3	0
			(34)			
19b	13	<2-4-3> (1)		1	3	.33
			—			
20	14	<2-1-4-3>		2	6	.33
			(12)			
21	15	<1-2-4-3>		1	6	.17
			(24)			
22	16	<1-4-2-3>		2	6	.33
			(234)			
24	17	<1-2-3-4>		0	6	0
			(12)			
25	18	<2-1-3-4>		1	6	.17
			(34)			
26	19	<2-1-4-3>		2	6	.33
			(13)			
29	20	<2-3-4-1>		3	6	.5
			(23)			
30	21	<3-2-4-1>		4	6	.67
			(234)			
32	22	<4-3-2-1>		6	6	1.0
			(234)			
33	23	<2-4-3-1>		4	6	.67
			(34)			
34*	24	<2-3-4-1>		3	6	.5
			(14)			

* There appears to be a misprint in the published version of the score in m. 35: in the composer's personal copy (Library of Congress, Seeger Collection), the C5 in Violin 2 is crossed out and a B4 is written in, and is tied to the B4 in m. 34.

Meas.	Sonority	Strand Pattern [hi-mid-lo]	Permutation	Degree of Twist	Max	N = Degree/Max
37a	25	<2-3-1-4>		2	6	.33
			()			
37b	26	<2-3-1-4>		2	6	.33
			(132)			
39a	27	<1-2-3-4>		0	6	0
			(34)			
39b	28	<1-2-4-3>		1	6	.17
			(142)			
40	29	<4-1-2-3>		3	6	.5
			(142)			
43	30	<2-4-1-3>		3	6	.5
			(13)			
45	31	<2-4-3-1>		4	6	.67
			()			
46	32	<2-4-3-1>		4	6	.67
			()			
47	33	<2-4-3-1>		4	6	.67
			(1342)			
49	34	<1-2-4-3>		1	6	.17
			(12)			
50a	35	<2-1-4-3>		2	6	.33
			(134)			
50b	36	<2-3-1-4>		2	6	.33
			()			
51	37	<2-3-1-4>		2	6	.33
			(23)			
53	38	<3-2-1-4>		4	6	.67
			(1234)			
56a	39	<4-3-2-1>		6	6	1.0
			(123)			
56b	40	<4-1-3-2>		4	6	.67
			()			
57	41	<4-1-3-2>		4	6	.67
			(23)			
58a	42	<4-1-2-3>		3	6	.5
			(14)			
58b	43	<1-4-2-3>		2	6	.33
			(234)			
59	44	<1-2-3-4>		0	6	0
			()			
60	45	<1-2-3-4>		0	6	0
			()			
61a	46	<1-2-3-4>		0	6	0
			()			
61b	47	<1-2-3-4>		0	6	0
			()			

309

Meas.	Sonority	Strand Pattern [hi-mid-lo]	Permutation	Degree of Twist	Max	N = Degree/Max
62a	48	<1-2-3-4>		0	6	0
62b	49	<1-2-3-4>	()	0	6	0
63a	50	<2-1-3-4>	(12)	1	6	.17
63b	51	<2-1-3-4>	()	1	6	.17
64	52	<2-1-3-4>	()	1	6	.17
65a	53	<2-1-3-4>	()	1	6	.17
65b	54	<2-1-3-4>	()	1	6	.17
66	55	<2-1-3-4>	()	1	6	.17
67	56	<2-1-3-4>	()	1	6	.17
68	57	<3-1-2-4-5>	()	2	9	.22
69	58	<3-1-2-4-5-6>	–	2	13	.15
70a	59	<3-1-4-2-5-6-7>	–	3	18	.17
70b	60	<3-1-4-2-7-5-6-8>		5	24	.21
71a	61	<3-1-4-2-7-5-8-6>	(68)	6	24	.25
71b	62	<1-3-2-7-4-5-8-6>	(13) (274)	5	24	.21
72	63	<1-3-2-7-4-5-8-6>	()	5	24	.21
73	64	<1-3-2-4-5-7-6-8>	(457) (68)	2	24	.08
75a	65	<1-4-5-2-7-6-8-3-10-9-11-12>	–	9	46	.20
75b	66	<2-1-3-4>	–	1	6	.17
75c	67	<3-4-2-1>	(14) (23)	5	6	.83
75d	68	<5-6-7-3-1-8-4-2>	–	17	24	.71
76	69	<2-3-1-4>	–	2	6	.33
77a	70	–	–	–	–	–
77b	71	–	–	–	–	–
			–			

Meas.	Sonority	Strand Pattern [hi-mid-lo]	Permutation	Degree of Twist	Max	N = Degree/Max
77c	72	<1-2-3>		0	3	0
			(12)			
77d	73	<2-1-3>		1	3	.33
			(132)			
78a	74	<1-3-2>		1	3	.33
			()			
78b	75	<1-3-2>		1	3	.33
			(13)			
78c	76	<3-1-2>		2	3	.67
			()			
78d	77	<3-1-2>		2	3	.67
			(123)			
79a	78	<1-2-3>		0	3	0
			()			
79b	79	<1-2-3>		0	3	0
			(23)			
79c	80	<1-3-2>		1	3	.33
			(23)			
79d	81	<1-2-3>		0	3	0
			()			
80a	82	<1-2-3>		0	3	0
			(23)			
80b	83	<1-3-2>		1	3	.33
			(23)			
80c	84	<1-2-3>		0	3	0
			(123)			
81a	85	<2-3-1>		2	3	.67
			(23)			
81b	86	<3-2-1>		3	3	1.0
			(132)			
81c	87	<2-1-3>		1	3	.33
			(13)			
82a	88	<2-3-1>		2	3	.67
			()			
82b	89	<2-3-1>		2	3	.67
			(13)			
82c	90	<2-1-3>		1	3	.33
			(13)			
83a	91	<2-3-1>		2	3	.67
			()			
83b	92	<2-3-1>		2	3	.67
			(23)			
84a*	93	<3-2-1>		3	3	1.0
			(123)			

---

* In the composer's score (Seeger Collection), a slur connects violin 2's pitch in m. 84 to its last note in m. 83, making the pitch a B♭ rather than B♮.

Ellie M. Hisama

Meas.	Sonority	Strand Pattern [hi-mid-lo]	Permutation	Degree of Twist	Max	N = Degree/Max
84b	94	<1-3-2>		1	3	.33
			(23)			
85a	95	<1-2-3>		0	3	0
			(23)			
85b	96	<1-3-2>		1	3	.33
			(132)			
86a	97	<3-2-1>		3	3	1.0
			(12)			
86b	98	<3-1-2>		2	3	.67
			(123)			
87a	99	<1-2-3>		0	3	0
			(123)			
87b	100	<2-3-1>		2	3	.67
			–			
88a	101	<2-3-1-4>		2	6	.33
			()			
88b	102	<2-3-1-4>		2	6	.33
			()			
90a	103	<2-3-1-4>		2	6	.33
			(123)			
90b	104	<3-1-2-4>		2	6	.33
			–			
90c	105	<1-2-3> (4)		0	3	0
			–			
91	106	<1-2-3-4>		0	3	0
			–			
94a	107	<1-3-4>		0	3	0

312

Does the Song Remain the Same? Questions of Authorship and Identification in the Music of Led Zeppelin

Dave Headlam

Scholarly writing on popular music of the post-World War II era, particularly the many varieties of rock music and their antecedents, has seen a dramatic increase in the past few years, in publications like the journals *Popular Music, Popular Music and Society*, and the *Journal of Popular Music Studies* and books initiated by authors Simon Frith, Andrew Goodwin, Richard Middleton, Robert Walser, and others.[1] From an earlier position of concern largely with history and biography, popular music writers have embraced developments in literary critical theory such as post-structuralism, deconstructionism, feminism, and postmodernism in efforts to explain the particular role of rock music in society of the last forty or so years, including its "social, psychological, visual, gestural, ritual, technical, historical, economic and linguistic aspects."[2] More recently there has been a turn toward what might be described as purely musical elements, or the "specific musical choices embodied in individual songs and organized by genres."[3] This laudable recognition of the importance of the sounds and their structures has, however, been accompanied by attacks on the approaches of "traditional" musicology and music theory not only for their inability to account for the "meaning" of popular music, but for the damage caused by misguided attempts to "legitimate" popular music by using analytical methods designed for "art" music.[4]

---

1   See, for instance, Simon Frith, *Sound Effects: Youth, Leisure, and the Politics of Rock 'n' Roll* (New York: Pantheon Books, 1981); Simon Frith, ed., *Facing the Music* (New York: Pantheon Books, 1988); and Simon Frith and Andrew Goodwin, eds., *On Record* (New York: Pantheon Books, 1990); Richard Middleton, *Pop Music and the Blues* (London: Victor Gollancz, 1972) and *Studying Popular Music* (Bristol, PA: Open University Press, 1990); and Susan McClary and Robert Walser, "Start Making Sense! Musicology Wrestles with Rock," in Frith and Goodwin, pp. 277–92; and Robert Walser, *Running with the Devil: Power, Gender, and Madness in Heavy Metal Music* (Hanover: Wesleyan University Press, 1993).
2   Philip Tagg, "Analysing Popular Music: Theory, Method and Practice," *Popular Music* 2 (1982): 40.
3   Walser, p. xiv.
4   For comments on such attempts, see McClary and Walser and Tagg. See Tagg, pp. 41–42, and Middleton, *Studying Popular Music*, on distinctions between popular and art music. Middleton and other writers have attacked Wilfrid Mellers, *Twilight of the Gods: The Beatles in Retrospect* (London: Faber and Faber, 1973) as an example of the misapplication of art-music techniques to popular music.

The rift between writers on popular music and music theorists and musicologists is not only unfortunate, for each side has much to learn from the other, but also, as I hope to show, unnecessary. After a brief summary of arguments from both sides, I will address an issue which, I believe, demonstrates the usefulness and integrity of including both points of view. The issue is one associated with both art and popular music, concerning authorship and identification, here in reference to the music of the rock group Led Zeppelin. As John Spitzer has noted, authorship in art music has many functions: establishing contexts, authenticating a corpus, bestowing and generating value and meaning, and providing a mythic link in a creative discourse.[5] Although Spitzer contrasts the importance of the author or composer in art music with that of popular music, where original authors are not always attributed or are difficult to define in an era when recorded songs result from the contributions of many people including performers, arrangers, and producers, it may be argued that authorship in the latter still fulfills many of the same functions as in the former. In regard to rock music, Andrew Goodwin has noted that, despite the difficulties in attributing authorship, the romantic notion of the single, authentic, creative force has persisted and continues to be central to critical and popular reception.[6]

In the course of studies on the music of Led Zeppelin, it has become apparent that many songs are compilations of pre-existent musical material from multiple sources, both acknowledged and unacknowledged.[7] Despite the tradition that fostered the group—the assimilation of American country and electric blues and rock and roll into "rock" music by British musicians of the 1960s—Led Zeppelin has been criticized for their use of existing material, cited as a lack of originality, or, even worse, a lack of authenticity. At the same time, however, these songs are strongly associated with the band and define its distinct and unique style. The band's continuing popularity has been based on listeners' consistently high level of identification of the songs and recognition of their role within the class of musical pieces defined by the author figure of Led Zeppelin. Thus we are presented with the paradoxical situation of songs like "Whole Lotta Love" and "Dazed and Confused" which are on the one hand not "authored" by Led Zeppelin, but

---

5 John Spitzer, "Authorship and Attribution in Western Art Music" (Ph.D. diss., Cornell University, 1983).

6 Andrew Goodwin, "Sample and Hold: Pop Music in the Digital Age of Reproduction," in Frith and Goodwin, pp. 258–74.

7 For Led Zeppelin and their use of borrowed material see J. D. Considine, "Led Zeppelin," *Rolling Stone* 587 (September 20, 1990): 56ff; Charles R. Cross and Erik Flannihan, eds., *Led Zeppelin: Heaven and Hell* (New York: Harmony Books, 1991); Stephen David, *Hammer of the Gods* (New York: Ballantine Books, 1985); Jimmy Guterman, "The Blues and Other Inspirations," in Cross and Flannigan, pp. 37–45; Robert Palmer, "Led Zeppelin: The Music," in Booklet, *Led Zeppelin Box Set Re-release* (New York: Atlantic Recording Corporation, 1990); and Dave Schulps, "Jimmy Page gives a History Lesson" in Cross and Flannagan, pp. 46–72.

on the other hand are virtual signatures identifying the band's musical essence.

An exploration of this paradox requires both what might be termed the traditional socio-cultural and critical concerns of popular music and the purely musical considerations which are central to music theory. For the former, I will review the musical tradition from which Led Zeppelin developed, with its changing attitudes toward authorship and originality, using a critical apparatus drawn from the writings of Roland Barthes and Michel Foucault, who reject the role of "author" as authority and question the validity of the traditional attribution of "authorship."[8] As described below, Foucault nonetheless outlines several features of the role of author which prove relevant to the case of Led Zeppelin. On the latter, musical side, I will identify the musical elements which define the sound and style of Led Zeppelin in three songs, "Whole lotta Love," "Babe, I'm Gonna Leave You," and "When the Levee Breaks," and use them as criteria for defining the band as authors, in particular by defining aspects of the "style class" created by the author figure of Led Zeppelin. I hope to demonstrate that, since music theory not only has much to contribute, but is essential to an explanation of the musical factors of this issue, it is reasonable to conclude that music theorists may have a useful role to play in the world of popular music, and that writers from the two worlds should act in harmony rather than react in dischord.

Music Theory and Popular Music

The field of music theory has long been dominated by the spirit of modernism, influencing both the chosen repertories and adopted methodologies. Music theorists tend to treat musical works as autonomous, self-contained entities with unified structures.[9] They usually study "masterpieces" of music from the Western art music tradition composed by acknowledged and revered "artists" who are admired for their ingenuity, individuality, and originality. These works, which invariably exist in relatively stable written forms, are analysed to reveal relationships among their formal components. Typically, theorists place a premium on the complexity and unity of the music, as well as on the logic of the analytical method.[10]

---

8 See Roland Barthes, *The Rustle of Language*, trans. Richard Howard (Oxford, 1986), and *Image, Music, Text*, selected and trans. Stephen Heath (New York: The Noonday Press, 1977); and Michel Foucault, "What is an Author," from *Language, Counter-Memory, Practise: Selected Essays and Interviews by Michel Foucault*, trans. Donald F. Bouchard and Sherry Simon, ed. Donald F. Bouchard (Ithaca: Cornell University Press, 1977); reprinted in Chandra Mukerji and Michael Schudson, eds., *Rethinking Popular Culture* (Berkeley: University of California Press, 1977).

9 I am speaking in general terms here; obviously, some music theory writings, such as those by Leonard B. Meyer, have different viewpoints.

10 The triumvirate of Schenkerian theory, set theory, and twelve-tone theory illustrates these tendencies in music theory.

Opposed to the formalist methodologies of music theorists, researchers into popular music adopt what might be termed a postmodernist stance. Taking their cue from writers such as Roland Barthes, they believe that popular songs are intersection points of elaborate social codes. Under this interpretation, question of complexity, originality, and authorship are less important than cultural or ideological function and meaning. This view stems, in part, from the production of popular music, a process in which materials emerge from collective experiences and are mass produced and disseminated in ways that include many people (eg., songwriters, arrangers, performers, producers, engineers, and record company executives). Thus, the focus of popular music researchers is, for the most part, not on the internal structure of the music, but rather on its cultural, sociological, and political contexts and effects on society. In general, these writers shift their attention from the work to its underlying "text," and from the music to its reception, or the "author" to the "reader."[11]

Differences between the methods and goals of music theorists and popular music researchers are reflected in the historically-based biases of the two groups towards the other's methodologies and repertoires. For instance, Heinrich Schenker had a dim view of popular music and the masses; in *Free Composition*, he wrote:

> to assemble and entertain 50,000 people—this can be accomplished only by bullfights, cockfights, massacres, pogroms: in short, a brutal ranting and raving, a demented and chaotic outcry. Art is incapable of uniting such large numbers.[12]

Another theorist decrying popular music was Theodor W. Adorno, who, in his essay, "On Popular Music," echoed Schenker's view that popular music is not interesting or complex enough to warrant close scrutiny. In Adorno's view, popular music has such exaggerated degrees of "standardization"—familiar features that remain the same across the genre, such as vocal range, length, formal structures, character, and harmonic schemes—that listeners do not perceive the music as a "whole," but only as a compilation of schematic details. In "serious" music, by contrast, details "derive their musical sense from the concrete totality of the piece

---

11 "Any text is a problematic embodiment of cultural motifs that transcend the author's employment of them and that subvert the author's intention for the text and the reader's impulse to interpret it as a coherent whole. What is missing or repressed or unspoken becomes more significant that what is said, and the task of criticism is to anatomize all the ways in which a text signifies something less or more than it was intended to—to rewrite the text so as to disclose how thought is captive to language and ideology." See J. A. Appleyard S.J., *Becoming A Reader: The Experience of Fiction from Childhood to Adulthood* (Cambridge: Cambridge University Press, 1990): 138.

12 See Heinrich Schenker, *Free Composition*, trans. and ed. Ernst Oster (New York: Longman, 1979), Appendix 4b, p. 159. I am indebted to Matthew Brown for this quotation.

which, in turn, consists of the life relationship of the details and never of a mere enforcement of a musical scheme." [13]

More recent music theory has taken its ideological position from the view of composition as a modernist occupation offered by Milton Babbitt. Despite his knowledge of American popular song literature, Babbitt has maintained a strictly isolationist attitude in his own work. His musical systems are self-contained sets of precisely defined twelve-tone relationships, which, although they share structural principles, are essentially unique to each piece. Babbitt's compositions and the analytical methods they have spawned stake out quintessentially modernist positions. [14]

Although music theorists have until quite recently largely ignored popular music, [15] writers on popular music have expressed negative opinions—grouping music theory with musicology—about the applicability of current theoretical systems to their repertoire. [16] According to Philip Tagg, music theory has difficulties "relating musical discourse to the remainder of human existence." [17] Furthermore, in Tagg's opinion, traditional theory has specific problems 1) associating musical expression with extra-musical phenomena, 2) dealing with music that is not written down, and 3) understanding those aspects of music—"sound, timbre, electro-acoustic treatment, ornamentation, etc."—that are not easily notated in traditional ways. [18] Paul Clarke extends his criticism to lyrics and music, noting that "The evaluation of rock music based on inappropriate criteria drawn from the *creative* arts generally takes two forms: the literary critical assessment of words, or the musicological-notational assessment of music. In both cases the aural artefact of rock song is valued only to the extent that it can be reduced to the form of a visual artefact." [19] A similar view is expressed by Peter Wicke, who notes the futility of

---

13 Theodor W. Adorno, "On Popular Music," *Studies in Philosophy and Social Science*, IX (Frankfurt am Main: Suhrkamp Verlag, 1941): 17–48; reprinted in Frith and Goodwin, pp. 301–14.

14 Of the composer's numerous writings, see Milton Babbitt, "Who Cares if You Listen?" (originally "The Composer as Specialist") *High Fidelity* 8/2 (February 1958): 38–40, 126–27; reprinted in Elliott Schwartz and Barney Childs, eds. *Contemporary Composers on Contemporary Music* (New York: Holt, Rinehart and Winston, 1967), pp. 243–50; and *Words About Music*, ed. Stephen Demski and Joseph N. Straus (Madison, Wis.: University of Wisconsin Press, 1987).

15 Signs of recent interest include Robert Gauldin, "Beethoven, Tristan, and The Beatles," *College Music Symposium* 30 (1990): 142–52; and the first rock music session at a Society for Music Theory Conference in Oakland (1990), with papers given by Graham Boone, Matthew Brown, John Covach, Walter Everett, and the present author on topics ranging through the Grateful Dead, Jimi Hendrix, Cream and the blues, Spinal Tap, and Jefferson Airplane.

16 Popular music writers' grouping of music theorists and musicologists is somewhat ironic, since the issues raised by popular music writers have actually divided the two groups in the past.

17 Tagg, p. 41.

18 Ibid., p. 44.

19 Paul Clark, "A Magic Science: Rock Music as a Recorded Art," *Popular Music* 3 (1983): 202.

applying the analytical standards of "serious" music to rock, concluding that "it is impossible to consider rock music without placing it in its social and cultural contexts."[20]

Susan McClary and Robert Walser also raise objections to musical analysis of popular music, especially with regard to fixations on pitch organization. These authors assert the following:

> Studies of popular music that try to locate meaning and value exclusively in pitch relationships are products of traditional musicological training, and they tend to make the music they deal with seem very poor stuff indeed. The blues suffer especially in the hands of unreconstructed musicologists, for the harmonic progression itself (simple and unvarying for the most part) cannot begin to explain what is significant about this repertoire. The music interest resides elsewhere, in the dimensions of music that musicology systematically overlooks.[21]

To "start making sense" of popular music, McClary and Walser propose that if theorists and musicologists could but kick their pitch habit and deconstruct their methods, they might join popular music writers in finding alternative explanations that address "how in material terms the music manages to 'kick butt.'"[22]

Ultimately, the conflicting views of theorists and popular music writers stem not from the music, but from the types of questions that each group finds of interest. For example, McClary and Walser may be correct in asserting that "meaning" and "value" can only be explained when a musical work is no longer treated autonomously, but these questions are ones which music theory is not designed to answer. While the latter's orientation is a source of constant criticism, however, the sophistication of analysis in music theory plays an essential role in analytical systems such as Philip Tagg's, which, despite the constant references to music's encoding of socio-cultural features, is firmly rooted in transcribed sounds.[23] Tagg's point that traditional music theory is characterized by "notational centricity" does not mean that analysis will not yield any useful information, only that popular music has aspects that require approaches sensitive to the problems of accurate pitch representation in the equal-tempered notational system. Similar notational problems arise for analysts when considering art music of the recent and remote past. As Richard Middleton points out, the issues that separate proponents from opponents of analysis in popular music are often similar to those for art music. In fact, Middleton devotes considerable energy to a definition for popular music, only

---

20 Peter Wicke, *Rock Music: Culture, Aesthetics, and Sociology*, trans. Rachel Fogg (Cambridge: Cambridge University Press, 1990), Ch. 1 and p. 73.
21 McClary and Walser, pp. 281–82.
22 Ibid., p. 290.
23 Tagg, passim.

to conclude that an airtight distinction between popular and art music does not exist.[24] The questions of authorship and identification raised here in Led Zeppelin's music might as well be considered with regard to Igor Stravinsky's *Pulcinella* (1919–20), Luciano Berio's *Sinfonia* (1968), or Peter Maxwell Davies's *Eight Songs for a Mad King* (1969). In these and other similar pieces, the questions raised prescribe the methods used to arrive at answers, and neither analysis nor context should be excluded outright.

Dissatisfaction with approaches which do not account for musical questions are being expressed even within the popular music field. In a recent book, Robert Walser rebukes some of his popular music compatriots, noting that the problem is not with music analysis, but with the concomitant ideology.[25] Reviewer Peter Winkler has commented approvingly that Walser includes a "close analysis of the music itself," even with "such arcana as the theory of modes," and combines a "solid understanding of musical structure," "immersion in the style as both a musician and a listener," and attention to what "fans, musicians, and others have to say about the music."[26] Although Walser's methodology of "locating meaning in musical structures by interpreting them metaphorically,"[27] firmly rooted in a venerable 19th-century tradition of music criticism, is currently out of fashion in the music theory world, most music theorists would not argue with Winkler's assessment of Walser's approach as appropriate.

Winkler's comments on Walser's book should also be considered in light of the tradition of transcription and analysis of playing, improvising, and composing styles that has existed in rock music magazines such as *Guitar Player* and *Guitar for the Practicing Musician*, and, more recently, *Bass Player*. These publications have long contained detailed discussions of modes and keys in articles and columns designed to help readers learn songs and styles. Despite denigrations like Theo Cateforis's comments that "analyses such as those found in *Guitar Player* ... empower the musical text [only] as an unquestioned technical achievement,"[28] the information in these magazines and popular music courses such as those offered at the Berkelee College of Music have long supported Walser's claims that "Musicians take such [musical] conventions and details seriously, and fans respond to them."[29]

---

24 Middleton, *Studying Popular Music*, p. 4. Ethnomusicologists have long considered similar questions. See, for instance, Chapter 3 in Constantin Brăiloiu, *Problems of Musicology*, ed. and trans. A. L. Lloyd (Cambridge: Cambridge University Press, 1984).

25 Walser, pp. 30–31.

26 Peter Winkler, review of *Running with the Devil* by Robert Walser, *Journal of Popular Music Studies* 5 (1993): 105.

27 Ibid., p. 104.

28 Theo Cateforis, "'Total Trash:' Analysis and Post-Punk Music," *Journal of Popular Music Studies* 5 (1993): 45.

29 Walser, p. xiv.

Dave Headlam

Authorship and Originality

In his study "Authorship and Attribution in Western Art Music," John Spitzer defines an author–composer as the originator of a basic core idea that is distinct, original, and maintains its identity with time. He lists the many functions of a recognized and defined author to the perception and existence of a piece: the ascription of an author 1) greatly affects the reception history; 2) defines and limits the critical discourse; 3) classifies a piece as an authentic representative within the canon, which in turn acts as a basis for style criticism and assessment; 4) creates value and meaning both creatively and as a commodity by imparting "prestige"; and 5) creates a mythic creative figure which allows listeners to participate in an interactive relationship with the composer as communicator. Spitzer illustrates the importance of the author function by using contrasting examples of works thought to be by acknowledged "great" composers which turn out to be "spurious" or by "lesser" figures and subsequently lose most of their critical and value status, and the reception of "anonymous" works, which never gain the rank of "masterwork" or the level of communication with listeners due to the lack of a defined "author."[30]

Spitzer contrasts the importance of the author in Western art music with certain types of non-Western, popular, and folk musics, where authorship may be less acknowledged than performing ability or ability to improvise, or even where creative power is ascribed to a higher spiritual power, with the human interpreter regarded as conduit only.[31] In at least one type of popular music, rock music, however, the author function maintains several of the characteristics Spitzer finds in Western art music. In the course of a discussion refuting the characterization of rock music in the age of samplers and other digital reproduction as quintessentially "postmodern," Andrew Goodwin points out that, despite the prevalence of digital reproduction, pastiche, quotation, and the increasing creation of music by committees of musicians, technicians, producers, and accountants, the "romantic aesthetic" of the creator, both originator and skilled interpreter/performer, remains extremely important. He illustrates the point by the counter-example of the "persistent failure of all those acts who are marketed as a self-conscious hype" in the tradition of the Monkees, and by the continuing existence of the live concert, in which fans go to experience the *presence* of the mythic creator and the personalized presentation of the music.[32]

In rock music, the equivalent of an art music "spurious work" or attribution is the realization that a group either does not "perform" or "write" their own music, as in the case of the lip-synching duo Milli Vanelli. This generally leads to a loss of

---

30 Spitzer, passim.
31 Ibid., pp. 30–33.
32 Goodwin, p. 267.

prestige and revenue. Goodwin even goes so far as to distinguish between "pop music" and "rock music" by defining pop as a manufactured product by a faceless conglomerate and rock as an authentic and original creation from a defined author/performer. While this distinction is certainly an overgeneralization, it seems to be the case that, although certain performers define themselves and maintain an enduring popularity and integrity without "writing" their own music, such as Elvis Presley, for the most part the lasting figures of rock, those now being inducted yearly into the Rock and Roll Hall of Fame, are both authors and performers of a defined repertoire and style.

Authorship and Led Zeppelin

Given the importance of authorship and originality, it is essential that a rock group maintain its status in this regard in the view of fans and critics. Led Zeppelin (1968–80) is generally considered to be one of the most influential and innovative rock bands of the late 1960s and early 1970s; a group whose distinctive sound on record and virtuosity in concert defined many of the following trends in rock music.[33] Yet, despite the strong identification between the band and its music, many Led Zeppelin songs are not "composed by" the group in the traditional sense. Pre-existent sources for many of the most characteristic songs have been uncovered in writings on the music, lawsuits between affected parties, and interviews with the individual members. Thus, we are confronted by a problem in defining the role of the band as authors: in what, if any, context may Led Zeppelin be considered the originator of its own most distinctive songs? The question, which includes historical, social, and musical aspects, is significant, for attitudes toward it, which change over time, have contributed greatly to the perception and critical evaluation of the group.

As a critical framework to consider the issue of authorship in Led Zeppelin's music, it is useful to turn to the role of the "author-function" propounded by Michel Foucault, in its connection to an earlier pronouncement by Roland Barthes. In an infamous passage Barthes declared that "the birth of the reader must be at the cost of the death of the author."[34] According to Michael Moriarity, Barthes's often misunderstood downgrading of the author was a reaction to the author as "authority" for definitive readings of literary texts in traditional academic

---

33 The British rock band Led Zeppelin consisted of guitarist Jimmy Page, singer Robert Plant, bass and keyboardist John Paul Jones, and drummer John Bonham. The band released 10 albums, the last, *Coda* (1982), after its breakup in 1980 with the death of Bonham. A recent digitally-remastered boxed set re-release of their ouevre (1990) has sparked renewed interest in the group. For sources on the band, see note 7 above.

34 Barthes, *The Rustle of Language*, pp. 61–67, and *Image, Music, Text*, p. 148.

criticism, where the author's life, beliefs, experiences, and values acted as the only allowable criteria. Barthes advocated space for the reader, where no one interpretation can claim authority. Moriarity argues that Barthes objected less to the presence of an author than to the appropriation of the author-function by critics as justification for authoritarian readings.[35] Barthes's attitude is reflected in writings by many popular music figures, who have similarly adopted an anti-establishment stance in the face of traditional musicology and music theory departments and their author-driven authoritarian studies which seemingly leave no room for interpretation of listeners.

In his essay of a decade later, "What is an author," Michel Foucault responded, examining "the empty space left by the author's disappearance," by reconsidering the notion of an "author" and the equally problematic concept of a "work."[36] Foucault proposed that "the function of an author is to characterize the existence, circulation, and operation of certain discourses within a society."[37] He then isolated four features of "authors" in their roles as functions of discourse.[38] Although he restricted his compass to authors of books or written texts, three of Foucault's categories are relevant for popular music in general and Led Zeppelin's music in particular.

The first of Foucault's categories states that authors are "objects of appropriation"; the author denotes a system of ownership and copyright, and legal responsibility for the finished product. Second, the significance of the author is not "universal or constant in all discourses"; throughout history the extent to which the status of works has depended on a recognized author has varied. Third, the definition of an author is a "complex operation": authors 1) create a class of texts which can be explained by reference to themselves; 2) constitute a unity to which not only evolution and maturity in output, but also inherent contradictions, can be related; and 3) are sources of expression manifested in complete or incomplete texts, such as fragments or drafts.[39]

Foucault's first category, the author as a system of ownership and copyright, points up a particularly problematic aspect of the tradition from which Led Zeppelin emerged.[40] The song "Dazed and Confused" from the first album

---

35 Michael Moriarity, *Roland Barthes* (Stanford: Stanford University Press, 1991), pp. 100–02.

36 Foucault, "What is an Author," from *Language, Counter-Memory, Practice: Selected Essays and Interviews by Michel Foucault*, ed. Donald F. Bouchard, trans. Donald F. Bouchard and Sherry Simon (Ithaca, N.Y.: Cornell University Press, 1977).

37 Ibid., p. 452.

38 Ibid., pp. 452–57.

39 Foucault's fourth category, concerning the author "characterized by a plurality of egos," has interesting implications for Led Zeppelin and many other rock bands, but will not be considered here.

40 See discussions of copyright and ownership in popular music in Simon Frith, "Copyright and the Music Business," *Popular Music* 7/1 (January 1988): 57ff.

provides an example. When in New York in 1965, the future guitarist of Led Zeppelin, Jimmy Page, went to a nightclub to hear folk singer Janis Ian, but was struck by the opening act, singer Jake Holmes, particularly the song "I'm Confused."[41] Page appropriated the most characteristic aspects of Holmes's song, particularly the descending scalar pattern ((E)–G–F$\sharp$–F–E (E) D–C$\sharp$–C–B), for a reworked version, first with the band the Yardbirds, then later with Led Zeppelin.[42] The song, renamed "Dazed and Confused," is attributed to Page. When released on Led Zeppelin's first album and played in their initial concert tours, it quickly became the song that defined and identified the band's style and sound. Although aware of the use of material from his song, Holmes did not contest the attribution and so the ownership and copyright of the song remained with Led Zeppelin.[43]

"Dazed and Confused" was supplanted as the song most strongly identified with Led Zeppelin by "Whole Lotta Love" (1969) from their second album. In concert tours, the latter became the anthem of the group and of a generation of listeners. Fourteen years after its release, in 1983, Willie Dixon's daughter played "Whole Lotta Love" for her father, and he recognized elements from his own song, "You Need Love" (1962). Dixon sued Led Zeppelin for their unattributed use of the earlier song in 1985, and secured royalties in 1987.[44] In the 1990 boxed set re-release of Led Zeppelin's music, however, the song is still attributed only to the members of the band. Led Zeppelin was also sued successfully in the 1970s by ARC records, who claimed that the song "Bring it on Home" was based on a song of the same name by Willie Dixon, and that the "Lemon Song" was based on "The Killing Floor" by Howling Wolf (Chester Burnett); the cases were settled out of court.[45]

When pressed on their use of pre-existent material, the members of Led Zeppelin and their proponents point out that questions of copyright and authorship are not always clear even when sources are cited. Page noted that "the

---

41 See Charles R. Cross, "Tales from Led Zeppelin's Recording Sessions," in Cross and Flannigan, p. 108. Stephen Davis, p. 34, cites Holmes's song as "Dazed and Confused."

42 The Yardbirds (1963–68) were seminal in the development of British blues-based rock by the mixing of genres—blues, psychedelic, Eastern, and pop—that characterized Led Zeppelin's style. Guitarists for the band included Eric Clapton, Jeff Beck, and Jimmy Page. Page, who joined in 1966, played in the Yardbirds until their demise in 1968, then formed "The New Yardbirds," which became Led Zeppelin. See Jon Pareles and Patricia Romanowski, *The Rolling Stone Encyclopedia of Rock & Roll* (New York: Rolling Stone Press, 1983): 606–07.

43 Davis, p. 54.

44 Willie Dixon with Don Snowden, *I Am the Blues* (London: Quartet Books, 1989; rpt. New York: Da Capo Press, 1990), pp. 217, 223. Muddy Waters's version of "You Need Love" was released on a promotional record in England.

45 Davis, p. 108. Reported in *Rolling Stone* (March 14, 1985), and *Variety* 317 (January 30, 1985).

traditional lyrics that we [Led Zeppelin] used predate the people they were associated with."[46] Robert Palmer has commented:

> [Led] Zeppelin has frequently been charged with plagiarism for uncredited use of blues riffs and tunes. It's one thing to run afoul of Willie Dixon, a professional Chicago songwriter and session bassist who wrote and copyrighted the original "You Shook Me" and "I Can't Quit You Baby," and successfully sued after Zeppelin released their considerably altered versions of those songs. Yet several of Dixon's copyrights are of material from the folk-blues public domain—tunes like "My Babe" were current in the South long before he claimed them. It is the custom, in blues music, for a singer to borrow verses from contemporary sources, both oral and recorded, add his own tune and/or arrangement, and call the song his own.[47]

The historical context that surrounds Led Zeppelin's adaptations of pre-existent material may be also considered in light of Foucault's second category, concerning the changing significance of the author in different time periods. Popular music, particularly traditions like that of the blues, frequently raises issues of the "text" and the "author." Blues songs exist in as many different forms as there are performers, and they are often compilations of various pre-existent musical materials and lyrics.[48] In many cases, it is impossible to attribute a song to an original "author." With regard to one of the most famous blues singers, Robert Johnson (1911–1938), Samuel Charters has noted that "Johnson was one of the first delta musicians who listened seriously to recordings. Verses, accompaniment patterns, melodies, even vocal inflections from recordings by Leroy Carr, Scrapper Blackwell, Joe McCoy, Willie Newburn, Kokomo Arnold, and Lonnie Johnson found their way into his own compositions. Even some of his delta pieces had elements that he'd taken from recordings".[49] Johnson's strength was, however, his own musical gifts: "Even in the songs that he took from his delta background Johnson had an immediacy that was distinctively his own."[50] Authorship and originality were not critical issues in Johnson's time; blues singers

---

46 Schulps, pp. 46–72.

47 Palmer, p. 3.

48 See Paul Oliver, "Blues," *The New Grove Gospel, Blues, and Jazz* (New York: W. W. Norton, 1986) pp. 36–178; Roy Pratt, "The Politics of Authenticity in Popular Music: The Case of the Blues," *Popular Music and Society* 10/3 (1986): 55–77; and Samuel Charters, *The Blues Makers* (New York: Da Capo Press, 1991).

49 Charters, *The Blues Makers*, Part I, p. 89.

50 Ibid., Part I, p. 90. Charters, in Part I, p. 172, 190–91, distinguishes "songsters," who performed songs essentially unchanged for social occasions in which easy recognition was desirable, from "creative blues singers," who changed songs and made them their own. Charters also noted that the same performer assumed both roles, depending on the audience. For early copyright issues, see Charters Part I, p. 130, and Part II, pp. 12, 21, 40, 115.

were measured by their musical ability to remake a song in their own style.

Although Led Zeppelin followed in the lineage of Robert Johnson, on the well-worn path through Muddy Waters and Chicago electric blues to the 1960s British rock scene, attitudes towards authorship changed in the climate of rock adaptations of blues songs. The change in attitude stemmed, in part, from negative

connotations attributed to "covers," or versions of pre-existing songs, in the 1950s. While different versions of songs have existed as long as recordings, with regard to recording practises in the middle 1950s, Arnold Shaw has identified and distinguished two categories: "reworkings" and "covers":

> The distinction inheres in the style and character of the new version. From the time that records became a major exposure device, all publishers tried to get as many versions of a new song as they could. But these versions were different, and, what is more significant, in the natural style of whatever artist recorded them. What happened between 1954–56 was a horse of a different colour.[51]

"Reworkings," in the natural style of the artist, are considered by Shaw to be a positive development. The "horse of a different colour" is "covers." Shaw referred to an area of recorded popular music of the time in which two repertories existed. One was rhythm and blues (R&B) records by black musicians for black audiences (which stemmed from the older "race" records); the other was pop records by white musicians for the larger white audience. In the early 1950s, record producers noticed that the growing young white audience was becoming more interested in R&B songs. These producers then took songs originally recorded by black groups or individual performers, and re-recorded, or "covered," them using white musicians. Since copyright law did not protect arrangements, studio arrangers of covers would copy existing arrangements, taking the characteristic features but cutting out the edges in "more polished, smoother" versions. The "raw and exuberant earthiness of rhythm and blues" was thus toned down for white audience consumption. The new versions would then enter the pop charts with access to a larger audience.[52] Thus, these covers have the negative connotation of blatant copies for quick profit (not to mention the underlying racism). The ones who suffered most were the original black artists, since the record and publishing companies and producers involved usually had royalites and copyright privileges, rather than the original writers and performers.[53]

---

51 Arnold Shaw, *The Rockin' 50s* (New York: Hawthorn Books, 1974) pp. 124–26.
52 Ibid., p. 125.
53 See Bill Millar, *The Coasters* (London: W. H. Allen, 1974) p. 34. See also Charles Keil, *Urban Blues* (Chicago: University of Chicago Press, 1966), Ch. III. Keil refers to an expression from a blues song by Sonny Boy Williamson, "Fattening Frogs for Snakes"; a reference to the ripoffs of black artists by record companies, agents, Artist and Repertoire executives (A and R men), writers, etc.

In Britain of the 1960s, many rock bands began life playing pre-existing material, blues and rock and roll songs, in styles that varied from faithful recreations to the increases in tempo and changes in instrumentation characteristic of the new rock styles.[54] Pioneering British blues musicians Graham Bond (1937–74), Cyril Davies (1932–64), Alexis Korner (b. 1928), and John Mayall (b. 1943) fostered a generation of blues-influenced players and bands, including the Yardbirds (1963–69), Cream (1966–68), the Rolling Stones (1962–), and eventually Led Zeppelin.[55] Many of the British musicians, particularly guitarist Eric Clapton (b. 1945), were conscientious about citing their sources and paying royalties to the original black artists. Unlike the negative effects of covers described above, many of these musicians finally received their due by the publicity gained through their association with famous British rock bands' performances of their songs.

By the time that Led Zeppelin began recording and touring in 1968, critics had "discovered" the original performers and writers of the blues songs on which many rock songs were based.[56] In spite of the positive effect of rock covers on the careers of many of these artists, critical attitudes turned against Led Zeppelin, and their borrowed material and covered tunes were described in negative terms as "rip-offs." In the changed atmosphere, "authorship" and "authenticity" became important aesthetic criteria, and, despite their lineage, Led Zeppelin's adaptations of pre-existent material were severely criticized.[57]

Another important factor in the borrowing practices of Led Zeppelin stemmed from the experiences of the lead guitarist and leader of the band, Jimmy Page, and the bass player/keyboardist, John Paul Jones, as studio musicians. Both spent years as performers and producers in studios, recording music of all different styles.[58] In their positions, stylistic compentency was a requirement—but one that did not exclude borrowing. Originality was not valued as much as the replication or

---

54 See Kurt Loder, "The Roots of Heaven," Booklet, *Led Zeppelin Box Set Re-release*; David Hatch and Stephen Millward *From Blues to Rock* (Manchester: Manchester University Press, 1978); and Wicke, Ch. 1.

55 Davis, Ch. 1.

56 Ralph J. Gleason, "Perspectives: Let's Spread the Goodies Around," *Rolling Stone* (May 3, 1969): 22, commented that the groups who used the music of the old bluesmen to great success should pay royalties and help to promote their sources. Gleason mentions Skip James, "I'm So Glad" a hit by Cream, a group which included guitarist Eric Clapton, from which James received royalites; he also noted that Chuck Berry made money from his songs on Beatles albums.

57 See Davis, p. 66; Cameron Crowe, "Led Zeppelin: Light and Shade," in Booklet, *Led Zeppelin Box Set Re-release*; and J.D. Considine, who refers to the first bad reviews given Led Zeppelin in *Rolling Stone* 29 (1968). Other bands were also criticized, such as the Rolling Stones (see Ed Ward, Geoffrey Stokes, and Ken Tucker, *Rock of Ages: The Rolling Stone History of Rock and Roll* (New York: Rolling Stone Press, 1986): 283).

58 Palmer, pp. 3–4.

recreation of the appropriate style. Page and Jones carried this attitude into Led Zeppelin. Thus, when the band covered the song "I Can't Quit You Baby," by Willie Dixon on their first album, Page recreated the style and used specific musical figures from Otis Rush's recording of the song, and added stylistically similar and actual borrowed materials from guitarists B. B. King and Jimi Hendrix.[59] This stylistic and quotational compilation was a natural outgrowth of the band members' previous studio experiences.

From the initial period of criticism, however, recent literature on Led Zeppelin has taken a more relaxed view toward authorship. The band is no longer castigated for their use of pre-existent material; in fact, band members are praised for their wide-spread knowledge of the repertoire, and influences are cited as evidence for the richness of the band's legacy. This view toward not only Led Zeppelin but many blues-based British musicians of the 1960s has been given a great impetus by the deification of Eric Clapton and the celebrating of his ties to Robert Johnson. Johnson himself has become a celebrity, as the declared originator of rock, despite his role more as a compiler of many influences from his own time.[60] In Shaw's terms, the view has changed from the negative connotation of "covers" to the more positive view of "reworkings" in a new style, with an element of homage or even reverence to the original performers and writers. Critics' changed responses to Led Zeppelin's authorship are also grounded in the music itself, which is now well-established. Originality has again taken a back seat to the effect and musicality of the new version, in a revival of criteria applied to Robert Johnson and other musicians in the blues tradition.

This return to the traditional view of creative activity in the blues resonates with Foucault's third category of authorship: the complex attribution of an author. In this view, the "author" constitutes a principle of unity among a class of works, somewhat akin to a theory, under which disparate works can be grouped together by their shared characteristics stemming from that authorship. Under this criterion, the role of Led Zeppelin as authors in different songs can be considered in terms of a musically-defined "style class."

In several of the songs adapted by Led Zeppelin, the closeness to the original does not allow for a significant enough identification of the songs with the style of the band for the attribution of "author." Two songs on the first album, "You Shook Me" and "I Can't Quit You Baby," both by Willie Dixon, are in this category. The Led Zeppelin versions are virtual transcriptions of the originals

---

59 Davis, Ch. 1. In addition, the final tonic chord of the blues progression in the Led Zeppelin version of "I Can't Quit You Baby," is altered by the addition of a chromatic I–♭II (A–B♭) chord motion—an alteration already evident in a John Mayall cover (July 1967) of the tune.

60 Johnson's popularity was demonstrated by the amazing success of the recent box release of the complete forty-one versions of his twenty-nine songs (*Robert Johnson: The Complete Recordings*, in "Roots 'n' Blues" [Columbia 46222, 1990]).

transplanted to a rock ensemble, with a minimum of transformation other than the solos, which, as mentioned, draw on a variety of influences.[61] The closeness to the original versions in these transplanted songs is characteristic of the "purist" lineage in British rock, which includes the Bluesbreakers and early Yardbirds and Rolling Stones.

In two other songs, "Bring it on Home," by Willie Dixon as recorded by Sonny Boy Williamson, and "Hats off to Roy Harper," derived from "Shake 'em on Down" by Bukka White, Led Zeppelin recreated the sound of old blues recordings, in the style of the originals, using studio technology.[62] These songs are deliberately uncharacteristic of the band's sound and style, and so do not display the shared characteristics attributable to authorship by the band. By the criteria of Led Zeppelin as a "style class," the band cannot be described as authors of these songs.[63]

In the case of other songs, however, in which the Led Zeppelin versions are "reworkings," radical transformations which create and define its own style, the unifying force of the band as "authors" may be identified.[64] The songs "Dazed and Confused," "Whole Lotta Love," "Babe I'm Gonna Leave You," the "Lemon Song," and "When the Levee Breaks" fall into this category. Although based on pre-existent material, the new versions of these songs feature the unmistakeable characteristics most strongly identified with Led Zeppelin's style, and their central place as defining elements within the band's output permits the attribution of "author" by the criteria of Foucault's third category of author as unity.[65] It is this category that is the most musically interesting, and is, I believe, definitive for the issue at hand. In the following section, I shall demonstrate, by musical analysis, the elements of the band's reworkings of three of these songs that define their style and

---

61 Davis, p. 78.

62 These versions have a precedent in Cream's cover of "Rollin' and Tumblin'," which is a recreation of a Baby Face Leroy recording of the tune, which features Muddy Waters on guitar. Cream anticipated Led Zeppelin in many aspects; for instance, Page's copying of the Otis Rush guitar solo on "I Can't Quit You Baby" recalls Clapton taking of Albert King's solo from "O Pretty Woman" for his solo on Cream's song "Strange Brew."

63 In the world of art music, Berio's *Sinfonia* third movement, which contains music from the third movement of Mahler's Second Symphony, as well as other quoted material, or Webern's transcription of the Ricercare from Bach's *Musical Offering*, raise similar concerns about the attribution of "author."

64 Note Page's comment in relation to "Gallows Pole," a version of an ancient ballad recorded by 12-string guitar pioneer Fred Gerlach, that "I used his version as a basis and completely changed the arrangement." See Cross, "The Song Remains the Same," p. 118.

65 An example from art music in this category might be Shostakovitch's adaptation of Beethoven's Moonlight Sonata and the fugue theme from the Piano Sonata Opus 110 in the final movement of his Viola Sonata Op. 147. Despite the borrowed materials, the assimilation by Shostakovitch to his own style allows for the attribution of "author." A more recent composer who has made a career from his reworkings of existing materials is Alfred Schnittke.

allow for their inclusion in the context of a larger body of works under the authorship of Led Zeppelin. Despite the importance of the historical and social conditions and factors in the question of Led Zeppelin's authorship, it is only through the examination of the musical evidence that satisfactory criteria may be defined to serve as the basis for a meaningful discussion of this issue.

Three songs by (?) Led Zeppelin: An Analytical View

As I pointed out above, questions raised about the attribution of Led Zeppelin as "authors" in songs with borrowed material inciting legal issues of copyright and historically-based attitudes toward originality must be balanced against the identification of these songs with the sound and style of the band. Led Zeppelin's distinctive style was largely fashioned from their skilful manipulation of borrowed materials. The authorship, if any, thus resides in the purely musical aspects of the band's reworkings, which can be uncovered only by comparative analysis of the original and recomposed versions. This is, of course, not to say that the musical analysis uncovers the only aspect or even the most important aspect of the music; it is merely a tool—albeit an essential one to this question—to achieve certain ends.

Of the thirty-six songs on Led Zeppelin's first four albums, thirteen, or approximately one-third, are known to contain borrowed materials; the songs are listed in Figure 1.[66] Three features stand out in the transformations of pre-existent material which define the style class of Led Zeppelin.[67] The first is the stripping down of musical material to an essential, repeated melodic/rhythmic motive or "riff." Such motives, usually based on pentatonic fragments, are highly characteristic of the influential Chicago electric blues songs by Muddy Waters, Willie Dixon, and Howlin' Wolf. The second is the creation of large, complex forms based on contrasting sectional blocks. These forms have precursors in the growing complexity of rock music following the Beatle's *Sgt. Pepper* album (1967), exemplified by the extended three-part form of the song "1983 . . . (A Merman I Should Turn to Be)" from *Electric Ladyland* (1968) by the Jimi Hendrix Experience. The third is the incorporation of electronic effects, including altered instrumental sounds, altered concrète sounds, and sounds from electronic sources. The use of these sounds was

---

66 Sources on Led Zeppelin's songs have already been cited (see note 7). I am also indebted to the staff at the *Bop Shop* in Rochester, NY for their help in locating source recordings, and to Matthew Brown for pointing out the the the influence of the song "Taurus" by the group Spirit on Led Zeppelin's song "Stairway to Heaven."

67 Led Zeppelin was not the first band to incorporate these three features into their reworkings of songs, but, along with Jimi Hendrix, they were arguably the most successful and influential. Precursors include the Yardbirds, Spirit, Cream, the Rolling Stones, the Beatles, Hendrix, and the Paul Butterfield Blues Band. See Davis, *Hammer of the Gods*; Loder, "The Roots of Heaven," and Ward, Stokes, and Tucker, *Rock of Ages*.

Led Zeppelin I

"Babe, I'm Gonna Leave You": Words and Music by Anne Bredon, by assignment from Janet Smith, *c.* 1963 by Ryerson Music Publishers. Recorded by Joan Baez. Attributed as "Traditional, arr. by Jimmy Page," changed to "Anne Bredon/Jimmy Page and Robert Plant" on boxed set re-release.

"You Shook Me": Attributed to Willie Dixon.

"Dazed and Confused": from "I'm Confused" by Jake Holmes, on "The Above Ground Sound of Jake Holmes" (Tower T5079, 1965). Yardbirds version on "Live Yardbirds from Anderson Theater in New York," (Epic E30615, 1968) and "Yardbirds Live featuring Jimmy Page." Unattributed. Solo riff added by Page from his own solo on the Yardbirds song, "Think about it" (Epic 5–10303).

"Black Mountain Side": derived from English folk riff by folksinger Annie Briggs, also from "Black Water Side" recorded by Bert Jansch. Unattributed, earlier version by Page with Yardbirds called "White Summer."

"Communication Breakdown": riff derived from "Nervous Breakdown" by Eddie Cochran. Unattributed.

"I Can't Quit You Baby": attributed to Willie Dixon. Modelled after versions by Otis Rush version (Cobra 1956) and John Mayall (1964), with influence of B. B. King and Jimi Hendrix.

"How Many More Times": lyrics from "The Hunter" by Booker T. Jones, recorded by Albert King, music from "How Many More Years" by Chester Burnett (Howlin' Wolf). Unattributed. Versions with Band of Joy and Yardbirds, guitar solo from "Shapes of Things" by Yardbirds.

Led Zeppelin II

"Whole Lotta Love": from "You Need Love" by Willie Dixon. Unattributed. Dixon sued and won royalties in 1985–87.

"The Lemon Song": from "The Killin' Floor" by Chester Burnett (Howlin' Wolf), with lyrics from "Travelling Riverside Blues" by Robert Johnson. Successfully sued by ARC records. Unattributed in UK version of album, on later albums re-titled as "Killing Floor" and credited to Chester Burnett (Howlin' Wolf).

"Bring it on Home": from "Bring it on Home" by Willie Dixon as recorded by Sonny Boy Williamson. Unattributed. Successfully sued by ARC records.

Led Zeppelin III

"Gallows Pole": from "Gallows Pole" recorded by Fred Gerlach on Folkways record. Unattributed. Labelled "Traditional, arr. by J. Page and R. Plant."

"Hats off to Roy Harper": from "Shake 'em on Down" by Bukka White. Unattributed. Labelled "Traditional, Arr. Charles Obscure" as inside joke.

Led Zeppelin IV

"Black Dog": riff derived from Muddy Waters song on collection, "Electric Mud."

"Stairway to Heaven": opening passage from "Taurus" by Spirit. Unattributed.

"When the Levee Breaks": by Kansas Joe McCoy. Recorded by McCoy and Memphis Minnie. Attributed only to Memphis Minnie.

Figure 1: Led Zeppelin Songs with Borrowed Materials on the First Four Albums

"You Need Love"

Verse 1
You got yearnin' and I've got burnin'
Baby you look so—-sweet and cunnin'

Refrain
Baby, way down inside, Woman you need love,
Woman you need love, You got to have
    some love, some love,
I'm goin' to give you some love,
    I know you need love. you need love etc.

Verse 2
You are frettin' and I am pettin'
Now the good thing, oh, you ain't gettin'

Refrain
Baby, way down inside, Woman, you need love,
I know you need love, Woman you need love
I know you need some love. Let me have
    some love.

Verse 3
I ain't foolin', you need schoolin'
Baby, you know, you need coolin'

Refrain
Baby, way down inside, Woman, you need love

You gotta have some love, mm . . .
You gotta have some love, mm . . .

"Whole Lotta Love"

Verse 1
You need coolin', baby I'm not foolin'
I'm gonna say it, yeah! Go back to schoolin'

Way down inside, honey you need it
I'm gonna give you my love,

I'm gonna give you my love,

Chorus
Wanna whole lotta love? etc.

Verse 2
You've been learnin', Baby I mean learnin'
All them good times, baby, baby, I've been
    yearnin'

Way, way down inside, honey you need it
I'm gonna give you my love
I'm gonna give you my love

Chorus
Wanna whole lotta love? etc.

Verse 3
You've been coolin', Baby I've been droolin'
All the good times, baby, I've been misusin'

Way way down inside, I'm gonna give you
    my love
I'm gonna give you every inch of my love
Gonna give you my love

Chorus
Wanna whole lotta love? etc.

Coda
Way down inside, woman, You need love,
    Shake for me, girl, I wanna be your
    backdoor man. Keep a'coolin' baby

Figure 2: Texts of "You Need Love" and "Whole Lotta Love"

associated, probably most famously in "Revolution no. 9" from the Beatles White Album (1968), with the increasing sophistication of the studio contributing to the recording process, as well as with drugs and psychedelia. With these three features as broad outlines, the Led Zeppelin songs "Whole Lotta Love," "Babe, I'm Gonna Leave You," and "When the Levee Breaks" are analysed below and compared with the progenitor versions known to the band members.[68]

"You Need Love"/"Whole Lotta Love"

In 1962, Muddy Waters recorded the Willie Dixon song "You Need Love."[69] In the late 1940s, 50s, and 60s, Dixon was a session writer and bass player at Chess Records, and briefly at Cobra Records, in Chicago. Perhaps more than any other figure he defined the Chicago electric blues sound and may be regarded as the authentic "author" of this music; many of his songs were covered by fledgling British rockers. Seven years after "You Need Love," in 1969, Led Zeppelin released their second album, which begins with the song "Whole Lotta Love." As mentioned above, Willie Dixon heard the Led Zeppelin song in 1983, and, upon recognizing elements of his own earlier song, he successfully sued Led Zeppelin for royalties, awarded in 1987.[70]

Muddy Waters's version of Willie Dixon's "You Need Love" features Muddy's vocals, along with a somewhat unusual instrumental combination for Chicago electric blues: organ, guitar, drums, acoustic bass played by Willie Dixon himself, and two tenor saxophones that enter only near the end. In the text (Figure 2), the narrator implores his woman, trying to convince her that she "needs love" and he could use some as well, with some thinly veiled sexual allusions by references to "way down inside" and "the good thing . . . you ain't gettin'." The strophic form, with three verses each followed by a refrain, is shown in Figure 3. The form is based on the vocal line and the text, since the accompanying E pentatonic-based harmony (notes E–G–A–B–D), instrumental timbres, and texture change very little, except for the added saxophones in the final refrain and fade out.

---

68 One objection to my analytical treatment of the songs might be that Led Zeppelin continually changed and evolved in their concert versions of these songs. For instance, concert versions of "Dazed and Confused" ran to 45 minutes (see Cross, p. 110). Despite these improvisations, however, each song has a fixed studio version that has become definitive, and formed at least the basis for improvisations on stage. I consider the studio versions justification for my analysis.

69 The song was released on Chess CH3 16500, MCA 8337, originally Chess single 1839. It was recorded on October 12, 1962, with Muddy Waters on vocals, J. T. Brown and Ernest Cotton on tenor saxes, John "Big Moose" Walker on organ, Earl Hooker on guitar, Willie Dixon on bass, and Casey Jones on drums. See liner notes to *Willie Dixon: The Chess Box* (New York: MCA Records, 1988): 10.

70 Dixon, *I Am the Blues*, pp. 217, 223.

Section	Duration (4/4 bars)
Introduction	3
Verse 1	4
Refrain	18 extended improvisation on last line of text
Verse 2	4 voice enters shifted by a half bar
Refrain	4
Instrumental	10
Verse 3	4
Refrain	7
Instrumental fade/saxophones	

Figure 3: Form of "You Need Love"

The verses consist of four bars each, but the irregular refrains are different lengths (Figure 3). The first refrain is extended to eighteen bars by a vocal improvisation, built from extemporizations on the last line of text accompanied by improvisatory variants on an anacrusis motive between the guitar, organ, and voice. The second refrain is only four bars long, but it is followed by an instrumental section of ten bars, featuring an organ solo (with no guitar) over a prominent bass line; this section has a function similar to the extended first refrain. The final seven-bar refrain leads to an instrumental coda and fadeout, with the added saxophones alternating motives with the guitar. The irregular lengths of the refrains and the continual imitative "call and response" commentary between the organ, electric guitar, saxes, bass, and voice throughout give the song its strongly improvisatory flavor.

A most notable feature of the song, both rhythmically and motivically, is the repeated statements of an anacrusis figure, which appears in various forms in all instruments. The opening eleven bars are given in my own transcription in Example 1a. The anacrusis figure leads into the downbeat of each measure, in the electric guitar and bass drums and blocks in the introduction, then the bass takes over the anacrusis in the verse while the electric guitar doubles the voice, and the organ adds imitative responses.[71] The rhythms, notated as dotted in duple divisions, are an approximation; while the opening guitar anacrusis is strictly dotted, other instances of the anacrusis rhythm tend toward "swing"-like divisions of the beats, between dotted and triplet divisions.

The remarkable rhythmic presence of the song is created by a contrast between the insistence of the anacrusis motive and a metric shift in the vocal and upper

---

71 The anacrusis in the drums is combination of bass drum and a higher, hollow block sound, which resembles a cow bell.

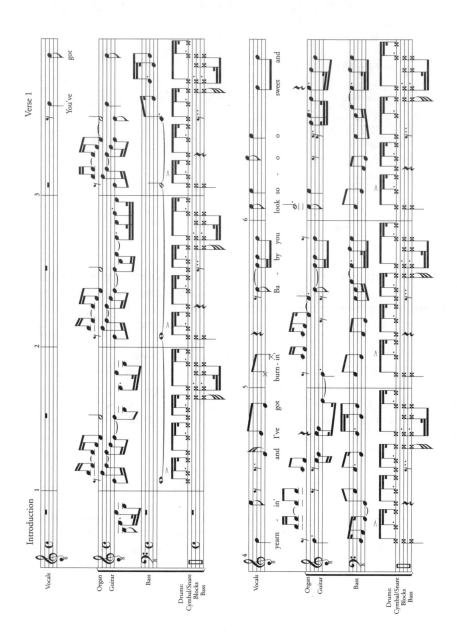

Example 1a: "You Need Love," Introduction and Verse 1
(All parts sound an octave lower, except guitar when doubling voice)

"You Need Love"

Written by Willie Dixon   © 1962, 1990 Hoochie Coochie Music (BMI) Administered by Bug Music   All Rights Reserved   Used by Permission

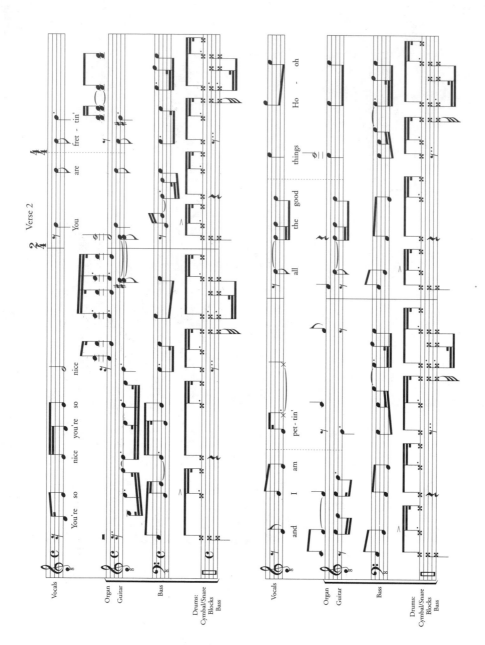

Example 1b: "You Need Love," End of Extended Refrain and Beginning of Verse

instrumental parts. Beginning the second verse, these upper parts shift over two beats, creating a tension between beats 1 and 3 which lasts for the rest of the song. In the first refrain, some emphasis is given to beat 3: in m. 8, the bass alters its pattern to play the anacrusis figure to beat 3, and the vocal line "Woman, you need love" (mm. 9–11) leads to an emphasis on beat 3 with the key word "love" (Example 1a, mm. 9–11). In the course of the extension to the first refrain, the guitar continues to double the vocal "Woman, you need love" rhythm, but also adds the anacrusis figure to beat 1, so that both beats receive emphasis. At the end of the refrain, leading into Verse 2 (Example 1b), the vocalist enters with his upbeat figure shifted by two beats, to coincide with the beginning of a bar, supported by the guitar and organ. As a result, the upper parts are shifted a half bar relative to the bass and drums, shown by the broken bar line in Example 1b. In effect, the vocalist adds a 2/4 bar, before continuing with Verse 2, and carries the upper instruments with him, leaving the lower parts in their established meter. In the organ solo following the second refrain, the organ shifts back to the meter of the lower parts, but then shifts again with the entrance of the voice for the third verse. The metric conflict between beats 1 and 3, which continues to the end of the song, provide a constant rhythmic and metric tension that subtly yet powerfully reflects the text.

The Led Zeppelin song "Whole Lotta Love" is clearly based on textual and musical materials borrowed from Dixon's "You Need Love." The texts are similar (Figure 2), with the sexual innuendo of the latter made more explicit by singer Robert Plant, and a chorus added, "Wanna whole lotta love," as well as an ending coda. The Led Zeppelin version retains the irregular lengths of the original in its outer sections, and it maintains an E pentatonic harmony from fifth-based "power chords" for long stretches, but adds a neighbor D-based fifth chord and a crucial, form-defining move to an A (IV) chord to end the vocal cadenza.

These additions and others change the Led Zeppelin version from a simple cover to a veritable transformation, with three principal distinguishing characteristics: 1) the use, in the outer sections, of a "stripped" down version of the anacrusis motive of the original, continually repeated in the same rhythm, metric position, and notes, as a "blues/riff" played on overdriven, distorted guitar within a pared-down ensemble of guitar, bass guitar, and drums; 2) the creation of a large-scale sectional form with an added contrasting middle "B" section consisting of a psychedelic, electronic fantasy,[72] and 3) a change in rhythm and meter from

---

72 The form of "Whole Lotta Love" is foreshadowed on two songs from the first album. In "Dazed and Confused," the riff borrowed from Jake Holmes has a similar three-part form built around it. After the opening section based on the riff, the middle part consists of repeating bass patterns under electronic effects on the guitar. The middle section is followed by a guitar solo with a cadenza-like section—as in "Whole Lotta Love"—then a return to the opening material. A similar ABA form with internal electronic section occurs in "How Many More Times."

The dual nature of the form of "Whole Lotta Love" and the incomprehension of the music

the original fluid rhythm with swing influences and a conflict between beats 1 and 3 to a straight rock rhythm with emphasized, insistent downbeats and strong syncopations.

Writers on Led Zeppelin inevitably refer to their use of repeated blues-derived pentatonic motives, or riffs, usually syncopated or with some rhythmic twist.[73] Repeated pentatonic riffs are a staple of Chicago electric blues songs, although usually with variation and as part of a larger texture—as in "You Need Love"— and in fluid rhythms without strongly defined downbeats. Led Zeppelin's riffs are essential, primal, stripped down statements—complete in and of themselves—a form of expression that gains its strength from the insistent repetition of its very minimal yet complete nature. Devoid of variation, the riffs are usually in syncopated rhythms against the emphatic, straight eighth-note meter. The syncopation usually occurs, however, in an anacrusis to the downbeat, articulating the metric arrival by its previous offbeat attacks. The combination of pitch simplicity and rhythmic and metric drive gives these riffs their memorable quality.[74]

The riff in "Whole Lotta Love" is clearly patterned after the 5–♭7–1-based anacrusis motive in "You Need Love," but without variation and pared down to an anacrusis to beat 1 only (Example 2a).[75] The "riff" continually repeats in the outer A sections (see Figure 4), reinforcing the meter each time, and gaining in urgency by its unwavering metric placement and power from the overdriven guitar

---

business of the time is illustrated by arrangements radio stations made of the song as a single, leaving out the middle section. In response to this single, Atlantic records released their own, edited version, over the strenuous objections of Peter Grant and Jimmy Page. Led Zeppelin released only a few singles, depending instead on the album sales and FM album format radio stations. See Charles Cross and Robert Godwin, "Collecting Led Zeppelin," in Cross and Flannigan, pp. 73–92.

73 Robert Palmer ("Led Zeppelin: The Music," p. 3) comments on Led Zeppelin's riffs: "Country blues and early Howlin' Wolf sides with staggered off-kilter rhythms had a lot to do with shaping Page's riff construction." Page observed that "I was always experimenting with riffs and things then [during the Yardbird years 1966–68] and began to see during that period that playing such music with a highly inventive rhythm section could move the music into new dimensions." See Jimmy Page," Interview," *The Guitar Classics* 3 (1990): 62.

74 Led Zeppelin's rock riffs follow in the tradition of the Rolling Stone's song "Satisfaction" and Cream's "Sunshine of Your Love" and were influential in the thousands of heavy riffs found in later heavy metal. See Guterman, in Cross and Flannigan, p. 37.

75 Transcriptions in Example 2 are from *Led Zeppelin Volume 1* (London: Warren Chappell Music Ltd., 1991). Despite the clear derivation of the riff from that of "You Need Love," Jones claimed that it arose from improvisation: "Today, none of the band members is sure when the monster 'Whole Lotta Love' riff first appeared. John Paul Jones ventured that it probably came from a stage improvisation during 'Dazed and Confused.'" See Crowe, "Led Zeppelin: Light and Shade," p. 3. Erik Flannigan claims that "Whole Lotta Love" evolved from a long jam in Led Zeppelin's first year of touring, based on the song "As Long as I Have You" which included the song "Fresh Garbage," see Flannigan, "Performances and Career Hghlights 1968–1990," in Cross and Flannigan, p. 166.

Example 2a: "Whole Lotta Love," Riff and Opening of Verse 1

© Superhype Music Publ.
Reproduced by permission of Warner Chappell Music Ltd

Example 2b: "Whole Lotta Love," End of First Verse Leading into Chorus

© Superhype Music Publ.
Reproduced by permission of Warner Chappell Music Ltd

Section		Duration
Introduction:		4 bars, anacrusis to every 2nd bar
A	Verse 1	9 bars
	Chorus	4 bars drums enter a bar early (on bar 9 of verse)
	Verse 2	9 bars
	Chorus	5 bars extended
B		Psychedelic fantasy, extended
Guitar cadenza		6 bars
A'	Verse 3	11 bars
	Chorus	5 bars extended to fermata
Vocal cadenza		free: definitive IV chord (A)
Coda/out		vocal extemporization to fade

Figure 4: Form of "Whole Lotta Love"

timbre and supporting bass and drums.[76] The only rhythmic variety appears in the chorus section, in variations on the anacrusis figure in the second guitar part, which introduces the neighbor D chord, and the drums (Example 2b).

In the outer, A sections, of "Whole Lotta Love, the verse/refrain text of "You Need Love" is combined into the verse alone (Figure 2). The harmonies are typical incomplete triads as "power fifths" played with distortion adding an array of harmonics, including those approximating the missing third. The added formal chorus is defined by a change in harmony, in which the anacrusis figure is harmonized by a D chord that functions as a lower neighbor to the song's prolonged E harmony, and by the definitive vocal line and text "Wanna whole lotta love" (Example 2b). The first chorus is anticipated by the entry of the drums in the extra ninth bar of the verse (m. 14 with a pickup), in a "formal syncopation." This added bar with the drum entry might be considered analogous to the syncopated entry of the voice in "You Need Love," in that it momentarily creates a metric tension.

The vocal line in the outer sections of "Whole Lotta Love" is modelled somewhat on the Muddy Waters version, but Plant employs a wider range and use of dynamics. The emphasis on beat 3 corresponding to the refrain section of

---

76 Mark Bosch ("Jimmy Page," *Guitar School* 1/1 (1990): 21) commented that "On Led Zeppelin II, Page's playing was more aggressive, breaking new ground in guitar overdubbing to create what he referred to as a guitar army. This is most evident in 'Whole Lotta Love' where he uses numerous tracks to thicken the main riff and superimpose slide guitar treatments with backward echo. The riff captures the essence of Led Zeppelin's vision of the original song, transplanted to a rock idiom."

the earlier song, on the words "(in)side," "need" and "love" (Example 2b) in the first verse, lasts only briefly, and is shifted back to the notated downbeat in the chorus (m. 14ff.). Except for the syncopated second beat entry of "Oh" in the added ninth bar of the second verse, the metric conflict of "You Need Love" is sacrificed to the metric drive of "Whole Lotta Love."

By the time Led Zeppelin recorded "Whole Lotta Love" electronic effects altering instrumental sounds, and as sound sources in and of themselves, had been explored by many groups and musicians, such as Pink Floyd, the Beatles, and Jimi Hendrix.[77] The middle section of "Whole Lotta Love," which features a collage of different sounds and effects recalling the roughly contemporary "Revolution No. 9" on the Beatles *White Album* (1968), includes "clamoring trains, women in orgasm, a napalm attack on the Mekong Delta, a steel mill shutting down, backwards echo, an electronic theremin, and vocals with backwards echo."[78] In concert a theremin was used extensively in this section, as part of long electronic improvisations.[79] A link between the A and B sections of "Whole Lotta Love" is provided by the drums that last throughout the middle section, continuing the insistent rhythm created by the riff in the opening. The high hat keeps a continuous beat, with improvisations on the cymbals, snare, toms, and bongos. The power and effect of "Whole Lotta Love," characteristic of Led Zeppelin's style, derives in a large part from the formal contrast and combination of the two seemingly disparate elements—driving, rhythmic blues-riffs and free-form psychedelic effects—into a coherent whole.[80]

---

77 Hendrix's song "1983 (A Merman I Should Turn to Be)" on his album *Electric Ladyland* (1968) is somewhat similar to the form of "Whole Lotta Love" with its electronic/effects middle section. A connection between Led Zeppelin and Hendrix is outlined by Page: "What happened was Roger Mayer, who later worked for Jimi Hendrix, came up to me when I was still in art school and had started to do a few sessions, and he said, 'I work for the Admiralty in the experimental department and I could make any sort of gadget you want.' So I said why didn't he try to make me this thing that I had heard years before on this Ventures record, 'the 200 Pound Bee'." in Davis, p. 17.

78 Davis, pp. 96–97.

79 A theremin was used previously by Spirit, a band well-known to Led Zeppelin—the two bands played at the same concert on Dec. 26, 1968 in Denver, Co. See Flannigan, p. 166. The theremin, invented in 1924 by a Russian scientist named Theremin, creates sounds by differences in frequencies generated by alternating current. The resulting sound is characterized by glissandi and indeterminate pitch frequencies. See Edwin M. Ripin, "Electonic Instruments," in Willi Apel, *Harvard Dictionary of Music* (2nd ed., Cambridge: Belknap Press of Harvard University Press, 1972), pp. 283–85.

In live versions of "Whole Lotta Love," the middle section was often the basis for long improvisations, with songs of different rock and roll vintages inserted. These live versions foreshadow the postmodernist contexts that Led Zeppelin's own music would encounter, as described in the Conclusion below.

80 Robert Palmer ("Led Zeppelin: The Music," p. 3) notes: "None of the musicians [in Led Zeppelin] was a blues purist, or collector, like say, the members of the Rolling Stones. Zeppelin played the blues, but blues filtered through a very individual group sensibility. Perhaps the most

Example 2c: "Whole Lotta Love," End of Cadenza Leading to Verse 3

© Superhype Music Publ.
Reproduced by permission of Warner Chappell Music Ltd

Following the B section, a transitional guitar cadenza links back to the return of the original A material, shown in Example 2c. The guitar solo employs the altered, or "bent" notes characteristic of the blues tradition (the smaller unstemmed notes preceding several notes in the example are the position from which the player bends up to the following note), the notes ♭3 G, ♯4/♭5 A♯/B♭, and ♭7 D are, as some of the rhythms, only an approximation, as boundary limits. The bends on the notes are each to a different position between the boundary notes; the differing extents of the bends contribute greatly to the expressive content of each figure. The downbeat-oriented rhythm of the accompaniment to the cadenza provides a powerful, marked change from the rhythm in the A sections. In the final bar of the cadenza, the drums provide the crucial link up with the riff itself and its anacrusis rhythm to begin Verse 3.

After the third chorus, a vocal cadenza in free rhythm marks the climax of the song (Example 2d). The cadenza is embellished with echo effects on the voice

familiar example is 'Whole Lotta Love,' which begins as a bluesy riff-cruncher but moves organically into pyschedelic sound-collage territory on the break ('That was Page and Eddie Kramer just going crazy twisting knobs in the studio,' an observer reported) without ever losing sight of the mood and intent of the original tune."

Example 2d: "Whole Lotta Love," Vocal Cadenza and Beginning of Coda

which both precede and follow the vocal entries. Within the cadenza the only definitive harmonic motion occurs, an accented IV chord. This chord change, basic to the traditional blues form, is reserved for the dramatic highpoint of the song—the "primal scream"—and it contains tremendous force by its uniqueness and placement. The attack of this chord marks the return of the metric drive, carried first in the voice, then picked up in the drums and finally the return of the riff. The cadenza is followed by a fade out on the A material with vocal improvisations.

"Whole lotta Love" was, and still is, a signature Led Zeppelin tune, with the characteristic elements of driving rhythm in an emphasized meter, sectional form, electric guitar-based instrumentation, improvisatory sexual lyrics, and screaming vocal quality. It is the rhythm of the riff, the psychedelic middle section, and the vocal cadenza that are most memorable, and most clearly mark the transformation from "You Need Love" to the style that defined the sound and essence of Led Zeppelin.

"Babe I'm Gonna Leave You"

According to Stephen Davis, at their first meeting, "Jimmy [Page] played Robert [Plant] some soft things, like Joan Baez doing 'Babe I'm Gonna Leave You . . .' as well as the Incredible String Band and other English folk airs."[81] The song on the first album, "Babe, I'm Gonna Leave You," from a version by singer Joan Baez, exemplifies folk influences on Led Zeppelin. Baez was part of a wider folk community of the 1960s which included Bob Dylan, the Byrds, Joni Mitchell, Buffalo Springfield, and Moby Grape in America, and Pentangle, the Incredible String band, and singers Bert Lansch and David Graham in Britain.[82] Other Led Zeppelin songs in this category include "Black Mountain Side" from the first album, "Ramble On" from *Led Zeppelin II*, the songs on the acoustic second side of *Led Zeppelin III*, and "The Battle of Evermore" and "Going to California" from the fourth album.

The song "Babe I'm Gonna Leave You" is a white blues, a cross between a "Southern Lyric lament (with its ties to the old ballads) and the Negro blues . . . Joan Baez learned it from Janet Smith at Oberlin College."[83] On the first Led Zeppelin album the song is labelled, "traditional, arr. Jimmy Page" but on the boxed set re-release it is attributed to "Anne Bredon, Page and Plante." In a collection of Joan Baez songs, it is attributed as "Words and Music by Anne Bredon, by assignment from Janet Smith, *c.* 1963 by Ryerson Music Publishers." The text of the song is an elaboration on the three line AAB blues format; the last line is repeated with a slight variant at the end, in an AA'BB' form. Verse 1 is given in Figure 5. Each verse begins with the distinctive verbal motive, "Babe," as a plaintive cry. Baez sings four verses, adopting the persona of a "rambler" who describes how she is going to leave in the summertime, in answer to the call of the highway to go westward, despite the fact that her heart tells her to stay. Each verse is accompanied by solo acoustic guitar arpeggiating chords in Spanish and folk styles. The texture and mood remain constant throughout.

> A   Babe, I'm gonna leave you
> A' Tell you when I'm gonna leave you
> B   Leave you, when our summertime, summer comes a rollin'
> B' Leave you, when the summer comes along.

Figure 5: Verse 1 of Baez Version of "Babe I'm Gonna Leave You"

---

81 Davis, pp. 51–52, also Schulps, p. 77.
82 Ibid.
83 Liner notes from *Joan Baez in Concert Part I* (Vanguard CV 2122, 1963). My transcription is from this live recording. In the transcription given in Example 3, the guitar part is notated on two staves to show the separate roles of the bass note and arpeggiated chords.

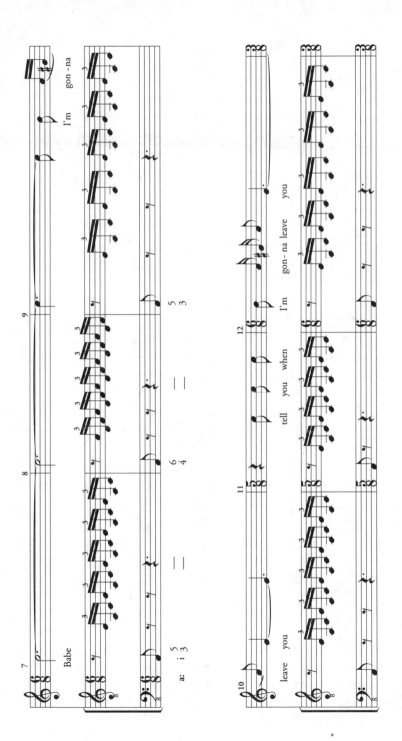

Example 3: Joan Baez Version of "Babe I'm Gonna Leave You," Opening Verse
(Guitar sounds down an octave.)

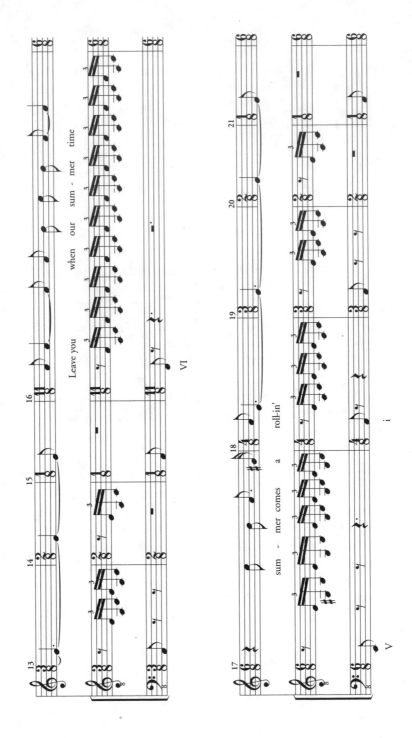

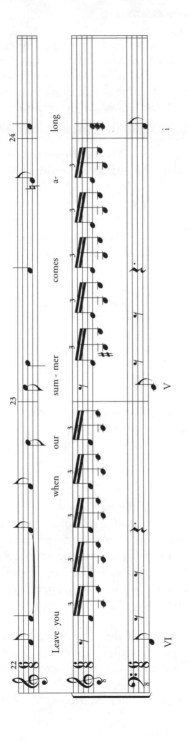

Example 3 (cont.): Joan Baez Version of "Babe I'm Gonna Leave You," Opening Verse
(Guitar sounds down an octave.)

Words and Music used by permiss on, Courtesy of Vanguard Records, a Welk Music Group

The song is in A minor and has just four chords: I, a neighboring 6/4 over the tonic bass note, VI, and V. A transcription of the first verse is given in Example 3. The most distinctive feature of the vocal part is the sustained scale degree $\hat{3}$, note C, dissonant and unresolved against the neighboring 6/4 chord in m. 8, notes D–F–A, setting the word "Babe." The $\hat{3}$/C is also dissonant over the V chord in mm. 17 and 23, but resolves as an appoggiatura. The C could have been harmonized by a more supportive 6/4–5/3 over V, but without that support, it gains in poignance as an exposed dissonance. The perseverence of the unresolved dissonant $\hat{3}$ against the pull of the harmony reflects the painful choice the singer has to make. A similar dissonance, which also reflects the conflict of the singer, occurs on the penultimate G in the voice, melodically ♭7 but also the ♭3 of the V harmony, sounding against the G♯ ♯3 of the same chord.[84] The voice part is also characterized by rhythmic freedom, moving between duple and triple divisions; the notation in Example 3 is only an approximation.

	intro	A		A'	B	B'
	I 5/3–6/4	I 5/3–6/4	5/3	I	VI V I	VI V I
V1	66 66 66	66	6 6	5 6 3 2 1	11 6 4 3 2 1	6 6 66 66
V2		66	6 6	6 6 3 2 1	12 6 3 2 1	6 6 66 66
V3		66	5 6	5 5 6 3 2 2 2 2	6 6 6 3 2 1	6 6 66 66
V4		66 66	6 6	6 5 5 ( )3 2 2	6 6 6 3 2 1	6 6 6 66 66

Figure 6: Form, Harmonies, and Irregular Groupings in Baez Version of "Babe I'm Gonna Leave You"
(Each number indicates a group defining a bar; e.g., 6 = 6/8;
I 5/3–6/4 groups two bars as 66.)

The pattern of harmonies in each verse of the song is given in Figure 6. The first verse begins with an instrumental introduction consisting of the tonic 5/3–6/4 alternation, and each verse ends overlapping into an instrumental extension that doubles as the introduction to the next verse. The first line of text, A, begins over the I 5/3–6/4 alternation but switches to repeated I 5/3 chords, followed by the second line, A', over I 5/3 chords. The third line of text, B, appears over the chords VI V I, and the fourth line, B', over the repeated VI V I progression, overlaps onto the tonic chord extension.

The most striking and beautiful feature of the rhythmic and metric structure in the song is the irregular groupings, primarily within the I 5/3 sections. The beginning of each group is articulated by a bass note, which creates a group

---

84 I am indebted to Rosemary Killam for suggesting this interpretation.

boundary analogous to a downbeat (Example 3). The pattern of grouping is shown in Figure 6. While the 6/8 meter and number of bars in the introduction and with the VI and V chords remain fairly consistent—except for the 11 beat VI chord in the first verse and the two 6/8 bars of VI in Verse 4 which signal the end of the song—the sections with straight tonic chords each contain a different number of bars and beats, varying from 1/8 to 6/8. For instance, in Verse 1, the A section of text has four 6/8 bars, then the A' text has bars of 5/8, 6/8, 3/8, 2/8, and 1/8. The VI chord part of the B text is 11/8, and the tonic chord ending the B text in m. 18 has bars of 4/8, 3/8, 2/8, and 1/8. Most tonic groups end with a successive foreshortening of the grouping units, as in the 3/8, 2/8, 1/8 pattern in Verse 1. Verse 4 has a slight pause before the foreshortening, to begin the preparation for the end of the song.

Both the acceleration provided by the metric foreshortenings and the pauses in the irregular tonic sections reflect the narrator's indecision—alternately wanting to leave and to stay. Thus, although the song is strophic, each verse has a distinct profile; the irregularities follow traditional solo country blues style, in which the singer alters the length of the tonic chord lines to fit the nuances of the text.

Led Zeppelin's version of "Babe I'm Gonna Leave You," transforms the song into a large sectional structure set for voice with some backing vocals, electric guitar, two acoustic guitars, bass, and drums.[85] The arrangment exemplifies a type of sectional formal construction that characterizes many of the band's songs. The Baez version is strophic, with similar textures, mood, and formal structures, but with internal groupings varied subtly in each verse in conjunction with the text. Led Zeppelin's version, diagrammed in Figure 7, transforms the song into two large, formal parts, each with internal repeating and contrasting sections, and the second varied from the first. Contrast is achieved by setting controlled, quieter arpeggiated "Verse" sections with single acoustic guitar, against a strummed "Break" section with acoustic guitar, bass, and drums, and the louder, more raucous, "Chorus" of heavy strumming on the chord progression of the verse with acoustic and electric guitars, bass, drums, and improvised vocals.[86] A reconciliation

---

85 "Babe I'm Gonna Leave You" was released as a single with "Dazed and Confused" on Atlantic promotional EP 1019. The transcriptions in Example 4 are from *Led Zeppelin Volume 1*, cited previously.

86 The sectional quiet/loud heavy form in Led Zeppelin's "Babe I'm Gonna Leave You" and other songs such as "What is and Should Never Be," "Ramble On," "Bring It on Home," "Gallows Pole," "Tangerine," and "Four Sticks," evolved into the continuous development of quiet, acoustic music into heavy electric textures that define one of the band's most famous songs, "Stairway to Heaven." The song "Gallows Pole," in particular, with its continuous buildup from the acoustic beginning, directly foreshadows the form in "Stairway."

With regard to the contrasting forms that characterize many of Led Zeppelin's songs, Davis (p. 58) referred to Page's "light/heavy scheme, a counterpart to the light and shade: acoustic white blues mutates into raunchy guitar and pounding drums." Jones commented that "['Stairway'] actually had a precedent in a song on the first album called 'Babe, I'm Gonna

arp = arpeggiated, str = strummed

Part I		Part II	
Intro 8 bars	arp acoustic guitar	Intro 8 bars	arp acoustic guitar solo acoustic solo
Verse 1 24 bars	vocals arp acoustic guitar	Verse 3 16 bars	vocals arp acoustic guitar bass
Break 8 bars	str acoustic guitar bass, drums	Chorus 8 bars	vocal improvisation heavy strum on verse chords electric guitar fills bass, drums
Verse 2 24 bars	vocals acoustic guitar solo acoustic fills bass	Verse 4 20 bars	vocals arp acoustic guitar solo acoustic bass
Break 8 bars	str acoustic guitar bass, drums	Chorus 16 bars	vocal/backing vocal improv heavy strummed verse chords
Break 8 bars	arp acoustic guitar slide electric gliss. bass		acoustic, electric guitars bass, drums
Chorus 20 bars	vocal improvisation heavy strum on verse chords acoustic, electric guitars bass, drums	Coda 14 bars	vocals str, arp two acoustic guitars
Break 8 bars	strum acoustic guitar bass, drums		

Figure 7: Form of Led Zeppelin's "Babe I'm Gonna Leave You"

between the two extremes appears in an arpeggiated "Break" section after the second verse. A large-scale evolution takes place by the replacing of the "Break" sections from the first part by the "Chorus" sections of the second part. Thus, the Led Zeppelin version creates drama by instrumental and textural contrast, as opposed to the mostly vocal shaping that occurs in the Baez version.

Leave You,' which had many of the same elements: the acoustic start, the build and the sort of 'heavy' end" (in Schulps, pp. 59–60). Palmer (p. 2) noted that "'Babe I'm Gonna Leave You' is a kind of initial blueprint for later songs that used multi-part structures, complex arrangements, culminating in Opuses like 'Stairway to Heaven' and 'Achilles Last Stand.'" Finally, Page opined "I always thought our mixing of the electric with the acoustic made us stand out as a band" (in Palmer, p. 2).

In Led Zeppelin's "Babe I'm Gonna Leave You," the A minor key is retained along with the arpeggiated texture and VI–V harmonic motion, and the tonic 5/3–6/4 progression appears in the "Break." The irregular groupings are evened out, however, in favor of a consistent meter of 4/4; some irregularity is maintained in the lengths of the verses and choruses, which change from Part I to Part II. Characteristically, singer Plant retained the lyrics of the first verse of the original, but altered the other verses and added two improvisatory verses, with stock blues lines such as "I gotta quit you." As with "Whole lotta Love," the vocal line is wider in register (a two octave span E3–E5) and dynamics than the original. In Plant's version, the text is more pleading with a wider contrast of mood, but a more static message.

The verse progression is a characteristic folk song progression using arpeggiated chords over a bass descent A–G–F♯–F–E, or 1–♭7–6–♭6–5 (Example 4a). The introduction to each part consists of a two-fold presentation of the four-bar descent, then the twenty-four bar verse progression consists of the four-bar descent four times, then a four-bar alternation of VI–V, and one more occurrence of the descent. Thus, the form of the entire verse reflects the internal form of the progression, with the expanded VI–V near the end. In Part II of the song the verses are sixteen bars in length, consisting of four descents only. Throughout, guitarist Page varies the progression, adding shaping motivic gestures in the melody to the underlying voice-leading.

The verse harmonies also appear in a heavy strummed version, labelled "Chorus" in Figure 7 (Example 4a). The Chorus section in Part I is twenty bars in length, following the verse pattern, but the final A–E descent of the twenty-four bar verse is omitted. In Part II, the Chorus material appears in two eight-bar statements and an extended sixteen-bar statement, without the VI–V chord alternation of the verse, which does not appear in Part II until the coda.

In Part I, the verse alternates with a "break," the I 5/3–6/4 sections, strummed in Spanish style. In the chords (Example 4b), the 6/4 has an added fifth, note E, above the bass to increase the dissonance—this dissonance is the counterpart to the held ⅜/C against the 6/4 in the Baez version of the song (Example 3). After the second verse, the break appears twice, first strummed, then arpeggiated, in the texture of the verse, and accompanied by a slide guitar in a slow ascending glissando with backwards echo, creating a mysterious and dreamy section. In Part II, the break is replaced by the heavy strummed version of the verse progression.

In several places, including the second verse, the introduction to Part II, and the verse accompaniment improvisation near the end of Part II, a second acoustic guitar adds flamenco-like arpeggiated figures and solos, and in Verse 4 a pedal steel guitar adds a slide part. The ending coda pauses on VI–V, then descends chromatically in a typical blues figure, with a final arpeggiated flourish ending with a frozen ninth suspension (Example 4c), as another reminder of the unresolved dilemma in the text.

Example 4a: "Babe, I'm Gonna Leave You,"
Introduction; Chorus with Strummed Chords of Introduction

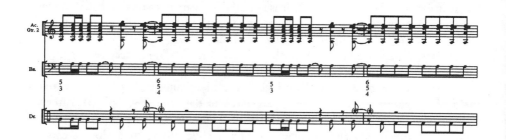

Example 4b: "Babe, I'm Gonna Leave You," Break

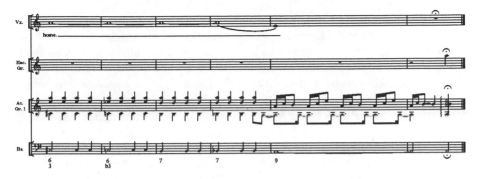

Example 4c: "Babe, I'm Gonna Leave You," Coda Progression

The overall impression of the Led Zeppelin reworking is the powerful contrast created by the juxtaposed formal blocks, each with its own instrumentation, dynamics, texture, and gestures. The subtle accompanimental changes of the original are abandoned for the force of regular repetition, with some high level formal irregularity retained. The personal tone and mood of the original are also transformed into the somewhat hysterical improvisatory pleadings and extreme expression of Plant's prototypical high tenor rock voice. By his verbal improvisations from stock blues figures, Plant also connects the song with its own lineage and to the style which feeds into Led Zeppelin.

"When the Levee Breaks"

The song "When the Levee Breaks" was written and sung by Kansas Joe McCoy (1905–50); McCoy recorded it with his wife at the time, Lizzie Douglas, under the name "Memphis Minnie" (1897–1973), on June 18, 1929. The song is for two guitars, with McCoy on accompanying guitar with Minnie playing melodic leads. It was released by Columbia Records on the 14000 race series on August 2, 1929, eventually selling around 6000 copies. Soon after their first recordings, Minnie was featured as vocalist, and she became increasingly well-known as the two played in Memphis in the 1920s, then in Chicago clubs in the 1930s and 40s, where Minnie split up with McCoy in 1935. McCoy's career ended at this point, but Memphis Minnie went on to make over two hundred recordings and was popular for over twenty years, into the 1950s. It is probably due to her popularity that "When the Levee Breaks" is attributed to Memphis Minnie, including on the fourth album and the recent re-issue of Led Zeppelin songs.[87]

The text of "When the Levee Breaks" is in nine verses, with each verse in the blues form AA'B (Figure 8).[88] According to Samuel Charters, the subject is the Mississippi flood of 1927, when the river flooded over the levees and homes were destroyed.[89] The levee breaking is also a metaphor for the breaking up of a relationship, where the rain symbolizes trouble falling, or crying. The narrator sits on the levee and tries to hold the water back, or tries to hold the relationship together, but to no avail.

In light of the later success of Memphis Minnie, "When the Levee Breaks" shows an important point in her early career, before she had even started singing. For Kansas Joe McCoy, this early song in 1929 marks a brief period where he sang and wrote for the duo. According to Samuel Charters, the song shows both the strengths and weakness of McCoy's writing:

> The first verses were strong and direct, though their effect was weakened by standard lines like "Thinkin' about my baby and my happy home" and "I ain't got nobody to tell my troubles to." None of the details was strong enough to give the song a vivedness that it lacked, though there was a clear overall mood. The thing that was most lacking was a definite self that dominated the song. The use of common verse material and the failure of the song to become more sharply visualized kept it from being a more successful blues text.[90]

Charter's comments criticizing McCoy for using stock lines are of interest in relation to the Led Zeppelin version, where Plant's use of such "standard lines" in his revised text help to create the strong links to the past, as a strength rather than a weakness.

---

87 "When the Levee Breaks" was released on the race record series Col 14439, along with "That will be alright." A version also appears on a compilation by Arhoolie BC C–215 Blues Classics. For McCoy and Memphis Minnie see Charters, Part II, Ch. 9, Sheldon Harris, *Blues Who's Who* (New Rochelle, N.Y.: Arlington House, 1979; rpt., suppl. New York: Da Capo Press, 1989); Mike Rowe, *Chicago Blues* (New York: Da Capo Reprint, 1975; originally *Chicago Breakdown*, London: Eddison Press, 1973); Bob Groom, *The Blues Revival* (London: Studio Vista, 1971), and *Blues and Gospel Records 1902–42* (London: Storyville Publications, 1969): 128–31; Mary Ellison, *Extensions of the Blues* (London: John Calder, 1989), and Alan Lomax, *The Land Where Blues Began* (New York: Pantheon Books, 1993), Ch. 8 for comments.

   Memphis Minnie's songs were re-released by Arhoolie in the early 1960's. The singer Jo-Ann Kelly in London put out an album in 1969 (Epic BN 24491) in styles close to Memphis Minnie and Robert Johnson, and may have sparked interest in the old recordings ("Record Reviews, *Rolling Stone* (December 27, 1969): 58. See also "Review," *Guitar Player* 12/8 (August 1978): 28ff). Plant apparently heard the original recording. See Schulps, p. 39.

88 The text is from Charters, Part II, p. 85.

89 Ibid., Part II, pp. 83–95.

90 Ibid., Part II, p. 87.

If it keeps on rainin' levee's goin' to break
If it keeps on rainin' levee's goin' to break
And the water goin' come and we'll have no place to stay.

Well, all last night I sat on the levee and moaned
Well, all last night I sat on the levee and moaned
Thinkin' about my baby and my happy home.

If it keeps on rainin' levee's goin' to break
If it keeps on rainin' levee's goin' to break
And all these people will have no place to stay.

Now look here, mama, what am I to do
Now look here, mama, tell me what I can do
I ain't got nobody to tell my troubles to.

I works on the levee, mama, both night and day
I works on the levee, mama, both night and day
I ain't got nobody to keep the water away.

Oh cryin' won't help you, prayin' won't do no good
Oh cryin' won't help you, prayin' won't do no good
When the levee breaks, mama, you got to move.

I worked on the levee, mama, both night and day
I worked on the levee, mama, both night and day
So I worked so hard to keep the water away.

I had a woman, she wouldn't do for me
I had a woman, she wouldn't do for me
I'm goin' back to my used-to-be.

Oh, mean old levee caused me to weep and moan
Its a mean old levee caused me to weep and moan
Caused me to leave my baby and my happy home.

Figure 8: Text of McCoy/Minnie's "When the Levee Breaks"

text	A	A		B		
harmony	I	IV	I	V	(IV)	I
bars	4	2	2	1	1	2

Figure 9: Standard Blues Form

The song is performed on two guitars with single vocal, and maintains its texture, tempo, and dynamics throughout. The form is based on a twelve-bar blues in A (Figure 9); in each verse the AA'B text is arranged in the customary manner, each line beginning on a different harmony, with a gradual acceleration of the harmonic rhythm from 4 to 2 to 1 bars. As in many early blues songs, the chord following the dominant only implies IV by the melodic motion.

The introduction consists of eight bars, beginning on the fifth bar, the first "IV" chord of the blues progression, followed by a complete twelve-bar form with solo, as shown in Figure 10. Each verse is a twelve-bar form. The first verse is given in my own transcription in Example 5a. Two important motives appear in the upper guitar part in mm. 1 and 7–8. After the fifth verse, an irregular solo appears: fifteen bars on I followed by the remaining eight bars of the progression. According to Samuel Charters, the extended solo grew out of a mistake: "They [Memphis Minnie and Joe McCoy] got confused in the first instrumental chorus following the vocal [Verse 5], when Minnie changed to the subdominant chord one beat too soon, but Joe changed to simple chording and held the rhythm until they got it together for the next chorus."[91] Actually, the soloist Minnie comes in one bar too soon with scale degree 4/E♭, which is to coincide with the IV chord, as shown in a transcription of the beginning of the solo in Example 5b. Minnie goes right back to the solo figure she had been playing, and Kansas Joe keeps "comping" (accompanying) on the I chord, returning to his original bass pattern two bars later, until they come back around for a second successful try at the IV chord. The irregular shape of this extended solo lends a memorable quality to the otherwise straightforward form, and, ironically, may have spawned the large irregular introductions in the Led Zeppelin reworking.

Led Zeppelin's version of "When the Levee Breaks," from the fourth album, reflects the band's concern for texture, layers, timbres, and colors. They combine the pounding drums, overdriven guitar sounds, and backward echo effects of rock with the moaning vocals, harmonica, and text of an old blues. The band members claimed that the sound of the drums was the original inspiration for their version of the song:

> We had amps in toilets, mikes hanging down chimneys. Sometimes when we were renting these big old houses to write in, we'd experiment with the sound there. Very often the sound would suggest a tune, and we'd write or arrange with that in mind—"When the Levee Breaks" is a good example of that."[92]

The blues idiom in Led Zeppelin's version is invoked by the harmonica and slide guitar in an open major chord tuning—a tuning typical for blues guitar, but in the

---

91 Charters, Part II, p. 87.
92 Davis, p. 133.

Example 5a: Kansas Joe McCoy's "When the Levee Breaks," Verse 1

Example 5b: Kansas Joe McCoy's "When the Levee Breaks," Beginning of Solo

Introduction:	8 bars IV I V (IV) I, then 12-bar form with solo
Verses 1–5:	each a 12-bar form
Solo:	15 bars on I, then remaining 8 bars of 12 bar form
Verses 6–9:	each a 12-bar form

Figure 10: Form of McCoy/Minnie "When the Levee Breaks"

unusual key of F, F–C–F–C–A–F—and the fluid syncopated bass.[93] The vocals, overdriven guitar, and harmonica with backwards echo exaggerate the wailing and moaning of the text, and the monolithic wall of water washing over the levee is represented by the pounding drum beat and continuous, reverberated sound from the guitar and harmonica. The most overwhelming impression is made by the drum track, in straight eighths on the high hat, emphasized beats two and four on the snare, and a syncopated attack on the bass drum before the third beat and following lead-in to the emphasized fourth beat, all given an echo delay of a sixteenth note (Example 6a). This unmistakable Led Zeppelin element, from the drumming of John Bonham, stamps the song as the band's own.

		Part I			Part II		
Intro:							
	drums	2 bars					
	I chord	18			I chord	14 bars	
	Break	5			Break	5	
A	Verse 1	7			Verse 3	8	
	Verse 2	7			Verse 4	6	
	Break	4			Break	4	
B	I–V–IV–I	12			I–V–IV–I	12	
			Coda		I chord to 3 bar cadence	20

Figure 11: Form of Led Zeppelin's "When the Levee Breaks"

Formally, Led Zeppelin abandoned the strophic twelve-bar blues form of the original, and created, as in "Babe I'm Gonna Leave You," a large, repeated two-part form, shown in Figure 11.[94] A transcription of the opening in Example 6a shows the ostinato drum pattern, the guitar in open F tuning repeating a figure based around F, with added blue notes A♭ (♭3) and E♭ (♭7), and the fluid bass similarly with A♭ (♭3). Both bass and guitar begin with a syncopated ♭3–1 pattern in two-beat units which complements the drum's downbeat stress and

---

93 See Example 6a. Open tunings for slide guitar, from the Spanish tradition, are usually E–B–E–G♯–B–E, E–A–E–A–C♯–E, or D–G–D–G–B–D. Capos are often used to transpose to different keys. The transcriptions in Example 6 are from *Off the Record: Led Zeppelin 4th Album* (London: Warner Chappell Music Ltd., 1990).

94 I find no musical evidence of Page's contention that in the song "each 12-bar section features a new texture" (Schulps, p. 106). The claim is echoed in Davis, p. 133, "different themes are developed each twelve bars." The song is not in twelve-bar units, except for the two B sections.

Example 6a: "When the Levee Breaks," Opening

© Superhype Music Publ.
Reproduced by permission of Warner Chappell Music Ltd.

Example 6b: "When the Levee Breaks," Break

© Superhype Music Publ.
Reproduced by permission of Warner Chappell Music Ltd.

Don't it make you feel bad when you're tryin' to find your way home, you don't know which way to go? If you're

Example 6c: "When the Levee Breaks," B Section Beginning

© Superhype Music Publ.
Reproduced by permission of Warner Chappell Music Ltd.

(a) McCoy   (b) Led Zeppelin

**Example 6d: Related Motives from the Two Versions of
"When the Levee Breaks"**

anticipation to beat 3. The overlaid harmonica part consists of an F scale, F–G♭/G–A♭/A–B♭/B–C–D–E♭, with the traditional ♭$\hat{3}$ and ♭$\hat{7}$, and, later in the introduction, with a distinctive emphasis on G, bent up from F and F♯, and sounding as a ninth over the F harmony. Both parts of the song begin with irregular length introductions based solely on the repeated I chord figures. These irregular introductions may stem from the extended 15-bar "mistake" solo in the original.

The two verses in each part are preceded and followed by a cadential break, which embellishes the F chord with a complex combination of two typical progressions and a changed rhythm (Example 6b). The slide guitar part plays a standard rock progression of ♭VI–♭VII then ♭III–I in alternation. Underneath the bass plays a typical blues progression of ♭III–IV then ♭III–I in alternation. The guitar and bass combine with the A♭–B♭ in the bass as the fifth of the D♭ and E♭ chords in the guitar, and thus create somewhat exotic "6/4" position chords. Rhythmically, the alternating ♭III–I progression in the second bar is set in a sharply syncopated pattern of sixteenth-dotted quarter, with a neighbor chord on the beat and the main chord immediately following. (This pattern is a highlighted version of the syncopation in the bass and guitar during the verse, cf. Example 6a.) At this point all instruments play the same rhythm, including the drums, which alters its ostinato pattern and adds cymbal crashes on the syncopated second sixteenth of each beat. Because of their relative harmonic and rhythmic instability, the breaks are unsettled, and lend the following tonic chords of the verse a strong quality of resolution.

The contrasting B section consists of a characteristic rock progression, I–V–IV–I— the rock adaption of the V–IV–I end section of a blues progression, shown in Example 6c. The melodic motive of this section, in a varied form, recalls the florid motive in the original version; the two are juxtaposed in Example 6d. The rhythm is characteristized by a dotted eighth–sixteenth division, the retrograde of the syncopated rhythm of the break. The drum beat again changes, supporting the guitar line and vocals.

In the vocals, Plant sings four verses of the original out of order: verses 1,9,6,2, with a few changes, including a reference to a "mountain man" (which probably stems from the song "Misty Mountain Hop" on the fourth album). The vocal line, again of a wider register and use of dynamics than the original, implies the traditional blues harmonic changes, but remains over a tonic pedal. The text's AA'B lines are set in consecutive two-bar units, but a one-bar repetition of the accompaniment creates odd lengths of seven bars in Verses 1 and 2, a two-bar repetition of the accompaniment creates an eight-bar Verse 3, and the extra accompaniment is omitted for the six-bar Verse 4 (Figure 11).

In the B sections, the text changes time and perspective to a commentary about going to Chicago, since there's no work in the south. This addition both musically and textually changes the song considerably, creating a second subject—drawn from the history of blues singers—and a different "speaker" to complement the contrasting formal section. The change in perspective complements the combined elements in the instrumentals—the mixture of a traditional country blues with the well-established (by the fourth album) sound, textures, and forms of Led Zeppelin. The song ends with a piling on of elements from throughout the song with ever-increasing echo effects until the final overdriven solo guitar E♭ (♭7), held for a moment, then swooping down in a glissando to the final consonant F chord, which reverberates in a powerful echo.

Conclusion

My purpose in this study has been to consider different aspects of authorship and identification in reference to several songs from Led Zeppelin's first four albums. In the blues tradition from which Led Zeppelin emerged, originality generally was considered subordinate to creativity, but this situation changed. Undoubtedly due in large part to the amount of money and the social issues involved, copyright, ownership, and royalties had become important critical and business concerns by the time Led Zeppelin was recording in the late 1960s, and they have continued to be concerns up to today, particularly with reference to sampling. From the initial criticism of the band for their appropriation of existing material, however, the intervening span of twenty-five years has softened the accusations, and Led Zeppelin is generally praised for its musical acumen in these days of box-set compilations.

Within the relatively short span of their first four albums, Led Zeppelin evolved a distinctive and influential style, with roots in the many directions British and American rock musicians had taken in the 1960s, including blues, rock and roll, rock, folk, country, electronic music, art rock, and psychedelia. The four members all developed at a time when "cover" bands were greatly appreciated, and American audiences cheered groups like the Rolling Stones and Cream as they performed songs originally written and performed by black musicians from Chicago unknown in the United States but who often toured in Europe. Led Zeppelin was also influenced however, by the original material of the Beatles, who "authored" highly original concept albums like Sgt. Pepper. In the wake of this and other unified albums, audiences came to expect distinctive sounds, instrumental virtuosity, and established, individualized styles. Led Zeppelin was so successful in this milieu that even today, the ubiquitous lists of "top 100 rock songs" inevitably include "Stairway to Heaven" and "Whole lotta Love" in the top ten.

Ultimately, the question of whether Led Zeppelin can be considered the true "authors" of their own music cannot be determined by copyright laws or attitudes toward proven or unproven influences or appropriation. The true evidence lies in the music itself, independently of the usual social and cultural concerns of popular music writers, and can only be discovered by analysis of the musical features themselves. The songs analysed above, "Whole Lotta Love," "Babe, I'm Gonna Leave You," and "When the Levee Breaks," all share musical elements with the original versions, but are transformed formally, timbrally, rhythmically, motivically, and harmonically into the defining features of the Led Zeppelin sound. Questions of authorship and originality arising from the legal and historical categories of authorship defined by Foucault must be weighed against the attribution of the songs to Led Zeppelin by their distinctive musical characteristics, in the context of Foucault's third category, the unifying effect of the author in a corpus of works. The distinction may be set in the terms given by Arnold Shaw, between "covers" and "reworkings," where the former is a cheap imitation but the latter is a recomposition into a new self-contained stylistic and musical world, one which does not rely musically on the original but can stand on its own. The transformation must be so complete that the reworking and original can stand side by side and both be accepted completely on their own terms, with an appreciation for the elements that bind and separate the two.

Finally, it is interesting and perhaps appropriate to note that Led Zeppelin also spawned its own tradition of "covers" and "reworkings." As is fitting, two types of "Led Zeppelin" bands have emerged. First, bands like "Physical Graffiti," which are a carbon copy of the band down to the last detail, offer the attraction that they recreate the band's live concerts and give succeeding generations the illusion of having seen Led Zeppelin in action. Thus, they are the definitive "cover" band, and have no identity of their own. Second are bands like "Dread Zeppelin," which transform the music of Led Zeppelin to create their own style. Dread Zeppelin does reggae versions of Zeppelin tunes with an Elvis Presley impersonator, "Tortleelvis," as the lead singer. Dread Zeppelin ahistorically combines the pre-Led Zeppelin influence of Elvis and the post-Led Zeppelin development of reggae in a quintessentially postmodern statement. Commenting on Dread Zeppelin, Plant claimed that Led Zeppelin themselves occasionally did reggae versions of "Stairway to Heaven" in warmups, anticipating their own successors and the continuation of the tradition from which they themselves emerged.[95, 96]

---

95 Considine, p. 109.

96 I would like to thank Matthew Brown for his many hours of conversation, comments, and ideas on the topic of this article.

Theories of Chordal Shape, Aspects of Linguistics and Their Roles in an Analysis of Pitch Structure in Berio's Sequenza IV for Piano

Richard Hermann

Introduction

Luciano Berio's *Sequenza* series of compositions for solo instrument is an on-going project that had its start near the beginning of his career. *Sequenza IV* for solo piano (1966) has, perhaps, the most complex pitch structure of this influential series of works.[1] Its opening, jagged chordal gestures present an interesting analytical challenge, since set-theoretic equivalence and similarity relations do not always support perceived similarity between chords.[2] The theories developed here attempt to model not only this author's perception of certain chordal shapes as derivations of others, but also to model the physical and registral groupings of

---

1 This essay is an extensive revision of two of my earlier essays: "Some New Analytical Techniques for the 'Post-Serial' Repertoire, Re: Luciano Berio," delivered at the 1983 meeting of the Society for Music Theory (New Haven, Conn.) and "An Analysis of Berio's *Sequenza IV* for Solo Piano" delivered at the 1989 annual meeting of the Music Theory Society of New York State at Baruch College (New York City).

  There is some disagreement as to the year of composition for *Sequenza IV*. Berio's Universal Edition catalog gives the year as 1966, but the corrected edition of 1987 gives 1965 at its end. The facsimile shows no date at all. The pianist of the New York City premiere (Berio was present), David Burge, wrote to me on November 4, 1989: "For the record, . . . the piece was definitely written in 1966."

  A recorded performance of *Sequenza IV* by Aki Takahashi can be found on *Piano Space 2* (EMI Angel Japan EAC–60154 Stereo LP, no date). Another by David Burge is on *Avant Garde Piano* (Candide CE 31015 Stereo LP, 197–).

  I extend my thanks to Brian Alegant, David Burge, Robert Morris, and Patrice Pastore for reading and making valuable suggestions upon the earlier essays mentioned above.

2 Techniques such as Rahn's ATMEMB and Forte's K/Kh complexes failed to relate strongly many pairs of chords that theories to be developed here do. In fact, these tools in general yielded rather unfocused analytical results for this piece. See John Rahn, "Relating Sets," *Perspectives of New Music* 18 (1979–80): 492–94 for information on the ATMEMB function between two pc-sets. ATMEMB measures and scales abstract subset content held in common between two pc-sets. The function returns a value from 0 to 1. The greater the value, the more closely related the two pc-sets are; the lesser the value, the less closely related. See Allen Forte, *The Structure of Atonal Music* (New Haven: Yale University Press, 1973), pp. 93–100, for detailed information on the Kh relation. Informally, the Kh relation between two set classes (hereafter, scs) holds when the scs can be mapped into each other's sc or each other's complementary sc.

364

pitches from the perspective of the performer, in light of pianistic technique. Throughout the development of this argument, inspiration is drawn from the field of linguistics, which was an interest of the composer's.[3]

Example 1 reproduces the first page of *Sequenza IV*; the chords displayed there form a rich catalog of 24 different pitch sets belonging to 22 different set-classes. These chords are labeled by italicized capital letters. Those chords labeled *A* through *J* without a superscript "v" are called "referential chords"; those chords with v superscripts are variants of the referential chord bearing the same letter name, for reasons to be developed more fully below.[4] The questions of how many referential chords exist in this piece, how the variant chords are related to the referential chords, why the referential chords are distinct from one another, and so forth are subjects addressed in this essay.

The Editions

Before exploring the relation between pianistic technique and chordal shape in *Sequenza IV*, performers and analysts alike must consider the fact that three editions of the work have appeared to date. These must be investigated in order to establish their relative authority as *Urtexts*.[5] The first two editions of the work were published in 1967. One was a facsimile of the composer's holograph and the other was a traditionally engraved edition. The first mentioned is called the "facsimile," and the second is called "engraved '67." The third edition looks similar to engraved '67, and it has the words "corrected 1987" in the lower right-hand corner of the score's first page. It is called "corrected '87." All are in the oblong format common to Berio's Universal Edition scores.

---

3 In the following statement, Berio dates his interest in linguistics: "I met [the great novelist, philosopher, and semiotician Umberto] Eco in Milan in the mid-fifties. We soon discovered that we took a similar interest in poetry and within it, onomatopoeia: I introduced him to linguistics and he introduced me to Joyce." See Rossana Dalmonte and Bálint András Varga, *Luciano Berio: Two Interviews*, trans. and ed. David Osmond-Smith (New York: Marion Boyars, 1985) p. 142.

4 The referential chords are labeled alphabetically in their order of appearance. Chords related by pitch-class (hereafter, pc) transposition may be considered distinct from one another for the reasons to be developed later. Chords may also have an Arabic number after the v superscript. These numbers are ordinal labels distinguishing between different variant chords related to the same referential chord.

5 Unfortunately, Universal Edition (London), has given all three the same plate number, 132724 mi. Engraver errors, poor proof reading, and some actual changes by Berio necessitate this brief look at the editions. For instance, the facsimile is 215 bars in length; however, the two engraved editions omit the bar line between measures 96 and 97, thus yielding a total of 214 measures. I have prepared a detailed critical report on the differences between the editions; some of these differences are summarized here as well.

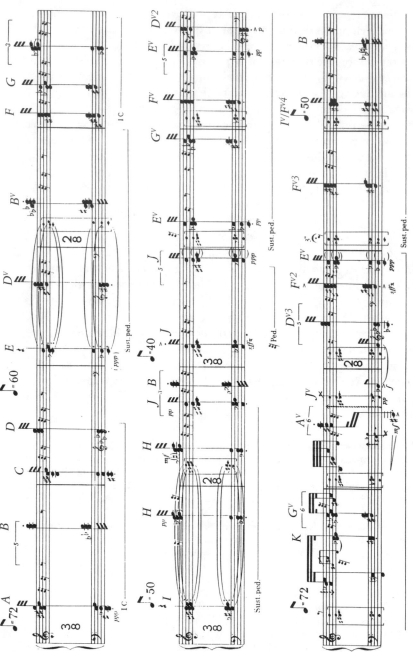

Example 1: Luciano Berio: *Sequenza IV* (1965)—First Page of the Corrected 1987 Edition

* The attack *sff* must always be as loud and as quick as possible. The pedal, when used immediately after this type of attack, should collect only random noises and resonances.

Differences among the three are many, and they range from the engraver's usual insignificant and easily spotted errors to medium and even large-sized errors. There also appear to be several changes by Berio in corrected '87. Unfortunately, the engraver introduced petty errors into engraved '67, which remain uncorrected by Berio. Perhaps the composer consulted his holograph or its facsimile and not engraved '67 when specifying the changes to the editor at Universal Edition. A missing bar line, a few changed pitches, some inaccurate rhythms, omitted accents, and so forth still stand.

Which edition are we to use? The facsimile edition is, for textural reasons, indispensable and the corrected '87 must be consulted for Berio's changes.[6] One should *not* follow engraved '67.

Although the engraved editions are indeed beautifully clear, well spaced and "easy" to read; they are so, however, at the cost of a rough congruence between the proportional spacing on the page and the attack-points of the pitches that is found in the facsimile. The most important benefit of consulting the facsimile is the evidence it contains for a layered method of notation, if not directly for a layered method of composition itself. This should not be surprising, since his *Sinfonia* and *Chemins* series of compositions are explicit in their use of layering.[7] There appear to be at least two stages in the process of notation: the first notated stratum is chordal and the second consists of both chords and lines laid upon the first. Examples of two different kinds of notational adjustments support the thesis of a layered compositional process for this piece. Example 2a shows that on pages 2 and 3 the very last 32nd note of the last measure on each page contains the exact same chord followed by a breath mark that is notated above and to the right of each page's last barline. Further examination of these measures yields other identities and variants. These breath marks and identical chords provide a "frame" for the later embellishing lines that complete the surface of these passages. In Example 2b, the fourth stave of page 5 was carefully extended into the right hand margin, and the first bar of the following stave holds a prominent chord in the piece, indeed a near repetition—only lacking one of the chord's nine pitches—of

---

6 Sadly, I suspect that copies of the facsimile edition are now rare. Berio's notation of the harmonic intervals of major and minor seconds occasionally deviates from usual practice and has been tacitly "normalized" in the engraved editions. Though altering a highly musically literate composer's notation is a suspect practice, I have yet to discern reasons for his notational "deviations."

7 On his works *Sequenza VI* for solo viola, *Chemins II* (which employs a chamber ensemble aurally surrounding *Sequenza VI* with its own material), and *Chemins III* (which employs an orchestra to further surround *Chemins II*) Berio has said: "The three pieces relate to each other something like the layers of an onion." The quote is found on the record jacket of *Berio Sequenza VI Chemins II Chemins III*, Walter Trampler, viola (RCA LSC–3168, 1970). For recent information on Berio's *Sinfonia* see David Osmond-Smith, *Playing on Words: a Guide to Luciano Berio's Sinfonia* (London: RMA Monographs, 1985).

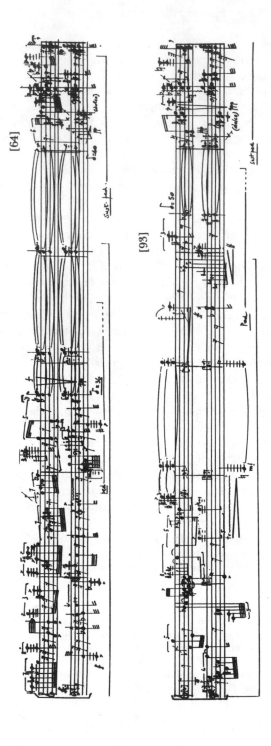

Example 2a: Luciano Berio: *Sequenza IV* (1965)—The Last Systems of Pages 2 and 3 from the Facsimile Edition

[137]

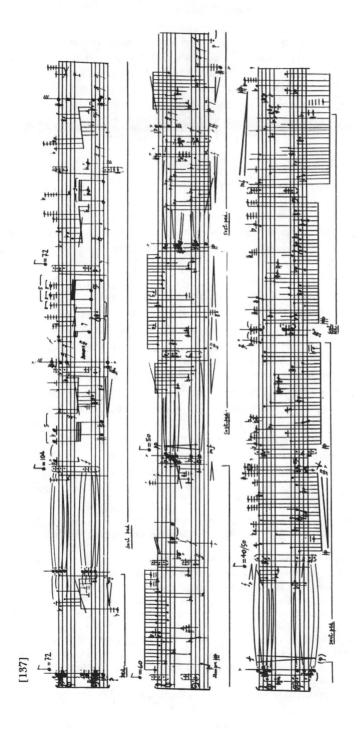

Example 2b: Luciano Berio: *Sequenza IV* **(1965)—The Last Three Systems of Page 5 from the Facsimile Edition**

the very first chord. As the composer evenly preruled the measures and then added the chords of the first layer, he needed here to extend the measure into the margin in order to hold all of the second embellishing layer's material. That embellishing material could not flow into the next stave because a chord was already placed at the beginning of the stave in the previous layer of composition. Had the composer not preruled the measures ahead of time and flexibly layed out the measures as he went along, the marginal extenstion would not have been needed.

Towards A Theory of Chordal Shape

In order to answer the question of why the referential chords are distinct from one another, we start with some thoughts on a theory of chordal shape. A chord is a set of pitches, and it consists of one or more "shape fields," which have the following properties: 1.) shape fields are chordal subsets of contiguous pitches; 2.) if a chord has more than one shape field, then the shape fields are disjunct and completely partition the chord; 3.) boundary intervals between adjacent shape fields must be equal or greater than some real number variable "x" times any interval found between adjacent pitches within either of the adjacent shape fields. This "x" variable could be set to some value appropriate to the musical dimension under consideration.[8] These definitions of chord and shape field provide reasonable methods for determining whether the pitches of a chord fuse into one perceptual entity or whether the pitches divide into perceptually distinguishable subsets.

Chords may also be partitioned by the performing techniques of the musical medium employed in sounding the chord. These partitions via performance techniques are called "chordal spans" or just "spans" for short. The division of chords between the pianist's two hands is a commonplace example of spans.

The ideas of chords, fields, and spans and their interrelations are roughly analogous to words, morphemes, phonemes, and syllables in linguistics.[9] An

---

8   I have been influenced by James Tenney and Larry Polansky's "Temporal Gestalt Perception in Music," *Journal of Music Theory* 24 (1980): 205–41 on employing a variable suitable for each musical dimension.

   Recent work on contour theory has also been a stimulus to this work. Please see the following: Michael L. Friedmann, "A Methodology for the Discussion of Contour: Its Application to Schoenberg's Music," *Journal of Music Theory* 29 (1985): 223–48; Friedmann, "A Response: My Contour, Their Contour," *Journal of Music Theory* 31 (1987): 268–74; Elizabeth West Marvin and Paul A. Laprade, "Relating Musical Contours: Extensions of a Theory for Contour," *Journal of Music Theory* 31 (1987): 225–67; and Robert D. Morris, *Composition with Pitch-Classes* (New Haven: Yale University Press, 1987), pp. 23–42.

   For a differing viewpoint on these issues, see Christopher F. Hasty, "Phrase Formation in Post-Tonal Music," *Journal of Music Theory* 28 (1984): 167–90, and Elizabeth West Marvin's contribution to this volume.

9   Berio's interest in linguistics can be seen in his widely known *Circles* (1960) for mezzo-soprano,

(a) Relations Among Chords, Spans, and Shape-Fields

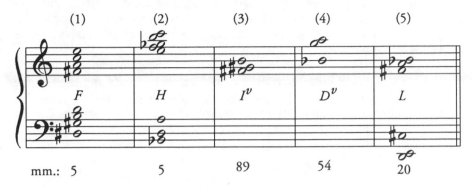

(b) Parts of Spans or Shape-Fields

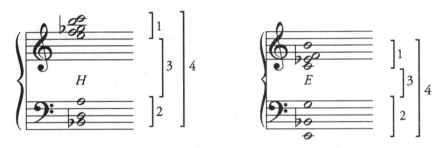

(1) Right Hand Span (2) Left Hand Span (3) Intrahand Span
(4) Total Span, Boundary Pitches, Boundary Interval

N.B. Referential Chord *E* is first found in measure 3.

Examples 3a–b: Chords, Spans, and Shape-Fields in Berio *Sequenza IV*

examination of Example 3a, will make the rough analogy clear enough. The word "a" is both a single syllable, and morpheme; furthermore, it is the phoneme [e]. The word "boy" is a single syllable and morpheme but consists of three phonemes: [b] and the two vowel sounds/phonemes [ɔ] and [i] that create the diphthong [ɔi].

---

harp, and percussion, which employs the international phonetic alphabet in the voice part. Berio's *Sequenza IV* may, thus, be thought of as a transfer of the selected linguistic concepts mentioned above into the musical dimension of pitch-chords.

The word "boys" has a single syllable, two morphemes ("boy" and English's plural morpheme "s"), and phonemes: [b] [ɔi] and [z]. The word "boyish" has two syllables (boy–ish), two morphemes ("boy" and "–ish"), and the phonemes [b] [ɔi] [i] [ʃ]. Thus, words, syllables, phonemes, and morphemes do not simply nest or map onto one another.[10]

Just as a variety of relations exist between the above mentioned linguistic entities, so too, many kinds of relations hold between chords and their shape fields and spans. Example 3a demonstrates this with chords from *Sequenza IV*. If the boundary interval variable mentioned above, "x," is set to 2.0 (in semitones), then chord 1 has one field and two spans, chord 2 has two fields and two spans, chord 3 has one field and one span, chord 4 has two fields and one span and chord 5 has two spans and three fields. Thus, while two or more of the analytical labels of span, field, and chord may be identical in application for some cases, they are not necessarily always identical as the cases from Example 3a explicitly show. Chords with more than one field will hereafter be called "multifielded" (as chords 2, 4 and 5 of the example); chords with two fields are "bifielded" (chords 2 and 4), while chords with a single field are "monofielded" (chords 1 and 3).

Example 3b displays other descriptive terminology demonstrated on referential chords *H* and *E*. Relevant dyadic pitch segments in these chords are labeled with numbered brackets denoting various parts of the chord's right- and left-hand spans. These dyadic segments may be used to define a measurement of a given chord's "sparseness" or "denseness." The *degree of* compactness, DOC, of a span, shape field, or chord is the ratio of its *boundary interval* (bi) divided by (n-1), where n equals the cardinality of the pitches. Hence, where X is a span, shape field, or chord, $DOC(X) = bi/(n-1)$. If the DOC function returns values that are equal for two different spans, shape fields, or chords, they are members of the same equivalence-class. This measurement gives an average distance between pitches; higher DOC values model relatively "sparse" chords, while lower values model "dense" chords. For this piece, it seems reasonable to call a span, shape field, or chord "sparse" when its DOC value is equal to or greater that 3.0, and it also seems reasonable to call them "dense" when that ratio is less than 3.0. Figure 1 gives the DOC values for the referential chords and their shape fields and spans.

Example 4 lists the referential chords. Questions remain: Why 14 referential

---

10 See Mario Pei and Frank Gaynor, *Dictionary of Linguistics* (New York: Philosophical Library, 1954), pp. 140, 167, 209, and 233 for concise definitions of morpheme, phoneme, syllable, and word; see Bertil Malmberg, *Phonetics: Physiological Phonetics, Experimental Phonetics, Evolutionary Phonetics, and Phonemics* (New York: Dover, 1963) for information on the international phonetic alphabet and on phonemes; and see Oswald Ducrot and Tzvetan Todorov, *Encyclopedic Dictionary of the Sciences of Language*, trans. Catherine Porter (Baltimore, Maryland: John Hopkins University Press, 1979), pp. 173–6, 199–203 for information on the relations among the concepts of morpheme, phoneme, syllable, and word.

RIGHT HAND SPANS OR SHAPE-FIELDS			LEFT HAND SPANS OR SHAPE-FIELDS		
bi/n-1	DOC	from Ref. Chord	bi/n-1	DOC	from Ref. Chord
3/2	1.500	K	2/1	1.000	L*
7/4	1.750	I	3/2	1.500	M
7/4	1.750	M	7/3	2.000	I
4/2	2.000	L	4/1	2.500	K
8/4	2.000	H	10/3	3.333	J
9/3	3.000	G	7/2	3.500	B
10/3	3.333	A	7/2	3.500	D
10/3	3.333	F	11/3	3.667	F
7/2	3.500	B	15/4	3.750	A
7/2	3.500	D	8/2	4.000	G
11/3	3.667	E	13/3	4.333	C
11/3	3.667	J	11/2	5.500	H
11/3	3.667	N	11/2	5.500	N
13/3	4.333	C	15/2	7.500	E

* Referential Chord L has two shape-fields played by the left hand, <D2,E2> and <C♯3>. As the second shape-field has only one element, bi/n-1 = 1/0 whose value is undefined. Because DOC gives an average of intervals between elements, a one element shape-field creates no intervals within itself and, thus, can generate no measurement. This is much like a single point in geometry. It has no magnitude; it merely has location.

MONOFIELDED REFERENTIAL CHORDS			MULTIFIELDED REFERENTIAL CHORDS		
bi/n-1	DOC	Ref. Chord	bi/n-1	DOC	Ref. Chord
16/8	2.000	I	13/4	3.250	K
19/6	3.167	G	23/7	3.286	M
16/5	3.200	D	28/5	3.571	B
25/7	3.571	F	41/8	5.125	A
26/7	3.714	J	38/7	5.429	H
31/7	4.429	C	32/5	6.400	L
29/6	4.833	N			
31/6	5.167	E			

Figure 1: DOC Values for Referential Chords and Their Spans and Shape-Fields

chords and not more or less, and how are the variants related to the proper referential chord? Some reasons for assigning a generator-like status to these 14 come from empirical observations: they are the chords that appear most frequently among apparently closely related chords, and, more importantly, they frequently assume boundary positions in the gestural form of the piece. The referential chords were statistically tested to see whether they would collapse into fewer referential chord categories, and the results indicate that these 14 are reasonably distinct from one another.[11]

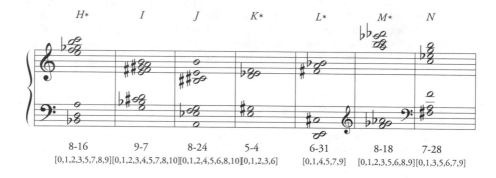

* = Multifielded Referential Chord

Example 4: A Catalog of Referential Chords for Berio's *Sequenza IV for Piano*

---

11 The statistical testing was was done by finding out the probability of each pair of chords having the number of pitch (not pc invariants) common tones that they actually do have. Those pairs of referential chords having improbably high numbers of common tones were considered possible candidates for merger into a single referential chord category. These pairs were also examined with the theory of chordal shape outlined above. They were considered sonically independent if they had significant differences in two or more of the following categories: total boundary interval, number of shape fields, degree of compactness, or set-class membership.

In my 1983 essay, referential chords were there called "archetypal chords," and they were 15 in number. Recent rethinking of what was, in my first essay, a more implicit theory of chordal shape and the statistical testing allowed me to eliminate one of those referential chords.

Some Interactions Between Performing Technique on the Piano and the Theory of Chordal Shape

Each referential chord as labelled in Example 4 has its own sonic signature created by differences of hand-position, registral location and pitch, pitch-class, intervallic and set-class design. Significant matching within these sonic realms can assure resemblance between a referential chord and a variant of it. Thus, the manner of playing chords is naturally tied to a theory of chordal shape that, in turn, contributes to the concepts of chordal shape identity and resemblance.

In considering how differences in chordal shape come about, some clues can be gleaned from the fact that Berio, a pianist himself, coordinates the pitch structure of his pieces to rethinkings of the medium's capabilities and the processes of performing in that medium.[12] Thus, I infer the piece to be an exposition of chordal playing and the list of referential chords detailed above (see Example 4) to be a catalog of the kinds of ways in which the pianist can deploy the hands in playing chords.

Four oppositions provide the means for understanding each chord's uniqueness: 1.) is the chord monofielded or multifielded? 2.) is it dense or sparse? 3.) does it have a high or low tessitura, and 4.) is it like or unlike other chords in pitch, pc, intervallic and sc design? The first of these oppositions describes the pianist's hand positions; informally, are they close together or far apart? Chord E (monofielded) is an example of the hands being close together, and the multifielded chord H is an example of hands spread further apart. The second opposition describes the positions of the fingers; informally, is the hand called upon to play many or few pitches, and does the chord force the fingers to stretch apart or contract toward one another? For instance, the right-hand of referential chord H is an example of a dense deployment: DOC(H's top field) = $8/(5-1)$ = 2.0. The left-hand span of referential chord E is an example of a sparse deployment: DOC(E's left-hand span) = $15/(3-1)$ = 7.5. The third opposition describes the rough location of the hands upon the piano: chord M is high in tessitura, and chord C is low in tessitura.[13] The fourth opposition is the subject of traditional atonal theory and some of the theory unveiled here.

---

12 Berio has commented (Dalmonte and Varga, p. 99): "Control of the development of harmony and melodic density is a feature common to all the *Sequenzas*, though it takes different forms because, in each case, certain aspects of the instrument's technique are examined critically."

13 *Pitch* transformations of transposition, inversion, and their combinations on chords naturally preserve chordal shape as a by product of preserving intervals. However, if both chords are not literal pitch-transpositions or pitch-inversions of one another, and if they inhabit different areas of the pitch spectrum, they can certainly still be related to one another through chordal shape-transformations. These transformations can only be suggested here. A transposition-like transformation called SHIFT, an inversion-like transformation called FLIP, and their combinations can create equivalence-classes that preserve chordal shape, boundary-interval spans, DOC

Another way to understand the differences between two chords through the third opposition, pitch-space location or register, is through the real value returned by a function called the "*degree of spatial overlap*," abbreviated DSO. The DSO function returns a number between 0 and 1; the closer the value is to 1 the closer the two chords are in pitch space, and the closer the value is to 0, the further apart they are. The DSO function consists of a relationship between two other functions: the "*element span*," abbreviated ES, and the "*overlap span*," abbreviated OS. The ES function applied to a chord returns the integer value of the interval (in semitones) formed between the lowest and highest pitches plus 1. Thus, the ES function counts all of the elements that could occupy the space described by that interval. The OS function applied to the two chords under consideration measures their overlap by taking the integer value of the interval formed between the higher value of the two chords's lowest elements and the lower value of the two chords's highest elements and adds 1. The DSO of chords X and Y equals OS(X,Y) divided by either ES(X) and ES(Y), whichever is lower. The range of the DSO function is between 0.0 for two chords that do not spatially overlap and 1.0 for two chords that overlap entirely. An example in pitch space follows. Returning to Example 1, consider the referential chords *C* from measure 2 and *H* from measure 5; recall from Figure 1 that they share the same sc membership, 8-16 [0,1,2,3,5,7,8,9]. The function ES(*C*) = 33 (the distance in semitones between C♯2 and G♯4 is 32) and the function ES(*H*) = 39 (the distance between B♭2 and C6 is 38 semitones). The OS(*C, H*) = 23 (since the interval between B♭2, the higher of the two chords's lowest pitches, and G♯ 4, the lower of the two chords's highest pitches, is 22). Thus, the DSO(*C, H*) = OS(*C, H*)/ES(*C*) = 23/33 = 0.697. Thus, *C* and *H* are not closely related through the opposition of pitch-space location, despite the fact that they belong to the same set-class.[14]

---

values, and relative relations of the chord's shape-fields or spans with one another. Certainly, similarity functions can be easily designed for the DOC function. Order transformations such as rotation could also be useful in describing relations between multifielded chords.

14 Because *C* is monofielded and *H* is bifielded, their chordal shapes are different and not chordal shape equivalent under operations suggested in footnote 13. Further, their degree of spatial overlap is not great (0.697). Even though the referential chords *C* and *H* share the same sc, these two referential chords are distinct from one another according to the oppositions as demonstrated above.

The operation of set intersection of pitches between chords can be thought of as describing their "literal overlap" in pitch space; the DSO function between two chords can be thought of as describing their "abstract overlap" in pitch space.

Towards a Theory of Chordal Shape Functions

Chordal shape functions give the specifics of how variant chords may be related to or generated from referential chords. Of the nine functions introduced here, seven involve literal pitch-subset and -superset relations. Example 5a presents referential chords *A*, *B*, *E*, and *K* which will be transformed into variant chords or other, non-variant-chords by chordal shape functions in Examples 5b, c and d. Extending the linguistic comparision, the chordal shape functions can be thought—at this level—as analogous to the linguistic transformations upon the morphemic, phonological and syllabic structure of words. Some of these linguistic trans-formations are declension, conjugation and adding prefixes, infixes or suffixes.

Example 5b shows the results of the chordal shape functions AddPitch, AddSpan, AddField, and AddChords as applied to the referential chord *K*. These chordal shape functions are abbreviated as AP, AS, AF, and ACS respectively. AP takes as its arguments a chord and the pitch set to be added to it. AS and AF also take a chord as its first argument and the span or shape field to be added to it as the second argument. The span or shape field to be added can be specified as a pitch set or by a number subscripted to a named chord, which represents a span or shape field from that chord. As a convention, spans or shape fields from chords of n spans or shape fields are numbered from lowest to highest, with the lowest called 0 and the highest n-1. For instance, the second chord of Example 5b could also be labelled $AF(K, B_0)$. ACS takes as its arguments all of the chords to be added. The chordal shape functions DeletePitch, DeleteSpan, and DeleteField take the same arguments as their add counterparts and give the expected results. These are illustrated in Example 5c and abbreviated as DP, DS, and DF respectively.[15]

The chordal shape function SubstitutePitch, abbreviated SP, takes three arguments: the first is a chord, the second is the ordered set of pitches to be replaced, and the third argument is the ordered set of pitches of the same cardinality to be substituted in their "places." The pitch substitutions are done by

---

15 All the contour-functions mentioned so far are mathematically classed as either "into" or "onto" functions. Under pitch transposition of 0 semitones, the mapping of referential chord *A* of measure 1—see Example 1 or 4—to measure 29's variant chord of *A*, A^v which consists of only the pitches A4, E♭5 and G5, is "onto" because each element or pitch of A^v has at least one element from *A* mapped onto it. Reversing the order of the mapping, A^v to *A* creates an "into" mapping because each element of A^v is mapped to at least one element of *A*. As this mapping pairs only one element of A^v with only one element of *A*, this mapping is a special case of an "into" function called a one-to-one function, abbreviated, 1–1. See David Lewin, *Generalized Musical Intervals and Transformations* (New Haven: Yale University Press, 1987), pp. 123–34 for his theoretical and analytical use of 1–1 functions as his "injection function."

Thus, all the contour-functions with "Delete" in their names are "onto" functions and all with "Add" in their names are 1–1 functions. For more on functions see Seymour Lipschutz, *Theory and Problems of Discrete Mathematics* (New York: McGraw-Hill, 1976), pp. 43–46.

Example 5a

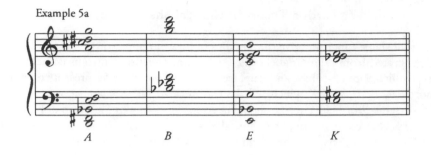

A   B   E   K

Example 5b

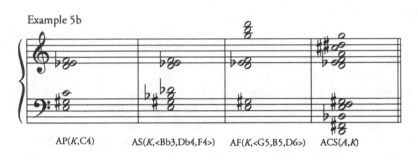

AP(*K*,C4)   AS(*K*,<Bb3,Db4,F4>)   AF(*K*,<G5,B5,D6>)   ACS(*A*,*K*)

Example 5c

DP(*K*,Eb4)   DS(*E*,<C4,Eb4,F4,B4>)   DF(*K*,<E3,G#3>)

Example 5d

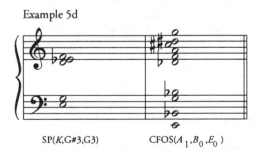

SP(*K*,G#3,G3)   CFOS(*A*$_1$,*B*$_0$,*E*$_0$)

Examples 5a–d: Results of Contour-Functions upon some Referential Chords

swapping pitches of the same ordinal numbers in arguments two and three.[16] The last chordal shape function to be introduced here is ConcatFieldsOrSpans, abbreviated CFOS. This function takes as arguments any number of shape fields or spans desired and concatenates them. The arguments can either be given in the form of pitch sets or in the form specified by the convention given above. See Example 5d for instances of their use.

These chordal shape functions can have interesting effects. For instance, ACS, AF, AS, and CFOS create chords with resemblances to more than one referential chord. Chords that refer to more than one referential chord are called "multi-variant chords." Further, the use of chordal shape functions in combinations can result in new chords with resemblances to multiple referential chords or to none at all.[17] When composite chordal shape functions change chordal shape and possibly sc membership and pc-sets as well, they are called metamorphic transformations.[18]

Some of the chordal shape functions can also be thought of in terms of the pianist's performing techniques in playing chords. Recall the oppositions of the pianist's relative individual hand-positions and the general registral placement of the hands mentioned above. The chordal shape functions of AP, and AS or AF can be thought of as addition-functions for the techniques of playing at the levels of finger- and hand-deployment respectively. Naturally, the chordal shape functions DP and DS or DF operate as subtraction-functions at the levels of finger- and hand-deployment. The function CFOS can be thought of as a technique of swapping the shape of hand-spans between parts of two different chords.

---

16 The chordal shape function of SubstitutePitch, SP, swaps one or more pitches of a chord for spatially adjacent pitches, no more than two semitones away. This function is a first cousin to Lewin's SLIDE operation which preserves the third of a tonal triad while changing its mode by altering (or substituting for) the chord's root and fifth. For instance, an F as the chordal third of a D minor triad after SLIDE-ing becomes the same chordal member of a D♭ major triad. See Lewin, *Generalized Musical Intervals and Transformations*, p. 178.

17 In answer to an interviewer's question on his compositional processes, Berio said the following (Dalmonte and Varga, p. 102): "It's not really a matter of manipulatory capacities (I find that a somewhat degrading expression), but of the ability to transform. We're always dealing with models, even those that we make for ourselves, and our work consists in widening the field of transformational paths until we manage to transform one thing into another, as in a fairy tale."

18 These chordal shape functions are closely related to analog electronic studio techniques of the time such as tape-splicing, band-reject-filtering, band-pass-filtering, amplitude-modulation, frequency-shifting and so forth. Needless to say, Berio was an early practitioner and master of them all. See David Osmond-Smith, *Berio* (New York: Oxford University Press, 1991), pp. 11–15, for a description of Berio's early interests in analog electronic compositional techniques. See Thomas Wells and Eric S. Vogel, *The Technique of Electronic Music* (Austin, Texas: Sterling Swift, 1974) for a contemporaneous view and definition of the electronic music terms used here.

Richard Hermann

Large-Scale Form Part 1: Referential Chord-Layers.

Figure 2 outlines the work's gestural form.[19] With a little practice, one way of hearing this work can be of considerable interest: that of following the succession of variant and multivariant chords, as they refer to specific referential chords, throughout the piece.[20]

Section Numbers	Subsection Numbers	Measure Numbers	Description
I			
	.1	mm. 1–17	Opening chordal section presents Referential Chords
	.2	mm. 18–49	Chords and Arpeggios
	.3	mm. 50–61	Cluster Chords and Arpeggios
	.4	mm. 62–70	Chords
II			
	.1	mm. 71–80	Chords with Repeated Notes and Arpeggios
	.2	mm. 81–82	Chords (flashback to the beginning?)
	.3	mm. 82–90	Chords with Repeated Notes and Arpeggios
	.4	mm. 91–94	Chords
	.5	mm. 94–102	Cluster Chords with Repeated Notes and Arpeggios
III			
	.1	mm. 103–166	All previous textures rapidly changing over sustained chordal "backdrops." Frequent and rapid tempo changes.
	.2	mm. 167–187	A gradual return of a chordal texture, "Retransitional"
IV			
	.1	mm. 188–215	A Varied "Reprise" of the Opening Chordal Material

Figure 2: A Gestural Description of Surface Formal Design
in Berio's *Sequenza IV for Piano*

---

19 For alternate analytical viewpoints on this piece, see John MacKay, "Aspects of Post-Serial Structuralism in Berio's *Sequenza IV* and *VI*," *Interface* 17 (1988): 223–39 and Gale Schaub's unpublished essay "Transformational Process in Luciano Berio's *Sequenza IV*," 32 pp. presented at at the 1989 annual meeting of the Music Theory Society of New York State at Baruch College. Other interesting information about this piece and other pieces for piano by Berio can be found in David Burge's *Twentieth-Century Piano Music* (New York: Schirmer Books, 1990), pp. 161–65.

20 Only a few chords receive metamorphic transformations, and these chords are difficult to assign as a variant to one or more than one referential chords. If the context does not assist, the analyst may assign it to one by applying the law of parsimony, the simplest of available

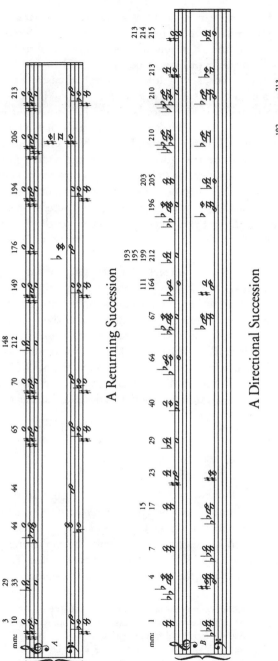

A Returning Succession

A Directional Succession

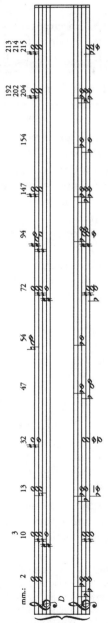

A Directional Succession

Example 6: Referential Chord Succession or "Sequences"

Here, one aspect of the work's form can be heard as an interlacing of multiple referential chord-layers. Example 6 gives these piece-wide layers for referential chords A, B, and D, their variants, and those multivariant chords that refer to them. Eight of the fourteen referential chord-layers begin and end on the same chord from the catalog of referential chords with at most, in several cases, a single pitch deleted. They are the referential chords A, C, E, H, I, J, L and N. The others, B, D, F, G, K and M, become changed by the chordal shape functions and end without returning to their original generator chords from the catalog of referential chords. Note that the B and D layers shown in Example 6 are both directional in that they do not return "home," and are transformed to the same ending point; they are the only pair to do so. Also, as mentioned before, they share membership in the same set class: 6-Z49 [0,1,3,4,7,9]. They share four of five adjacent intervals, too, and they are the only pair to share n-1 adjacent intervals.[21] These properties shared by referential chords B and D and their merging as a frequently repeated hybrid chord (a multivariant chord) in the last measures of the piece make for a striking and fitting "ending" signal.

The relation of B and D to C is also of interest. The first page of the score, previously given as Example 1, shows that B and D are constantly repeated and reordered and, further, it shows C as presented just once in the opening after which it is temporarily abandoned. While referential chords B and D and their variants occur throughout the piece, C and its variants resurface only twice at measures 50 and 66 to "round off" the first section. (Recall Figure 2.) They reappear much later in the piece from measures 132 on, where, in conjunction with B and D, they appear to act as a kind of catalyst for closure. Referential chord A, on the other hand, seems to function as a "start" signal for many of the sections and subsections of the piece.

Contiguous or Surface Pitch Relations

Example 7 contains four quite brief passages from *Sequenza IV* that form the subject matter for a more detailed analysis of contiguous pitch structure. In the analysis, the results of composite chordal shape functions are presented one function at a time, and those intermediate results will be labelled by the referential chord's letter and a suitable numerical superscript. As a chord is returned from a chordal shape function and as it becomes the input for the next chordal shape

---

explanations, or may embrace the ambiguity as intentional and integral to the piece. (At a later date I will offer some statistical and other theoretical tools to assist with employing the first option.) In this context, recall Berio's comment cited in footnote 17 above.

21 However, B is bifielded and D is monofielded, and DOC(B) = 26/5 = 5.2 and DOC(D) = 17/5 = 3.4, DSO(B, D) = 18/26 = 0.692; they have only 1 of 6 possible pitches in common, G5, for 0.167%. By the measures introduced in this essay, these chords are dissimilar.

function, its superscript is incremented. The final result is given the v superscript and an appropriate ordinal number, if needed.

Example 7a contains measure 136 and the beginning of the next measure. The first chord, specified by the temporary variable X, resembles or perhaps evokes referential chords A and K. Referential chord A's relation to X is described by applying the following chordal shape functions: $DP(A, \{D2, F\sharp2, F3, A4\}) = A^1$, $SP(A1, \{F3\}, F\sharp 3) = A^2$, and $AP(A^2, \{C5\}) = A^v$. Referential K's relation to X is described by the following chordal shape function: $DP(K, \{E\flat4\}) = K^v$. Finally, we have $X = ACS(A^v, K^v)$. In this instance, listing X's multiple references as a set of chords well reflects the fact that A^v spatially envelops K^v, $DSO(A^v, K^v) = 1.0$, hence $\{A^v, K^v\}$ is an appropriate label for this chord, a multivariant chord. The second chord is an arpeggiated variant of N: $AP(N, \{D4\}) = N^v$.

Measure 117 is presented by Example 7b. This chord also has multiple references; they are to referential chords H and L. This chord is the result of the concatenation of H's lower field, H_0, and L's highest field, L_2. However H_0 has been subjected to a *pitch* transposition that lowers the field two semitones. This chord is described as follows: $CFOS(T_{-2}(H_0), L_2)$. As neither field spatially subsumes the other, the chord's label is given as an ordered set starting with the lowest sounding field and proceeding in order towards the highest sounding field. In this case the chord is labelled $< T_{-2}(H_0), L_2 >$.

Example 7c displays a slightly more complex passage found in measure 64 and the beginning of measure 65. Here six chords are numerically labelled with the last being a literal appearance of referential chord A. The others are variant or multivariant chords. The first chord, X1, is multivariant, here referring to H and L. The chordal shape functions upon L are as follows: $AP(L_2, \{G\sharp4\}) = L_2^1$; $SP(L_2^1, \{F\sharp4\}, \{F4\}). = L_2^v$. The chordal shape function upon H is as follows: $DP(H_1, \{B5, F5\}) = H_1^v$. Finally, $X1 = CFOS(L_2^v, H_1^v)$; its label follows the convention set above for Example 7b: $X1 = < L_2^v, H_1^v >$. The second chord, X2, has resemblances to N and K. Two chordal shape functions upon N contribute: $AP(N_1, \{E\flat6, A5, F\sharp5\}) = N_1^1$; $SP(N_1^1, < B5, E\flat5 >, < B\flat5, D\flat5 >) = N_1^v$. Likewise, two chordal shape functions upon K contribute: $AP(K, \{F\sharp3\}) = K^1$; $DP(K^1, \{E\flat4\}) = K^v$. Thus, $X2 = CFOS(K^v, N_1^v)$, and its label also follows the convention set above for Example 6b: $X2 = < K^v, N_1^v >$.[22] The third chord, X3, is generated as follows: $SP(F_1, < E5, C5, A4, F\sharp 4 >, < E\flat5, C\flat5, B\flat4, F4 >) = F_1^v$; $SP(N_0, < F4 >, < E4 >) = N_0^1$; $AP(N_0^1, \{C\sharp4\}) = N_0^v$; $X3 = CFOS(F_1^v, N_0^v) = < N_0^v, F_1^v >$. Chord four is generated as follows: $SP(M_1, < F\flat6, E\flat6, A5 >, < G\flat6, D\flat6, A\flat5 >) = M_1^1$; $AP(M_1^1, \{D5\}) = M_1^2$; $X4 = DP(M_1^2, \{B5\}) = M^v$. Chord five is as follows: $AP(F, \{B\flat4\}) = F^1$; $X5 = SP(F^1, < F\sharp4 >, < F4 >) = F^v$.

Measures 70–72, given at the top of Example 7d, show other aspects of

---

22 The second chord of the facsimile has a different pitch content than in corrected 1987. The facsimile lacks the pitch G5 and has F5 and G4 for F♯5 and F4 respectively.

(a) Measures 136–37

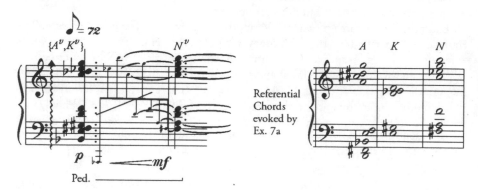

(b) Measure 117

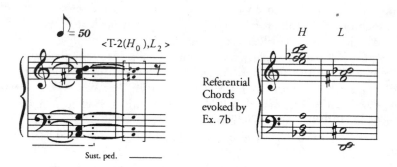

Examples 7a–d: Analysis of Surface Pitch-Structure in Brief Passages
from Berio's *Sequenza IV*

(c) Measures 64–65

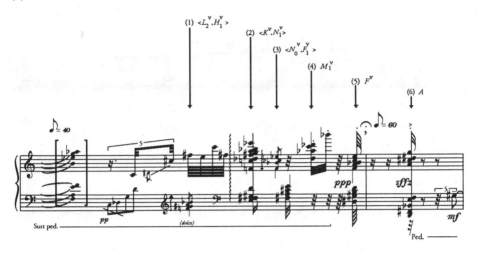

Examples 7a–d (cont.): Analysis of Surface Pitch-Structure in Brief Passages
from Berio's *Sequenza IV*

(d) Measures 70–72

Examples 7a–d (cont.): Analysis of Surface Pitch-Structure in Brief Passages from Berio's *Sequenza IV*

analytical technique using chordal shape functions. The excerpt consists of three chords with a *fioritura*-like passage of pitches played by the right hand between the last two chords.[23] The bottom system gives the referential chords evoked by this passage. As before, the three chords may be generated as follows: $SP(F, < D\sharp3, D4 >, < D3, D\sharp4 >) = F^1$, $X1 = DP(F^1, \{G\sharp3, B3, C5\}) = F^v$; $SP(A, < B\flat2 >, < B2 >) = A^1$, $X2 = DP(A^1, \{D2\}) = A^v$; $SP(A_1, < A4, D\sharp5 >, < G\sharp4, E5 >) = A_1{}^v$, $SP(B_0, < D\flat4, F4 >, <D4, F\sharp4>) = B_0{}^v$, $X3 = CFOS(B_0{}^v, A_1{}^v) = <B_0{}^v, A_1{}^v>$.

The middle two systems show how the *fioritura* may be generated as arpeggiations of chords 2 and 3 along with the use of the SubstitutePitch, SP, chordal shape function. Half-notes indicate chordal pitches and the quarter-notes indicate substituted pitches; the arrows make the connections between substitute pitches and chordal pitches clear. The second chord's arpeggio occurs after that chord is struck—a "post-chord" arpeggio—and the third chord's arpeggio occurs before the chord is struck—a "pre-chord" arpeggio, perhaps here retrospectively understood. This later case is a slightly more complicated situation but similar to that of the second chord, N^v, from the previously discussed Example 7a.[24]

The vertical dotted lines point out the same pitches between the two middle systems; these show the area of connection between the two arpeggiations. Note how the crescendo to *ff* and the appearance of rests in the left hand point out the only two pitches in common between the chords, G5 and C$\sharp$5. Further, the diminuendo starts upon the arrival of a chordal pitch, A$\flat$4, from chord 3.[25] The first and fourth pitches connected by the vertical dotted lines also serve a transitional purpose between the chords. The first note is in anticipation of a pitch from the next chord to come, and the fourth note has its function reinterpretated; it starts as a chordal pitch, and then it becomes a substitute pitch for A$\flat$4, the one just mentioned above.

When referential chords can clearly be established within a piece, theories of chordal shape and chordal shape functions can give some account not only for polyphony but even for some rudimentary "voice-leading" techniques as the preceding discussion demonstrates.[26] The theories of chordal shape and chordal

---

23 I wonder whether Berio had passages like this in mind when he said to David Burge after hearing him play this work before its New York City premiere: "Just play it like Chopin." The quote is from David Burge's letter of November 4, 1989 to this author.

24 As these chords and the contour-functions upon them are manipulations of pitch-space and not pc-space, there is no question of quasi-Schenkerian "unfoldings." Unfoldings may rely upon pc- and name-class equivalence in reaching a *Stufe's* chordal member not previously present as a pitch in the initial appearance of the *Stufe*. See Joseph N. Straus, "The Problem of Prolongation in Post-Tonal Music," *Journal of Music Theory* 31 (1987): 1–20 for more detailed discussion of these issues.

25 Corrected '87 has the diminuendo starting on the preceding F4; however, the facsimile has it starting on A$\flat$4 as notated in my Example 7d.

26 For an alternate view on "atonal voice-leading," see Fred Lerdahl, "Atonal Prolongational Structure," in *Music and the Cognitive Sciences* 4, ed. Stephen McAdams and Irène Deliège (Paris: Centre National d'Art et de Culture 'Georges Pompidou,' 1989): 65–88.

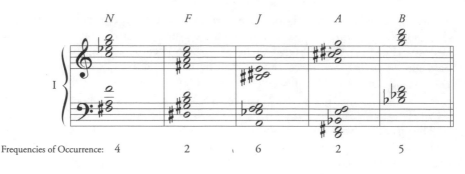

Frequencies of Occurrence: 4   2   6   2   5

Frequencies of Occurrence: 2   2   2   2

Example 8: Chaconne-Like Model Sequences of Sostenuto Pedal Emphasized Chords in Berio's *Sequenza IV for Piano*

shape function may also be of particular importance when traditional atonal theoretical tools and the newer contour theory tools seem to provide unfocused results. They, of course, also provide alternate theoretical and analytical instruments for theorists and analysts and may be suggestive for composers.

Large-Scale Form Part 2: Two Chaconne-Like Sequences

Taking up hints gathered from the study of the facsimile and Berio's comments favoring a layered method of composition, a deeper layer of structure, created by the use of the sostenuto pedal, is shown in Example 8. Here, two chaconne-like, model successions of referential chords are displayed. They are labeled with Roman numerals I and II. Unlike a conventional chaconne, the harmonic succession is not always present in the piece nor, when one of the chaconnes occurs, are all the chords of the harmonic succession necessarily present or present as a pure referential chord. A variant chord or multivariant chord may take its referent's place in the sequence, and a "DeleteChord" function, DC, may omit one or more of the chordal locations from that sequence. Further, the chords in these harmonic designs are only ordered with regard to their place within the sequence, there is no durational patterning or meter implied.[27]

Chaconne I, occurs six times in the piece, while Chaconne II, appears only twice. The frequency that each referential chord, its variant, or multivariant appears in one of the chaconnes's successions is shown by the numbers given below each of the two chaconne models of Example 8. Note that the first element of Chaconne I and the last element of Chaconne II are the same referential chord or are variants of it. This ability to overlap the two is exploited in both of the second chaconne's appearances. The importance of the sostenuto pedal in creating a subsurface layer — featuring the chaconnes—upon which other material is projected is paramount. The greater use, durationally, of the sostenuto pedal over the other pedals underlines its importance.[28]

Figure 3a provides a chordal shape function analysis of all chords found in each appearance of Chaconne I, and Figure 3b does the same for Chaconne II. In those figures, the top rows are labeled I.0 and II.0, and they represent the two chaconne models. The chaconnes, however, never appear in their model forms. The referential chords of each model form the top elements of the columns under which each of the model-variant's chords are aligned, and their chordal shape functional derivation from their respective referential chords are shown. Each chord in the succession of a model variant is separated by a semicolon. When several chordal shape functions are employed, commas separate each chordal shape function statement from the next. Frequently space does not permit all members of the row to appear on the same line, and statements are aligned under each other in their respective columns. Note that in the last entry for Chaconne I.3, the dashes between pitches mean that all pitches between those pitches are also included. In *Sequenza IV*, the same chordal shape functions that generate the work's detail from the referential chord catalog are also employed in generating the deeper-layer, sostenuto-pedaled chaconne sequences from the chaconne models.[29]

---

27 The use of a transformed chaconne-like structure should come as no surprise in Berio's work. He has said the following on the uses of the past (Dalmonte and Varga, p. 66): "No, there can be no *tabula rasa*, especially in music. But this tendency to work with history, drawing out and consciously transforming historical 'minerals', and absorbing them into musical materials and processes that don't bear the mark of history, reflects a need—that has been with me for a long time—to organically continue a variety of musical experiences, and thus to incorporate within the musical development different degrees of familiarity, and to expand its expressive design and the levels on which it can be perceived."

28 The use of the other pedals is the pianistic equivalent of panning between speakers in an analog electronic-music studio. This, together with the over-dubbing effect of the layered surface of the piece, radical changes of dynamics, chord density and location, seems to generate an effect of shifting distances and depths of sound.

29 Berio has said the following (Dalmonte and Varga, p. 103): "But if the deeper structure is to

(a) Chaconne I

I.0   < N, F, J, A, B >

         (Chaconne I model)

I.1 $DC(N)$; $DC(F)$; J; $DC(A)$; $SP(B,\{F4\},\{E4\}) = B^v$.

I.2 N; $DC(F)$; $DP(J,\{A2,F3,C\sharp4,E4\}) = J^1$,
                    $SP(, <E\flat3,G3>,<E3,G\sharp3>) = J^v$;

            $DP(J,\{A2,B\sharp3,B4\}) = J^{v2}$;
                 $DC(A)$; $SP(B_0,<B\flat3,D\flat4,F4>,<B3,C4,F\sharp4>)$
                           $= B_0^{v2}$, $SP(N_1, <B5,G5,E\flat5>,$
                           $<B\flat5,A\flat5,D5>) = N_1^1$, $DP(N_1^1,\{C5\})$
                           $= N_1^v$, $CFOS(B_0^v,N_1^1) = < B_0^{v2},N_1^1 >$.

I.3 $AP(N,\{D4\}) = N^v$;
       $SP(F, <D\sharp3,D4>, <D3,D\sharp4>) = F_0^1$,
       $DP(F_0^1,\{B3\}) = F_0^v$;

             J; $DP(A,\{F3\}) = A^v$;

                     $AP(B,\{G\flat3-A3,B3,C4,D4-E4,E5-F\sharp5,$
                     $A\flat5-B\flat5,C6,C\sharp6,E\flat6\}) = B^{v3}$;

I.4 N; $DC(F)$; $DP(J,\{B\sharp3,B4\}) = J^v$;
                 $DC(A)$;   See entry at I.2.

I.5   See I.3;   See I.3; J;   See I.3; $SP(B_0,<B\flat3,D\flat4>,<B3,D4>) = B_0^1$,
                               $AP(B_0^1,\{A4\}) = B_0^{v4}$,

I.6 $DC(N)$; $DC(F)$; J; $DC(A)$; $SP(B,\{B\flat3\},\{A3\}) = B^{v5}$.

Figures 3a–b: A Contour-Function Analysis of All Chaconne Appearances

The layout of all chords that employ the sostenuto pedal, including the chaconnes, is given in Example 9. In order to save space in that example, chords are simply labelled by the referential chords to which they refer. The instances of each chaconne sequence are indicated by brackets underneath the staves. The members derived from Chaconne I are given in solid brackets and those derived from Chaconne II are shown in broken-lined brackets. The Roman numerals identify which of the two chaconne models is present, and the arabic numeral gives

influence what we hear *structurally*, then there must be many links, a hierarchy of many different signals that can at least potentially be deciphered and recognized—even though sometimes these signals are destined to disappear, to be swept away and absorbed by the events that they have themselves initiated . . . ."

(b) Chaconne II

II.0 $< L,$ $K,$ $A,$ $N >$

(Chaconne II model)

II.1 $CFOS(T_{-2}(H_0),L_2) = <T_{-2}(H_0),L_2>$;

$AP(K,\{B\flat4\}) = K^v$; $DP(A,\{D2,F\sharp2,B\flat2,A4,D\sharp5\}) = A^1$,
$AP(A^1,\{E\flat4\}) = A^v$;

$AP(N,\{D4\}) = N^v$.
(Same as I.3)

II.2 $DP(J_1,\{C\sharp4,E4\}) = J_1{}^v$, $CFOS(L_0, L_1, J_1{}^v) = <L_0, L_1, J_1{}^v>$;

L_2;

$AP(K,\{C\sharp4,B\flat4\}) = K^v$;

$DP(A,\{D2,F\sharp2,B\flat2,A4,D\sharp5\}) = A^1$,
$AP(A^1,\{E\flat4\}) = A^v$;

$AP(N,\{D4\}) = N^v$.
(Same as I.3 & II.1)

Figures 3a-b (cont.): A Contour-Function Analysis of All Chaconne Appearances

the respective ordinal number of its appearance. Those chords indicated with black diamond-shaped note-heads are chords "played" by silently depressing those keys.

The bottom two systems show a similar pattern of chaconne-successions with an overlap. These describe a pitch-structural design of A B B'. In this example, then, each system represents one of those pitch-structural design sections. Note that the first occurrence of a succession generated from the first chaconne model has an interpolated E variant indicated by an asterisk in Example 9. Of interest is the first appearance of the referential chords M at the end of the "A" section, and N which forms the start of the "B" section. These two referential chords were missing from the original presentation of the other twelve referential chords at the opening of the piece. Their first appearances seem reserved especially as signals for these locations of structural articulation.

Two other ways of organizing the chaconnes within the sostenuto-pedaled layer are shown in Figure 4. The top row recalls previous comments made about Example 9. The middle row has an upper and lower arrow tipped brackets which point out Chaconne I pairs that greatly resemble one another. Four of their five entries in their harmonic sequences are identical, and the remaining sole entries resemble one another closely. This can be confirmed by consulting either Example 9 or Figure 3a. The pair I.1 and I.6 provide a frame for the whole; continuing the

Example 9: Structural Layer Created by the Sostenuto Pedal

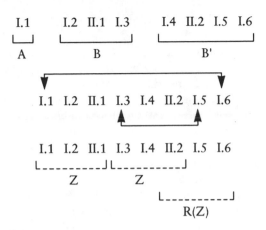

Figure 4: Three Structural Designs for the Chaconnes from the Layer
of the Sostenuto Pedal

metaphor, the other pair, I.3 and I.5, provide weight bearing walls for the interior. The bottom row displays another design that emerges from the previous observations. The "Z module" is here a succession of two successive and different iterations derived from the Chaconne I model followed by an appearance of an iteration derived from Chaconne II. A retrograde equivalent pair of Z modules, using the "frame" pair of Chaconne I appearances, begins and ends the work. Another Z module is also shown in the figure, and all three appearances account for all instances of the chaconnes.

Comparing the pattern of deeper layer sostenuto-pedaled chords as given in the top row design of Figure 4 with the surface articulations of form given previously in Figure 2, we find some striking correspondences and differences. The Chaconne I's first appearance marks the end of the opening gestural form's first subsection—the presentation of the referential chords. The start of the sostenuto-pedaled B section nearly coincides with the gestural division at measure 104. The "retransitional" section of the gestural form, starting at measure 167, is also marked by the last appearances of a Chaconne II derived iteration. Important differences include the lack of gestural marking of the sostenuto pedal's B' section and the lack of confirmation with the sostenuto-pedaled layer for the gestural "reprise" at measure 188. These correspondences and differences make for some large-scale formal design and pitch-structural "cross rhythms" that contribute to the interest of the piece. Note that C appears only once in the sostenuto-pedaled layer of structure at the very end. Again, it takes on the function of an ending signal as mentioned in the preceding discussion of referential chord successions.

Linguistic Analogies/Reprise

Earlier discussions mentioned some analogies with linguistics, one of Berio's long standing preoccupations, and we now can fruitfully expand the analogies. The piano's total pitch-space may be thought of as the alphabet, the catalog of referential chords as a lexicon, the chordal shape functions as means of producing new lexical units from the lexicon, and the theory of chordal shape as a means of determining what are distinct lexical elements and what are the principles of combining the elements to form "words."[30]

At the next levels of syntactical structure, the analogies become less precise but they are still of some interest and use. How are words combined into phrases, clauses, and sentences? Here in *Sequenza IV*, the chaconne sequences from the sostenuto-pedaled layer seem likely candidates for sentences. The two chaconne models may be thought of as the kernel sentences or deep structures of these actual sentences. The chordal shape function DeleteChord may be thought of as a transformational rule which changes the deep structure of a chaconne model into a surface structural chaconne sequence, much like the imperative-mode transformation that changes the deep structural sentence of "You will open the window." into the surface sentence of "Open the window."[31] As noted before, the other chordal shape functions are used to explain surface details of the chords

---

30 A lexicon differs from a dictionary or a word list in that all semantic elements such as word "roots" and other non-word morphemes are also included as independent items in a lexicon. See Adrian Akmajian, Richard A. Demers and Robert M. Harnish, *Linguistics: An Introduction to Language and Communication*, 2nd ed. (Cambridge, Mass.: MIT Press, 1984), pp. 260–65.

31 Many readers will note technical terms from Noam Chomsky's transformational grammar are employed throughout this paragraph. For a good and gentle tutorial on transformational grammar that includes discussion of some of the main differences between Chomsky's first two books, see John Lyons, *Noam Chomsky*, revised ed. (New York: Penguin Books, 1977).

   On another and related note, Chomsky's first book, *Syntactic Structures* (The Hague: Mouton & Co., 1957), introduced his initial version of transformational grammar, and it made him a figure of international prominence in linguistics. From 1955 on, he has resided in Cambridge, Massachusetts and taught at the Massachusetts Institute of Technology. His next book, *Aspects of the Theory of Syntax* (Cambridge, Mass.: MIT Press, 1965) introduced a completely reworked transformational grammar—now called the "standard theory." In his own words from page vii of the preface of the second book dated and placed at Cambridge, Massachusetts, October 1964, "The writing of this book was completed while I was at Harvard University, Center for Cognitive Studies..." The corrected edition of 1987 for *Sequenza IV* gives the date of 1965 and the location of Arlington, Massachusetts (a suburb of Boston across the Charles river from Cambridge) at the end of the score. Further, David Osmond-Smith writes: "In the autumn of 1964, Oyama [Susan, soon to be Berio's second wife] began her doctoral research at Harvard University, where Berio also took on a semester's teaching." See Osmond-Smith, *Berio*, pp. 28–29. It is difficult not to draw conclusions about possible influences of Chomsky upon Berio's compositional thought—for at least this work— given the coincidences of interest, time, and location between these two men.

projected upon the sostenuto-pedaled layer and also to describe the derivation of the chaconne sequences of the sostenuto layer from the chaconne models. While other transformational rules for generating the surface chaconne sequences from the chaconne models could be devised, the analogical point has been made.

The compositional process underlying this work could be viewed as ways of generating surface and subsurface layers of structure through the use of a few well chosen procedures (chordal shape functions) upon a few distinct and well chosen referential chords (theory of chordal shape). These are clearly related to the technique of playing chords upon the piano as demonstrated above. The work's economy of means and materials place quite manageable demands upon the auditor's memory and associative capacities; these are the keys that permit auditors to follow the various aspects of the work's pitch structure. This economy allows for enormous variety of new "words" and "sentences," perhaps seemingly infinite, and it enables the auditor from being completely overwhelmed by the various layers of sound. Should attentive and reasonably experienced listeners, competent listeners, become temporarily lost, they can always find a way back "into" the piece because of these economies. Further, these economies enables auditors to "bootstrap" themselves into hearing as much of the work's pitch structure as they may wish through repeated hearings. This economical and "bootstrapable" approach seems to separate Berio's work from that of his Darmstadt colleagues of Boulez and Stockhausen at various points in time in their careers. Oddly enough in that regard, it also connects him with some American composers of a formalist bent who also concern themselves with creating hearable—that is, for competent listeners—musical structures in their works. Berio, however, disagrees with many American compositional and theoretical preoccupations because of their reputed lack of historical connection and their deemphasis of process. [32]

Returning to linguistics, the seemingly infinite generative capacity and yet manageable demands upon memory and associative capacities described by this analysis of, and speculative comments upon, Berio's compositional process for *Sequenza IV* mirrors some of transformational grammarians' analyses of natural languages. [33]

---

32 Berio's criticism of formalist composers and theoretical thought has been plentiful and long standing. See George W. Flynn, "Listening to Berio's Music," *Musical Quarterly* 61 (1975): 393–94 for a concise summary of Berio's criticisms.

33 Ray Jackendoff in his *Semantics and Cognition* (Cambridge, Mass.: MIT Press, 1983) pp. 5–6 and 7 says the following on these economies in natural languages: "Linguistics is the study of grammatical structure—what Chomsky (1965) calls *linguistic competence*. Psycholinguistics is the study of the strategies employed in processing grammatical structure in real time—*linguistic performance*. Obviously these two inquiries have a natural influence. On the one hand, a theory of language processing presupposes a theory of linguistic structure; on the other hand, one crucial test of a theory of linguistic structure is whether it can be integrated into a theory of processing. Moreover, many phenomena are amenable to either structural or processing

While other analogies with natural languages could be made, a brief look at a few of the important ways in which the analogies break down is worth pursuing. Before we begin, we should remember that other fields of endeavour, such as linguistics, need only to serve as stimuli for a composer's compositional process. There is no need—nor should there be an expectation—for any given composer to "translate" one field, lingusitics in this case, into another. Influences from past musical work and from other fields also are likely to contribute significantly to the poietics of musical composition.

On the syntactical level, an important difference is in the simultaneous layers of pitch structure, such as the chaconnes and referential chord sequences. The main model for such simultaneity found in natural language use is from the theatre: there multiple characters can concurrently speak or sing. No individual character's line of discourse directly or indirectly conveys the entire situation to the audience. It is the clatter of the competing lines that represents the emotional states of characters who find themselves in some particular situation together. The collective emotional relationships are, perhaps, what is most importantly portrayed by this device, not the sum of the possible meanings of each character's individual lines. To my knowledge, linguistics has not attempted analyses of these kinds of language uses.

Of course, this theatrical meaning leads us to another main branch of linguistics, semantics. Meanings set forth here are naturally my own, though my arguments receive some support from Berio's thought.[34] These meanings fall under the headings of the extra-musical and the purely musical; however, meanings assigned to one of the categories are not always completely limited to that one category.

Berio's colleague, Umberto Eco, has made the case that coherent writing in natural languages contains very significant correlations of meanings between individual readers.[35] However, extra-musical meanings for *Sequenza IV* do not appear to be easily expressed by natural language. Associations made within this

---

description, and it is often an interesting question how to divide up the power of the theory between the two elements.

"In particular, one must always remember that a theory of mental information structure must eventually be instantiated in a brain. This imposes two important boundary conditions on the theory: (1) the resources for storing information are finite; (2) the information must somehow get into the mind, whether through perception, learning, or genetic structure."

For those familiar with Chomsky's work, the use of functions to describe natural language-like phenomena in music should come as little surprise. John Lyons has said of Chomsky: "The revolutionary step that Chomsky has taken, as far as linguistics is concerned, has been to draw upon this branch of mathematics (finite automata theory and recursive function theory) and to apply it to natural languages, like English . . ." (Lyons, *Noam Chomsky*, p. 59).

34 Please recall notes 3, 7, 12, 17, 27, and 29 for Berio's thoughts on these matters cited in this essay.

35 See the witty introduction to Umberto Eco, *The Limits of Interpretation* (Bloomington: Indiana University Press, 1990), pp. 1–7.

realm are most likely to be quite idiosyncratic and with little correlation between individual listeners. Certainly, the linguistic analogies and mathematical modelling are extra-musical meanings too; however, if these structures are hearable, then they also have a purely musical meaning. The modelings and analogies are then merely tools used to help the inexperienced listener focus upon some aspects of the purely musical meanings (musico-structural and self-referential meanings) present in a sensitive and intelligent performance of the score.

More purely musical meanings also fall into two categories whose various constituent meanings, again, are not necessarily mutually exclusively assigned to one or the other category. They are on one hand the "diachronic" meanings or more historically based relations between the work and preexisting works and techniques and, on the other hand, the "synchronic" meanings or self-referential relationships found within the work itself.[36]

Among the diachronic relationships in *Sequenza IV* are the following: the reexamination of the technique of chordal playing on the piano, the reinterpretation of the chaconne technique for generating large scale pitch-structural units, the multiple references of the multivariant chords which recall the *Mehrdeutbarkeit* of traditional tonality's fully diminished seventh chords, the rethinking of variation technique as described by the chordal shape functions, and the simultaneous layers of pitch structure recalling—among other works—moments from Ives's *Fourth Symphony*.

The synchronic relationships found within *Sequenza IV* and touched upon in this essay are the following: its gestural form with the special formal functions for referential chords A, B, C, D, M and N; the narrative created by following chordal shape functional variation upon the referential chords; the means—displayed in Figure 4—of organizing the derived chaconne sequences into larger pitch-structural units; the rhythmic interactions of gestural form with larger pitch-structural units as they go in and out of phase with one another; the transition-like spaces inhabited by multivariant or metamorphic chords between the "nodes" of the network that contains the referential chords; and the dramatic narrative of shifting the listeners attention between the various simultaneous layers of pitch structure through the imaginative use of the piano's pedals, and dynamic, durational and articulative contrasts. My favorite metaphors for this piece are that of multiple partially overheard and followed conversations at a dinner party or that of the mind's self-reflection upon its own "stream of consciousness."

Although I've made fairly extensive analogies between linguistics and Berio's *Sequenza IV*, it should be clear that this work can not be "reduced" to those analogies. They merely point to a "way in" for the inexperienced listener. Even the combination of the linguistic analogies with mathematical modelling techniques are

---

36 See Ducrot and Todorov, *Encyclopedic Dictionary of the Sciences of Language*, pp. 137–44 for discussion of the linguistic concepts of diachrony and synchrony.

not sufficient for a critical assessment of Berio's *Sequenza IV*. That combination omits the work's diachronic and narrative references and its transformations of them.

This essay might, therefore, give pause to those in the fields of philosophy, linguistics and artificial intelligence who solely equate mind with thought, thought with natural language, and the anatomical structures of the brain that instantiate natural language with potentially adequate working models of the mind.[37] In a letter to Marc-André Souchay of October 15, 1842, Mendelssohn wrote "People often complain that music is ambiguous, that their ideas on the subject always seem so vague, whereas everyone understands words. With me it is exactly the reverse— not merely with regard to entire sentences, but also as to individual words. These, too, seem to me so ambiguous, so vague, so unintelligible when compared with genuine music, which fills the soul with a thousand things better than words."[38] That thought might also apply to the hope of finding fully adequate interpretations of any sort for sophisticated music; nonetheless, the continuing process of interpreting sharpens our perception and understanding.

---

37 See Pamela McCorduck, *Aaron's Code: Meta-Art, Artificial Intelligence, and the Work of Harold Cohen* (New York: Freeman, 1991) for a flawed but interesting account of these same issues—among others—with regard to visual art. In *The Open Work*, trans. Anna Cancogni, intro. David Robey (Cambridge, Mass.: Harvard University Press, 1989), first published in Italy as *Opera Aperta: Forma e indeterminazione nelle poetiche contemporanee* (Milan: Bompiani, 1962), Umberto Eco realizes that critical theory and aesthetics must engage non-linguistically based art works too. In fact he starts out that work with discussion of contemporary musical compositions including Berio's *Sequenza per flauto solo* of 1958. A rewritten version of that opening appears later in his *The Role of the Reader: Explorations in the Semiotics of Texts* (Bloomington: Indiana University Press, 1979).

38 See *Letters of Felix Mendelssohn Bartholdy from 1833 to 1847*, trans. Lady Wallace, 1864 cited in Ruth Halle Rowen, *Music Through Source & Documents*, (Englewood Cliffs, New Jersey: Prentice-Hall, Inc., 1979), p. 261.

Stylistic Competencies, Musical Humor, and *"This is Spinal Tap"*

John Covach

I

As its title suggests, this study focuses upon matters of humor and musical style, specifically the ways in which musical numbers in the 1984 Rob Reiner film *This is Spinal Tap* elicit an amused response.[1] On first pass, one might wonder how such seemingly diverse concerns as nineteenth-century German philosophy, recent theories of musical style, and late 1960's rock and roll could possibly intersect: one could hardly imagine a more incongruous trio of figures than Arthur Schopenhauer, Leonard Meyer, and the fictional Nigel Tufnel, lead guitarist of the equally fictitious rock group "Spinal Tap." I hope to demonstrate not only that there are music-analytical concerns that make for these rather strange bedfellows, but also that the notion of incongruity itself plays a pivotal role in this eclectic combination.

The present study will explore the various ways in which three Spinal Tap numbers elicit an amused response from listeners. I am primarily concerned with the ways in which humor is created through specifically musical means. In the context of the film, there are many factors at work in the Spinal Tap songs that contribute to their humorous impact; each song, for instance, is accompanied by visual images (shots of the performers, audience, off-stage shots, etc.). Each song is also situated in the context of the unfolding of the story itself, and can elicit an amused response according to these relationships. In addition, each song has lyrics that elicit an amused response. There are, for example, a number of factors creating humor in the Spinal Tap song "Big Bottom," and perhaps the most obvious of

---

1 "This is Spinal Tap," Rob Reiner, dir., written by Christopher Guest, Michael McKean, Harry Shearer and Rob Reiner, Embassy Pictures, 1983, video cassette 1987 (ISBN 1–55847–103–0). All musical examples are drawn form the original soundtrack album, *Spinal Tap* (Polygram Records, 817–846–1–Y1, 1984).

For those unfamiliar with the film, Spinal Tap is a fictitious British heavy-metal rock band. The film poses as a documentary ("rock-umentary") of what appears to be Spinal Tap's last American tour. The tour falls apart as the group makes its way from the East Coast to the West Coast; by the time they reach Los Angeles the band has almost broken up completely. The film features concert footage, glimpses backstage, interviews, and flashbacks.

these components is the lyrics; but another component creating humor in the tune is that all three guitarists play bass guitars—the drummer plays only low tom-toms and the keyboard player only low notes on the synthesizer—and two of the guitarists "spank" the third with the necks of their guitars at the end of the tune. The rhyme scheme that produces the many references to the *derrière* (which will not be quoted here) is a literary-verbal technique; the low-end instrumentation—one sees three bass guitars in the film—and the spanking of guitarist Tufnel are visual cues. Ultimately one must consider each of these aspects, and their inter-action, in accounting for the humorous effect of a song such as "Big Bottom"; humor arises in the Spinal Tap songs in multiple contexts and these contexts tend to reinforce one another. This study will, nonetheless, focus attention on those factors that create humor in the songs by purely musical means; I am concerned with examining how the musical materials themselves, thought of in their own contexts, elicit an amused response.

My discussion of the Spinal Tap songs below will rely on theories of humor that have been developed in the field of the philosophy. In order to lay the groundwork for the musical analysis and discussion that will follow, then, a brief overview of philosophical writings on laughter and humor will be helpful. In his book, *Taking Laughter Seriously*, John Morreall discusses the three basic theories of laughter.[2] The first is the "superiority theory," which originates with Plato but is articulated most forcefully by Thomas Hobbes. Hobbes asserts that laughter results from a feeling of superiority over others—a laughing *at* others.[3] A second theory is set down by Herbert Spencer and later taken up by Freud; this is the "relief theory." Spencer asserts that our laugh is a release of nervous energy. Freud refines this theory by further classifying the types of energy that laughing releases.[4] The third theory, found in the writing of Immanuel Kant and Arthur Schopenhauer, is referred to as the "incongruity theory." Our laughter is the result of some perceived incongruity between concept and object.[5] Morreall points out that laughter and humor are not synonomous and that laughter exists without humor and humor without laughter. For Morreall, each of these three theories says something about our laugh-response, but each is incomplete.[6] For the purposes of the present investigation, the third theory of

---

2   John Morreall, *Taking Laughter Seriously* (Albany, NY: State University of New York Press, 1983). A shorter overview may be found in John Morreall "A New Theory of Laughter," reprinted in Morreall, ed., *The Philosophy of Laughter and Humor* (Albany, NY: State University of New York Press, 1987), pp. 128–38.

3   Morreall, "Taking Laughter Seriously," pp. 4–14.

4   Ibid., pp. 20–37.

5   Ibid., pp. 15–19.

6   Morreall divides his book into two parts: the first deals with laughter, the second with humor. Clearly laughter can occur without humor and humor without laughter, and Morreall argues that this distinction is a crucial one. He provides a table divided into nonhumorous and

laughter is most useful, primarily because it sheds considerable light on the specifically musical means at work in eliciting an amused response.[7] I will therefore concentrate throughout the following discussion on the incongruity theory.

In volume two of his *The World as Will and Representation*, Arthur Schopenhauer defines his "theory of the ludicrous" as follows:

> According to my explanation, put forward in volume one, the origin of the ludicrous is always the paradoxical, and thus unexpected, subsumption of an object under a concept that is in other respects heterogenous to it. Accordingly, the phenomenon of laughter always signifies the sudden apprehension of an incongruity between such a concept and the real object thought through it, and hence between what is abstract and what is perceptive.[8]

By way of example, Schopenhauer puts forth the following:

> Of this kind is also the anecdote of the actor Unzelmann. After he had been strictly forbidden to improvise in the Berlin theatre, he had to appear on the stage on horseback. Just as he came on the stage, the horse dunged, and at this the audience were moved to laughter, but they laughed much more when Unzelmann said to the horse: "What are you doing? don't you know that we are forbidden to improvise?"[9]

In this anecdote, the representation of the horse dirtying the stage is viewed through the concept of theatrical improvisation; the fact that the horse's action falls outside what is "in the script" allows for this otherwise unlikely pairing of concept and representation. We laugh when we realize the incongruity of percept and concept.

Let us say, then, that we accept the notion that perceived incongruity can give rise to an amused response.[10] The next step is to determine how this would

---

humorous laughter situations. Thus situations like solving a puzzle or problem or winning an athletic contest are instances of nonhumorous laughter, while hearing a joke, a clever insult, or a pun are humorous instances (see "Taking Laughter Seriously," pp. 1–3). After a thorough discussion of laughter, Morreall proposes the following definition: "Laughter results from a pleasant psychological shift" (p. 39). His theory of humor, on the other hand, is based on the incongruity theory (pp. 60–84). The present study takes up the incongruity theory as a theory of *humor*.

7 The superiority and relief theories might be used to unpack the humorous effects of these songs that occur in the other dimensions that this study does not directly address. To a certain extent the superiority theory is taken up in Scruton's notion of irony discussed below.

8 Arthur Schopenhauer, *The World as Will and Representation*, vol. II, trans. E. F. J. Payne (New York: Dover, 1969), p. 91.

9 Ibid., p. 93.

10 Bearing in mind the distinction made earlier between laughter and humor, this statement does not preclude the possibility that perceived incongruity may also give rise to another response,

apply to humor in music. To say that something is incongruous is to appeal to some set of norms. In the world of everyday life, we share certain ideas of what is normal, or at least, of what is common. The comic artist is especially sensitive to these commonly held notions about the world and uses them to create the incongruity that so amuses us. In the world of music, then, one must determine what norms could give rise to incongruity and account for how these could be manipulated to humorous ends. One area of research that identifies musical norms is the study of musical style. Much of the work done by Leonard Meyer, Leonard Ratner, and Robert Gjerdigen has demonstrated that common-practice Western art music (especially the music of Viennese classicism) operates according to certain normative procedures.[11] Meyer, for example, defines style as follows:

> Style is a replication of patterning, whether in human behavior or in the artifacts produced by human behavior, that results from a series of choices made within some set of constraints.[12]

Further, Meyer's notion of style change involves a consideration of compositional choices that fall outside the constraints of the style—that is, musical-stylistic incongruities. The replication of these new choices can produce style change.[13] Obviously, these stylistic incongruities can also produce humor and the music of Peter Schickle's fictitious P. D. Q. Bach bears this out.[14]

---

or that an amused response may be elicited in some other way. The claim is only that an amused response *may* be triggered by a perceived incongruity.

11 Robert Gjerdingen, "The Formation and Deformation of Classic/Romantic Phrase Schemata," *Music Theory Spectrum* 8 (1986): 25–43; and *A Classic Turn of Phrase: Music and the Psychology of Convention* (Philadelphia: University of Pennsylvania Press, 1988); Leonard Meyer, "Innovation, Choice, and the History of Music," *Critical Inquiry* 9 (1983): 517–44; "Toward a Theory of Style," in *The Concept of Style*, ed. Berel Lang (Ithaca, NY: Cornell University Press, 1986), pp. 21–71; *Style and Music: Theory, History, and Ideology* (Philadelphia: University of Pennsylvania Press, 1989); and Leonard Ratner, *Classic Music: Expression, Form, and Style* (New York: Schirmer Books, 1980).

12 Meyer, "Toward a Theory of Style," p. 21.

13 In his "Innovation, Choice, and the History of Music," Meyer sets out his position as follows (p. 518): "Put simply: save as a curious anomaly, a single, unique innovation, however interesting in itself, is of little import for the history of music. What is central for the history of an art is, I suggest, neither the invention of novelty or its mere use—whether in a single composition or in the oeuvre of a single composer—but its replication, however varied, within some compoosition community." Though this study limits itself to considerations of stylistic norms, it is certainly possible to view the congruity/incongruity dialectic in other analytical contexts.

14 A good example of stylistic incongruity can be found in P. D. Q. Bach's "My Bonnie Lass She Smelleth"; in this parody of Elizabethan madrigal singing, one vocalist sings a cadenza that quickly becomes an improvisatory jazz skat-singing solo. The humor depends on the perceived incongruity between these two musical styles. See *The Wurst of P. D. Q Bach*, Peter Schickle

If there exist certain stylistic norms in art music, they are certainly also present in popular music; in fact, Theodor Adorno's main complaint with popular music, or at least the pop of the late 1930s and early 1940s, is that it is formulaic in an empty and mechanized way.[15] If pop-style norms exist, then so does the possibility of stylistic incongruity, and therefore, humor in popular music. While the notion that pop songs can be humorous may seem obvious to those who know popular music, bear in mind that our concern is with specifically *musical* humor; there have, of course, always been songs with funny words.

II

Let us examine the stylistic incongruity that occurs in Spinal Tap's "Heavy Duty" (supposedly from their 1976 LP "Bent for the Rent").[16] Example 1 provides sixteen measures from the song's chorus: the style is that of mid-1970's heavy-metal rock. The final occurrence of this chorus is followed immediately by the music shown in Example 2. Clearly we perceive the insertion of a classical-style minuet—in this instance the well-known minuet from Boccherini's *String Quintet in E major*—into a heavy-metal song as incongruous, not to mention the additional incongruity of the "power-chords" that accompany the melody, which is itself played by the lead guitar. These incongruities are the key to the humor here: in a tune that aspires to "heavy-duty-osity," an instrumental interlude in the classical style is desperately out of place. This example might be viewed as a musical analogue to Schopenhauer's horse story and confirms that incongruity can produce specifically musical humor. Here the incongruity resides between two very different, even antithetical, musical styles.

(Vanguard VSD 719/20, 1971). Robert Gauldin has collected a number of humorous examples from the Western art-music repertoire and organized them in a way similar to the examples that follow. I wish to thank Dr. Gauldin for sharing his collection of taped excerpts and outline with me.

15 Theodor Adorno, "On Popular Music," reprinted in Simon Frith and Andrew Goodwin, eds. *On Record: Rock, Pop, and the Written Word* (New York: Pantheon Books, 1990), pp. 301–14.

16 All the Spinal Tap songs under consideration are composed by Christopher Guest, Michael McKean, Harry Shearer, and Rob Reiner. Of these four, perhaps Guest is the only one with well-known previous work in musical satire. He was a cast member of National Lampoon Lemmings, a Woodstock satire, in which he parodies James Taylor, in addition to cowriting three songs. See *National Lampoon Lemmings* (Blue Thumb Records, BTS–6006, 1973). He also composed songs for and performed on *National Lampoon Radio Dinner* (Blue Thumb Records, BTS–38, 1972).

None of the three Spinal Tap numbers under consideration in the present study occurs in its entirety in the film. References are always to the complete versions that appear on the soundtrack LP. All examples are transcribed and arranged by the author.

Example 1: "Heavy Duty," final appearances of chorus
(Example includes lead vocal, backup vocals (in parentheses), and rhythm guitar
part, with some of the lead-guitar part.)

By Michael McKean, Chris Guest, Rob Reiner and Harry Shearer
Copyright © 1984 EMI BRILLIG MUSIC, INC,
Reprinted by Permission of CPP/Belwin, Inc., Miami FL All Rights Reserved

"Heavy Duty," then, depends for its humorous effect on an obvious stylistic
incongruity. Consider, on the other hand, "Cups and Cakes," a single produced in
1965 when Spinal Tap still called themselves "The Thamesmen." The humorous
effect of "Cups and Cakes" is achieved somewhat differently from that of "Heavy
Duty." Here, the entire number is in a single style: the so-called "British-invasion"
style, prevalent in popular music between 1963 and 1967.[17] Unlike "Heavy Duty,"

---

17 For more about the British invasion, see Ed Ward, Geoffrey Stokes, and Ken Tucker, *Rock of
    Ages: The Rolling Stone History of Rock & Roll* (Englewood Cliffs, New Jersey: Rolling Stone
    Press/Prentice-Hall, 1986), pp. 277–89; and Charlie Gillett, *The Sound of the City: The Rise of
    Rock and Roll*, 2nd. ed. (New York: Pantheon, 1983), pp. 261–84. "British-invasion" is an
    American term; the British refer to the same style as "beat music."

Example 2: "Heavy Duty," insertion of the minuet from Boccherini's
String Quintet in E Major
(Example includes lead, rhythm, and bass guitar parts.)

there are no passages in "Cups and Cakes" that produce incongruity by radical stylistic juxtaposition. In fact, most of the song's musical characteristics are *congruent* with the norms of the British-invasion style. In order to understand the role played by stylistic incongruity in "Cups and Cakes," we need to first explore in some detail the ways in which the tune matches the style.

Let us turn to the music. The song begins with a five-measure introduction employing piano, string quartet, and trumpet, with electric bass entering at the end of the fifth measure to lead into the first verse. One notices immediately the use of trumpet and string quartet, instruments more often associated with "high-brow" music, and their pseudo-Baroque scoring. The first and second verses are shown in Example 3. The text of the first verse is sung solo to the accompaniment of pseudo-Baroque piano, along with electric bass, and tambourine. A cello line in the eighth measure of that verse leads into the second verse, which is sung by a second solo voice to the same accompaniment, augmented now by harpsichord.

At the bridge (see Example 4), the voice, piano, and electric bass are joined by the string quartet, and the tambourine is replaced by snare drum and tom-toms

405

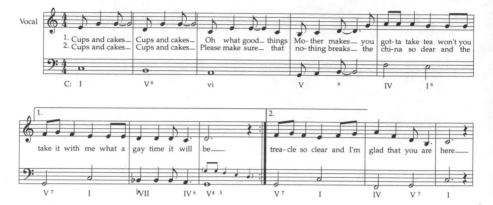

Vocal

1. Cups and cakes— Cups and cakes— Oh what good— things Mo-ther makes— you got-ta take tea won't you
2. Cups and cakes— Cups and cakes— Please make sure— that no-thing breaks— the chi-na so dear and the

C: I   V⁶   vi   V   ⁶   IV   I⁶

1.
take it with me what a | gay time it will | be——

2.
trea-cle so clear and I'm | glad that you are | here——

V⁷   I   ♭VII   IV⁶ V⁴³   V⁷   I   IV V⁷ I

Example 3: "Cups and Cakes," Verses One and Two
(Example includes melody and reductive representation of bass movement and
harmonic progression.)

By Michael McKean, Chris Guest, Rob Reiner and Harry Shearer
Copyright © 1984 EMI BRILLIG MUSIC, INC,
Reprinted by Permission of CPP/Belwin, Inc., Miami FL All Rights Reserved

Vocal

Milk and sug-ar | bread and jam— | yes please sir and | thank you ma'am— | here I am—

E: I   V   ♭VII   ♭VI   I   V   ♭VII   ♭VI

C: I   IV   V

Example 4: "Cups and Cakes," Chorus

(played to sound like tympani). This is followed by an instrumental interlude
featuring the trumpet, accompanied by piano, electric bass, and tambourine. The
harmonic progression in this five-measure interlude is identical to that of the
introduction until the fifth measure, where a modulation up one whole step, from
C major to D major, occurs through the introduction of the new dominant
sonority. The final verse, though transposed to D, is identical to the second verse
up to its seventh measure. The harmony in measures 8–10 of the last verse
progresses as follows:

D: vi –♭VI | iv–♭VII | I | I ||

The instrumentation is identical to the first verse with the addition of string quartet.

As Susan McClary and Rob Walser have pointed out, the music of one's own culture often seems completely transparent and requires very little mediation to achieve its effect.[18] While the listener who knows the British-invasion style will surely recognize it in "Cups and Cakes," describing how one can identify such a style often poses a number of difficulties.[19] The ability of listeners to identify a particular style results from what will be termed a specific "stylistic competency." At a low level of competency one can merely identify the style; at a higher level of competency, one can acutely identify the significant incongruities from the style within a single work.[20] Stylistic competencies are frequently tacit: a listener is able to perceive a stylistic incongruity—in fact, the incongruity may seem obvious—but is often unable to articulate the perception in a systematic or technical way.

While the stylistic incongruity that occurs in "Heavy Duty" requires that the listener possess a low-level competency in two styles—one needs to know only that the juxtaposed styles are 1970s heavy metal and classical-period art music, not that there are any deviations within those styles—the fullest appreciation of the humor in "Cups and Cakes" depends on a rather advanced British-invasion stylistic competency. This claim is supported by the fact that so many features of "Cups and Cakes" are congruent within the style.

One way of identifying the ways in which "Cups and Cakes" is congruent with the British-invasion style is to compare it with genuine tunes from the style. Figure 1 enumerates some of the correspondences between "Cups and Cakes" and a number of other songs in the British-invasion style.[21] The introduction to "Cups and Cakes" uses string quartet and trumpet. "Classical-sounding" instruments are typical in mid-1960s British-invasion music, and one need look no further than the Beatles' "Yesterday" or "Eleanor Rigby" for strings and their "Penny Lane" for

---

18 Susan McClary and Rob Walser. "Start Making Sense! Musicology Wrestles With Rock," in Frith and Goodwin, *On Record,* pp. 277–92.

19 In fact, I am always surprised, when I ask pop musicians to identify the possible targets of this gag, how many different responses I get.

20 The term "stylistic competency" is used in a way similar to Robert Hatten's usage. See Robert Hatten, "Toward a Semiotic Model of Style in Music: Epistemological and Methodological Bases," (Ph.D. dissertation, Indiana University, 1982).

21 These are, of course, only suggestions and everyone will have his or her own set of associations. Please note that the chart includes correspondences in instrumentation, an area that is generally thought to fall under the auspices of arranging or production, and which is, to follow Meyer, non-syntactic. The aspect of production is crucial to the perception of the style in this instance, however, and could be thought of as one of Meyer's secondary parameters. See Meyer, "Toward a Theory of Style," p. 41.

Text	"You Were Made For Me," Freddie and the Dreamers (1965)
	"Mrs. Brown, You've Got a Lovely Daughter," Herman's Hermits (1965)
	"I'm Henry VIII, I Am," Herman's Hermits (1965)
	"Sunday For Tea," Peter and Gordon (1967)
Accent	"Mrs. Brown" (1965)
	"I'm Henry VIII" (1965)
Strings	"Yesterday," Beatles (1965)
	"Eleanor Rigby," Beatles. (1966)
	"As Tears Go By," Rolling Stones (1966)
	"Sunday For Tea" (1967)
Harpsichord	"Lady Jane," Rolling Stones (1966)
	"Yesterday's Papers," Rolling Stones (1967)
	"Sunday For Tea" (1967)
Trumpet	"Penny Lane," Beatles (1967)

Harmonic movement of "Cups and Cakes" (verse = C: I–V^6–VI–V–IV–I^6–V^7–I–$\flat$VII–IV^6–V; bridge = E: I–V–$\flat$VII–$\flat$VI) and melodic movement and rhythm fall within the style generally. The use of inversions suggests a "learned" aspect. Last verse modulates up a whole step (see also "Penny Lane").

Figure 1: Stylistic Correspondences in "Cups and Cakes"

trumpet. The eighth-note rhythm of the strings in the introduction to "Cups and Cakes" is especially reminiscent of the eighth-note strings in "Eleanor Rigby," and the trumpet solo of "Penny Lane" might easily have been the model for the one here.[22] The harmonic root-progression is common enough in this style; the use of inversions lends a certain "learned" aspect to the movement, further reinforcing the pseudo-Baroque aspects of the arrangement. The melody features the characteristic eighth-note syncopation found in many pop styles. The lyrics are silly, but so are the ones to "Mrs. Brown You've Got a Lovely Daughter" or "I'm Henry the Eighth, I Am" by Herman's Hermits.[23] Both those numbers also feature the heavily

---

22 It is the use of a trumpet in a British-invasion style tune that is most significant. The trumpet melodies in both "Penny Lane" and "Cups and Cakes" imitate "classical music," but that is as far as the resemblance goes. In the documentary film *The Compleat Beatles* (videotape, Delilah Films Inc., 1982), Beatles producer and arranger George Martin states that Paul McCartney heard the piccolo trumpet in a performance of Bach's *Brandenburg Concerto* (no. 2) and wanted to make use of the instrument in music the Beatles were recording at that time. For an account of the composition of the trumpet part in "Penny Lane," see George Martin with Jeremy Hornsby, *All You Need is Ears* (New York: St. Martin's Press, 1979), pp. 201–2. I cannot resist pointing out that the trumpet solo also uses a particular riff that strongly resembles one in the theme music to the 1980's TV series "Dynasty."

23 Both of these songs are found on the compilation *Herman's Hermits XX, Their Greatest Hits* (Abkco, AB 4227, 1972).

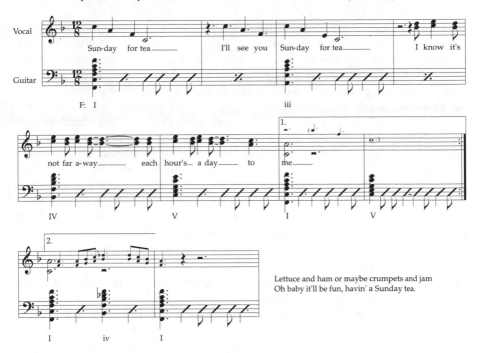

Lettuce and ham or maybe crumpets and jam
Oh baby it'll be fun, havin' a Sunday tea.

Example 5: "Sunday for Tea," Verses One and Two
(Example includes vocal parts and an arrangement of the accompaniment as it
appears on the recording.)

accented voice of Peter Noone, making him the likely model for the overdone
accent in "Cups and Cakes."

In many ways, however, "Cups and Cakes" is most reminiscent of Peter and
Gordon's "Sunday for Tea."[24] To begin with, both sets of lyrics deal with tea
time and use instruments commonly associated with high-brow music. The five-
measure introduction to "Sunday for Tea," for instance, is played by harpsichord

---

24 "Sunday for Tea" is found on the Peter and Gordon compilation cassette *A World Without
Love* (Capitol Records, Inc., 4XL-9288, 1985).

solo in a pseudo-Baroque style. The first and second verses are each eight measures in length, but are in a pop-folk style, with vocal duet accompanied by strummed acoustic guitars and acoustic bass (see Example 5). The eighth measure of the first verse features an interjection from the harpsichord, and the second verse adds a xylophone, which does not constitute a strong reference to high art, to the accompaniment. The eight-bar bridge introduces a pop-style tambourine to the ensemble, while the twelve-measure third verse incorporates a now "chord-comping" harpsichord throughout. An eight-measure instrumental interlude follows with the music from the second verse scored for traditional piano trio only. The remainder of the song consists of a repetition of the bridge, followed by verse three; concluding with the introduction, which is used as a codetta. Thus one may note the use of "classical music" instrumentation throughout the song, with the instrumental interlude for piano trio and the introduction and codetta for harpsichord the most obvious references to high-brow music. Considering the correspondences enumerated here, both in comparison with the British-invasion style and with an original British-invasion tune like "Sunday for Tea," it is not at all clear how incongruity could be at work creating humor in "Cups and Cakes."

The British philosopher–aesthetician Roger Scruton, in considering Schopenhauer's theory of incongruity, cites caricature as a counter-example. In discussing a caricature of the former British Prime Minister, Scruton writes

> The caricature amuses, not because it does not fit Mrs. Thatcher, but rather because it does fit her, all too well. It is true that it must also contain an exaggeration: but the exaggeration is amusing because it draws attention to some feature of *her*. If one wishes to describe the humor of a caricature in terms of incongruity it must be added that it is an incongruity which illustrates a deeper congruity between an object and itself.[25]

Later, Scruton adds that ". . . satire at least possesses, when successful, the quality of accuracy."[26]

Scruton's remarks further refine the incongruity model by introducing the notion that a dialectical tension exists between congruity and incongruity, and his observations on satire and caricature shed important light on the questions that arise in comparing the bogus Spinal Tap number with the genuine one by Peter and Gordon, as well as with the British-invasion style generally. "Cups and Cakes" *does* fit the style and this accounts for the correspondences which are found in Figure 1 (the number of correspondences could be increased quite easily). But, to follow Scruton, does "Cups and Cakes" contain some kind of exaggeration?

---

25 Roger Scruton, "Laughter," reprinted in Morreall, *Laughter and Humor*, p. 161.
26 Ibid., p. 162.

Let us again consider "Sunday for Tea." The lyrics poke fun at conservative and affluent British high society. The use of harpsichord and piano trio is motivated by the use of these instruments in drawing rooms and gardens of the elite (or, at least it is rooted in the popular association of these instruments with aristocracy). This interaction of lyric and instrumentation produces a kind of gentle irony, and the tune is surely meant tongue-in-cheek. The music hall element is not far off in this number, and the music-hall style played a prominent role in Peter and Gordon's previous single "Lady Godiva," which made use of tenor banjo and tuba.[27] The irony of "Sunday for Tea" amounts to a criticism of high society—albeit a not-so-direct one—and one can find many songs from the same period that took a more direct aim at their targets.[28]

When the Thamesmen/Spinal Tap adopt this style there are indeed exaggerations. Trumpet and string quartet do not really interact with the lyrics, which are even plainer and sillier than those of "Sunday for Tea." Further, how do we make sense of the tympani-like drumming in the bridge, especially when the lyrics are "milk and sugar/bread and jam/yes please sir and thank you ma'am/here I am"? There is no gentle irony or underlying social commentary here. While "Cups and Cakes" abounds with features typical of the style, certain ones are exaggerated or are combined with others in ways that produce an exaggeration within the style. These exaggerations, to follow Scruton, draw attention to particular and real features in the style—features that are, nonetheless, ripe for a humorous treatment. None of this produces an amused response, however, unless the listener can tell the difference between the real thing and the exaggeration; it is the listener's stylistic competency that permits this crucial discrimination. Without the ability to make such a judgement (no matter how tacitly or overtly this is done), "Cups and Cakes" could pass for a legitimate song in the style (though probably a below-average one). While one knows that in context of the film "Cups and Cakes" is supposed to be funny, the listener highly competent in British-invasion music can detect the stylistic incongruities even when the song is heard in isolation.[29]

One might also posit that there is a kind of "threshold region" within a listener's stylistic competency. An incongruity that is easily perceived falls below this threshold, one that is too difficult to perceive falls above it. When an incongruity falls into the area where it challenges the stylistic competency, without boring it or confusing it—when it balances on this threshold—then the greatest amused response is aroused; the key to eliciting the amused response would seem to depend

---

27 Peter and Gordon's "Lady Godiva" may also be found on *A World Without Love*, cited above.
28 The Kinks' "A Well Respected Man" (1965), the Beatles' "Nowhere Man" (1966), and "Penny Lane" (1967) are just three examples of many that can be cited.
29 This is confirmed to a certain degree by the fact that in the film one hears only the very end of the tune; on the soundtrack LP, however, one finds the entire song. Most of the features of "Cups and Cakes" discussed here are not obvious from the short excerpt of the tune one hears in the film itself.

on just the right kind of dialectical tension between congruity and incongruity. In short, what is obvious is not as funny as what requires a little more thought; or as our two Spinal Tap guitarists say during a philosophical moment in the film, "There's a fine line between clever and . . . stupid." With regard to the satire of Spinal Tap, the movie's most effective numbers are those that nearly pass for authentic ones; the stylistic exaggerations offer a challenge to the listener's powers of detection.

III

In "Heavy Duty," the obvious incongruity between styles accounts largely for the humorous effect of the tune. In "Cups and Cakes," those characteristics that are congruent within the style and those which are incongruent enter into a dialectical relationship. The Spinal Tap number "(Listen to the) Flower People," however, elicits an amused response in a way slightly different from the two preceding examples.

We are to believe that "Flower People" was released in 1967, perhaps during the celebrated "summer of love." The tune begins with a six-measure introduction that features electric-guitar arpeggiation around a D-major chord. Two eight-bar verses are followed by an eight-measure chorus (see Example 6). Next there is an instrumental interlude of fifteen bars. Two eight-measure verses follow, played as before except that two beats are inserted between bars four and five of the first verse. The music from the instrumental interlude is used as the basis for a psychedelic-style ending.

There are some fairly obvious gags in this song: the use of the famous theme to Mozart's *Eine Kleine Nachtmusik* at the words "it's like a Mozart symphony" in verse three produces an obvious interstylistic incongruity (this is, of course, similar to the appearance of the Boccherini minuet in "Heavy Duty," discussed above). The whispered "shhh" after each occurrence of the word "listen" in the text and the phase-shifted "no" after "it's not too late" are exaggerations of stylistically typical vocal effects.[30]

"(Listen to the) Flower People," like "Cups and Cakes," is in the British-invasion style. "Flower People," in addition, relies heavily on stylistic traits usually associated with "psychedelic rock"; but this stylistic mixture is also typical of late British-invasion pop. "Flower People" has many of the typical psychedelic features: reversed-tape effects, exotic scales (the ending especially), and the use of sitar.[31]

---

30 In Herman's Hermits' 1967 hit, "There's a Kind of Hush," the word is sung "hushhh." See *Greatest Hits*.

31 In this instance a "Coral Sitar" is used, an instrument manufactured by the Danelectro Company that sounds somewhat like a sitar but is tuned like a guitar. For more on the

Example 6: "(Listen to the) Flower People," Verses One, Two, and Chorus
(Example includes lead and backing vocal parts and an arrangement as it appears
on the recording.)

By Michael McKean, Chris Guest, Rob Reiner and Harry Shearer
Copyright © 1984 EMI BRILLIG MUSIC, INC.,
Reprinted by Permission of CPP/Belwin, Inc., Miami, FL All Rights Reserved

Reverse Tape	"Rain," Beatles (1966)
	"I'm Only Sleeping" (ending), Beatles (1966)
	"My White Bicycle," Tomorrow (1967)
Sitar	"Norwegian Wood," Beatles (1965)
	"Paint It Black," Rolling Stones (1966)
	"Shapes of Things" (sitar-like), Yardbirds (1966)
	"My White Bicycle" (sitar-like, reversed), (1967)
Lyrics	"San Francisco," Scott McKenzie, (1967)
Vocal Whispers	"There's a Kind of Hush," Herman's Hermits (1967)
	"My White Bicycle" (1967)

Figure 2: Stylistic Correspondences in "Flower People"

Figure 2 shows a table of correspondences for "Flower People."[32]

While "Flower People" has many of the general features of late British-invasion music, it also models features of certain specific tunes rather closely. The harmonic progression of the verse (see Figure 3) is I–II–iv–I. Consider the Beatles' 1965 hit "Eight Days a Week" which progresses I–II–IV–I, or their 1966 hit "Nowhere Man" which moves I–V–IV–I–ii–iv–I. "Flower People" can be seen as a conflation of those two. Further, "Eight Days a Week" features the guitar introduction shown in Example 7. The introduction to "Flower People" (Example 8), while much simpler, is nevertheless similar.

"Eight Days a Week"	D: I–II–IV–I
"Nowhere Man"	E: (I–V–IV)–I–ii–iv–I
"Flower People"	D: I–II–iv–I

Figure 3: Correspondences in Harmonic Progression

<hr>

psychedelic movement and the groups that played psychedelic music, see Ward, Stokes, and Tucker, *Rock of Ages*, pp. 328–87.

32 Another example—an obscure one, to be sure—that makes use of some of the psychedelic features discussed here is a tune by the British psychedelic band "Tomorrow"; it is their 1967 British hit "My White Bicycle," which appears on the group's LP *Tomorrow* (Import Records, Inc./EMI Records Ltd., IMP 1003, 1968). Here one notes the reverse-tape effects, exotic-scale guitar passages, simple-minded lyrics, and whispered back-up vocals. The lead guitarist in this recording is Steve Howe. Howe, as a member of the British supergroup Yes, went on to be an extremely influential figure on the 1970's progressive-rock music scene. Howe is certainly the target of the backstage scene in "This is Spinal Tap" in which lead-guitarist Nigel Tufnel (played by Christopher Guest) leads film maker Martin Di Burge (played by Rob Reiner) through his dozens of collectible guitars. The Yes group becomes one target of Spinal Tap's progressive rock send-up numbers—pieces entitled "Stonehenge" and "Rock and Roll Creation."

Example 7: Introduction to "Eight Days A Week" (Lead-Guitar Part Only)

The introduction to "Flower People" bears an even stronger resemblance to the opening of the Byrds' 1965 hit "Mr. Tambourine Man" (Example 9).[33] While the Byrds' Roger McGuinn uses his characteristic Rickenbacker electric twelve-string and the Spinal Tap introduction does not, the voicings, and the guitar fingerings that go with them, are very similar. The similarity between the introductions to "Mr. Tambourine Man" and "(Listen to the) Flower People" is further reinforced by the similar electric bass guitar parts that accompany each. Further, the musical texture employed in both tunes after the introduction consists of chords arpeggiated on the twelve-string low on the neck against a second guitar that articulates short, rhythmic high voicings (see Figure 4).

"Flower People" demonstrates a closer kind of modelling than either "Heavy Duty" or "Cups and Cakes." Despite these many close correspondences, though, there is something about "Flower People" that keeps it from being mistaken for an authentic example of either British-invasion pop or psychedelic rock. And it is precisely this stylistic "near miss" that elicits the amused response.

In his 1981 book, *Sound Effects*, sociologist Simon Frith distinguishes between pop and rock.[34] Pop music is made with the consumer in mind: it is commercially motivated and aims to give the listeners "what they want." Rock, on the other hand, lays claim to authenticity and sincerity: the musician expresses him- or herself without regard for commercial gain. Frith points out that most rock musicians reside somewhere in between these opposite poles. Frith's book provides

---

33 It should be pointed out that the Los Angeles-based Byrds cannot be considered British invasion, but are usually thought to be part of the "American response." For a discussion of the American response, see Ward, Stokes, and Tucker, *Rock of Ages*, pp. 303–14. For a fuller consideration of the Byrds, see Johnny Rogan, *Timeless Flight: The Definitive Biography of the Byrds*, 2nd ed. (Essex: Square One Books, 1990).

34 Simon Frith, *Sound Effects: Youth, Leisure, and the Politics of Rock and Roll* (New York: Pantheon Books, 1981), p. 11.

Example 8: Introduction to "Flower People" (Guitar and Bass)

Example 9: Introduction to "Mr. Tambourine Man" (12-String Guitar and Bass)
(Please note that octave doublings that result from the tuning of the third and fourth strings are represented in parenthesis.)

a clear (and accurate) description of these contradictory pressures.[35] But anybody who has ever taken rock music seriously will not need to read Frith's elegant prose to understand the meaning of "selling out." In fact, the desire to play a music that

---

35 In his *Studying Popular Music* (Milton Keynes: Open University Press, 1990), Richard Middleton cautions that a simple binary opposition like the pop-rock one presented here can be misleading (p. 43). It is clearly possible that the artist who builds a career on the directness and authenticity of his or her music may be just as likely to be manipulating this image—or have it manipulated by a manager or record company—for commercial gain as the most cynical pop star. In using Frith's distinction in the present discussion, however, I am less concerned with the reality of whether artists are *really* what they appear to be, than with the notion that listeners perceive authenticity in musical, and specifically stylistic, terms. The idea is that in absence of any other information, the competent listener can *hear* the artist either "selling out" or remaining faithful.

"Flower People" (1967!)	"Mr. Tambourine Man" (1965), Byrds
12-string arpeggios (acoustic) in verse with high-voiced chord accompaniment (6-strg.)	12-string arpeggios (electric) in verse with high-voiced chord accompaniment (12-strg.)
arpeggio intro (6-strg.) with sliding bass accomp.	arpeggio intro (12-string) with sliding bass accomp.*

* see also Eight Days a Week for acoustic 6-strg. + elec. 6-strg. (and similar intro). For another 12-strg. intro, see "Ticket to Ride," Beatles (1965), or "Turn, Turn, Turn," Byrds (1966).

Figure 4: Modeling in "Flower People"

has a high degree of integrity, and the desire to make some kind of living through doing so, come to seem irreconcilable to many rock musicians; some quit, some sell out, and some get jobs teaching music theory or musicology. Some rock musicians are able to strike a balance between the pursuit of their musical goals and the demands of the music industry, at times achieving notable commercial success.

What makes "(Listen to the) Flower People" not fit the British-invasion/ psychedelic-rock mold, what makes it seem not quite right, is this: "Flower People" is a sell out, and the stylistically competent listener can discern this. To use Frith's distinction, it is all pop and no rock. It arouses an amused response because it tries every stylistic trick in the book in an effort to be current, and in 1967 current means psychedelic. But psychedelia was the voice of the counterculture, a culture that advocated "peace, love, and dope." Psychedelic music was high in commitment to the ideals of the "flower people movement"—or was at least perceived to be so—and the rock pole eclipsed the pop one in this music—or, again, was as at least *supposed* to.

Into this context comes Spinal Tap, which is presumably looking for a hit single in the United States and "flower power" is "in." In order not to offend, however, they attenuate the elements in the music that might be considered objectionable. There is a kind of stylistic neutralization that takes place—a sort of entertainment-business "spiffing up" that makes the tune acceptable to parents everywhere. The liner notes to the soundtrack LP (which also play along with the gag) inform us that "Flower People" is the single from Spinal Tap's 1967 LP "Spinal Tap Sings 'Listen to the Flower People' and Other Favorites." [36] In a 1984 mock interview published in *Guitar Player* magazine, Nigel Tufnel (Christopher Guest) reflects on Spinal Tap's 1967 hit:

---

36 Liner notes to Spinal Tap, *Spinal Tap*.

Interviewer: ... In 1967 you did "(Listen To The) Flower People," which seems like a complete departure. Why?
Tufnel: Well, to be honest—and only because I like you I'm telling you—we tried to jump on the bandwagon. There was such an enormous sort of public clamoring for that sort of *garbage*, frankly, we thought we might as well reap some of the benefits. So we dished that one out, and it really did well for us, actually.[37]

The broadest amused response to "Flower People," then, is aroused by challenging the listener's stylistic competency for British-invasion and early psychedelic-rock music. "Flower People" is so close to the real thing that it could easily pass for authentic. One does notice the incongruity of the psychedelic features with their pop application. But unlike "Heavy Duty," stylistic juxtaposition alone is not enough to mark "Flower People" as a satire; there are genuine tunes that mix these stylistic features. To return to Scruton, the listener is amused only upon recognition that some particular stylistic incongruity is an exaggeration; we say: "This couldn't be real!" It is not so much the presence of psychedelic features in a tune that is directed at a broad pop audience that triggers the humor, as much as it is that the use of these features is a little heavy-handed and desperate. Spinal Tap goes a little too far—they are perhaps too eager to please—and the listener realizes that the incongruity is too great to be genuine. The humor then ultimately lies in issues of stylistic authenticity, or in the blatant lack of it.

IV

Schopenhauer's incongruity theory, when extended by Scruton's notion of a congruity–incongruity dialectic present in satire, provides a useful model for understanding the humor in the three Spinal Tap numbers examined here. Most important to this study, however, is the fact that the incongruity theory can be combined with theories of style to explain incongruity both between styles and within a single style.[38]

The discussion of the incongruities in these three Spinal Tap songs might suggest, however, that an amused response arises from a sense of superiority: we laugh at the band's inadequacy. Again, Roger Scruton's remarks are useful: he

---

37 Nigel Tufnel, "Volume For Volume's Sake: Nigel Tufnel of Spinal Tap," interview by Teisco Del Ray, *Guitar Player* 18/10 (October, 1984): 43.
38 For an examination of incongruity within the style of one specific group, see John Covach, "The Rutles and the Use of Specific Models in Musical Satire," *Indiana Theory Review* 11 (1991): 119–44.

distinguishes between sarcasm and irony. The former is a "laughing at" action which entails rejection. Irony is, on the other hand, a "laughing at" action without rejection; it is kinder and entails a certain aspect of laughing at ourselves. In ironic humor, the character becomes more endearing through his or her inadequacies; irony is involved in a mental act Scruton calls "attentive demolition." The Spinal Tap songs, and the film generally, evoke this ironic response.[39]

Spinal Tap, with their endearing inability to ever get anything quite right, is not the ultimate target of the musical humor in "This is Spinal Tap," however. The dialect of congruity/incongruity in the bogus songs that triggers the humor also forces a reconsideration of the model; in the moments that the listener hears this parody, not only does "Cups and Cakes" seem silly, but the whole British invasion itself seems silly. The Spinal Tap group, as well as the songs they play, serves as a kind of "lens" through which one views the model style. The richness of the humor in these numbers arises not simply because the tunes themselves are funny, nor because they are performed in a funny way, but because they also provide a humorous perspective, through clever distortion, on the models. This is not to claim that one emerges from this experience convinced that the music of groups like the Beatles or the Rolling Stones is foolish; after all, one's experience of a parody of something need not forever strip it of the possibilty of subsequent serious consideration. Instead, the full humorous effect of each Spinal Tap number relies on the listener's ability to identify references within a rich network of intertextuality.[40]

The relationship between the kind of amused responses discussed above and the more serious, aesthetic response requires further exploration. As Scruton, Morreall and others have suggested, these two modes of contemplation can share the quality of disinterestedness. In fact, the act of "distancing" oneself from the model, both specific and general, plays a crucial role in eliciting the amused responses described above. But the stylistic competency that allows one to identify intertextual references need not only elicit an amused response; the detection of stylistic incongruities is crucial to the aesthetic response in music generally. Though an

---

39 Scruton, "Laughter," pp. 167–69. Scruton contends that "devaluation" is an important aspect of ironic response (p. 168): "Irony devalues without rejecting: it is, in that sense, "kind." For example, Joyce's ironic comparison of Bloom with the wily Odysseus de-values the former only to insert him more fully into our affections. His shortcomings are part of this pathos, since they reflect a condition that is also ours. Irony of this kind causes us to laugh at its object only by laughing at ourselves. It thus forces upon us a perception of our kinship."

40 For a discussion of intertextuality in music, see Robert S. Hatten, "The Place of Intertextuality in Music Studies," *American Journal of Semiotics* 3/4 (1985): 69–82. Hatten also uses style theory to explain intertextual references in music, and he provides a number of examples. In the same issue, see Thais E. Morgan, "Is There an Intertext in This Text?: Literary and Interdisciplinary Approaches to Intertextuality" (pp. 1–40), for an extremely helpful survey. The issue of intertextuality and style theory is discussed further in Covach, "The Rutles."

examination of how the amused response differs from the more serious aesthetic one is beyond the scope of this study, it seems clear that the respective response mechanisms are highly similar.[41]

The "Flower People" example is suggestive in a second, related way: if issues of authenticity can arouse an amused response, they can also arouse an aesthetic one. In fact, it is fairly evident that many serious rock fans demand authenticity from the musicians they follow and that many musicians stake their reputations on a defiance to sell out; Eric Clapton's departure from the Yardbirds is the classic example.[42] Many rock listeners develop very advanced stylistic competencies and in listening to a rock song weigh every stylistic incongruity against a complex (though often tacit) model. The listener accepts incongruities that are judged to be innovative and rejects others that are judged to be corruptive or derivative. By this process the listener comes to an aesthetic evaluation of the music. This again suggests that the mechanisms that produce humor are very like those that produce aesthetic appreciation.

While this study has focused primarily on the ways in which humor can be created through specifically musical means, it is clear that the musical humor in each tune interacts with other contexts that are not specifically musical but nevertheless participate in eliciting an amused response. Thus the musical means that create humor in these songs can only be isolated from the larger context of the film itself provisionally; humor is created in the film in many ways and music plays only one part—albeit a crucial one—in the overall effect. Despite the fact that the musical text itself is situated among other contexts in the film—and even on the soundtrack LP—it is clear that there are specifically musical means of eliciting an amused response in each song examined above. Just as the musical context is situated within the larger context of the film itself, however, so too is each specific Spinal Tap song situated within a larger body of musical works. The musical humor arises from setting each bogus Spinal Tap number against the appropriate musical repertory, and it is the song's position within this network of other songs

---

41 Two complementary kinds of instance suggest that these two mechanisms are highly similar:
 1) a listener whose stylistic competency is insufficiently developed will not detect the incongruities in a parody, and may respond to the piece aesthetically;
 2) a listener whose stylistic competency is insufficiently developed will mistakenly identify incongruities, perhaps mistaking a serious work for a parody.
 In the first instance, I have often noted that listeners unfamiliar with popular music find the Spinal Tap songs to be typical stylistically, even judging them to be boring or uninventive. In the second instance, one could easily lead a group of listeners generally unfamiliar with twentieth-century music into believing that an acknowledged masterwork such as Arnold Schoenberg's *Pierrot Lunaire* is a parody. This kind of interpretive mix-up surely hinges on the stylistic competencies involved.

42 Ward, Stokes, and Tucker, *Rock of Ages*, pp. 282–83; Gillett, *The Sound of the City*, pp. 278–9. The reader is reminded that I am concerned here with authenticity as it is perceived in specifically musical terms.

that gives it its significance and allows it to achieve its effect. The source of the humor then is ultimately *relational,* and the humor lies not so much in the song itself, but rather in the relationship between the specific song and a large number of other songs that it invokes.[43]

---

43 Earlier versions of this paper were read before the International Association for the Study of Popular Music (New Orleans, 1990), Music Theory Midwest (Evanston, 1990), University of Rochester Symposium on Rock Music (1990), and the Society for Music Theory (Oakland, 1990). I would like to thank Robert Hatten, Robert Gauldin, and John Morreall for reading an earlier draft and offering many helpful suggestions.

Music Theory and the Postmodern Muse: An Afterword

Nicholas Cook

As its title implies, *Concert Music, Rock, and Jazz since 1945* covers a range of musics created by musicians of quite different backgrounds, whose only common feature is that they were working in North America or Europe during the past fifty years (or a little more, in the case of Ruth Crawford). It is not easy to say what the variety of approaches on offer have in common, except that they generally focus on the music itself (whatever that problematical formulation may mean) rather than on the contexts surrounding its conception, production, and reception. But then, that is just the point of the book. It encapsulates the diversity of musical styles found in the Western world during the second half of the twentieth century, and equally it encapsulates the diversity of approaches to music that have evolved during the last decade or so; most of these essays would have been unlikely, and some of them quite unimaginable, as recently as 1980.

The tone is set by the opening essay, Jonathan Kramer's "Beyond Unity: Toward an Understanding of Musical Postmodernism." Part of his aim in this essay is to show how recent music should be understood within the context of postmodernism, as a broad cultural and intellectual movement linking what used to be distinguished as "high" and "low" art (the apparently effortless linking of which is one of the most significant characteristics of this book). But Kramer's principal aim is to stimulate ways of *thinking* about music that are fully informed by these values, and that would be as applicable to modern or premodern music as to music specifically composed under the emblem of postmodernism. So he sets out some of the essential issues around which postmodernism revolves: the death of the author, the principle of unity, and the relationship of work and text. Most of the essays in this book have a bearing on one or more of these issues, and so I shall use them to structure my own comments.

The Death of the Musical Author

The notion of the death of the author is drawn from one of Roland Barthes's most famous proclamations, cited by Kramer in a footnote: "the birth of the reader must be at the expense of the death of the author" (note 43). In its positive aspect, this statement refers to the general shift of critical attention from production to reception, from the intentions of the author (or composer) to the meaning that a reader (or listener) finds in or creates out of a literary or musical text. In its negative aspect, it denies that the author is a free agent, the source from which meaning flows; instead the author is seen as a construction of ideological forces, and meaning is seen as being negotiated between those forces and the reader.[1] Now these ideas are far from new in literary theory; Barthes's essay "The Death of the Author" was written in 1968. As Kramer puts it, "Barthes throws down a challenge to which literary critics have responded but which music analysts are only now, a quarter of a century later, beginning to consider" (note 43). Once again, it seems, thinking about music lags behind the other arts.

But it is primarily historical musicology, not analysis, in which the "author" is still live and kicking; musicologists try to set composers' thinking into its original context, editors try to find the most faithful way to notate what composers intended, and performance practice experts try to reconstruct how composers wanted their music played. Contemporary analysis developed precisely as talk about composers' intentions gave way to explanations located in "the music itself," and this is a transformation that began long before Barthes was writing. To this extent, theory might be said to be a discipline *predicated* on the death of the author: Heinrich Schenker affirmed as much when he wrote of the genius-composer that "the superior force of truth—of Nature, as it were—is at work mysteriously behind his consciousness, guiding his pen, without caring in the least whether the happy artist himself wanted to do the right thing or not. If he had his way in following his conscious intentions, the result, alas! would often be a miserable composition. But, fortunately, that mysterious power arranges everything for the best."[2] In this way, Schenker saw his theory as explaining the principles according to which Music, and not the composer as such, operates.

This is hardly the way theorists write nowadays. But they frequently give no more scope to the composer as a free agent than did Schenker. I can illustrate this in terms of Andrew Mead's essay "Twelve-tone Composition and the Music of Elliott Carter," in which Mead explains some of the principles governing row organization in Carter's music. Mead adopts the same explanatory strategy as Schenker did in *Der freie Satz*: he sets out abstract structures and then shows how they are "realized" or "manifested" in the finished composition. One might well

---

1 Of course, Barthes sets up an opposition between author and reader with which not all literary critics agree, as Robert Cogan points out in the conclusion of his essay, "The Art-Science of Music after Two Millennia." Cogan (pp. 51–52) prefers the interpretive framework proposed by the Russian philosopher–critic Mikhail Bakhtin, whose work—developed from the early decades of this century—allows a multiplicity of voices and a dialogue between author and reader.

2 *Harmony*, ed. Oswald Jonas, trans. Elisabeth Mann Borgese (Chicago: The University of Chicago Press, 1954), p. 60.

argue that this model of the compositional process reflects the academic environment in which much contemporary composition (and almost all commentary on composition) is carried out: pure research, conceived in abstract terms, is followed by the application of the research within concrete contexts. The emphasis is not so much on what composers *create* but on what they *discover*, and this is reflected by Mead's repeated use of the metaphor of compositional "exploration," the colonization of new compositional "terrain."

I see no reason to suppose that composition as discovery leads to results that are less musically satisfying than composition as creation. Nevertheless, this distinctly Platonic concept of composition[3] imposes limits upon the composer's authority that are hardly less severe than Schenker's. There are two points in Mead's essay where this issue surfaces. One is in a footnote where Mead cites a statement by Carter to the effect that his use of register is based on instrumental practicality rather than structural logic; Mead comments, with apparent justice, that "Carter's subtle handling of both pitch and pitch class leads one not to take this statement too literally" (note 22). The other is less obvious and more telling. At the beginning of his final paragraph, following mention of a number of features that Carter's music shares with that of Martino and Babbitt, Mead writes (pp. 101–02):

> we should emphasize that observations regarding the various intersections between Carter's music and the work of others should in no way diminish our sense of the composer's originality. On the contrary, such intersections are unavoidable given the inevitable restrictions imposed by the inherent abstract structure of the twelve-pitch-class total chromatic, and our appreciation of those commonalities can only increase our enjoyment of the individualities of each composer's music.

What is interesting is the fact that Mead feels called upon to allay such worries about originality, which are essentially out of place if composition is seen as the discovery of abstract, and in that sense eternal, principles. Mead rationalizes composition as discovery, but values it as creation. The "author" may be dead in music theory, but his ghost continues to haunt us.[4]

So far we have explored only half of Barthes's proclamation. If music theory is predicated on the death of the author, that does not necessarily mean that it has thereby given birth to the reader. We might evaluate this in terms of the interpretive freedom a theoretical approach gives its reader. In general such freedom varies inversely with the authority annexed to itself by the theoretical approach. I can

---

3 See Peter Kivy, "Platonism in Music: A Kind of Defense" and "Platonism in Music: Another Kind of Defense," in *The Fine Art of Repetition: Essays in the Philosophy of Music* (Cambridge: Cambridge University Press, 1993), pp. 35–58, 59–74.

4 "His" because I am assuming that romantic and modernist ideology constructs the author as male.

clarify this by comparing Andrew Mead's essay with Jonathan Bernard's "Theory, Analysis, and the 'Problem' of Minimal Music." The abstract structures set out by Mead provide a basis for understanding the note-to-note compositional strategies behind Carter's music, and in at least one instance, Mead is prepared to overrule Carter's own statements where these contradict the analytical demonstrations; as Mead presents it, theory is (or aims to be) both authoritative and comprehensive. But in Bernard's essay, it is neither. Indeed, Bernard writes that "an analytic approach to minimal music might prove more viable if it were less exclusively bound up with exactitudes" (p. 266), and he goes on to propose a number of visual analogues to the music of Reich and Glass, drawn from minimalist painting and sculpture.

Of course, these visual analogues can't represent the pitches of the music or its registral or rhythmic patterns; indeed, they may not have any correspondence to the music's temporal unfolding. What they *do* share with the music is one or more of its qualities or attributes—for instance a certain relationship between sparsity and density, or an emphasis on surface rather than depth. By focusing attention on a particular attribute of the music, these visual analogues elicit a corresponding "way of 'seeing' the music," as Bernard puts it (p. 266). Moreover, the possibility of matching alternative images with the music, and so "seeing" it in different ways, creates the kind of interpretive space that minimal music has often been accused of abolishing (as in the once common labelling of it, cited by Bernard [p. 263], as "trance music"). In this way, Bernard empowers the listener, turning him or her into a free agent instead of a passive recipient. Barthes's dictum would imply that, in that case, Bernard must be killing off the composer. This isn't his stated intention; indeed, Bernard quotes Reich's stated aim of arriving at "a compositional process and a sounding music that are one and the same thing" (p. 261). At the same time, it is the prying apart of what is produced from what is experienced (or, in Jean-Jacques Nattiez's terms, the poietic from the esthesic)[5] that lies at the heart of Bernard's approach.

Some might object that Bernard is driven to this by a repertory that stubbornly refuses to present analytical problems and is therefore resistant to analytical solutions; they might suspect that the principles he enounces have no possible application to other musics. But I don't think so, because Ellie Hisama's "The

---

5   Jean-Jacques Nattiez, in *Music and Discourse: Toward a Semiology of Music*, trans. Carolyn Abbate (Princeton: Princeton University Press, 1990), defines three dimensions of the symbolic phenomenon (pp. 11–12):

> (a) *The poietic dimension*: even when it is empty of all *intended* meaning ... the symbolic form results from a *process of creation* that may be described or reconstituted.
> (b) *The esthesic dimension*: "receivers," when confronted by a symbolic form, assign one or many meanings to the form ...
> (c) *The trace*: the symbolic form is embodied physically and materially in the form of a *trace* accessible to the five senses.

Question of Climax in Ruth Crawford's String Quartet, Mvt. 3" is based on a complex, modernist composition, and yet achieves precisely what Bernard achieves: the creation of interpretive space and the empowerment of the listener (or at least the reader). And what is more, Hisama apparently achieves this without the sacrifice of the author. Her argument has two starting points. One is the personal situation in which Crawford found herself at the time she composed her string quartet, as a result of what Hisama calls her "social, gender-based exclusion" (p. 292), and Hisama provides some interesting documentation of this. The other is the climax that occurs at measure 75 of Crawford's movement; "as a remnant of earlier musical procedures," says Hisama, "it seems incompatible with the work's otherwise wholly modernist technique and aesthetic" (p. 285).[6] What Hisama wants to do, of course, is to find some connection between the two.

First, she outlines the notion of double participation, or double-voiced discourse, according to which members of oppressed groups outwardly conform to the mores of dominant groups, while subverting them from the inside. Then she invents an analytical function called "twist," which measures the extent to which the registration of the four instruments deviates from the normative string quartet pattern according to which the first violin is at the top of the texture, and the cello at the bottom. Next, she compares the values for twist throughout the movement, and finds that they are completely out of kilter with the climax structure to which register and dynamics are subordinated. Finally she concludes that Crawford is subverting the traditional, and therefore characteristically male, climax structure by means of the hidden dimension of twist; true to the principle of double participation, says Hisama, Crawford "managed to speak the language of the 'great tradition' while also maintaining a space of resistance in her art" (p. 305).

One possible limitation of Hisama's theory has to do with the conclusions she draws from her analysis of twist. If we are to interpret any instance of non-isomorphism between parameters as evidence for the subversion of male hegemony, and given that a proficient analyst can just about always find *some* kind of non-isomorphism, then can't we read just about *any* piece of music as a feminist double-voiced discourse? But to put the question this way is to prejudge the issue; it is a *reductio ad absurdum*. Indeed, I would argue that the idea that music is intrinsically double-voiced, and that it therefore has a privileged status as gendered discourse, is by no means absurd. As an activity that had come to be seen as essentially feminine by the middle of the nineteenth century,[7] music represented a

---

6 I don't really agree that these two are incompatible; the idea of climax is deeply rooted in the music of Schoenberg, whom I take to be the archetypal modernist in music, and, as Hisama demonstrates, the entire registral and tensional morphology of Crawford's movement is carefully structured round its climax.

7 See, for instance, Hayden White, "Form, Reference, and Ideology in Musical Discourse" (in Stephen Paul Scher, ed., *Music and Text: Critical Inquiries* [Cambridge: Cambridge Universtiy Press, 1992], pp. 288–319), p. 303.

socially accepted context within which men could evade the gender stereotyping characteristic of patriarchal society; music became a medium for the expression of gender-ambivalence. Moreover, if we accept the widespread gendering of the rational as male and the irrational as female, then talking about music provided a rare opportunity for men to publicly defend values based on intuition and personal expression against the dominant values of scientific positivism. In this way, and despite Charles Seeger's characterisation of composition as "a groove . . . definitely flavored with machismo" (in Hisama, p. 305), music has historically represented an arena for double participation by both men and women.

This might at first seem to cast doubt on Hisama's identification of the climactic structure of Crawford's movement with "a dominant, masculinist musical narrative" (p. 293) and hence on her characterization of it as "not just revolutionary but also distinctly feminist" (p. 293). But then, Hisama herself stops well short of claiming that Crawford intended the movement as a feminist statement (p. 293, note 14). And I don't think that arguments about historical fact represent the best way to approach what Hisama has to say. Just as she offers us the image of a marginalized composer who subverted the accepted practices of a male-dominated art, so Hisama leads the reader to "see" Crawford's music from an avowedly marginal perspective, and the result is to throw the entire edifice of accepted analytical practice off balance. It's not that Hisama shows conventional analysis to be wrong, by revealing a previously unrecognized dimension of musical design; what makes Hisama's essay so successful is its ability to rupture the apparently seamless continuity of the poietic and the esthesic planes. Hisama transforms Crawford's movement into a parable of the subversion of authority. Perhaps, then, we should value Hisama's essay not so much for its reconstruction of historical fact as for the reading of Crawford's music that it enables; not so much for what it represents as for what it *does*.

Musical Unity and Disunity

Maybe the frank dissociation of the poietic and the esthesic planes is the hallmark of postmodernist analysis. Kramer advances something like this as one of the criteria of postmodernist thinking about music: "the listener's perceptual unity/disunity," he says, "is not identical to the music's textual unity/disunity" (p. 14). The attempt to collapse these two planes into one is an important thread connecting nineteenth-century romanticism to twentieth-century modernism; the listener's duty to accept the composer's work on its own terms, as advanced by such nineteenth-century critics as Adolph Bernhard Marx, became the basis for the astonishing twentieth-century exercise in aesthetic engineering known as the music appreciation movement. Max Ernst used to tell the story of how "when his father was painting in his garden, and a tree in the picture irked him, he painted it out,

427

and then wondered whether he ought not to remove the real tree as well. 'At the time it occurred to [Max] that there was something amiss in the relationship between painter and subject.'"[8] Kramer suggests that this kind of illegitimate identification of the poietic with the esthesic is the basis for what he calls the "totalizing meta-narrative of textual unity" (p. 32) that has characterized musical analysis up to the present day.

According to Kramer, "we have well-developed theories of musical unity but nothing comparable for disunity. Traditional analysis studies similarity, not difference (difference is central to postmodern thinking in other disciplines, but not yet in music analysis)" (p. 12). If Kramer is right, then there are good historical reasons why this should be so. It is hardly going too far to say that analysis as we know it was invented to deal with Beethoven's symphonies.[9] More precisely, it was designed to show how Beethoven's symphonies made sense despite their apparent incoherence—their erratic thematic and formal organization, their abrupt discontinuities of register, texture, and tonality, and so forth. What was obvious was the diversity of the music; what was not obvious and therefore needed explaining, in order to justify the almost universal approbation of Beethoven's achievement, was its underlying unity. In this way the characteristic features of analysis as we know it were there almost from the beginning: the emphasis on unity, the rhetoric of apparent versus underlying structure, the subordination of the obvious to the non-obvious, and the concern with aesthetic legitimation. One could plausibly argue that it is these characteristics that give musical analysis its disciplinary identity.

In "The Art-Science of Music after Two Millenia," Robert Cogan likewise criticizes analysts' apparent fixation with unity; "much thought and energy in the aesthetics and theory of music have been devoted to the processes of unity," he says, "while comparatively little have been devoted to the necessary complementary processes of diversity and opposition" (p. 40). But his mention of the "complementary processes of diversity and opposition" suggests a counter-argument to Kramer. "Schenker's theory is essentially *oppositional*," Cogan reminds us. "Only at a work's conclusion does the linear path, or *Urlinie*, resolve to the tonic goal; until then, the essential tension of the work results from the open conflict, the irresolution, between that line and its ultimate goal" (note 30). Certainly the language of opposition, of strife, of social and personal disorder runs through Schenker's writings like a *leitmotif*; his passionate desire (it is more than just an aim) is to show how in spite of all this there is a higher unity, a purpose, that gives meaning to what he calls "the chaos of everyday life."[10]

---

8   Uwe M. Schneede, *The Essential Max Ernst* (London: Thames and Hudson, 1972), p. 8.

9   I have heard Charles Rosen say this.

10 Sylvan Kalib, *Thirteen Essays from the Three Yearbooks "Das Meisterwerk in der Musik" by Heinrich Schenker: An Annotated Translation* (Ph.D. diss., Northwestern University, 1973), ii, p. 239.

But a pole has two ends, and in the same way what Kramer calls a theory of musical unity is equally a theory of musical disunity; it just depends which way you point it. Schenker's theory is a means of relating unity to disunity. We generally think of it as a mechanism that takes foreground disunity as its input, and yields background unity as its output. But it makes equally good sense to think of Schenker's theory as a means of demonstrating the diversity, the lack of continuity, the incongruity—in a word, the disunity—of the foreground; it is precisely the comparison with the unified background that makes these qualities stand out in relief. Moreover, Schenker can be read as dramatizing the tensions between levels of structure rather than just as demonstrating their conformance. As I have written elsewhere, "any motivic parallel across different structural levels must, by definition, involve the apparent similarity of formations that have different generative sources; hence motivic parallels don't impose unity, as has been generally assumed, but rather highlight the discrepancy between surface and structure."[11] If the same argument can be extrapolated to other analytical methods, then responding to Kramer's call for us to focus on disunity rather than unity may not necessarily mean abandoning our existing analytical tools, as Kramer implies; it may rather mean applying them with a new sense of purpose.

There is a further assumption that I would like to tease out of Kramer's argument. As I mentioned, his essay is about postmodernism in both music and writing about music, and the underlying principle seems to be that writing about music should reflect the music itself. In one sense, of course, this is obvious and uncontroversial. But there is another sense in which one might argue just the opposite. Early analysts tried to demonstrate the unity of Beethoven's symphonies precisely because all they could hear in them was disunity. Webern promoted the aesthetics of unity but wrote music that struck most listeners as episodic and disconnected; hence the enormous investment of post-war theory in methods for demonstrating how his music is unified after all. On the other hand, as we have seen, Bernard seeks means of articulating the diversity of minimalist music in order to counteract its immediately perceptible unity, just as Hisama tries to controvert what she sees as the unified surface design of Crawford's quartet movement. There is a general principle here. In the dialectic of unity and disunity, the role of analytical writing is as often as not to *oppose* the music's phenomenal qualities. And in this sense one might directly challenge Kramer and assert that difference constitutes the basic logic of analysis.

The issue of unity brings to light an interesting divergence between theory and practice in this book. The three introductory essays (Kramer's and Cogan's, plus Robert Morris's "Aspects of Confluence between Western Art Music and

---

11 "The Future of Theory" (*Indiana Theory Review*, 10 [1989], pp. 70–72): 71. For an example of a Schenkerian reading that thematizes inter-level conflict, see Kevin Korsyn, "Towards a New Poetics of Musical Influence" (*Music Analysis* 10 [1991], pp. 3–72): 35.

Ethnomusicology") all argue in one way or another for an aesthetic that espouses disunity, methodological pluralism, and value-neutrality; Morris calls this the "ethnomusicological perspective" (p. 55). But such values are much less evident in many of the applied analyses that follow. While Mead, for instance, avoids overt talk of unity, the entire explanatory thrust of his essay is to bring to light the connected structures that underlie the richly variegated surface of Carter's music. And the vocabulary he applies to these structures explicitly associates them with aesthetic values; over the course of the essay there is a gradual crescendo of terminology from "striking" through "fascinating," "elegant," and "vivid," to "poignancy and power." [12] Shortly after using these last words, he writes that "a full appreciation of the richness and subtlety of Carter's music can be greatly aided by an understanding of the principles that underlie his approach to composing within the total chromatic" (p. 99). Like Richard Hermann's analysis of Berio, to which I shall return, Mead's essay aims to initiate the reader (or in Hermann's words the "inexperienced listener" [p. 397]) into an esoteric inner drama from which she or he might otherwise be excluded.

Issues of unity move into the foreground in Dave Headlam's "Does the Song Remain the Same? Questions of Authorship and Identification in the Music of Led Zeppelin." Headlam's starting point is the difficulty of applying traditional concepts of authorship to popular music in general, and to Led Zeppelin in particular. The issue on which he focuses is the relationship between what classical musicians would call "arrangement" and "composition." Translated into the terms of rock practice, the distinction is between the essentially parasitic "cover" and the genuinely creative "reworking"; only the latter involves the creation of a distinctive artistic identity, and thus fulfills the criteria for authorship. Headlam's procedure is to compare a number of Led Zeppelin's songs with the originals from which they were derived, evaluating the extent to which they "contain the unmistakable characteristics most strongly identified with Led Zeppelin's style" (p. 328)—in other words, the more the songs sound like Led Zeppelin, the more Led Zeppelin can be considered their authors.

But his rationale for the process is more sophisticated than this might initially suggest. It is based on Foucault's inversion of the relationship of author and text as traditionally conceived: instead of seeing the author as creating the text, Foucault sees the text as creating the author. In other words, he sees the author as an explanatory construct, an organizational principle in relation to which texts can be interpreted. (We might say that the Ruth Crawford who emerges from Hisama's essay is an author in the Foucauldian mold.) But Headlam gives Foucault's argument a distinctive spin. As he puts it, "the 'author' constitutes a principle of unity among a class of works, somewhat akin to a theory, under which disparate works can be grouped together by their shared characteristics stemming from that

---

12 See, for example, Mead, pp. 76, 81, 83, and 99.

authorship. Under this criterion, the role of Led Zeppelin as authors in different songs can be considered in terms of a musically-defined 'style class'" (p. 327). Unity, in other words, is seen as correlative with authorship, just as it is within the romantic and modernist tradition of thinking about music. And so, when Headlam concludes that "the power and effect of 'Whole Lotta Love' . . . derives in large part from the formal contrast and combination of the two seemingly disparate elements—driving, rhythmic blues-riffs and free-form psychedelic effects—into a coherent whole" (p. 341), this is to be understood as as an argument for regarding Led Zeppelin as the song's authors.

Headlam's essay freely mixes modernist and postmodernist thinking; and that is exactly what he intends. While he is keen to extend the concept of authorship into new areas of repertory, his underlying motivation is essentially traditional; after all, it is only in terms of the romantic and modernist ideology of artistic creation that the distinction between cover and reworking actually *matters*. And John Covach displays a similar mixture of postmodernist thinking and traditional theoretical concerns in his "Stylistic Competencies, Musical Humor, and 'This is Spinal Tap,'" There is more to this than the extension of theory to new areas of repertory; Covach focuses on the way in which the songs of Spinal Tap disrupt or subvert the norms of rock music. But he does not offer us a postmodernist celebration of disruption. Instead, he is using the humor that derives from stylistic incongruity as a kind of probe, a means of elucidating the stylistic norms that govern aesthetic reception.[13] His real topic is what it means to listen to rock music (and perhaps, by extension, any music) as a competent listener; and his central argument is that music must be understood relationally. You can't understand any piece of music in isolation, he is saying; it derives its meaning—that is, its humorous or aesthetic effect—from the network of comparable or incommensurable pieces of which it forms a part, and knowledge of which constitutes listening competence. To say this is, of course, to suggest that the boundaries between one piece and another, or between a composition and its context, are more blurred than theorists were at one time inclined to think.

Covach, then, works from a postmodernist concern with strategies of disruption toward more traditional issues of aesthetic perception, and back again to an equally postmodernist critique of the autonomous work; he compounds post-modernism and music theory. Whether such a compound can ever be stable is open to question. The disciplinary identity of theory, after all, has historically been predicated on the concept of the autonomous musical work. And while Covach explicitly states that the humor of the Spinal Tap songs is ultimately inseparable from the larger context of Rob Reiner's film, his focus on the creation of humor

---

13 For a parallel exploration of the "analogies . . . between understanding a joke and understanding a musical composition" see Kendall L. Walton, "Understanding Humor and Understanding Music," *Journal of Musicology* 11 (1993): 32–44.

"through specifically musical means" echoes old controversies between theoretical and contextural approaches to music; the same might be said of Headlam's concern to show how Led Zeppelin's authorship can be determined "by purely musical values." The language is reminiscent of Hanslick, Schenker, and Réti. And in some ways the battle currently being fought in popular music studies is comparable to that between the absolutists and the referentialists; Headlam and Covach are trying to carve out a space for music theory in a territory over which sociologists and cultural theorists have long claimed exclusive rights. But it is clear that a latter-day formalism will not suffice for their purposes. If such a thing as a fully post-modernist heory of music is possible, the study of popular music is perhaps the most likely place for it to emerge.

And yet of all the essays in this book, it is another of those on rock music— Walter Everett's "The Beatles as Composers: The Genesis of *Abbey Road,* Side Two"—that adheres most strongly to the values traditionally associated with music theory. Of course, Everett's choice of analytical method is determined in part by the strongly tonal language of the music. Yet despite the title, and the very interesting information he cites regarding the recording process, Everett's study is really directed towards the aesthetic qualities of the finished product, particularly issues of expression and musical design. He uses Schenkerian techniques to show how the eight-song medley that makes up the largest part of the side is unified into what Jonathan Dunsby would call a "multi-piece."[14] And having demonstrated that the entire medley can be subsumed under a $\hat{3}$–$\hat{2}$–$\hat{1}$ *Urlinie,* he "searches for an overarching theme in this group of songs that were chosen and joined in a very conscious manner" (p. 227), finding it in a meaning that is more than just musical: the need for self-gratification to be outweighed by generosity. "It seems rewarding," Everett concludes, "to hear this uplifting message as a very personal final gift from McCartney to his mates, as well as from the Beatles to the world" (p. 227). Such a reading is "rewarding" because it draws out from the music its potential for moral improvement. In this way, Everett's essay shows how the music of the Beatles displays the ethical qualities that have since the Romantic period been seen as the hallmark of great art. It is, as I see it, an exercise in aesthetic legitimation, an argument for the inclusion of the Beatles along with Bach and Beethoven in the basic curriculum of a liberal arts education.

Popular music neatly encapsulates the tensions implicit in the idea of a post-modernist music theory. It presents, in the most pressing manner, issues relating to the identity (or lack of identity) of the musical work and the separation (or inseparability) of the work and context; in these respects, any adequate theory of popular music must address the central concerns of postmodernism. But, at the

---

14 Jonathan Dunsby, "The Multi-piece in Brahms: *Fantasien* Op. 116," in Robert Pascall (ed.), *Brahms: Biographical, Documentary, and Analytical Studies* (Cambridge: Cambridge University Press, 1983), pp. 167–189.

same time, the emergence of popular-music theory reveals the contradictory impulses of aesthetic legitimation and canonization—impulses with which music theory has been closely associated since the time of Beethoven. Why is it that the essays about popular music in this book tend to betray more of these traditional concerns than the essays on what used to be called "serious" music? The answer is obvious: you make use of established concepts in order to legitimize repertories that have not up to now been taken seriously. Where the legitimacy of the repertory is not in question, you can afford to be much more adventurous in your approach; you can afford to take risks with the music. Who knows what Ellie Hisama could do with Beethoven?

Musical Work and Text

Robert Cogan writes that "most often we regard the musical work as a single object—fixed, knowable, immutable, unified—rather than as a set of opposing, mutable, surprising, open-ended possibilities" (p. 40). Postmodernism has sensitized us to the conceptual baggage that attaches to the idea of a musical work. After all, composers don't write "musical works"; they write scores or, to use another word, texts. And a text is, as Cogan puts it, full of opposing, mutable, surprising, open-ended possibilities. Or to put it another way, a text doesn't have meaning; rather, it has the *potential* of supporting an indefinite variety of meanings. What turns texts into works, then, is interpretation. And what gives rise to the traditional concept of a work—as fixed, knowable, immutable, unified—is an interpretation to which such authority is attached that the work is identified with the text, as if no other interpretation were possible or, at any rate, legitimate.

There is, then, an intimate link between the concept of author and that of work; to put it crudely, text plus authority equals work. By shoring up the traditional concept of authorship in the uncertain and treacherous terrain of popular music, Headlam reinforces the idea that groups like Led Zeppelin create works. But this is a problematic idea, if only because it is not very obvious what we might mean by text when dealing with popular music. Headlam foresees the difficulty and takes evasive action: "One objection to my analytical treatment of the songs might be that Led Zeppelin continually changed and evolved in their concert versions of these songs . . . Despite these improvisations, however, each song has a fixed studio version that has become definitive, and formed at least the basis for improvisations on stage. I consider the studio versions justification for my analysis" (note 68). There is really no other choice if you want to assimilate popular music within the framework of traditional analytical and aesthetic thinking, based as it is on the duality of work and performance. And yet to adopt this approach is to eliminate at a stroke the vast body of recorded material on which a study of these dynamically evolving songs might be based. We don't have any choice about this with premodern music, for which only documentary evidence is available; that is why traditional interpretive approaches center on scores. But this is no reason for applying the same approach to Led Zeppelin; instead of tailoring the music to our thinking, we could be trying to tailor our thinking to the music. I shall return to this.

Cynthia Folio's "An Analysis of Polyrhythm in Selected Improvised Jazz Solos" centers on acoustic rather than notated texts. Her analysis is mainly based on her own detailed transcriptions of recorded solos by Thelonious Monk, Ornette Coleman, and Eric Dolphy; she shows how note-to-note rhythm, pitch content, and articulation give rise to interlocking metrical frameworks, sometimes on several levels of structure at once. She is of course perfectly aware that any transcription is an idealization of the music on the record; she says of one of the transcriptions that "in fact the notation of this tune is a very 'square' representation of what is actually played; the material is not in alignment with the notated meter, as the example suggests" (note 38). In other words, the transcription is itself an analysis, rationalizing what Coleman and Cherry played by assimilating it to the regular common-time meter; the music has in effect been filtered through the notation. Her multi-layered interpretations may stike some readers as excessively complex: does anybody hear all this? At the same time, it seems intuitively clear that the music is full of the kind of polyrhythmic implications that Folio renders explicit, even if these implications seem to be generically sensed rather than specifically perceived. Maybe her analyses are best seen as superimposing everything that might possibly be experienced in the course of an indefinite number of hearings, and so representing the total potential of the music for cognitive realization by the listener.

There is one respect, however, in which I think the intervention of notation may have imposed its own values upon Folio's interpretation. Western notation maps musical time onto space; it leads us to think of the passage of time in terms of directed motion. So it is not surprising that Folio characterizes polyrhythm by means of terminology that clearly implies such motion: she speaks of dissonance (which is defined by its tendency towards resolution) and tension (which is defined by its tendency towards release). And accordingly she concludes that polyrhythm "invariably creates . . . an anticipation of resolution, and a sensation of forward momentum" (p. 111). Now of course this is very characteristic of at least some of the music she analyzes, such as the Coleman solo in "Lonely Woman"; Folio's description of the separation and rejoining of the various rhythmic layers in this solo is very reminiscent of the later stages of a North Indian *raga* performance. But it is not so characteristic of other styles of polyrhythmic music, among them West African drumming. Polyrhythm is as capable of sustaining pulsating but direction-less musical textures as it is of creating forward momentum. Maybe characterizing polyrhythm by means of a term such as "density," which lacks the directional implications of "dissonance" and "tension," would facilitate the extension of Folio's approach to a broader range of musical styles.

A more wide-ranging example of the difficulties notation poses for analysis is suggested by Liang Mingyue's transcription that accompanies Robert Cogan's discussion of the Chinese *ch'in* (long zither) piece *Yu-lan*, or "Elegant Orchid." The transcription uses staff notation (Cogan's Example 1), but Cogan's analysis approaches the music from a phenomenological viewpoint, using spectrograms derived from a recorded performance of *Yu-lan* for much the same purpose that Bernard uses images drawn from minimalist painting and sculpture: to draw attention to qualities of the music that traditional score-based approaches tend to de-emphasize.

It is natural for a Western reader of this book to think of Cogan's Example 1 as a score, the graphic trace of a musical work. But the *Yu-lan* Cogan is talking about is as much a performance as a work, or perhaps it would be better described as lying uneasily between the two. The cause for the unease is the disparity between staff notation and the traditional notation of *ch'in* music, which is in effect a tablature, specifying the manner in which the right hand should strike the string, and the point at which it is to be stopped with the left.[15] However, it lacks any direct specification of rhythm; some of the performance instructions have rhythmic implications, but these fall far short of the overall rhythmic specification that Western notation provides. *Ch'in* tablature, then, represents the music as essentially no more than a chain of gestures; it is up to the interpreter to decide how fast the music should go, how the notes should be grouped into phrases,[16] which notes should be longer or shorter than others and in consequence which should be projected as more or less structural than others. In this way aspects that are seen as fundamental to a work's identity in the Western tradition are left almost wholly indeterminate, and there is no way of knowing how far modern *ch'in* performance conforms in these aspects with what was done in Tang times.

Cogan's Example 1 is not a direct transcription of the original notation. It is a translation of the original notation, by means of one particular recorded performance, into the quite different patterning of determinacy versus indeterminacy that characterizes all Western staff notation. Transforming the original chain of gestures into a determinate rhythmic structure, it represents a modern performance practice tradition as much as it represents *Yu-lan*. Such realizations of pieces from the ancient *ch'in* repertory have traditionally been communicated aurally from teacher to pupil, gradually evolving in the process, before becoming fixed in the present century through the use of staff notation and,

---

15 Cogan's Figure 1 is an example of the earliest *ch'in* tablature, which is essentially a prose description of what the player is to do. Most *ch'in* repertory survives in tablatures based on schematic characters, the upper part of which specifies what the left hand should do, and the lower the right. As the information is essentially the same, the following discussion applies to both types of notation.

16 In some *ch'in* notations small circles are used to indicate a break.

more recently, sound recordings. But this pattern of gradual change has traditionally been complemented by one of what might be called catastrophic change, in which musicians go back to the original notation and attempt to reinterpret it from scratch. This process, which is called *da pu*, has been set out in an authoritative article by Bell Yung,[17] and consists of three main stages. The first involves a study of the poetic or other inscriptions which normally accompany the tablature, in order to establish the intended representational and affective qualities of the music. (In the case of *Yu-lan*, the title relates to Confucius's comparison of himself, as a superior man who lacks recognition, with an orchid growing amid weeds.)[18] The second is similar to the Western concept of performance practice research; it consists of in-depth study of the original notation, combining research into contemporary notational practices (*ch'in* notation has changed through the centuries) with experimentation in playing techniques. The final stage, which is the most personal of the three, involves synthesizing the results of the previous two, resulting ideally in a performance that fully realizes the music's poetic qualities.

Yu-lan highlights the problems of relating works to texts. If text plus authority equals work, then who is its author? The Confucius of the no doubt mythical ascription? The unknown individual responsible for the original notation of *Yu-lan* (which itself may well have been a reworking of an earlier piece or performance tradition)? The musician responsible for the *da pu* process on which any given performance or performance tradition is based?[19] The performer on any given occasion of performance? We have here a continuum of creative acts which cannot be mapped onto binary oppositions of work and performance, composition and interpretation. That may not be surprising since we are applying Western terminology to music from another culture. But I want to suggest that these binary oppositions may not do justice to our own musical culture either. Read for its variety rather than its unity, a song like "Whole Lotta Love" is not so much a work as a performance tradition, within which we might distinguish two levels of variance: routine or gradual change from one occasion of performance to another, taking place within some kind of invariant framework, and catastrophic change, such as when Led Zeppelin reworked Willie Dixon's original. And in such a context, traditional notions of authorship and authority clearly need rethinking.

---

17 Bell Yung, "*Da pu*: the Recreative Process for the Music of the Seven-string Zither," in Anne Dhu Shapiro (ed.), *Music and Context: Essays for John M. Ward* (Cambridge, Mass.: Department of Music, Harvard University, 1985), pp. 370–84.

18 Liang Mingyue, *Music of the Billion: An Introduction to Chinese Musical Culture* (New York: Heinrichshofen Edition, 1985), p. 182. [Editor's Note: Liang Mingyue appears in some catalogs, and in Cogan's article, as (David) Ming-Yueh Liang.]

19 While Cogan's Example 1 is taken from the Liang Mingyue transcription, the modern performance history of *Yu-lan* derives from Yang Zhongji (1865–1933), who published it in a modern notation that specifies rhythm. See Liang, *Music of the Billion*, pp. 152–53.

A Postmodern Analyst's Toolkit

The three remaining essays are all firmly based on the textual plane, in the sense that they deal with relationships that can be explicitly modelled in terms of notational symbols. Elizabeth West Marvin's "A Generalization of Contour Theory to Diverse Musical Spaces: Analytical Applications to the Music of Dallapiccola and Stockhausen" is not so much a series of musical readings as the exposition of an analytical methodology illustrated by examples. She begins by outlining some traditional approaches to contour, but her real starting point is Robert Morris's generalized definition of contour as "a set of points in one sequential dimension ordered by any other sequential dimension" (p. 150). So she presents ways of correlating not only time with pitch class, time with dynamics, and time with register, but also pitch class with dynamics, dynamics with register, and so forth. And by representing these relationships numerically, she makes it possible to categorize them into equivalence classes. Simple in conception but sophisticated in realization, her essay generalizes from the familiar to the unfamiliar; it has the mind-bending quality of the best theory. Also like much of the best theory (I am thinking for instance of Réti and Forte), it presents models of relatedness that are so powerful that practically anything *could* be shown to be related to practically anything else. Faced with this not unfamiliar situation, analysts usually emphasize the need to proceed with discretion; in a footnote, Marvin remarks that "in general, analytical choices and segmentation have been guided here by the ear as well as the eye" (note 31).

But there is an alternative, which is exactly the opposite: to use the theory as a mechanical discovery procedure, looking for all possible relationships and evaluating them statistically. Outside the most restricted musical contexts, this is impossible without the use of computers. But since the relationships that Marvin deals with can be fully reconstructed from conventional score notation, there is no reason in principle why her methodology could not be implemented in software. And this is equally true of the relationships of similarity and equivalence that Richard Hermann discusses in his "Theories of Chordal Shapes, Aspects of Linguistics, and Their Roles in Structuring Berio's *Sequenza IV for Piano*." Unlike Marvin, Hermann focuses on a single parameter, chordal shaping. He shows how *Sequenza IV* is based on a chord series, apparently composed first, which he describes provocatively as "a catalog of the kinds of ways in which the pianist can deploy the hands in playing chords" (p. 375); he then shows how this chord series is elaborated by superimposed layers of decoration, modelling the process of elaboration by means of variables and functions that are clearly modelled on programming languages.

The possibility of computer implementation is even more obvious in Jane Piper Clendinning's "Structural Factors in the Microcanonic Compositions of György Ligeti." The substance of Clendinning's essay lies in the series of analytical graphs, which build on approaches applied previously by Bernard and others to the representation of Ligeti's music. In each case one of the axes is time, but the other may be pitch, pitch class, the number of pitches sounding, or the number of entries taking place at any time point. The graphs are computer generated, but only in the sense that they have been created by means of a graphics program; the data have all been entered by hand (note 20). In principle, however, there is no reason why the entire analysis could not have been carried out by computer on the basis of the score, using any appropriate music representation language. Indeed, as Clendinning mentions, Alexander Brinkman and Martha Mesiti have developed software that takes DARMS code as its input and produces graphs essentially similar to Clendinning's as its output.[20] The software is technically complex, involving the compilation of the DARMS code (which is closely coordinated with traditional staff notation) into a data format that renders structural information accessible to mechanical discovery procedures. But instead of considering what Brinkman and Mesiti's software does, I would like to throw reality to the winds and fantasize about an analytical dream machine that would implement everything discussed by Marvin, Hermann, Clendinning, and Cogan.

The dream machine that I envision can represent music graphically, numerically, spectrographically, or in terms of staff notation, as well as outputting it as sound. Graphic views allow any parameter to be correlated with any other (unlike Brinkman and Mesiti's software, in which the horizontal axis is always time). And editing can be done within any of these music views (as is the case in the piano-roll windows of commercial sequencing software, which are otherwise identical to Clendinning's "range graph"); the results of input in any one view are instantly reflected in all other views. Or data can be entered from scratch within any of these views. You can enter or edit data at any structural level and in terms of any configuration of parameters, from inputting single notes by means of a MIDI keyboard to digital manipulation of live performances or drawing pitch class/dynamic contours with a mouse; where the music is defined only in global terms, note-to-note patterns are created by routines based on random number generation. You can reverse or invert contours, or paste them from one set of parameters to another, or from one level of structure to another. You can highlight a set of notes in the staff notation window and select any chordal shape function. (Who knows, there might even be a "twist" tool.) And of course there is an undo button so that any operation can be tried out and, if necessary, reversed. The dream machine is, in short, not just an analysis environment, but a composing environment too.[21]

19 Alexander Brinkman and Martha Mesiti, "Graphic Modeling of Musical Structure," *Computers in Music Research* 3 (1991): 1–42.

20 Brinkman's work with Mesiti has already realized some of the graphic potential for the "dream machine." Likewise, Brinkman's Contemporary Music Analysis Package (CMAP), co-authored with Craig R. Harris, can carry out many of the analytical functions of the machine proposed

In the eighteenth century, before music pedagogy became institutionalized, composition and analysis were essentially coextensive; basic analytical concepts (what goes with what, where the breaks are) were acquired and expressed through strict composition, keyboard accompaniment, and arrangement. As analysis acquired its own disciplinary identity, it became increasingly divorced from compositional practice. But the same aesthetic and intellectual approaches informed both composition and analysis. Just as musical modernism encompassed a plethora of subsidiary "isms," each claiming a monopoly on artistic truth, so analysis became fragmented into a variety of mutually exclusive approaches, each with its own proprietary methods. It is entirely characteristic of present-day practice, however, that both the editors of this book characterize their own analytical methodologies as complementary to set-theoretical and other approaches. And their writing conveys a sense of being part of the same enterprise as contemporary composition; indeed Hermann specifically mentions that his theories of chordal shape "may be suggestive for composers" (p. 388). If there is a disjunction between such contemporary theorizing and composition, it arises not so much from ideological or methodological difference as from the drag induced by the spoken or written medium of analytical demonstration. The dream machine integrates analysis and composition into a single musical activity because the results of any operation are instantaneous.

So how does all this square with what I said earlier about the role of analysis being, as often as not, to oppose the music's phenomenal qualities? If postmodernism means anything for music theory, it means that this is a non-issue; there is no *one* correct role for analysis because there is no *one* such thing as analysis. Different analytical approaches represent different music views, and they are positioned along a continuum that extends from Clendinning's range graphs (which can be derived from score notation and implemented as computer views) to Bernard's and Hisama's oppositional models. They extend, in other words, from composition to critical reflection. And this book offers not only a rich repertory of such analytical approaches, but a celebration of their diversity.

---

here. What makes the dream machine unique is its interface between compositional and analytical applications, using MIDI and music notation capabilities.

Index

*Page numbers appearing in **boldface** denote pages containing musical examples; page numbers appearing in italics denote pages containing figures. Information found in footnotes is indicated with a lower-case letter n adjoining the page number. Movements of a musical work are indicated by an upper-case Roman numeral.*

441